P9-CJW-957

LONELY PLANET'S
Guide To
TRAVEL WRITING

EXPERT ADVICE
From The
WORLD'S LEADING
TRAVEL
PUBLISHER

~ DON GEORGE ~

VIA AIR MAIL

LONELY PLANET PUBLICATIONS
Melbourne + Oakland + London

LONELY PLANET'S
GUIDE TO TRAVEL WRITING

3rd edition – August 2013
First published – March 2005
ISBN 978 1 74321 688 0

Published by
Lonely Planet Publications
Pty Ltd
ABN 36 005 607 983

text © Lonely Planet 2013
'Sri Lanka' by Harriet O'Brien © *Traveller* / Condé Nast Publications Ltd
'Guitar Central' by Christopher Reynolds © *Los Angeles Times*
Reprinted with permission.

photographs © photographers as indicated

Cover design Mark Adams

10 9 8 7 6 5 4 3 2 1
Printed in China

LONELY PLANET OFFICES

Australia - Head Office
Locked Bag 1, Footscray, Victoria 3011
03 8379 8000, fax 03 8379 8111
www.lonelyplanet.com.au/contact

USA
150 Linden St, Oakland, CA 94607
510 893 8556, fax 510 893 8572
info@lonelyplanet.com

United Kingdom
Media Centre, 201 Wood Lane, London
W12 7TQ
020 8433 1333, fax 020 8702 0112
go@lonelyplanet.co.uk

CONTENTS

INTRODUCTION

Travel writer. Those two words are among the most alluring in the English language. No less a luminary than Mick Jagger has said that if he couldn't be a rock star, he'd like to be a travel writer. Drew Barrymore has claimed the same.

It is an enticing image. There you are, lying on a chaise longue on a white-sand beach by an aquamarine ocean, describing how the palm trees rustle in the salt-tinged breeze; sipping a café crème in a Parisian café, scribbling impressions in a battered notebook; bouncing through the African bush, snapping photos of gazelles and lions, then ending the day listening to spine-tingling tales over gin and tonics in the campfire's glow.

If you love to travel and you love to write, it doesn't get any better.

TRAVEL WRITING & YOU

Every year a few dozen people around the world make a living travelling and writing full-time – and if that's your goal, go for it! This book will give you all the information and inspiration you need to try to reach that dream.

But you don't have to get paid full-time or even part-time to profit from your travel writing. Whatever your goals as a traveller and writer, the rewards of travel writing – and of approaching travel with the travel writer's mindset – are numerous. First and foremost, you become a better traveller. You arrive at your destination having already learned something of its history, culture and important sites, making you far better able to explore and appreciate what it has to offer. Also, as you are on the lookout for trends, unique places to visit and hot spots, you gradually build up a store of knowledge, becoming more and more of a travel expert.

When you are on the road, travelling as a travel writer will force you to pay attention. You will look more closely, listen more clearly, taste more carefully – and continually reflect on what you're experiencing. As a result, your travels will be deeper and richer. In addition, you will often be able to go behind the scenes at a restaurant, shop or hotel, to take advantage of special access to a historical site or museum exhibit, and to speak with intriguing people – from archaeologists and curators to chefs and shamans – whom everyday travellers would not be able to meet.

Finally, after you have returned home – or if you're blogging, while you're still on the road – you will be able to relive your journey in the course of writing about it. And when your account is published, sharing your travel experiences with others – whether in a magazine, newspaper, travel website or personal blog – will further multiply your pleasure, forging connections with others who share your passions. All these effects will broaden and extend the significance and depth of your travels.

These riches come with a corresponding responsibility, of course. As a travel writer you will have a fundamental commitment to your reader to explore a place deeply and fully, and to report the information your reader needs to know by writing an honest, fair, objective and accurate portrayal of that place. Integrity is the travel writer's compass and key.

A (VERY) SHORT HISTORY

Travel writing is an ancient impulse: people have been sharing accounts of their journeys ever since they first began to wander. The earliest wall paintings present the prehistoric predecessors of Bill Bryson and Paul Theroux recounting their adventures in the larger world. The Greek historian Herodotus is generally credited with writing the first travel book, *History of the Persian Wars*, with its vivid depictions of exotic sites, rites and fights, in 440 BC. Through the ensuing centuries, traders and explorers from Marco Polo and Christopher Columbus to Henry Morton Stanley and Charles Darwin wrote diaries and dispatches describing their adventures and discoveries in far-flung lands. In the 20th century, travel writing came into its own as a flourishing independent genre with the emergence of such extraordinary writer-travellers as Patrick Leigh Fermor, Wilfred Thesiger, Eric Newby, Colin Thubron and Jan Morris.

Travel writing has continued to evolve in the past quarter-century in the work of such masters as Paul Theroux, Bill Bryson, Pico Iyer, Tim Cahill, Stanley Stewart, Kira Salak, Anthony Sattin and Rory MacLean. Now, a new generation of 21st-century 'content creators' is pushing the boundaries ever further, merging text, audio and video content in inventive creations.

What this means is that travel publishing today presents an unprecedented wealth of mentors to learn from, outlets to target and platforms to construct.

PUBLISHING OPPORTUNITIES

The world of travel publishing has experienced a kind of accelerated evolution over the past two decades. The technological development and popular expansion of the internet as a publishing platform has profoundly affected its media siblings. Traditional publishers have adapted their print publications to fit the age of the internet, in most cases expanding their presence on the web, re-designing and re-formatting their content for publication on tablets and a range of other mobile devices, and cutting back on their printed pages. At the same time, the network of web-only publishers has expanded exponentially. This online proliferation has mirrored the historical evolution of media: starting out with text-centric websites, the internet is now extravagantly abloom with the contemporary equivalents of radio (podcasts) and TV (videos). Where this media convergence/divergence, expansion/contraction is heading is unclear. But it is clear that today's travel writers can choose from a greater range of potential subject matter and a more extensive and varied range of publishing opportunities than ever before. Here is a brief overview of these possibilities; we will cover them in detail in Part II.

Newspapers

Many newspapers in the UK, US and Australia publish separate sections devoted exclusively to travel. While some of these, particularly in the US, have shrunk substantially in size over the course of the decade, they continue to represent a significant market for both beginning and established writers. In the US, major newspapers' travel sections are usually published on Sunday and range in size from four to 20 pages. In the UK most quality newspapers have travel sections of between four and 24 pages on Saturday and Sunday, and some also feature travel during the week. Major Australian newspapers also feature separate travel sections on Saturday and Sunday, ranging from four to 24 pages. In addition to these, local newspapers often include some travel coverage.

Magazines

While the magazine world has confronted serious challenges to retaining readerships and revenues over the past decade, publishers continue to produce beautifully designed glossy publications that focus on travel, and lifestyle/general-interest magazines also regularly include travel coverage in their pages. In addition, virtually every airline has its own in-flight magazine, which publishes articles about the destinations to which it flies, and niche publications focused on specific subjects, activities or regions often feature travel pieces. Subcategories within the travel world have also developed audiences and publications of their own, including family travel, business travel, gay and lesbian travel, and adventure travel.

The Internet

The internet is the Brave New World of travel publishing. This sector has experienced explosive growth over the past decade, and its opportunities are limited only by your imagination and technological sophistication. From traditional articles to blogs to photo galleries to podcasts to videos, more travel content is being created and disseminated now than ever before. Making money through internet publishing is still a challenge, but as the medium expands and evolves, opportunities continue to emerge and develop.

Travel Literature

Many major publishers produce works of travel literature on a regular basis; these tend to come from writers with already established reputations, but some newcomers break into the ranks every year. Smaller publishers represent much better opportunities for writers who are not already well known. Travel anthologies remain an excellent market for narrative travel writing.

Guidebooks

Guidebooks continue to stretch in scope and speciality, offering writers a range of opportunities, from proposing and writing new books to updating subsequent editions of already published titles. While guidebook publishers contend with questions of how to complement print and online publishing, they remain vigilantly on the lookout for excellent writers and fresh ideas from knowledgeable travellers.

Other Avenues

There are hundreds of alternative outlets for the budding travel writer, from product descriptions for a travel-clothing manufacturer to travel brochures for tourist boards to catalogue copy for tour operators. In recent years, the expansion of online options for imaginative and entrepreneurial content creators has been striking; this burgeoning trend promises to keep growing in range, volume and velocity.

All of these opportunities are covered in more detail in Part II.

THE JOURNEY

Being a travel writer is not all palmy bungalows, Parisian cafés and safari sunsets. It's hard work. But Mick Jagger and Drew Barrymore had it right: travel writing is one of the globe's dream jobs. That doesn't mean it's beyond your reach. The world of travel writing is open to everyone; if you love to travel and you love to write, it's a natural. No one can guarantee that you'll be successful, but it is guaranteed that you'll never be successful if you don't try.

The aim of Lonely Planet's *Travel Writing* is to get you started – wherever you may be and wherever you may be travelling. The book is divided into three parts:

Part I focuses on the art of good travel writing. It aims to give you the strategies and tools to identify your best story subjects from your travels, and then to evoke each of those subjects in a transporting and compelling account. Part II focuses on the craft and business of travel writing, presenting hard-won advice on how to make sure you get your stories in front of as wide an audience as possible – and get paid for them, too. Part III provides an extensive compilation of UK, US and Australian resources, from publications and publishers to writers' groups and websites, reference books and travel literature classics.

Throughout the book you'll also find a treasure trove of tips and tales, including interviews with prominent UK, US, Canadian and Australian travel writers and editors, and examples of exemplary travel articles, to guide you on your journey.

One last point about that journey. This book is intended for writing travellers of all kinds – from aspiring professional travel writers to postcard scribblers and journal jotters, blog-abonds and tome raiders. In the end, you don't have to make money to profit from travel writing; sometimes the richest rewards are in the currency of experience. The goal of this book is to reveal the varied possibilities that travel writing offers, and to inspire all travellers to take advantage of those opportunities. That's where the journey begins; where it takes you is up to you.

Part 1

THE ART OF GOOD TRAVEL WRITING

WHETHER YOU'RE WRITING AN ARTICLE FOR
A MAGAZINE, NEWSPAPER OR WEBSITE, OR CREATING A
BOOK-LENGTH WORK OF TRAVEL LITERATURE,
THE SAME PRINCIPLES OF CRAFTING A STORY APPLY.

WHAT CONSTITUTES GOOD TRAVEL WRITING?

What makes a wonderful travel story? In one word, it is *place*. Successful travel stories bring a particular place to life through a combination of factual information and vividly rendered descriptive details and anecdotes, characters and dialogue. Such stories transport the reader and convey a rich sense of the author's experience in that place. The best travel stories also set the destination and experience in some larger context, creating rings of resonance in the reader.

THE GOALS OF GOOD TRAVEL WRITING

The goals of good travel writing are to present an accurate and compelling evocation and assessment of a place, to bring that place and the writer's experience to life so vividly that the reader is transported there, and to enhance the reader's understanding of the world (whether the reader is moved to plan a journey to that place, or simply content to visit it vicariously). In some cases, a secondary goal is to present the essential information the reader needs to visit that place and duplicate the author's experience.

How do you create good travel writing? The journey begins well before you set finger to keyboard.

FINDING & FOCUSING YOUR STORY

THE RIGHT SUBJECT

The very first step in writing a good travel story is finding the right subject. If the topic is right, the chances of writing a compelling piece – and of getting that piece published – will be maximised.

A good topic is usually a marriage of passion and practicality. As a writer, you want to choose a subject that will allow you to infuse your story with a sense of connection and conviction; at the same time, you need to write about a topic that will capture an editor's attention and will fit well with the publication you've targeted.

Today's publishing world offers a bountiful variety of outlets for travel writing, so it is critically important to know the market. Study the publications and websites that you'd like to write for, reading several editions of each to analyse the focus, tone, approach and length of the articles they publish.

At the same time, it is equally important to know yourself, and to focus on subjects or places that especially interest you. Are you particularly drawn to food, crafts, festivals or nightlife? Do you prefer five-star resorts or no-frills guesthouses? Do you like to explore the heart of a city or far-flung hinterlands? Finding your passion will help you narrow the publication targets for your stories – but don't narrow your field too much. If you love luxury resorts, you may think that you couldn't possibly write for a budget travel magazine – but what about a story on finding luxury for under £50 a night? If you're not passionate about food, you probably wouldn't think of approaching a food and wine magazine, but a humorous piece on surviving a week in Tuscany with a fervent foodie could be right on target.

EXERCISE 1

What are your travel passions? Think about your three most recent trips. What activities were common to all three? What are the things you seek out when you travel, the experiences that really move you? Why? Make a list of three things you love to do. Consider each. Why do you love it and what have you learned by doing it? Could this be the nucleus for a story?

TRAVEL TRENDS

As you try to marry passion with practicality, it's critical to stay abreast of travel trends. There are three kinds of trends you should monitor in order to find good story ideas and get to know your market.

Objective Travel Trends

Objective travel trends reflect traveller behaviour: where people are going, how they are getting there and what they are doing when they get there. Are ski resorts in North America suddenly all the rage with Europeans? Are more Americans barging their way along European waterways than before? Is Austria a hot destination for Australians? Does camping have a new cachet for Canadians? Is train travel booming around the globe? Are airlines or tour operators opening operations in any new destinations?

Whenever possible, anticipate these trends. If you read that a country is planning a major tourism campaign in six months, pitch a story about that country right now. When a city is chosen as a future Olympics site or future European Capital of Culture, you know that travellers – and editors – will be interested in knowing more about them as their time in the spotlight approaches.

STAYING UP TO DATE WITH TRAVEL TRENDS

Finding fresh material, spotting travel trends and keeping up to date with industry and consumer changes are essential practices for all travel writers. Part III of this book contains a wealth of global and regional information sources, and is a good place to start.

Scanning newspaper travel sections, travel magazines and websites will give you a feel for what your competitors are writing about, and will give you ideas for new stories. If you follow this practice you will also avoid the embarrassment of offering an editor a story similar to one that has just been run. Reading one or two industry magazines a week will keep you informed of what airlines, tour operators, hotel groups and others in the travel industry are up to. In the UK, subscribe to *Travel Weekly* and *Travel Trade Gazette*, or read www.travelweekly.co.uk and www.ttgdigital.com (much cheaper). In the US, subscribe to the American version of *Travel Weekly* or peruse its website, www.travelweekly.com. In Australia, read the fortnightly *Travel Weekly* (www.travelweekly.com.au) for Australian travel professionals.

Various online publications and websites are also important to watch, such as the UK-based TravelMole (www.travelmole.com) and Lonely Planet's travel forum, the Thorn Tree (http://thorntree.lonelyplanet.com). Other online resources that provide excellent updated information and analysis include Joe Brancatelli's informative newsletter (www.joesentme.com), OAG Traveler (www.oagtravel.com), Travel News (www.ttgweb.com) and World Travel Watch (www.worldtravelwatch.com), a website produced by James O'Reilly and Larry Habegger. An extensive list of online travel trade publications can be found at www.ehotelier.com/browse/magazines.php.

You should also look regularly at websites that provide tourism facts, figures and statistics; for a comprehensive list by region, see the Facts, Figures & Statistics sections of Part III. Major websites for UK travel writers include National Statistics Online (www.statistics.gov.uk), the UK Tourism Industry website (www.visitbritain.org) and the European Travel Commission (www.etc-corporate.org). In the US, try the US Travel Association (www.ustravel.org) and the Office of Travel and Tourism Industries (http://tinet.ita.doc.gov/research/reports/basic/index.html).

Useful Australian websites include the Australian Bureau of Statistics (www.abs.gov.au) and the Tourism Australia website (www.tourism.australia.com).

It's also a good idea to visit the websites of the World Health Organization (www.who.int/en), the UK's Department of Health (www.doh.gov.uk), the US Centers for Disease Control and Prevention (www.cdc.gov) and the Australian Department of Foreign Affairs & Trade (www.smartraveller.gov.au). Also compare the foreign office websites maintained by the governments of the UK, the US, Australia and Canada. Sometimes the differences in their respective travel advisories can be eye-opening.

Another useful way of finding out about what's happening in the travel world is by joining the press mailing lists of several travel companies. Ring up the companies you're interested in and speak to their PR departments, or contact them through social media sites, but try to be selective because you don't want to be flooded with press releases. Jaded travel writers or editors will tell you that 99 per cent of what you will be sent will go straight into the rubbish bin, but if that remaining one per cent forms the basis of a fresh travel article that you can sell, then it's worth it. And don't discount the fact that perusing a press release and learning about a new travel initiative adds to your overall body of travel information and may well be valuable one day.

Identifying a trend can become the nucleus for a story. You may create a story about the emergence of the trend itself – or you may be able to adapt that trend to a place you want to write about. For example, if you see that an editor has published a cover story on farm stays in Portugal, consider if there is a version of the farm-stay experience in New Zealand or Argentina that might interest the same editor. If the publication routinely features articles on extreme adventures, come up with an adrenalin-charged story in a destination they haven't covered yet. It's also important to remember that most newspaper travel sections are inundated with stories on hard-to-get-to places halfway around the globe, but are desperate for great writing on easy-to-visit places closer to home. Try proposing a long-weekend story – they're easier and cheaper to research, and your odds of getting published are considerably higher.

Subjective Travel Trends

These trends are anecdotal and often qualitative. Are the travellers who once flocked to Thailand now heading to Laos? Do up-market travellers consider the spa resorts in the Maldives passé and, if so, where are they going instead? Is Belize the new Costa Rica, Brno the new Prague? Are baby boomers turning to volunteer vacations to add meaning to their lives? Are eco-cruises suddenly in vogue?

Editorial Travel Trends

Editorial trends are indicated by changes in the weight of coverage given to different regions or types of travel. For example, these days almost every serious British newspaper regularly devotes coverage to European city breaks – a sharp contrast from a decade ago when such coverage was patchy. Stories on luxury spas might be on the decline while articles touting green travel options are on the increase.

YOUR PROFESSIONAL NICHE

To make a decent living as a travel writer, you need to be able to turn your hand to a variety of travel articles. However, it can be very much to your advantage to find the niche that best fits your expertise as a writer. By narrowing your field, you can focus on a particular slice of the travel world and so become an authority on it. Travel editors, and possibly broadcasters, will begin to recognise your expertise, and will think of you when they are looking for a story or comment on your subject. Specialising in this way should mean *more* paid work, not less, because your particular expertise will be recognised. In addition, writing on something that you know about means less research, and less research means more time to write – and in the end, writing is what you're paid for.

Choosing a niche will involve looking for a decent gap in the market – there's very little point in specialising in a subject that everyone else has chosen as their particular field. Obviously, you also need to select something that truly interests you and fits your lifestyle; it might be travel with children, no-frills airlines, a particular form of transport or a specific part of the world. Travel guidebook writers are in a great position to become experts on a region or country and its beliefs, customs and lifestyle. In addition, many journalists who are successful at being recognised as an authority in their area have done so by writing a book about their subject. Creating a specialist blog or website and posting on social media platforms are both excellent ways to get your expertise recognised. Of course, you may change your niche over time, as you adapt to changes in the world and in your own life.

DEVELOPING YOUR STORY

Whether you specialise or widen your view, each new trip poses the same question: how do you develop a story from scratch? You've researched the publications that interest you, the passions that arouse you and the subjects that are currently popular. Now it's time to put your research to work.

A fundamental issue, particularly for aspiring newspaper and magazine writers, is the question of timing. Should you come up with story ideas before you travel or after you return? In the beginning you may find it easier to pitch articles from trips you've already taken – you know the place, and know exactly what you want to write about, making it infinitely easier for you to write a convincing proposal, or query letter, for that article. (We'll talk more about proposals and query letters in Part II.)

As you develop a collection of published articles (known as a 'clip file') and a reputation, you may want to try pitching ideas for subjects and trips you haven't yet made. The difficulty is knowing what exactly you want to write about before you've made the trip. To be convincing, you'll need to do a good deal of research so you can paint a compelling portrait of your subject and of its relevance to the publication in question without having experienced it. (A more advantageous situation is when you have visited a place in the past and are returning to update your impressions and experiences.)

Pretrip Research

Whether you're hoping to pitch your story pre- or post-trip, in order to get the most out of your journey, you'll need to do some research. Start by buying a few good guidebooks and conducting an extensive web search to get a thorough grounding in the place you're planning to visit – everything from history and cultural background to specific events and attractions. These days many destinations have English-language newspapers or magazines. You may be able to track down copies before you leave home, depending on the destination, and you can find and read many of them online. Reading these publications and other regionally focused websites will give you a sense of local flavour and help you discover what news stories and events are capturing residents' interest. You can also use social media to solicit information and suggestions from both travelers and locals. Finally, reading travel literature set in the country you're planning to visit can also open up story ideas and offer deeper insights into the character of the place.

After you've done all this research – studied the markets, the trends, yourself and the place you're preparing to visit – you should have a well-grounded idea of what you're likely to find in that place and what experiences or topics are most likely to impassion you. One more factor to consider, however, is that the best travel stories are often the unanticipated ones that you stumble onto when you're actually in a place. The best practice is to have a story idea in mind before you take your trip, and at the same time be open to discovering an even better story while you're there. Having a preconceived idea will give your trip preparations and itinerary a focus and framework. Of course, if you've interested an editor in a particular story pretrip, you'll usually need to write about that. But if you find something extraordinary on the spot, all the better – your article possibilities will have doubled.

Researching on the Road

Of course, all that pretrip research is just the prelude to the journey itself. Once you're aboard the train, bus, ferry or plane, the real work begins. As you travel, stay alive to the world around you. Cultivate encounters. Ask questions. Gather brochures and other printed information. If something catches your fancy, follow it. When you can, let serendipity be your guide.

Use your camera to capture the look of a place; use your audio recorder to capture conversations, evocative sounds and snatches of your own impressions when it's impractical to write them down; use your journal to record on-the-spot notes that will bring your experience back to you later. (For more about these essential tools of the trade, see Part II, p226.) Absorb as much as you can, but remember to constantly filter what you're absorbing, so you retain and focus on the aspects of the trip that most appeal to you and offer the best potential story subjects.

HINTS & TIPS

Most destination articles include a fact box or fact file (also called a sidebar in the US) that presents essential travel information: how to get there, where to stay and eat, etc. An editor will tell you if they are planning to publish a fact box with your story, but if you are not working in advance with an editor, it is always a good idea to include one. Ask yourself what readers need to know in order to duplicate your experience. If you're writing about food stalls in Singapore, you'll want to tell them how to get to the stalls you mention, the days and times they are open, and particular specialities. If you're writing about discovering the riches of Riga, your editor will most likely want to tell readers the best way to get there, and places to stay and eat. For examples of fact boxes, see the reproduced articles at the end of Part I (p54).

EXERCISE 2

Play traveller for a day in your backyard. Visit a local museum and pick up all the information you can. Is it open on holidays? Are there any special days when admission is free? What are the upcoming exhibitions and their dates? What artwork moved you the most; how and why? Have lunch with friends or family at a restaurant and take notes. What's the atmosphere like? What were the other diners like? What was the best dish? How much did it cost? When is the restaurant open? Does it take reservations? Walk around a favourite neighbourhood and take notes. After you've finished your visit, write three 300-word descriptions – one of the museum, one of the restaurant and one of the neighbourhood – in a way that evokes them for someone who's never been there.

FINDING YOUR FOCUS

We have already discussed a number of ways to help you narrow your focus before and during your trip, but now let's consider the aftermath of the trip. You've just returned from three weeks in France and everything was great – every day brought new discoveries and treasures, and you want to write about them all. Tempting as that may seem, writing about everything you did on holiday should be kept strictly between you and your diary; you need to find the theme that will interest an editor. If you sounded out a few travel editors before you set off, you'll already know which stories might be of interest to whom. But if you didn't, or if you want to try other editors now that you've returned, how do you decide what to write about?

Ask yourself this simple question: what most impassioned you? When you meet people and they say, 'So, how was France?', what's the first story that comes to mind? Focus on that story, because for some reason your internal filter has decided that that particular story embodies the quintessence of your trip. Analyse why the story especially appeals to you, and ask yourself if other people would be interested in reading about it. Also ask yourself why you are choosing to describe that particular aspect of your trip. Think about the connection and resonance your focus has created. Does it capture an illuminating characteristic of French culture or French manners or French food? Does it tie in neatly with something that's highly topical today or with something that will be news in the future, such as an anniversary or event? Or is it so unusual that it stands out simply as an extraordinary travel experience?

This is the seed of your story: seize it, explore it, look at it from different angles, draw it out. Think about what it means to you, but remember that the

EFFECTIVE NOTE-TAKING & INTERVIEWING TECHNIQUES

Central to the success of your travel research and writing is the ability to take good notes and to carry out efficient, effective interviews.

Taking Notes

Notes taken on the spot provide reliable and vivid building blocks for your story. They are also poignant keys that can unlock a flood of images and details from a particular place and experience – even when you're writing your story half a year later. Fragments often do the job just fine. You might write 'red poppies, white columns' or 'pine scent, silvery sea' or 'grandmother in blue fur, lilac perfume, Mozart from window'. You just need a few words that capture the essence of the thing you want to remember. At other times you'll want to write a more complete portrait of a moment, as the words written on the spot are inevitably the most vivid depictions of all.

One of the secrets to good note-taking is simply paying attention. Slow down and take the time to stop, absorb and reflect on your surroundings and on the things that have happened so far on your journey.

Interviewing Techniques

Effective interviewing is an art of a different kind. Before you begin, you need to know what you want to get out of the interview. In many cases you will simply be trying to gather hard information, and so these interviews are not likely to be particularly controversial or confrontational. But since the interview will most likely be your only opportunity to talk with this particular individual, you need to make sure you have thought out in advance everything you want to learn from your meeting.

Basically, your interviews will fall into one of two types: the official and the unofficial. The official, or expert, interview involves anyone who represents a place. This might be a museum curator or the director of an archaeological site; a tourism official or guide; a hotel owner or chef. In every case, your job is to glean as much relevant information from this expert as possible. You want to be friendly and nonthreatening, but you also want to be sure to get the information you need. If you ask a question and don't get a satisfactory answer, ask it again.

In this kind of formal interview it's vital to use an audio recorder. This will liberate you from note-taking so that you can focus on the answers and your questions. Whenever possible, get contact information so you can follow up if a question occurs to you long after your meeting.

If you have a particularly intransigent interview subject, one trick is to turn off your recorder, put away your notes and prepare to leave. Then stop and say, 'You know, one more question has just occurred to me.' This may be the question you walked into the interview most wanting to ask, but if you had asked it directly during the formal part of the interview, you would not have received a useful response. Now, in that unguarded setting, you may get just the candid answer you need.

The unofficial interview is usually a conversation with a fellow traveller or a local, often used to provide a different perspective and voice for your story, or to fill in background information. Your interviewing technique can be more indirect and conversational. You may decide not to use an audio recorder, so the person you're talking to will feel at ease and converse freely. (Writers who are just starting out may feel that using an audio recorder or notebook will make them seem more 'professional'. This is not necessarily the case, and if such equipment makes your subject nervous or self-conscious, you may not get the free-flowing stories, information and quotes you're hoping for.) Ask for anecdotes that illustrate a point. Ask for memories. If you are not using an audio recorder or taking notes during the interview, write down all the important points from your conversation as soon as you possibly can.

If you are planning to name and quote your interviewee you should let them know before you begin the interview. In an informal situation where you won't be naming the speaker, you don't necessarily need to say that you're interviewing them for publication, but sometimes it's easier to approach someone if you say you're gathering information for a story. If you're using an audio recorder or taking notes, you will certainly want to explain why. And, of course, there are times when you will be interviewing people by phone or by email, as many travel pieces these days are researched and written from home. Finally, if you do quote someone (without naming them) in a story on a sensitive topic, be very sure that they cannot be recognised from your writing. You do not want to inadvertently imperil someone because they gave you important information or freely expressed their views to you.

In all cases, it is absolutely essential for you to be accurate in quoting people you've interviewed, and it is important to have records from your interview – either audio or extensive notes – that you can give to an editorial fact-checker, if asked, to verify the authenticity of your quotes.

story isn't about yourself. A very common mistake that inexperienced travel writers make is to put too much of themselves into a piece; your job as a writer is to be the reader's portal into a deeper understanding of the place and of the experience of being a traveller there.

Now, think about other experiences from the trip that support this aspect or in some way complement it. You can begin to fashion your story in this way, establishing a central theme and then building on it. Your final piece will be an exploration of this theme and how it was present in your trip, and ideally you will lead up to it step by step. If you feel you've got many seeds from your trip, then that's great – you'll be able to write a variety of different articles covering each one for a range of different outlets.

This process should help you avoid one of the most common traps for travel writers: the fear of the known. Writers often feel paralysed when trying to write about a familiar subject. How can I write about Paris, they say, when a million stories have already been written on the subject? A million stories have been written about Paris, it's true – but there could be a Paris you experienced that no one else has ever known. Let's say you love puppets and you stumbled onto a dusty puppet-maker's shop in an alley in the 13th *arrondissement*. You spent an hour talking about puppets and puppetry with the white-haired owner, who looked a little like a puppet himself. Here's the perfect subject for your story, a subject no one else could write about with as much authority, presence and passion as you.

Ultimately, travel is all about connections – connections outside us and connections inside us. If you can bring those connections to life in your work, readers who may have never been to Paris or who may not care a whit about puppets will be brought in touch with similar connections they have made in other countries, in other places. They will connect with your sense of connection, and so the piece will in some metaphorical way build a powerful bridge and remind us all over again of one of the great and fundamental joys of travel: the stretching of personal boundaries, the flinging of bridges across cultures.

EXERCISE 3

After your next trip, or thinking back to your most recent trip, finish these sentences: I've just returned from _____. My most memorable experience there was _____. It was memorable because _____. The experience taught me _____. Think about how you could expand on this to build a personal and compelling anecdotal bridge to that place.

HINTS & TIPS
Never underestimate the power of serendipity – and of being open to serendipity – to hand you a wonderful story. Early in my travel writing career, I was talking with a Japanese friend in Tokyo about my upcoming visit to Kyoto. He casually mentioned that a friend of his had just visited Kyoto and had stayed in a temple rather than a hotel. A temple, I thought – what a great idea for a story! So I arranged to stay at Myokenji temple in the heart of Kyoto and subsequently wrote an article about my stay for *Signature* magazine.

To achieve this connection we move to the next stage: the writing. You've done your research, analysed the market, studied yourself and found a subject that marries publishability with passion. Now you need to write to that passion. Explore it, savour it, draw it out in your prose – paint such a complete, compelling, sensually full description that your readers will experience it just as you did.

CRAFTING A STRUCTURE

As a writer, you are a sculptor working with words, moulding the clay of experience. An essential part of your job is to give that experience a shape that makes it accessible and understandable to a reader who hasn't shared it. The way you introduce and evoke your experience, the structure you give your story, is key.

A good travel article is structured, or shaped, like a good short story, with a clear beginning, middle and end. Broadly speaking, and of course varying with the overall length of the story (travel stories for the UK and Australian markets tend to be shorter than those for the US market), the beginning is made up of approximately the first two to seven paragraphs. The aim of the beginning is to create a thematic or narrative lead (spelled 'lede' in the US) that immediately interests and engages the reader, drawing them into the article. Often the beginning will set the story's scene, and sometimes it will hint at why the writer is there, but the prime purpose of the beginning is to grab the reader's attention. The middle is the long and winding road of the story, where the destination is brought alive for the reader, using your experience there as a filter. The end – and again, this is usually no more than the last two to seven paragraphs or so – wraps up the story and offers a kind of closure, tying the story back to its beginning but with a larger, enhanced sense of the whole.

COMPELLING BEGINNINGS

Let's begin with the beginning and study leads from published pieces that work well and in differing ways. Five of these stories are reprinted in their entirety at the end of Part I (see p54).

In 'The Wonderful Thing about Tigers', published in *Wanderlust* magazine, William Gray describes a jungle expedition in India. To begin that description, he chooses to pull us immediately into an electric moment, and to keep us there:

> It was almost as if the tiger had flicked a switch in the forest. One moment it was quiet and calm – the trees swathed in webs of early morning mist – the next, the air was charged with tension. Gomati had heard the distant alarm calls – the shrill snort of a spotted deer, the indignant bark of a langur monkey – and her mood suddenly changed. She blasted a trunkful of dust up between her front legs, then shook her head so vigorously that I had to clutch the padded saddle to keep my balance. Gomati's mahout, sitting astride her neck, issued a terse reprimand before urging the elephant into the tangled forest. There was no path; Gomati made her own. Soon the air was infused with the pungent aroma of crushed herbs and freshly-bled sap. Spiders and beetles drizzled from shaken trees; our clothing became wet with dew and stained by moss and lichen. We sounded like a forest fire – crackling, snapping, trailblazing. But through all the noise came a single piercing cry. Gomati stopped and we heard it again – the tell-tale alarm call of a spotted deer.
>
> Manoj Sharma, my guide, leaned towards me. 'When the tiger moves, the deer calls,' he murmured. 'We must be close.' I nodded slowly, my eyes chasing around the shadows of the forest. Sunlight sparked through chinks in the canopy, but the understorey was still a diffuse patchwork of muted greens and shadows-within-shadows – the perfect foil for tiger stripes. Apart from an occasional rumble from Gomati's stomach, the forest was silent. No one spoke or moved.

Gray's beginning offers an effective example of a literary technique called *in medias res*, which sets you right 'in the middle of things'. This technique has a long and honourable literary pedigree – Milton employed it in *Paradise Lost*, beginning the epic in the middle of the story. Without warning, we readers are plucked from our easy chairs and set in the middle of the jungle, tensely wondering what will happen next.

Former US Poet Laureate Robert Hass employs the same technique to riveting effect in his powerful story about Korea, 'The Path to Sokkuram', which originally appeared in *Great Escapes* magazine. Hass takes a couple of notable risks in his opening. He begins with a very long first sentence that propels the reader into the story with a stream-of-consciousness momentum, and he begins his narrative with a character in mid-speech:

HINTS & TIPS

If you can't find your beginning, one strategy is to think of the moment when you first felt a connection with the place you are describing, when you were first drawn into that place. (But please try to avoid: 'My plane landed on the tarmac at _____.' That lead was already stale in the time of the Wright brothers.)

'The thing you need to understand about Korea,' said the dissolute, cheerful-looking British shipping agent I had run into at six in the morning in the fish market in the harbour at Pusan – we were drinking coffee at an outdoor table in the reek of fish and the unbelievable choral din of the fish merchants, beside tanks of slack-bodied pale squid and writhing pink and purple octopus – 'is that it's Poland. I mean, as a metaphor it's Poland. Caught between China and Japan for all those centuries like the Poles were stuck between the Russians and the Germans. The Japanese occupied the place from 1910 to the end of the war, and in the '30s they simply tried to eradicate Korea as a nation. Outlawed the language. Everybody in the country over 40 went to school when the teaching of the Korean language was forbidden.'

An old woman pushed past with a cart full of fist-sized reddish-green figs. McEwan, the shipping agent, called her over. 'Try one of these,' he said. 'Damned good.' They were, red-fleshed, packed with seeds. McEwan was waving down a waiter with one hand, clutching a torn-open fig with the other. 'They demand soju, don't they?' Soju is a transparent, fiery, slightly sweet Korean brandy, perfect with figs, I was sure, but beyond me at that moment. I had been out the night before with a surprisingly hard-drinking lot of professors from Pusan National University, and wandered afterward rather aimlessly through the night market. Just before leaving America I had come to the end of a long marriage, and I had spent my first few days in Korea, when I did not have to concentrate on a task, in a state of dazed grief. In the night market the families had fascinated me, at one in the morning shutting down their produce stalls, loading up their boxes of fennel and cabbage and bok choy, moving swiftly in and out of the arc of light thrown by a hanging propane lamp, husbands and wives and drowsy children, working easily side by side. I drank beer at a stall and watched the market close down, and then went back to my hotel and couldn't sleep, and so got up again and walked down the hill in the pre-dawn coolness to the wharf.

In just two paragraphs Hass imparts a wealth of information about Korean history and culture – and about himself, an essential context for understanding his subsequent perceptions of and experiences in Korea. We are immersed in the Pusan fish market, ready to explore.

EXERCISE 4

Considering the trip you wrote about in Exercise 3 (p22), try to write an *in medias res* (in the middle of things) lead for your story. Think of the pivotal or most emotionally intense moment in your piece. Describe the prelude to that moment – the instance before the tiger, literal or figurative, appeared. Write two to four paragraphs – 400 words maximum – that place your reader right there with you in that scene. Could you begin your story this way?

Not all travel stories need to begin so dramatically. Here's a good example of a thematic beginning from an article that UK author Stanley Stewart wrote about rodeos in the American West for the *Sunday Times*:

At the rodeo you notice that horses and cowboys are kind of alike. Horses stand around a lot, flicking their tails, breaking wind, doing nothing in particular. Cowboys are like that. They lean on fences, looking at horses. Sometimes they spit, sometimes they don't. With their hats tipped down over their eyes, it is never easy to tell if they are asleep, like horses, on their feet. The similarity disguises a major difference of temperament. Cowboys are soft-spoken mild-mannered fellows. In the West it's the horses that are the outlaws.

To the newcomer, cowboys are the surprise of the American West, like finding Romans in pleated togas waiting for the trolley buses on the Via Appia. Towns like Laramie and Cheyenne and Medicine Bow and Kit Carson are full of people who seem to have wandered off the back lot at MGM. They wear boots and ten gallon hats and leather waistcoats. In town they drink in saloons with swing doors and stand around on street corners in a bowlegged fashion. Back at the ranch their nearest neighbours are miles away. The men are lean laconic figures with lopsided

grins. The women look like their idea of a good time would be to rope
you and ride you round the corral awhile. The women are rather chatty.
With cowboys there is a lot of silence to fill.

The West is America's most vibrant sub culture with its own music, its
own fashions, its own political orientation and its own folklore. They care
nothing for the suburban world that is the American mainstream. They
talk of Washington and back east as if they were part of Red China. It is
one of the pleasures of Wyoming to find Americans who are as cantanker-
ous and as sceptical as the regulars of any Yorkshire pub. If the West is
the spiritual home of America's ardent individualism, it is the landscape
that is to blame. Between the Missouri River and the Rocky Mountains
lies a vast swathe of country that early cartographers called the Great
American Desert. They were wrong but you can see where they got the
idea. The West is a landscape of skies and infinities. In the loneliness of
this place, self-reliance becomes a kind of religion. When the first settlers
tried to farm this land, it broke their hearts. The West did not take kindly
to the idea of fields. It was a vast sea of grass, a landscape for horses.

The rodeos that are held in small towns all over the West are like
church fetes with Budweiser tents and bullriders, a chance to meet the
neighbours and complain about the government. They are also the mo-
ment for the big showdown between the cowboys and the horses.

With this beguiling beginning, Stewart introduces a multifaceted theme: visiting rodeos is a singular method of developing an appreciation for the history,
quintessential qualities and contemporary culture of the American West.
Through five spare paragraphs he paints a vivid and compelling portrait of
the ensuing tale's main characters: cowboys, horses, and the infinite landscape they inhabit. By the end of that beginning, Stewart has already given
us a good notion of where he's going – in search of rodeos – and a seductive
sense of the riches and mysteries we'll find if we accompany him on the ride.

The article 'Las Vegas', by British travel writer and editor Simon Calder,
published in the *Independent* newspaper, begins with this quirky angle on that
singular city:

Neon: you need to know two things about this gas. The first is that it is,
in elementary terms, a relative newcomer; even though it is present in
small quantities in the air we breathe, it was identified only a century
ago by a French scientist named Georges Claude. The second is that,
being inert, neon is intrinsically dull. Oh, unless you pass an electric
charge through it, as M Claude did. Do that, and it can light up the
desert and dazzle the world.

Las Vegas was just a flicker in the eye of the San Pedro, Los Angeles and Salt Lake City Railroad when M Claude announced his discovery. The first neon sign in North America was sold in 1923 to a Packard dealership in Los Angeles.

At the time, the Mormons mistakenly thought they had discovered a promised, and morally safe, haven in the middle of the Mojave Desert. By the Thirties, they had lost faith with Las Vegas – and the rest of the world had lost interest in the fact that neon glows red in the dark and that, when mixed with a little mercury, its elementary cousin argon turns bright blue. But Las Vegas had barely begun to experiment with the extreme right-hand side of the Periodic Table of Elements.

Helium radiates a lurid magnolia when suitably fired up; krypton issues a steely silver; while xenon emits the palest blue. These elementary truths helped Las Vegas find its place in the world.

CREATING A COMPELLING BEGINNING

So how do you create a compelling hook to capture your readers' attention and propel them into your story? A few writers I know refuse to write any other part of their piece until they find that attention-grabbing introduction. I've sometimes found that a beginning will occur to me as I'm shaping the piece in my mind. When that happens I write it down immediately, as it can be a key that unlocks the rest of the story.

In most cases you'll only find the beginning in the process of writing the story. So my advice is to move on, and not get stuck on the start. You can, as Douglas Adams said so memorably, 'stare at a blank piece of paper until your forehead bleeds' but, if you're waiting for the perfect beginning, you may never get your story written. So just start writing.

You'll find that as you write, all sorts of ways to start your article may pop into your mind. Write them down and leave them at the top of your screen or page until they become so compelling that you feel forced to stop writing the body of your article to start writing its beginning.

Remember the serendipitous Kyoto temple stay I described on p23? To set up that story, I wanted to show the importance of temples in Kyoto – and then suggest the value of a temple stay. How to do that? Here's the beginning I came up with:

Perhaps more than any other place in the world, Kyoto is defined by its temples. There are 1,650 temples in this city of 1,480,000: more

By presenting Las Vegas in this unexpected light, Calder prepares us for – and entices us into – a new appreciation of this much-described city.

Adventure writer and novelist Kira Salak begins her powerful article 'Libya: The Land of Cruel Deaths', published in *National Geographic Adventure*, with these simple, compelling sentences:

> *'You come, Madame,' the man says to me.*
>
> *He wants to show me something – something 'special.' And maybe it's the sincere look in his eyes, the supplication, the knowing, but I follow this complete stranger across Tripoli's Green Square and through the stone gate of the ancient medina, or historic Arab quarter. It's my first night in Libya; I arrived only three hours ago in a country that's still a mystery of culture shock and conjecture.*

Who could resist following her – and her mysterious guide – into the medina?

> *than one for every 1,000 residents. Imagine New York City with 7,000 churches! The grand temples – Kiyomizudera, Kinkakuji, Sanjusangendo, Ryoanji, Kokedera – are known throughout the world, but if you wander the thoroughfares and back alleys, you will come away convinced that there is one temple – with its attendant scruffy dog and potted plants carefully tended by neighborhood women – for every block.*
>
> *On earlier visits to Kyoto, I had always done what most visitors do: toured the temples by day and retreated to a Western-style hotel at night. Then a Japanese friend told me that I had not really experienced Kyoto if I had not stayed overnight at a temple. Staying in a temple, he said, revealed an entirely different face of the city, a place of ancient rites and rhythms hidden from those who confined their explorations to day. It was only after the visitors left that the temples truly came to life, he said. I was instantly hooked.'*

By the end of this 184-word lead, the reader should have a good idea where this story is going: we're going to stay at a Kyoto temple and discover the riches of this off-the-typical-tourist-path experience – and gain new insights into the quintessential spirit and character of Kyoto along the way.

EXERCISE 5

Consider a recent trip. What was the first moment you really felt drawn into the place you were visiting? How did that happen – was it a person who drew you in, or a scene? What was the first connection? And what occurred when you, like Kira Salak, took those first steps into the metaphorical medina? Write a 200- to 300-word lead, drawing your reader into your story by depicting the way you were drawn into a particular place.

Finally, an example of a beginning that combines the narrative and thematic approach. This comes from a story of my own, published in *Signature* magazine:

There are no tavernas, no discotheques, no pleasure boats at anchor. Nor are there churches, windmills, or goatherds. Delos, three miles long and less than one mile wide, is a parched, rocky island of ruins, only 14 miles from Mykonos, Aegean playground of the international vagabonderie. Once the center of the Panhellenic world, Delos has been uninhabited since the first century AD, fulfilling a proclamation of the Delphic oracle that 'no man or woman shall give birth, fall sick or meet death on the sacred island.'

I chanced on Delos during my first visit to Greece. After three harrowing days of seeing Athens by foot, bus and taxi, my traveling companion and I were ready for open seas and uncrowded beaches. We selected Mykonos on the recommendation of a friend, who also suggested that when we tired of the Beautiful People, we should take a side trip to Delos.

HINTS & TIPS

If you're having difficulty starting, try making a list of the most important experiences you had on your trip, and then organise them in terms of their effect on you. I employed this method when struggling to begin an article about the South Pacific island of Aitutaki, and instantly a framing connection appeared: on my first night I'd attended an island-wide event to choose candidates for the annual Cook Islands dance competition, and the climactic experience of my stay was dancing a traditional Cook Islands dance on stage with local performers. So I began my story this way: 'Four drums pounded a deep, incessant rhythm through the sultry South Pacific night. A ukulele plunked plangent notes into the air. A smiling-eyed young beauty with copper skin and flowing hair, wearing a palm-frond skirt and a coconut bra, took me by the hand. "Will you dance with me?"'

On arriving in Mykonos, we learned that for under $3 we could catch a fishing trawler to Delos (where the harbor is too shallow for cruise ships) any morning at eight and return to Mykonos at one the same afternoon. On the morning of our fourth day we braved choppy seas and ominous clouds to board a rusty, peeling boat that reeked of fish. With a dozen other tourists, we packed ourselves into the ship's tiny cabin, already crowded with anchors, ropes and wooden crates bearing unknown cargo.

At some point during the 45-minute voyage, the toss and turn of the waves became too much for a few of the passengers, and I moved outside into the stinging, salty spray. As we made our way past Rhenea, the calluslike volcanic island that forms part of the natural breakwater with Delos, the clouds cleared, and the fishermen who had docked their caiques at the Delos jetty greeted us in bright sunlight.

At the end of the dock a white-whiskered man in a navy blue beret and a faded black suit hailed each one of us as we walked by: 'Tour of Delos! Informative guide to the ruins.' A few yards beyond him a young boy ran up to us, all elbows and knees, and confided in hard breaths, 'I give you better tour. Cheaper too.'

This approach is more purely chronological than the *in medias res* method. It provides a thematic framework for the piece, promising that the rest of the story will detail how my experience in Delos offered encounters and lessons that deepened my appreciation of Greece.

Each of these beginnings successfully draws the reader into the story and induces them to keep reading because they are intrigued by the possibilities and want to know what happens next. Each hook promises that the reader will be entertained if they continue reading, and introduces questions that can only be answered by plunging deeper into the text.

What beginning will work best for you? Think about where you want the reader to be at the start of your story. How do you want your tale to unfold? What is the main point of your story? What's the best way to get that point across?

However you structure your beginning, remember that it is the doorway to your story – and that in the eyes of an overworked editor, it's also your calling card. The beginning is your one chance to inspire the editor to read more. Many editors read hundreds of submissions a week; in effect, when they take your story in hand, they are looking for a reason to reject it as quickly as possible. If your beginning doesn't work, the editor will not read any further.

THE MIDDLE SECTION

Most travel stories are structured by following either a thematic or narrative strategy. If your story is thematic, you will develop the middle section as an ascending succession of examples leading to your overriding point. If it's a narrative, you will most likely develop the central section of your story as a chronological sequence of anecdotal incidents that embody and reveal the main points of your piece.

As you'll see when you read the complete stories at the end of Part I (p54), most of the pieces we've chosen to reproduce are organised along chronological, narrative lines, with the authors focusing on selected moments in their travels to draw out the most important aspects of their tales. In the Korea story ('The Path to Sokkuram'; p101), for example, Robert Hass takes us through his explorations, journeying deep into the countryside to visit the ancient capital of Kyongju, interweaving the themes of alienation and independence, pain and passion, introduced in the story's first paragraphs. Along the way we are presented with indelible portraits of people and places, history and culture, all interconnected in the unfolding of the author's experience – and all culminating in unexpected revelations and resolutions before the Buddha of Sokkuram. The result is an exemplary illustration of a moving and multilayered travel tale.

HINTS & TIPS

When making a list of highlight events, it's helpful to jot down a few notes about the significance of each. For example, here's the list of events I made for the Aitutaki article mentioned earlier (p30), along with the qualities each one represented, or illuminated, for me:

1. dinner at Café Tupuna (island cuisine using all local ingredients, friendliness of people)
2. the Cook Islands dance competition (culture)
3. island driving tour (landscape, history – *marae*: pre-Christian ceremonial site)
4. meeting local woodcarver and pareu-maker (culture, arts)
5. visit to One Foot Island (beauty, tranquility)
6. church service in Arutanga (history, island spirit and tradition)
7. dinner at Samade restaurant (cuisine)
8. dancing on stage with performers at Samade (dance, tradition – climax of stay).

I ordered these events in terms of their chronological order and emotional impact, and that order became the 'roadmap' for my article.

MODULATING YOUR MIDDLE

Let's say I want to write an article expressing my conviction that Croatia is the next big destination for travellers. First, I'd ask myself why I feel this way. Well, let's see: it's beautiful, it has a rich history, the people are warm and it's great value. I've isolated four salient points to support my theme, so the next question is order of importance.

To organise my story in terms of accelerating emotional connection, I'll lead with the point about value for money as it's the least emotional and most practical or logical consideration. History begins to involve the heart but is still fundamentally intellectual, so that would be second. Beauty is a more emotional consideration, drawing readers into the story via their soul. The people connection represents what I think is the climax of my trip, and the climax of travel itself, so that would come last. My final point is the top of the pyramid, but every step along the way contributes to my story's overall resonance and effectiveness.

Next, I'll search through my notes and draw out the experiences that brought these points to life. The hostel in Dubrovnik that cost just £15 a night, or that extraordinary meal under the stars that was £5. That's where I learned how inexpensive the place was, relatively speaking. The historical richness of the country came to life in Dubrovnik, when I walked along the walls of the old city and saw old roof tiles shattered during the war lying side by side with new roof tiles built to replace them – a poignant reminder of the constant presence of the past, but also an inspiring example of how tourism can help rebuild a place.

Croatia's beauty was obvious: the rocky coast and the shadowing cypresses, the wildflowers in bloom and not a person in sight.

And then it all came together for me on my last night in Dubrovnik, when I went out to dinner with a local tour guide and she told me about how her family had suffered during the war, how the entire country had suffered, but there was now new hope blooming in the land.

On reviewing these experiences, I realise that the historic part of the piece has more emotional resonance for me than the beautiful landscape. And so, I rearrange the segments. I start with the prices, then move on to the beauty and the history, and end with my meal with the tour guide. I'll have to make sure I pay attention to the transitions between the sections, but the piece is already taking shape in my mind. I've figured out how to structure the middle, and now it's just a question of bringing the individual examples to vivid life.

EXERCISE 6

Considering the trip you wrote about in Exercise 4 (p26), list the eight most important events that occurred during that journey. Order them by their importance to your understanding of the place or the impact of the place on you. Do you see a thread connecting at least some of these events? Does this thread lead to some conclusion or revelation? Does it illuminate something important about the place, or about yourself? If so, you may hold the itinerary of your story right there in your hands. Choose the four most important events and write 300-word descriptions of each.

CONCLUSIONS THAT LEAD TO NEW DIRECTIONS

The end of your article needs to achieve three intricately related objectives: bring the focus of your piece to a satisfying conclusion; tie the story back to its beginning; and deliver the reader back to the world.

The article about Las Vegas by Simon Calder quoted earlier in this chapter (p27) concludes with a reference that nicely brings the piece full circle:

> *Thanks to the physical properties of neon, a trip to Las Vegas can have much the same effect as expensive designer drugs.*
>
> *The home town of indulgence looks and feels like Toytown for tycoons. But beware staying here too long. On my last evening I got so lost trying to find a way out of Binion's Horseshoe Casino that I had to ask for directions back to real life.*

In the Aitutaki article mentioned earlier (p30 and p32), I began by describing the dance invitation, then explained the reason I had come to Aitutaki:

> *I longed for quietude, simplicity and a sense of things as they used to be. I was pining for qualities I associated with islands and with the South Pacific: a lush, slow, wild beauty, a barefoot tranquility, a balmy, palmy, sea-scented sensuality.*

To end that piece, I returned to the dance and the quest:

> *After we had feasted, a half-dozen musicians trooped in bearing ukuleles and wooden drums, then young dancers stepped onto the floor in pandanus skirts and coconut bras. Their passion and energy were infectious, and with the warm, caressing air, the delicious food, the music mingling with the stars, and the dancers' supple limbs and exuberant smiles, it was easy to get lulled into the spirit. I found myself on the floor, hips swaying.*

FINDING THE RIGHT CONCLUSION

In the article about my Kyoto temple sojourn (p23 and p28), I described the highlights of my stay – first impressions of the temple and my room; meeting the master of the temple, Yamada-sensei, and discussing the temple's history and his own hopes; and then wandering around the ground late at night, when that history seemed to come magically to life.

To conclude the piece, I wanted to find and describe one all-embracing moment that would embody the effect the temple had had on me and at the same time would allow me to prepare readers for re-entry into the world outside the article – just as I was preparing for re-entry into the city beyond the temple. In evoking this threshold moment, I wanted to be sure that the temple impression lingered – like a pebble dropped in a pool – in the reader's mind. Here are the two final paragraphs that comprise the end:

> The next day I arose at five to join the monks' morning service. The garden was obscured in a rice-paper mist, and the floor chilled my stockinged feet.
>
> I followed the six resident monks and nun in their rustling robes to the main hall, and sat as they did on the tatami mats. Yamada-sensei, sitting in front, began to chant – a low, deep, long wail – and the monks took up the prayer, breathing in, bellowing out, filling the hall with sound. One monk slowly tolled a huge gong; all around gold and red lacquer and deeply polished wood gleamed, incense spiraled into the air, and the chants and gongs surged and subsided, rose and fell, rose again – until the temple seemed one huge vibrating voice, and we its chords. Ahead was the Kyoto of day, of trolleys and tourist buses, but for me, just then, there was only this Kyoto of incense and chant and gong, of stone lantern and paper screen, of priest and monk and nun, this place of waking dream.

Time slowed, and the discoveries of my five-day stay coursed through me: the island's slow, stately pace, the warmth of the people, the soul-soaring beauty of the place, the bountiful humor I had encountered, the sense of plenty in mango and pawpaw, the sense of peace in palm tree, lagoon and beach. The leg-thumping and heart-pumping rhythms reached my deepest core like a key, turning and turning, unlocking mysteries that seemed even older than me.

Suddenly I found myself in a place I'd never been but knew instinctively. Drums pounded, hips swayed, gardenia perfumed the scene. In an instant I recognized this South Seas culmination: I had found the island of Salvation.

EXERCISE 7

Re-read the beginning you wrote in Exercise 4 (p26) and the descriptions you wrote in Exercise 6 (p34). Now describe in 250 to 300 words what happened right after that moment you wrote about in your lead, and what you learned as a result. Is this the climax of your story, the place where all the pieces of the puzzle come together? If so, you have a natural ending to your account. And by combining Exercises 4, 6 and 7, you have a first draft of your story. Well done!

A similar effect informs the Delos story. The extract reproduced earlier in this chapter (p30) ended with the introduction of an old man and a young boy, both of whom offered a tour of the island. The story goes on to describe how I spontaneously decided to miss the boat back to Mykonos in order to spend the night on the island, and depicts a raucous dinner with a Hungarian physicist who is also spending the night there, concluding with this description of the following morning:

Streaming sunlight awakened me. I turned to look at my watch and disturbed a black kitten that had bundled itself at my feet. In so doing, I also disturbed the ouzo and retsina that had bundled itself in my head, and I crawled as close as I could to the shadow of the wall – 6:45. I pulled my towel over my head and tried to imagine the windy dark, but to no avail. The kitten mewed its way under my towel, where it took to lapping at my cheek as if it had discovered a bowl of milk.

I stumbled down the stairs and soaked my head in tepid tap water until at last I felt stable enough to survey the surroundings. Behind the pavilion a clothesline led to the rusting generator. Chickens strutted inside a coop at the curator's house. Rhenea stirred in the rising mist.

Again I wandered through the ruins, different ruins now, bright with day and the reality of returns: The tourists would return to Delos, and I would return to Mykonos. I ate a solemn breakfast on the terrace with the physicist, then walked past the sacred lake and the marketplace to the Terrace of the Lions. Standing among the five lions of Delos, erected in the seventh century BC to defend the island from invaders, I looked

over the crumbling walls and stunted pillars to the temples on the hill.
Like priests they presided over the procession of tourists who would
surge onto the island, bearing their oblation in cameras and guidebooks.
As the trawler approached, a bent figure in a navy blue beret hurried to
the dock, and a boy in shorts raced out of the curator's house past the
physicist, past me, and into the ruins.

You can see how the story circles back to its beginning – the old man and the
young boy rushing to meet the new day's potential clients – but everything
else has changed. The reader has spent 24 hours on Delos with me, and so
now has an entirely different impression of the island. At the end of the story,
readers are led back to the world outside Delos and outside the article – but
with an enhanced understanding of Delos and, ideally, with a renewed appreciation of the planet.

EXERCISE 8

Re-read the beginning you wrote in Exercise 5 (p30). Now that you can
look back on your finished journey, consider if there is another moment
later in your trip that recalls this same experience and theme. Can you
find a thematic circularity? Does the second moment complement and
complete the first? Describe the second experience in 250 words. These
may be the 'bookends' of your piece.

Finally, it's critical that you pay special attention to the last word of your
story. This is where you leave the reader, literally and figuratively. It is your –
and your story's – last point of connection with the reader, and the reader's
threshold to the world outside the story. Where do you want to leave the reader?
What do you want their last – and lasting – impression of your story to be?

BUILDING BLOCKS

One fundamentally important element to consider when shaping your story
is its structural development. Think of each story as a set of building blocks.
The beginning lays the foundation, and the middle builds on that foundation. It is essential that each part of the story builds upon the part that came
before. This building up needs to be logical – that is, the progression of
ideas and events in the story has to make sense – but it should also be thematic and emotional.

When you are editing your own article, ask yourself if each section advances the story in the direction it needs to go, and whether each section builds upon the one before. In order to answer these questions, you need to be clear about your article's overall aim – this is absolutely fundamental to a successful travel article. As long as you know your story's goal, you'll be able to tell if your story is proceeding clearly and powerfully, block by block. With each new addition, ask yourself: does the reader need to know this? Does this take the reader one step closer to the overall point? If you stray from your overall aim, you'll lose your reader.

EXERCISE 9

Think about a travel experience or destination that you passionately want to write about. What is it about the experience or destination that you want to convey to your reader? What is the fundamental point of your piece? Try to reduce that point to one sentence. For example: 'Spending a night on the Greek island of Delos offered life-changing lessons in the history and character of that sacred island.' Write that sentence at the beginning of your story. As you write your story, this sentence will be your compass and map; refer back to it continually. Is every building block in your story leading toward conveying this point to your reader?

TRANSITIONS

In crafting a story, transitions are one of the writer's most important tools, linking one paragraph to another, and one section of a piece to the next. If you think of your article as a journey, the transitions are the stepping stones or tiny bridges that help the reader along – without them, the reader would fall into the chasm of incomprehensibility. Transitions give your piece coherence; they make sure your story follows logically from one step to the next, and they make sure you don't lose your reader along the way.

Transitions from one paragraph to another usually pick up a detail, image or theme from the last sentence in the preceding paragraph. In a chronological description, the sequential rush of events generally provides its own transitions, but when you leap from one event to another, you need to make sure that the reader leaps with you. Occasionally, you will find that there is no appropriate transition at a particular place in a story, or that you don't want to craft a transition – you want to make a clear break in the narrative.

THE ACCORDION THEORY OF TIME

Students often ask me how to craft a description of an entire trip in a few words. Say you have between 1500 and 2500 words to write about a five-day journey. If you tried to write about everything that happened on that journey, you would have the travel equivalent of *War and Peace*. (You would also end up with a piece that was more suited to your personal travel diary than the very public pages of a newspaper or magazine.) So what you have to do is edit your reality. You have to think about all the pertinent experiences in your trip and then you have to choose those very few – three or four – that embody and illuminate the main points you want to make about your journey.

In order to do this well, you are going to end up focusing very precisely on those four experiences, and skimming over all the other experiences of your trip. This is where the accordion theory of time comes in. Your narrative focus moves in and out, in and out. You expand the accordion to full arm's length in order to focus closely on a moment in time, then you push it in to skim over whole days; then you draw it out again to focus on the next significant experience, then push it in to jump over more days.

Study almost any travel narrative, and you'll see that the author is playing the accordion of time. The writer isolates the cardinal events in their experience, analyses how they fit into the pattern of meaning they are trying to evoke, and focuses on the details of those events to render them in a way that will enable the reader to live them just as they did. They may lavish three pages on an incident that happened in five minutes, then summarise the next five days in five sentences. The narrative proceeds in this way – in and out, in and out – singling out for scrutiny and expanded description the events that form the building blocks of the story. The full meaning and impact of the story is created through the accumulation, organisation and integration of these event blocks.

This is the place to use a section break, indicated in the text by a line break or a graphic element, which signals to the reader that you have ended one sequence and are beginning another. The reader will leap with you over the break, but without that visual cue, the reader will expect you to lead them along by the hand.

BRINGING YOUR STORY TO LIFE

How do you bring your story to life with the kind of lively prose that editors say they want? Here are some of the most important tools and principles.

DIALOGUE

Dialogue helps to enliven a piece aurally, varying its rhythm. On another level it can be used to humanise a story, injecting characters into your article in a way that creates warmth and resonance for the reader. It can also help to illuminate a place. Remember how Robert Hass began 'The Path to Sokkuram'? He employed dialogue to push the story thematically along. His account ends at another café with dialogue of a different kind:

> The waitress returned with a little paper packet of roast silkworms. On the house. She pointed at a shy boy at the next table and bit her lip before proceeding very deliberately. 'My friend is so exciting only to have this opportunity to speak practical English and having sharing Korean culture.' I understood. He was treating me to the silkworms. We were going to argue about politics. I ordered another bottle of wine and gestured him over. He sat down opposite me. Two of the waitresses joined us. The silkworms tasted vile, and I smiled gratefully trying to get one down. The girls laughed and the wine came. 'Korea,' the young man began, and shook his head. He said the word as if it were a synonym for life. Then he sighed happily and said it again. 'Korea, Korea, Korea.'

Dialogue gives a piece human context and contact. It can also help supply critical information in a nontextbook way. For example, a local resident or museum docent can enter the story to reveal the history of the town or the special qualities of the painting on display. And dialogue can introduce human quirks – turns of phrase, colloquialisms, patterns of speech – that help warm a story as well. The key is to use dialogue sparingly, keeping it crisp and authentic.

Dialogue should never be invented or embellished to suit your purpose. If you are altering reality in any way – compressing sentences spoken by three different people at three different times into one cocktail party dialogue, for example – then you have to make it clear that you are doing so. It's perfectly acceptable to clean up dialogue by removing repetitious pauses such as 'um' and 'ah', but you must adhere scrupulously to the truth of what the person is saying. You must not distort their words or misrepresent their meaning.

EXERCISE 10

On your next trip, near or far, engage someone you encounter in conversation. It might be a fisherman or a flower seller, museum docent or
metro conductor. Afterward, in no more than 250 words, reproduce your
dialogue as closely as you can, so that someone who wasn't there can
'hear' the content and flavour of your conversation. What essential information did they convey? Can you picture the person from their words?

Paul Theroux is a master at dialogue. Open any of his travel books and
you'll quickly find economical, illuminating conversations, as in this excerpt
from his wonderful book, *Ghost Train to the Eastern Star.* Here Theroux
recounts a conversation with a woman in Hanoi who had been a teen at the
time of the infamous US Christmas bombing of that city:

'*Do you remember the Christmas bombing?*'

'*I remember everything. I remember the day the bombs fell on Kham
Thien Street,*' she said, drawing her silk scarf close with her slender fingers. '*It was the nineteenth of December. A thousand people died there
that day, and most of them were women and children. Every home was
destroyed. It was very terrible to see.*'

'*You saw it?*'

'*Yes. My aunt and my mother took me to see the damage,*' she said.
'*We saw many cratères – yes, craters – big holes in the road. And the
dead, and the fires. I was so frightened. But my aunt and my mother
said, "We must see this. What has been done to us." There's a monument on that street now.*'

'*Were you living near there?*'

'*We were just outside Hanoi.*' She hesitated, then, seeming to remember, said, '*We didn't have much to eat. In fact, we had very little food all
through the war. We were always hungry. Even after the war was over
we had so little rice. And it was stale rice – old rice.*'

'*Because of the destruction?*'

'*No. Because of the American embargo, and the Chinese invasion.*'...

'*We were told that the targets were military bases.*'

She smiled sadly at this and said, '*Everything was targeted. The whole
city. Especially roads and bridges. Our bridge was bombed by the B-52s*' –
this was the Chuong Duong Bridge, across the Red River to Haiphong.
'*But we repaired it. Factories were especially targeted, no matter what
they made. The bombings continued for years. Everything was bombed.*'

Here Theroux conveys not just essential historical information but equally essential emotional information – without having to do any analysing or explaining himself. The dialogue says it all. This emotional context and connection is critical for the reader to understand how deeply Theroux will be moved by his experience in Vietnam – by the country's current prosperity and by its extraordinarily warm and open-hearted welcoming of him, an American.

CHARACTERS

The introduction of characters is often critical to the success of a travel piece. Characters can illuminate places, and often help to propel and enliven a story. The human connection is arguably the most powerful element of travel, spanning cultures and backgrounds. Conveying a sense of human connection through the effective introduction of character is a great and powerful art. So pay attention to characters and don't shy away from bringing local people – or fellow travellers – into your story. Their presence in a story creates a human bridge between the story and the reader, just as they themselves are a human bridge between their home and you.

A character can be memorably painted using just a few brushstrokes. Consider this figure from James D. Houston's heart-touching Hawaiian tale, 'Everything Come Round', published in the anthology *The Kindness of Strangers*. Houston is locked out of his car on an isolated island road:

> *I turned and saw a huge Polynesian fellow, Hawaiian or, perhaps, from the size of him, Samoan. His dark features were etched and fierce. Black hair was drawn back into a stubby knot. His mouth arced in what seemed a permanent scowl, as he regarded me in the twilight of this otherwise empty parking lot....*

HINTS & TIPS
To help in capturing dialogue, I always carry a pocket notebook with me. Whenever I have a conversation I want to remember, I immediately jot down as much of the conversation as I can. It's often awkward to start writing in front of the person I'm quoting, so if I'm talking to someone over a meal in a restaurant, for example, I'll excuse myself and go to the restroom, then write feverishly. Paul Theroux once told me that he uses this same technique. Now, whenever I'm waiting interminably for someone to vacate a restroom, I imagine Paul Theroux is inside, scribbling.

I glanced past him, wondering if there were others, though he didn't need any others. His brown arms, purpled with tattoos, were the size of my legs. His thighs were as thick as nail kegs. He out-weighed me by a hundred pounds, and it wasn't fat. If he came at me, I was finished....

That's all we need in order to see the hulking fellow and to feel Houston's fear. Happily, as it turns out, the gentle islander produces a coat hanger from his own car and proceeds to expertly unlock Houston's rental car – and to unlock some truths about stereotypes and human goodwill as well.

EXERCISE 11

Describe one of the most memorable people you've ever met. Begin with this simple sentence: The most memorable encounter I've ever had was _____. Think of what the person looked like. What were they wearing? How did they act? What did they say? What made the encounter so memorable? What did you learn from it? Why does it live so vividly inside you still? Write a 250- to 400-word description of this encounter that focuses on the most telling, the most revealing, details and events. What does a reader need to know to understand the impact of this encounter on you?

ILLUMINATING DETAILS & ANECDOTES

Details hold the key to a good description and can be full of meaning, embodying the most important characteristics you want to convey. The more precise you can be in identifying and isolating the right details, and the more fully you can evoke those particular details in the reader's mind, the more powerful, compelling and effective your description will be.

You can never squeeze all the details of a place into a description. If you tried to do so, you could write a book as long as *Ulysses* about the room you are sitting in now. You have to edit reality. You have to isolate the most telling details, asking yourself which ones most powerfully and precisely convey whatever it is about the scene that is most directly relevant to your story, which details will best establish the points you want to make.

In Simon Calder's description of neon, he didn't tell you everything he knows about neon, just the facts that pertain to his eventual point about Las Vegas. And in Robert Hass' depiction of his Korean pilgrimage, he doesn't add extraneous details about the country or his experience there – he focuses solely on the information the reader needs to know in order to relive his journey.

Consider this portrait of a table-maker named Pierrot from Peter Mayle's delightful 'A Year in Provence':

> We knocked and went in, and there was Pierrot. He was shaggy, with a wild black beard and formidable eyebrows. A piratical man. He made us welcome, beating the top layer of dust from two chairs with a battered trilby hat which he then placed carefully over the telephone on the table.

With just these few key details, Mayle masterfully conveys a sense of this impetuous, larger-than-life eccentric.

The same is true of places. You just need a few details, but the right details, to paint a persuasive scene. Here is how Kira Salak evokes the ruins of Leptis Magna in her Libya article:

> I'm not the kind of person who usually gets into Roman ruins, can only handle about a day of them. But here at Leptis Magna – Latin for the Great Leptis – the city is so well-preserved that it allows you to dream. There are the marble-covered pools of the Hadriatic Baths, great Corinthian columns rising 30 feet. There is the nearly intact coliseum, three stories high, where you can crawl through lion chutes and explore the gladiators' quarters. They don't make cities like this anymore, every architectural detail attended to, no plan too lavish, no material too dear. Bearded gods gaze down from friezes. Maidens and warriors lounge among the carved porticos. Even the communal toilets remain nearly unscathed, the marble seats shined by thousands of ancient buttocks.

How wonderfully those bethroned buttocks bridge the centuries!

A few paragraphs later, Salak brings another scene – the remains of a caravan town – to equally poignant life:

> Ghadamis is less a town than a gigantic labyrinth of narrow passageways that cut around and beneath adobe homes. Living here is like living in a subterranean world, the sun and its heat cut off by the rise of centuries-old buildings, each built into the next and accessed by an interlocking tunnel system. Now deserted, the town has an eerie quality of being just unearthed. Feeling like an archaeologist, I explore the dark, empty passageways with my flashlight, coming upon dead ends and mysterious chambers built from Roman columns. I squeeze through an open palm-wood door, climbing dusty stairs to the highest floor. Part of

the ceiling has fallen in, incongruous sunlight gleaming on white walls
painted with cryptic red Berber designs.
   Maneuvering through crumbling piles of adobe bricks and debris, I
reach the roof and gaze out on a scene out of Arabian Nights: *countless*
white-washed terraces spreading toward the setting sun and the distant
sand hills of Algeria. Nearby, palm gardens resound with birdsong and
the burbling of aquifer water. The call to prayer wails from the squat
mud minarets of a nearby adobe mosque, and I can only take it all in
silently, reverentially, like a devotee.

EXERCISE 12

Situate yourself somewhere comfortable – a café, say, or an open-air
market, a city square or a beach. Quietly and intently observe for 15
minutes or half an hour, then write as precise a description as you can
in 300 words. What are the most important, defining elements of the
scene – the points of the place? What are the things you need to convey to make someone else understand those points? Repeat the same
exercise in the same place the following day. Refine your description,
paring it to the essentials.

Anecdotes are simply a larger, expanded version of details. Just as a scene is
composed of myriad details that need to be filtered, so a journey is composed
of myriad anecdotes. Your job is to choose just those anecdotes that capture,
crystallise and convey the point of your piece.

EXERCISE 13

On your next trip, keep a record of your journey. At the end of each
day, list the main events of that day – try for at least three different events each day. At the end of the journey, choose the six most
important events of the entire trip. These are your prime anecdote
candidates. Can you see connections between them? A thematic or
emotional development from one to the next and the next? Focus on
this development. Where does it lead? What characteristics or lessons
does it reveal? Re-create these anecdotes for the reader, striving to
faithfully and precisely duplicate your experience, so that the reader
learns what you learned, as you learned it.

ACCURACY

One especially critical element in re-creating a travel experience is accuracy. Travel pieces must be accurate in two ways. First, they must be factually accurate in their reporting. This means getting the population of the African village right, precisely conveying the colour of the church in Nova Scotia and getting the year that the Spaniards settled on the coast correct. There is simply no excuse for getting your facts wrong, and you should not expect sympathy (or future work) from an editor if you do.

The second kind of accuracy is in perception and description. It is far more difficult to capture, but is equally critical to the depth and success of travel writing.

Let's say you are trying to describe a field in France. You write: 'I saw a field in France.' Does this bring any image of the field into the reader's mind? No. So you think some more about the field and write: 'In France I saw a field the size of a football pitch.' This helps a little – at least we have a sense of size – but we still don't see the field. So you dig back into your memory – and your notes – and write: 'In France I saw a field the size of a football pitch, filled with red poppies.' Suddenly the image blazes to life. We can see the field, the poppies extending toward the horizon. Now you're back in the scene, remembering the morning, and you write: 'In France I drove by a field the size of a football pitch, filled with red poppies and bordered on three sides by rows of lavender, whose sweet scent so filled the air that I had to stop.' Now we're right with you. Not only do we have a sense of size and colour, we now also have another sense involved – the sense of smell – as well as the action of you stopping. You have successfully engaged your reader.

A good travel story is basically the accumulation of such details of perception and description. But you can't put these descriptive details into your stories unless you experience them first. You have to experience the world with a fearless curiosity, and then render that curiosity and the discoveries it brings in clean, clear, compelling prose. Do that and you'll get somewhere. And you'll take the reader with you.

Tim Cahill presents a compelling on-site lesson in accuracy in this passage from his extraordinary tale 'Among the Karowai: A Stone Age Idyll', about a river journey deep into the wild heart of Papua New Guinea:

> William spent several hours teaching me to finally see the swamp. The tall trees? The ones over there that grow from a single white-barked trunk and have elephant-ear-size leaves? Those are called sukun, and the Karowai eat the fruit, which is a little like coconut.

Stands of bamboo often grew on the banks of the river, in a green starburst pattern that arched out over the water. Banana trees also grew in a starburst pattern of wide flat leaves. They reached heights of seven or eight feet, and yielded small three- and four-inch-long bananas.

Rattan, a long tough vine used to lash homes together, to string bows, or to tie off anything that needed tying – the local equivalent of duct tape – was identifiable as a slender leafless branch, generally towering up out of a mass of greenery like an antenna.

Sago, the staple food, was a kind of palm tree that grew twenty to thirty feet high, in a series of multiple stems that erupted out of a central base in another starburst pattern. The leaves were shaped like the arching banana leaves but were arranged in fronds ...

So – sukun, rattan, bamboo, banana, sago – the forest was no longer a mass of unvariegated green. Naming things allowed me to see them, to differentiate one area of the swamp from another. I found myself confirming my newfound knowledge at every bend of the river. 'Banana, banana,' I informed everyone. 'Sukun, sago, sago, rattan, sago, bamboo...'

The more accurately we apprehend the world, the more deeply we can penetrate it – and it can penetrate us.

USE ALL YOUR SENSES

Most travel articles include good visual descriptions of the places where the stories are set, but writers far too frequently ignore their other senses in their depictions. Think of it: when you walk into an Italian restaurant, what are the first senses that accost you? Not sight, but probably sound and smell. There's the raucous ruckus of the patrons, the waiters pushing through the crowd, the garlicky snap and sizzle of food flipped in frying pans. The aromas may be the first sensory impression of all: the garlic that insinuated itself into the preceding sentence's sizzle, the mozzarella and tomatoes wafting from the kitchen, the mingled smells of veal piccata and pasta al pesto. So if you are going to describe this Italian restaurant in your article, you could begin with its smells and sounds – not forgetting, of course, the tastes.

When we travel we experience the world with all of our senses – so why do we focus so exclusively on sight in our articles? Cultivate the fine – and rewarding – art of paying attention to all the senses. Let your ears and nose and taste buds and fingers do as much work as your eyes.

EXERCISE 14

Return to the scene-setting you did for Exercise 12 (p45). Rewrite the description, in no more than 350 words, using as many of the five senses as you can. What did the place smell like? What could you hear? What was the texture of the sand beneath you or the stone pillar by your side? Could you taste the sea-salt in the air? Now read both pieces of writing aloud. See how using all the senses in your description brings the place to life? It's more satisfying for you and for your reader.

SHOW, DON'T TELL

If you've ever taken a creative writing class, you will have had this maxim drilled into your head. Don't tell what your characters are feeling – show it. Reveal their inner selves through what they do and say. Let the reader draw the conclusions. The same is true for travel writing. Your piece will be much more powerful and successful if you engage the reader in the creative process of figuring out how the people in your tale are being affected. By the same token, don't spell out the fact that you were moved by an experience – make the reader feel moved by the way you describe the experience. Re-create the experience so that the reader is in your shoes – and is moved just the way you were.

AVOID CLICHÉS

Clichés have a way of creeping into our writing – it's difficult to come up with something fresh every time. Sometimes, without our even realising it, a well-worn phrase that we've picked up from who-knows-where slips surreptitiously into our prose. Reread your writing with your cliché-meter on high, and avoid

HINTS & TIPS
One of my first assignments for *Travel + Leisure* was a description of great places to go in Northern California, including famed Muir Woods. The most striking aspect of that sacred place – and an aspect featured in every article I'd read – was how the sunlight filters through the high branches of the trees, creating an effect like stained glass in a cathedral. As I approached the place, I wondered: how can I avoid writing the same description as everyone else? Then I came up with a solution – I walked around Muir Woods blindfolded. Suddenly an entirely different place – of rough-textured bark, crackling pine needles and crisp evergreen scent – came to life.

those tired descriptions – land of contrasts, tropical paradise, bustling thoroughfare… Whenever you come to a phrase that sounds wooden, stop and ask yourself if there might be a better way of expressing what you want to say, one that more truly reflects your take on it.

One of the culprits editors most frequently cite when they talk about bad travel writing is the use of clichés. So be a vigilant self-editor. Always make your words and descriptions your own.

ELEMENTS OF STYLE

The following critical elements also help to determine the success – or failure – of a travel story.

VOICE

Travel stories need a warm human voice. Don't try to write like a fact-checker or reporter who is simply recording their surroundings, without any sense of engagement. You are undertaking a fundamentally human adventure – encountering new people and a new culture, whether it's in a different region of your own country or somewhere halfway around the world. Your humanity should be one of the fundamental strengths of your story.

Your voice should be a reflection of your personality and style, whether romantic, reflective, funny, sarcastic or informative. Read the examples at the end of Part I (p54), and note how each writer employs a different tone. Over time you will come to be identified with the voice you project in your stories, so it is imperative to write in a way that feels natural to you and to the particular story.

Another aspect of voice is its use to express opinion and judgment. Readers – and editors – are relying on your expertise and discernment to steer them away from scams and disappointments, and to point them in the direction of the best on-the-road experiences. Informing your voice with opinion when appropriate is an essential part of your job.

PACING

What kind of pace do you want your story to have? It can be headlong and breathless or slow and measured. Make sure the pace fits your piece, and that you're in control of the pacing of your story. It's fine to speed up and slow down – it can make the reading a richer experience – just don't let the story career out of control like a South American mountain bus crossing a snow-patched pass and then heading downhill when suddenly the brakes give out and the driver can't stop and the landscape is whizzing dizzyingly by and before you know it the reader is gone – pfff! – like the bus into the South American sky.

ATTEND TO THE MUSIC OF THE LANGUAGE

Think of English as a musical instrument. You are using that instrument to create great music. Read your writing out loud, and listen to the music of your writing. What kind of mood are you creating? Are you keeping the pace lively or is it wooden? Are you varying the tempos in your writing? Are you using devices such as internal rhyme and alliteration?

Take any book by Jan Morris, open it at random and begin to read aloud. Listen to the way she modulates your journey through the story. Revel in her masterful use of the intrinsic music of our language.

Here's a luminous example of Morris' art from her essay 'Chaunrikharka', about a Sherpa home where she was nursed back to health when she fell sick in Nepal:

> Outside the house everything steamed. The monsoon was upon us. The rains fell heavily for several hours each day, and the gardens that surrounded Chaunrikharka's six or seven houses were all lush and vaporous. My room had no window, but the open door looked out upon the Sonam family plot, and from it there came a fragrance so profoundly blended of the fertile and the rotten, the sweet and the bitter, the emanations of riotous growth and the intimations of inevitable decay, that still, if ever my mind wanders to more sententious subjects, I tend to smell the vegetable gardens of Chaunrikharka.
>
> The taste of the potatoes, too, roasted at the family hearth, seemed to me almost philosophically nourishing, while the comfort of the powerful white liquor, rakshi, with which the Sonams now and then dosed me, and the merry voices of the children, frequently hushed lest they disturb my convalescence, and the kind wondering faces of the neighbors who occasionally looked through the open door, and the clatter of the rain on the roof and the hiss of it in the leaves outside, and the enigmatic smiles of those small golden figures in their half light at the end of the room – all built up in my mind an impression not just of peace and piquancy, but of holiness.

Study the musicality and modulation here. Those last two sentences go on and on – and yet you never lose your place in them. Morris builds them – and conducts us through them – phrase by phrase, detail by detail, until a sturdy, sensual and spiritual edifice is complete.

MAKE YOUR VERBS ACT & YOUR WORDS COUNT

One of the biggest traps for novice writers is the urge to make prose powerful by overwriting, using high-flown adjectives and adverbs. You can feel the sentences collapsing under the weight of such words. Use active verbs, and don't use three words when you can use one. Rather than writing 'He walked as quickly as he could up the crater', write 'He raced up the crater' or, even better, 'He scrambled up the crater'. Reread your work slowly, and ask yourself if you really need each word. Remember that less is more.

EXERCISE 15

Choose a few paragraphs from your favourite travel writer and type them into your computer. Now edit those paragraphs. Analyse their choice of words, especially the verbs they use. Does every word do as much 'work' as possible? Are there any words you can delete or improve? Now type a few of your own paragraphs. Read those sentences with the same critical eye. Can you delete or strengthen any of your word choices?

CONSISTENT VERB TENSE

You would be amazed how many writers, even very established writers, mix up their verb tenses in their stories. Unless you're doing this on purpose and with a sure sense of control, you shouldn't begin your story in the present tense and then flip into the past tense, and then into the present tense and then back into the past tense again. You might think this is an obvious point, but just watch

HINTS & TIPS

One of my most memorable writing mentors is the great John McPhee, longtime staff writer at the *New Yorker*. I was one of the lucky students in his first groundbreaking nonfiction writing workshop at Princeton, called The Literature of Fact. One of his favourite assignments was to pass out 250-word pieces from the 'Talk of the Town' section of the *New Yorker*. Though these had been meticulously edited and re-edited by the magazine's staff, until they had been pared to the editorial bone, he would delightedly tell us to cut 10 words from each piece. We would groan, but the value of this exercise was immeasurable. It taught me to read each sentence word by word and to ask: Is this word really necessary? Is this one? When I read my own pieces with that same mindset, any superfluous words stood out.

yourself the next time you write a travel piece. Reread it very carefully and see if at some point you too don't fall prey to inconsistencies of tense.

Writing in the present tense has become something of a vogue recently, largely due to the internet and the more immediate prose the medium has encouraged and cultivated. Somehow, the web feels like a present-tense medium. But writing in the present tense can have its pitfalls. As a narrator you can have no more sense of what's coming than your reader. You cannot possibly know what happened two days after the day you're describing, and you need to take particular care not to let that knowledge colour your narrative in any way. You have to re-create the ignorance you had at the moment you are describing, and never divulge more about your trip than you knew at that time.

Writing in the past tense, on the other hand, liberates you. You already know what happened at the end of the trip, so in that sense writing in the past tense is a much more natural choice. But it's up to you – just be sure to be consistent and in control of your choice. If you're not, the reader will get lost – and your piece won't get published.

HINTS & TIPS
When I was starting out, I wrote a commissioned piece for a magazine. I was pretty naive about the business of travel writing, and fashioned myself an artist – a poet of the road. And so I purposefully crafted my work in the present tense. The editor asked me to rewrite it in the past tense. After initially exploding with righteous anger (note: this is not recommended as a way to impress an editor), I recast the piece and discovered that in fact it made hardly any difference at all. I had written it in the present tense because I wanted to convey a sense of immediacy; I wanted the reader to feel they were right there with me. But the truth is that the reader will still feel that way when the piece is written in the past tense.

EXERCISE 16

Choose a particularly compelling encounter, event or activity from a recent trip and describe it in 200 to 300 words in the present tense. Then write the same account in the past tense. Which one works better? Which is more powerful? Does one feel more restricting or liberating than the other? Keep these differences in mind as you craft your stories. The tense you choose can help or hinder your ability to tell your tale.

REWRITING & SELF-EDITING

Different writers have different strategies for rewriting and self-editing. Some rewrite as they go along; others wait to rewrite until they've completed a first draft of the entire piece.

A good practice is to write three drafts of an article. In the first draft, try to get down everything that's in your mind about the story – all the important incidents, impressions and lessons. In this phase it's best to write as quickly as possible, rather than pausing to rewrite.

The second draft of your article is where you undertake the macro-editing phase. Read the story for flow and logical development, possibly looking to move sections in order to clarify and refine the movement and development of the piece. Also look to remove any sections that do not add to the story and identify any gaps that still need to be filled. Ask yourself if you've supplied all the information a reader needs to know in order to re-create that experience. Does the story build up coherently to its main point?

The third draft is the micro-editing phase, where you read very slowly and precisely, paying close attention to the style of the prose. Have you made every word count? Are you re-creating your experience as vividly and truly as possible? Are all the transitions there? How about the music of the piece?

After you have finalised the third draft you should be ready to send the story to an editor. At this stage many experienced writers show their work to a 'trusted reader', whether that be their spouse, a good friend or their agent, before they send it off to be published – sometimes even the most capable writers are too close to their work to see something that an objective eye can pick up. Of course, after the editor has read it, you may be asked to rework the piece further, but that is an essential part of the process, too.

The editor will have their own view of the piece, and of where and how it fits into the puzzle of their publication. It is the writer's job to work with the editor to come up with a story that satisfies both parties. If you feel very strongly that you do not want to make an editorial change, you should state your case and discuss that point with the editor by all means, but you should be careful not to alienate them. Just as finding a great story entails a marriage of passion and practicality, so too publishing a story entails marrying the editor's and the writer's views of the story. The examples of good travel writing that follow present some successful examples of this marriage.

EXAMPLES OF GOOD TRAVEL WRITING

We have discussed the various elements that comprise the art of creating a great travel story, from finding your focus, to researching before and during a trip, to identifying and evoking just the right details that convey the essential point of your piece. To end this section we are presenting seven travel articles, published in a variety of publications, that embody and illustrate the principles we have already described.

We hope our selection will inspire you by revealing the literary spectrum that travel writing encompasses. We also hope it will help you consider what kind of writing best suits you, or suits the subject of a particular piece you are trying to write.

Choosing these stories was a daunting task, and we do not mean to suggest in any way that they are the best travel stories published in the past decade. They are simply representative stories that illustrate many of the principles of successful travel writing that we have discussed throughout this section.

Pick up the current issue of any of the newspapers or magazines mentioned within these pages and you will find other excellent examples of travel writing.

MASTERFUL MENTORS

Listings of classic works of travel literature are included in the Resources section in Part III (p299, p315 and p330). In particular, I recommend that you peruse the works of the following writers, who are contemporary masters of travel writing and who publish in both periodicals and books:

Jan Morris (you can learn from anything she's written, but take a look at the essays collected in *Journeys and Destinations* for a starter); Paul Theroux (his first travel book, *The Great Railway Bazaar*, and his three-decade-later follow-up, *Ghost Train to the Eastern Star*, are arguably his best); Tim Cahill (his collections are audacious and illuminating; as an appetiser, try *Pass the Butterworms*); and Pico Iyer (all his books are elegant and insightful, but begin with *Video Night in Kathmandu*, which still pulses with an eclectic, electric intelligence and passion decades after its publication).

LAS VEGAS
by Simon Calder

Simon Calder is the Senior Travel Editor of the *Independent*, where this story was first published. This fact-packed article offers a witty illumination of neon's past and presence in Las Vegas. The story's surprising beginning signals that we are in for an offbeat approach to a city we may feel we already know well. We learn midway through the article that the piece is pegged to a specific exhibition on neon at the Nevada State Museum, but the larger point Calder makes is that all of Las Vegas is an 'amorphous neon museum'. Also note Calder's lively use of puns – 'the fall-out of constant re-invention' in a paragraph on Nevada's nearby atomic explosions; 'tuition is better than intuition' – and the way he compresses and connects ancient (Luxor) and modern (the Mormons, the railroad company, the atomic tests) history with the timeless character of the city itself. He uses the 'Neon Unplugged' exhibit to reveal the entire city in a new light.

Neon: you need to know two things about this gas. The first is that it is, in elementary terms, a relative newcomer; even though it is present in small quantities in the air we breathe, it was identified only a century ago by a French scientist named Georges Claude. The second is that, being inert, neon is intrinsically dull. Oh, unless you pass an electric charge through it, as M Claude did. Do that, and it can light up the desert and dazzle the world.

Las Vegas was just a flicker in the eye of the San Pedro, Los Angeles and Salt Lake City Railroad when M Claude announced his discovery. The first neon sign in North America was sold by M Claude's own company in 1923 to a Packard dealership in Los Angeles.

At the time, the Mormons mistakenly believed Las Vegas presented a promised, and morally safe, haven in the middle of the Mojave Desert. By the Thirties, they had lost faith with Las Vegas – and the rest of the world had lost interest in the fact that neon glows red in the dark and that, when mixed with a little mercury, its elementary cousin argon turns bright blue. But Las Vegas had barely begun to experiment with the extreme right-hand side of the Periodic Table of Elements.

Helium radiates a lurid magnolia when suitably fired up; krypton issues a steely silver; while xenon emits the palest blue. These elementary truths helped Las Vegas find its place in the world.

55

Whatever your desire, especially if it was illegal and/or frowned upon in the rest of the US, it could usually be found in Nevada's largest city. Drinkers could slake their thirsts, gamblers could stake their shirts and lovers could make (or fake) their vows. In short, it was a gas, with neon at the top of the elementary tree.

'Welcome to Fabulous Las Vegas' shrieks the iconic sign. When you see the city's emblem close up, in the unforgiving glare of a Nevada noon, it looks pitifully plain. You spot it as you head north along Las Vegas Boulevard at the intersection with Main Street. Las Vegas Boulevard is stripped down to 'the Strip' by almost everybody. All the grand monuments from the turn of the 21st century, from the Venetian to Camelot (not a lottery operator, but a re-enactment of the court of King Arthur), cling to the southern part of the Strip.

Downtown Las Vegas is where M Claude's new gas found its raison d'être, and helped the city claw an identity from the shadowy desert. Neon helped to define Las Vegas, and now the city is returning the favour. Time in Las Vegas seems to revolve around 33 times faster than real life. So the relics that have seen the city through since its foundation in 1905 are, relatively speaking, as ancient as the antiquities in Luxor – established in Egypt 1570 BC, established in Las Vegas 1993. This was the same time as the Dunes – a shining light on the strip – was snuffed out. It was imploded to make room for Bellagio, the flashy Italianate hotel-casino (that hyphen welds the two together with a permanence not often found in Las Vegas) where Europe meets America and gambles away the rest of the night.

Las Vegas did not always have such global pretensions. In the early days, the city experimented freely with newly discovered elements on the blank canvas of the Mojave Desert.

Evidence of innovation is scattered around the city, but you have to raise your gaze from the baize gaming tables to see it. Downtown is like an amorphous neon museum, whose exhibits are scattered around the streets. The first item was the horse and rider from the Hacienda, now frozen in mid-leap at the corner of Fremont Street. Other exhibits, such as the flame that illuminated The Flame Bar and Grill, are tucked away in culs-de-sac.

But this month, the definitive exhibition of electrical potential has plugged itself into the traveller's need to know. For the rest of this year, 'Neon Unplugged' is on show at the Nevada State Museum, a modest (for Las Vegas) building in Lorenzi Park, a couple of miles west of Downtown.

'Elvis slept here' used to be the boast of the Normandie motel, whose sign has been recovered from the boneyard (scrap-heap) to play a leading part in the new exhibition. 'If you wish to bet,' goes the catchy slogan of another exhibit, El Rancho, 'there's nothing better than roulette.'

There is, actually. Place a bet on Oxford to be selected as European Capital of Culture 2003, at the outrageously long odds of 10 to 1, then spend your winnings on a flight to Las Vegas to see the new exhibition. It opens with the long and ridiculously curly R of the Desert Inn – a 1950s casino demolished to make way for La Reve, the city's latest $5bn venture. You can see images of Moulin Rouge, 'The resort wonder of the world', now a dowdy shell on Bonanza Avenue but about to be replenished as Las Vegas rediscovers its roots.

Neon wasn't the only experimental element to feature in Las Vegas. In the Fifties, above-ground atomic explosions on the Nevada Test Site, north (but not very north) of Las Vegas were regarded as tourist attractions. Thousands of citizens and tourists flocked to Mount Charleston, 45 miles north of the city, for a radioactive picnic. Binion's Horseshoe Casino produced postcards of the events, while the Sands Motel staged a 'Miss Atomic 1957' parade. The fall-out of constant re-invention is the continuous scrapping of Las Vegas heritage. Happily, some of the most ancient signs

are preserved in Fremont Street, together with a free light show that puts the 'o' into ostentatious.

Among the bright lights, there is a dark side to Las Vegas. Paradise: that was what the destination board on the front of the bus promised. But as the CAT ('Citizens Area Transit') bus lurched from stop to stop along Paradise Avenue, which carves a messy track through the south-eastern wastes of suburban Las Vegas, my self-appointed tour guide in the next seat was not instilling confidence.

'Go any further east along Fremont and it's just crack-heads and whores,' she cautioned. 'We'll be passing by Crack Alley in a minute or two.'

A New Yorker who had just blown $4300 (£3000) in a marathon, four-day roulette session, insisted on spelling out in words, as well as figures, the measure of his personal catastrophe: 'Forty-three hundred dollars.'

Las Vegas takes the world to extremes. Spending time in Las Vegas without spending money in the casinos is to defy the purpose of the place; hey, everyone, let's chip in – you should see the size of the electricity bill. But when it comes to serious gambling, tuition is better than intuition. To help gamblers lose money more slowly, Caesar's Palace offers free blackjack lessons every morning. So long as you understand that the odds are against you, and that in the unlikely event of your being ahead you should quit, there are few more pleasurable ways of losing the odd $50. But bear in mind the gambling maxim: if, after half an hour at the table, you can't spot the sucker – it's you.

Thanks to the physical properties of neon, a trip to Las Vegas can have much the same effect as expensive designer drugs.

The home town of indulgence looks and feels like Toytown for tycoons. But beware staying here too long. On my last evening I got so lost trying to find a way out of Binion's Horseshoe Casino that I had to ask for directions back to real life.

TRAVELLER'S GUIDE

Getting there: the only airline with non-stop services between the UK and Las Vegas is Virgin Atlantic, which flies from Gatwick on Thursdays and Sundays. A return fare is typically £500.

Staying there: rates for most Las Vegas hotels are very flexible. At quiet times, particularly midweek, you could pay $79 (£53) for a room in a top hotel such as New York New York. On a Saturday night, the price could rise to $259 (£165).

Neon Unplugged: this exhibition runs until 4 January next year. It is part of the Nevada State Museum; call 001 702 486 5205 for more information, or visit www.nevada culture.org.

NEW DAWN
by Harriet O'Brien

Freelance writer Harriet O'Brien wrote this article for the UK's *Condé Nast Traveller*. It is an excellent example of how a writer can skilfully interweave a densely informative 'service story' on accommodation options in Sri Lanka with a vivid evocation of the country. The first few paragraphs immerse us in history and place – who can resist the brilliant beginning? – then O'Brien reveals the point of her piece: a hotel tour of this newly alluring destination. As she leads us on this tour, O'Brien uses specific details to bring to life the unique characters and amenities of each hotel. She avoids the fawning, purpled prose hotel critiques often inspire in less-seasoned writers; rather, she presents her own judgments about each place in an authoritative way, grounded in fact and precise description, so that we end the story with an overall impression of the island's attractions and an appreciation of what each property offers.

In the afternoon sunshine a couple of little brown monkeys sprawled indolently beside the king's swimming pool. Belly up, the small sunbathers looked preposterously human, as if deliberately apeing the insouciance of the monarch and his courtiers who enjoyed this leisure centre back in the 5th century. With their imperial airs, the resident creatures appeared to be the de facto inheritors of the colossal palace complex of Sigiriya, disdainfully ignoring larger visiting primates who clambered slowly up steep stairways and exclaimed in awestruck tones at the jungle panoramas that rewarded their efforts.

Such effusion is inevitable. The views at Sigiriya are astounding, while the remains of its pools and fortress constructions beggar belief: moats, ramparts, water gardens and, towering above them, the vestiges of a 1500-year-old citadel built into, and on top of, a mighty granite rock, its caverns still adorned with frescoes of big-breasted women. Yet this is by no means the only jaw-dropping sight in Sri Lanka. The interior of the island is strewn with ancient Buddhist shrines and with other excavated remnants of historic kingdoms. And quite apart from these is the promise of more forgotten riches lurking undiscovered in the undergrowth where snakes as well as monkeys now preside.

Other wildlife casually adds colour to this antique land. Bee-eaters flash iridescent plumage as they dart across rice fields; kingfishers perch on electricity wires, scrutinising irrigation ditches for tiny fish; brilliant white egrets stalk the shallows of lakes festooned with the pink bloom of lotus flowers. Less ubiquitous are the leopards that still roam Sri Lanka's mountain forests and the herds of wild elephants which periodically cause havoc in lowland villages. Meanwhile black eagles soar over tea estates that exude an atmosphere of the British Raj and around the island's coastline are coral reefs harbouring at least 1000 species of fish.

With its beaches, beasts and age-old emblems of a spiritual culture rooted in the very soil, Sri Lanka presents a halcyon package. Much of the island is reasonably accessible; prices are for the most part low, yet the abject poverty of the country's gigantic neighbour India is mostly absent; and the Sri Lankans themselves are courteously old fashioned and welcoming. About the size of Ireland, the island is traditionally described as a pearl, pear or tear drop off the south of India. Until recently the lachrymose image was the most apposite: like Ireland, the country has, of course, been troubled. Driving around the island, I was struck by the number of lottery ticket vendors sitting at the roadside in tricycles modified to allow propulsion from cranklevers on the handlebars. These landmine victims provide abrupt reminders of the civil war that has riven Sri Lanka.

However, prospects are promising. The Norwegian-brokered ceasefire between the majority Singhalese and the northern Tamils demanding a separate state has held for more than a year. Local opinion is optimistic – and also pragmatic. 'So far so good, but we've still got a long way to go,' commented one hotel owner and resident of the capital, Colombo. 'Peace talks are being negotiated, and at the moment we seem to be inching towards some sort of federalism. But there is a possibility that violence could flare up again. That said, it would probably be contained within northern and eastern parts dominated by the Tamil Tigers – the main holiday regions are unlikely to be affected.' With conciliatory enthusiasm, others are quick to point out that the Tamil secessionists were among the first to provide aid to the mainly Singhalese area around the southern city of Ratnapura when recent floods nearly devastated the region.

Natural disasters aside, the mood is buoyant and business is starting to boom. Alongside familiar advertisements for perfume and cosmetics, the June issue of SriLankan Airlines' magazine *Serendip* somewhat eccentrically included at least five large notices inviting passengers to invest in real estate. Meantime the travel industry is falling over itself to acquire property in Sri Lanka and quite apart from a rash of new openings, many old colonial hotels, oozing nostalgia, are being snapped up. Rumours are rife that Amanresorts is moving into the market, although the Hong Kong–based luxury hotel group is reticent about such interests. Not that Sri Lanka has been entirely lacking stylish accommodation: given the troubles, a surprising number of plush hotels were established in the 90s, many of them designed by the country's renowned architect Geoffrey Bawa who died in May this year. While some properties in the tea-clad hills are being refurbished and a few eastern beach areas are opening up to tourism, for the moment the finest places to stay are concentrated in Sri Lanka's cultural interior and along stretches of its relatively undervisited southwest coast.

CULTURE

The country's historic heartland, now known as 'The Cultural Triangle', contains a mind-numbing array of ancient sites with impossible looking names. Highlights include Anuradhapura and Polonnaruwa, respectively capitals from the 3rd century BC and the 11th century AD; Mihintale, a sacred monastic centre of caves and temple ruins; the great cave complex of Dambulla, housing hundreds of Buddha images, its walls coated with 16th-century paintings; and the extraordinary rock palace of Sigiriya. Other, less visited places range from the monumental Aukana Buddha, a vast statue hewn out of a solid rock face purportedly in the 5th century, to the royal hunting fortress of Ritigale, so hidden in dense forest it remains a semi secret. It would require superhuman effort to take in more than a few of these shrines, palaces and monuments, and besides, in the sapping heat the density of history and legend becomes bewildering – which makes relaxing accommodation all the more desirable.

Set more or less in the middle of the Cultural Triangle, between Sigiriya and the Dambulla caves, Elephant Corridor opened in March this year. The 22-suite hotel has been carefully constructed to make minimal impact on its 200 acres of wilderness and has recently acquired a resident naturalist to advise on planting so as to attract more bird-life – peacock, drongo, bulbul and more. Facing the jungle and offering fine views of the weird and wonderfully shaped Kandalama hills, separate thatched chalets, each with plunge pool and outdoor area, have been built on a slight

ridge so as to deter larger wildlife intrusions – a herd of elephants roams the area, hence the hotel's name. Nature in super luxury is the theme. Co-owner Susanne Filippin is an Al Maha enthusiast and describes the hotel as a jungle version of the desert eco-resort in Dubai. She is keen to emphasise that this is a sanctuary: there are no plans for more building save, possibly, for a helipad and an organic dairy farm. Meanwhile, privacy and seclusion are the catchwords of the management team, although given the large landholding it seems something of an oversight that most of the accommodation is grouped together like a line of up-ended dominoes, gardens well within earshot of each other. Not that there is any sense of being cramped: bedrooms, containing every conceivable amenity of TV, CD player and mini-bar (there is no eco-fastidious holdback here), are large, bathrooms huge if hot. Fine tuning, though, should soon improve ventilation and other slight design flaws such as overly discreet lighting. The 'romantic' suite I stayed in had a four-poster bed complete with mirrored ceiling (not entirely welcome), which blocked out the overhead lights. Requests for a table lamp so as to avoid reading in bed with a torch failed to be understood. With 120 employees, and a staff-to-guest ratio of 4:1 (far more in low season), service should be a shining feature but at the time of my visit in late May it was lacking in finesse. However, teething problems aside, Elephant Corridor is a stylish retreat, remote yet offering easy access to some of the most stunning sites in Sri Lanka. And with its dramatically sited restaurant, ayurvedic spa with swimming pool, archery, golf putting and small stable, it provides an agreeable range of resort facilities.

On the shores of Kandalama Lake nearby, the Kandalama Hotel is less exclusive although equally as spectacular, in an idiosyncratic way. At first sight the exterior looks like an urban complex from the 70s literally gone to seed and sprouting great fronds of greenery. It is, though, a mid-90s design by Sri Lanka's architectural giant Geoffrey Bawa who devised the hotel as an eco-resort that would embrace the surrounding nature. Birds flit through the open-sided corridors and bar areas, which at times pulse with so much wildlife that it seems as if the building has germinated from the jungle around it. Other environmentally friendly efforts are less visible and are concentrated where they matter most: water treatment and garbage disposal. The 162 slightly boxy bedrooms are replete with mini bar, TV and all the expected accoutrements of an international, quality hotel. And with three swim-

ming pools, tennis courts, and an ayurvedic health centre, facilities match those of other luxury establishments. Although guests are not brow-beaten over eco-concerns, nature watching is encouraged, with guided bird-spotting tours on offer every morning and elephant-back safaris readily available.

It is no coincidence that many hotels in the region share an eco-focus. Not only is the area rich in wildlife, most of the accommodation has been built in the last 10 years, during which environmental issues have become a big consideration. Over on the western fringes of the Cultural Triangle Ulpotha offers perhaps the ultimate blend of relaxation and ecological commitment. This hidden haven is not designed to appeal to everyone, but those seeking chill-out tranquillity tend to become hooked – when I was there one guest was on her third visit from Britain within less than a year. It is a working village rather than a hotel, whose community was founded on an abandoned coconut plantation in the mid-90s: the mission being to develop the surrounding farmland so as to revive traditional agricultural practices for the benefit of both the land and the people. Since 1997 paying guests have been welcomed for just a few weeks of the year, helping to fund the non-profit making operation and joining the rural lifestyle – one without electricity, hot running water or alcohol. All of which may sound absurdly ascetic, particularly given that a holiday here does not come cheap by local standards. Yet this is far from being a back-to-basics bootcamp. Traditional accommodation has been adapted for considerable comfort. The open-sided mud-hut bedrooms are beautifully and simply furnished with local fabrics, rush mats and pottery. Each grouping of three huts shares a stylish bathroom area complete with wooden-seated flush loos and outdoor showers where, in the heat, the water is naturally tepid. Meanwhile the lack of electricity seems a bonus in the soft lamp-lit evenings. There are no waiters or maids, yet the discreetly attentive hospitality of the villagers during my stay rivalled the best service offered by Sri Lanka's formal hotels. In a health-farm-meets-houseparty atmosphere, meals are nutritious, vegetarian feasts served communally to guests (the maximum capacity is 19) in a central pavilion. Yoga, mainly led by teachers from London, is the chief attraction for most visitors, however there is no pressure to join the classes. Reading, snoozing in hammocks, swimming in the reservoir, visiting the local temple, and receiving massage and ayurvedic treatments are the other principal entertainments. Occasionally day trips are arranged to Sri Lanka's great archaeological sites and to the pretty city of Kandy.

At the southern tip of the Cultural Triangle, Kandy is beautifully situated in a bowl of green hills. The last bastion of Buddhist power before the country was fully annexed by the British in 1815, it is still the lively centre of Sri Lanka's performance arts and contains a number of fine old buildings dating back over the last three centuries. Not least of these is the Dalada Maligawa, the octagonal Temple of the Tooth, housing Buddha's left eye-tooth. This sacred and much travelled relic attracts a steady stream of tourists and pilgrims who come to pay homage during daily, frangipani-filled ceremonies. Given the volume of visitors, the city's limited choice of chic accommodation is surprising.

Helga's Folly, famously atmospheric and eccentric, has long been a favourite with British travellers. The 40-bedroom home of the illustrious de Silva family has attracted a glittering list of celebrities – Zandra Rhodes being one of the more recent visitors. Awash with colour and flamboyant murals, the hotel is either hilariously outré or simply too much. 'A trip, a dream – who knows, who cares?' reads one entry in the visitors' book. Whatever the answer, the food here is a serious plus: dinner of aubergine salad with a kick and delicately seared tuna was the best meal I ate in Sri Lanka.

On the other side of town, Stone House Lodge is a model of peaceful understatement. A plantation-style bungalow lined in teak, it is furnished with antiques and wicker, its spacious garden filled with hibiscus and birdsong. For the moment, the elegance is unmatched elsewhere in Kandy, although plenty of properties have promising potential. Most notable of these is the Queens Hotel, a splendid 1844 building in the centre of the city, aching for a makeover and currently the subject of negotiations over new ownership.

COAST

Although for the most part unspoilt, Sri Lanka's southern beach area is not the pristine-white idyll of the coral coasts around the Maldives further west in the Indian Ocean. Frankly, it's not that bland. From toddy tappers in the canopies of coconut palms to fishermen perched on stilts in the sea, looking like human herons, and great Buddha statues peacefully presiding at busy road junctions, the shores are packed with local activity. And dotted with emblems of the country's colonial past, too. Although the Dutch never conquered the entire island, in the 17th and 18th centuries they dominated maritime trade

and many of their substantial forts are still thriving, if crumbling, seaside towns.

A few kilometres east of the dusty old fort of Matara, Tangalle has become the beach area of choice for those in the know. Empty, pink-tinged sandy bays border a cheerfully unassuming little town with a large Methodist church and a bustling main drag. There are just a few hotels in the locality – as well as an increasing choice of villas providing truly exclusive accommodation. Commanding spectacular views over sweeping, palm-fringed sands, Lansiya is one of the latest private properties being developed here. Owned by Colombo residents Anitra and Dirk Caldera, the villa has been designed to take full advantage of its ample, secluded grounds, with wide balconies and a shower room set outdoors in an attractive courtyard. A congenially laid-back atmosphere is in part attributable to the cook, Dilip, a jolly ex-mariner with a penchant for chatting and a considerable talent for concocting superb meals which are presented with due flourish.

Service is a more formal matter at the neighbouring Beach House, giving the villa the air of a private hotel rather than a holiday house. With its play of blue-and-white furnishings, its open-air master bathroom splendidly featuring a tub on claw feet, and its magical infinity pool set in an elysian, agave-filled garden, it would be difficult to improve on the sheer sense of style here. The colonial, four-bedroom villa was bought in the 1990s by the late Douglas Johnson, an American painter whose artworks still hang on the walls and who painstakingly restored the property with the help of his friend and mentor Geoffrey Bawa.

The Beach House is now run by Geoffrey Dobbs, an English entrepreneur with a string of equally glamorous properties along the south coast. Taprobane, west of Matara, is an almost impossibly romantic island-villa eccentrically accessible only by wading through the sea. Further west, just outside the walls of the Dutch fort of Galle, the Sun House is an elegantly refurbished mansion built by a Scottish spice merchant in the 1860s. Opposite is Doornberg, or the Dutch House, a 1712 building once home to the commander of the Netherlands's forces garrisoned in the old town below.

This four-suite boutique hotel opened last year to much acclaim. It has been beautifully and sensitively developed, a new wing added to the original ochre-washed building and a sublime infinity pool positioned at the edge of the hotel's tree-clad hilltop. Furry black monkeys were pinching mangoes overhead as I took a dreamy dip here, while beside the loungers a glass of lime juice appeared as if by magic, provided by evanescent staff. The subtle attentiveness is reflected in the care over detail. Two varieties of lawn grass carpet the neatly clipped gardens. Raffia sun hats for guests' use hang in the spacious bedrooms, which feature capacious four-poster beds and are filled with antiques – a huge hunt took place to find just the right period doors. The large bookshelves in my room offered an eclectic supply of reading material, from *Running in the Family*, Michael Ondaatje's reminiscence of a childhood in Ceylon, to the *Mini Owner's Workshop Manual*. Flower-filled bathrooms are thoughtfully supplied with such imaginative amenities as cinnamon body scrub and ayurvedic toothpaste. However, a possible downside to the hotel is the lack of a dining room, yet it is not much of a hardship for guests to pop across the road for dinner in the excellent restaurant at the Sun House.

Beach zealots, though, might find the location of both hotels disappointing. The principal attraction of Galle itself is the architecture of the old fort: lined with timeworn Dutch buildings, its quiet streets offer an absorbing meander while its north walls provide a good vantage point for watching cricket matches in the stadium below. But the nearest sizeable stretch of sand with safe swimming is Unawatuna Bay about 5km away. Once rated among the world's top 12 beaches, the golden shores are now perhaps a little too crowded with daytrippers and are peppered with busy cafes.

On the long strand of Bentota Beach, equidistant from Galle and Colombo, are two quietly elegant properties, both developed in the 70s by Geoffrey Bawa. One was an existing Dutch villa he restored and redevised; the other he built next door in the same style for his friend, the hotelier S M A Hameed, whose family home it became. Both houses have since been turned into small hotels. Management of the former, Villa Mohotti, has recently been taken over by Ajai Zecha. Operating independently of his father, Adrian Zecha of Amanresorts, he is taking this already beautifully decorated and furnished residence even more upmarket. The latter, Club Villa, is not quite as stylish but exudes cheerful charm – and is a great deal cheaper. Both villas are well placed not just for beach activities but also for boat trips along the Balapitya River and for excursions to the glorious garden of Brief, the creation of Bawa's brother, Bevis. And both villas also have a railway line cutting a clanking path between their long lawns and the beach. For some guests the intrusion is disconcerting; others, however, find that the periodic appearance of rusty, tooting trains adds a certain wacky charm, entirely in keeping with the intrinsic spirit of Sri Lanka.

HOW TO GET THERE

SriLankan Airlines (020 8538 2001) flies direct from Heathrow to Colombo: return fares in November around £620 including taxes. Emirates (0870 243 2222) flies from Heathrow or Gatwick to Colombo via Dubai: return fares in November around £560 including taxes.

TOUR OPERATORS

Colours of Sri Lanka (298 Regents Park Road, London N3 2TJ; 020 8343 3446; www.partnership travel.co.uk) offers tailor-made holidays taking in any of the above destinations and properties: prices for a 10-day holiday with accommodation at Elephant Corridor, Helga's Folly, Lansiya and the Dutch House from £1668 per person (based on two sharing) including international flights and private transport in Sri Lanka.

Other tour operators providing tailor-made travel to Sri Lanka include: Handmade Holidays (First Floor, Carpenters Buildings, Carpenters Lane, Cirencester, Glos GL7 1EE; 01285 642555; www .handmade-holidays.co.uk); Scott Dunn (Fovant Mews, 12 Noyna Road, London, SW17 7PH; 020 8682 5010; www.scottdunn.com); and Carolanka (01822 810230).

WHERE TO STAY
Cultural Triangle

Elephant Corridor, Sigiriya (00 94 66 83333; hotel@elephantcorridor.com; www.elephantcorridor.com). Suites from US$150 (accommodation only and excluding service charges and government tax).

Kandalama Hotel, Dambulla (00 94 66 84100; kandalama@aitkenspence.lk; www.aitkenspenceholidays.com). Double rooms from US$121 (accommodation only, including service and tax).

Ulpotha (bookings through Neal's Yard Agency, BCM Neal's Yard, London WC1N 3XX; 0870 444 2702; info@ulpotha.com; www.ulpotha.com). Open to guests from late May to early July and from November to March. Holidays are for two-week periods (although occasionally one-week stays are offered), with an all-inclusive cost of £980 per person earlier in the year and £1200 high season for the fortnight. The price includes group transfers from the airport and all yoga, massage and ayurvedic treatments.

Other options include Culture Club on the shores of Kandalama Lake near Dambulla (00 94 66 31822; cdchm@sltnet.lk; www.connaissanceceylan.com). Less happy-clappy than the name (and website) suggests, the hotel takes Sri Lankan traditions of hospitality as its guiding theme. Accommodation is in 92 chalets and 11 new 'eco-lodges' while facilities include an ayurvedic health centre, swimming pool, tennis courts and jogging track. Double-room chalets from $77 (room only, excluding service and tax).

Kandy

Helga's Folly, off Mahamaya Mawatha (00 94 8 234571; chalet@sltnet.lk; www.helgasfolly.com). Double rooms from $90 Nov–Dec, $100 Jan–Oct (room only, including service and tax).

Stone House Lodge, 42 Nittawella Road, Nittawella (00 94 8 232769; stonehse@sltnet.lk). Double rooms from $55 (room only, excluding service and tax, credit cards not accepted).

Other options include Earl's Regency, Kundasale (00 94 8 422122; erhotel@sltnet.lk; www.aitkenspenceholidays.com). In lush greenery yet within easy reach of the centre of town, the 85-room hotel offers every comfort in slightly unimaginative surroundings. Double rooms from $75 (room only, excluding service and tax).

Coast

Tangalle: Lansiya (book through Colours of Sri Lanka, 020 8343 3446). Sleeps two, although a further three bedrooms are due to be added during the low season next year. £140 per person per night including all meals.

The Beach House (enquiries through The Sun House, 00 94 74 380275; sunhouse@sri.lanka.net; www.thesunhouse.com). Accommodation for seven people. The rate of $495–$1000 per night depending on low/high season includes tax, staff costs (except tips) and a traditional Sri Lankan curry on arrival, other meals are between $10–$15 per person.

Other options include Mahawella, at the end of an unspoilt beach about 7km from Tangalle (enquiries to Tim and Sarah Jacobson at sarahjac@netvigator.com). Owned by a Hong Kong–based family, this is the last private house to be designed by Geoffrey Bawa, with gardens sweeping down to the beach, a courtyard swimming pool, shady verandahs and five double bedrooms. Rental prices per night range between $550–$750 depending on the season (meals, prepared by five resident staff, are extra). Eva Lanka (00 94 47 40940; eva.lanka@mail.ewisl.net; www.eva.lk), an Italian-run hotel set on a hillside overlooking a sandy bay, is well equipped for families, with three swimming pools and a long waterslide in addition to an open-sided restaurant, a bar and an ayurvedic health centre. Accommodation is in 29 chalets from $75 per night for two people (room only, extra bed for children up to 12, $5. The rate includes service and tax).

Weligama, near Matara: Taprobane (00 94 9 22624; sunhouse@sri.lanka.net; www.thesunhouse.com). Accommodation for up to eight people. The rate of $750–$2000 per night, depending on high/low season, includes tax, staff costs and a welcoming Sri Lankan meal; all other meals as well as drinks are extra.

Galle: Doornberg/The Dutch House, 23 Upper Dickson Road (00 94 9 22624; sunhouse@sri.lanka.net; www.thesunhouse.com). Double room from $330 per night inclusive of breakfast and afternoon tea as well as tax. Dinners at the Sun House are around $30 per person.

The Sun House, 18 Upper Dickson Road (00 94 9 22624; sunhouse@sri.lanka.net; www.thesunhouse.com). Double rooms from $120 including taxes.

Other options include Lighthouse Hotel and Spa, Dadella (00 94 9 23744; hotels@jetwing.lk; www.jetwing.net). The 163-room hotel looks down over quiet but at times rough beaches where the Indian Ocean can put on a spectacular show. It is another 90s building by Geoffrey Bawa, with comfortable if pricey rooms and extensive facilities including two swimming pools, a large spa and tennis and squash courts. Ideal for an active holiday but this is no hideaway. Double rooms from $180 (room only including service and tax). The Secret Garden, just off Unawatuna Bay (00 94 74 721007; secretgardenvilla@

msn.com; www.secretgardenvilla
.lk). This secluded villa and chalet
complex has a separate pavilion for
yoga practice, and can be shared
with other guests or privately rented
in entirety. Villa, sleeping seven to
nine plus two children from $210
per night; double-room chalet from
$35 (accommodation only and
including maid service as well as
service and tax; meals, provided by
the resident cook, are extra).

Bentota: Villa Mohotti Walauwa
(00 94 34 75311; reservation@
thevilla.eureka.lk). Doubles from
$195 high season (room only,
excluding service and tax).

Club Villa (00 94 77 362984;
clubvilla@itmin.com; www.club-
villa.com). Doubles from $90 high
season (room only, excluding service and tax).

Other options include Taru Villas Taprobana, 146/4 Galle Road,
Robolgoda (00 94 34 75618;
taprobana@taruvillas.com; www
.taruvillas.com). In quiet gardens
just off Bentota Beach, this boutique hotel has recently been refurbished by fashion designer Taru.
The nine bedrooms, furnished with
antiques, are set off a central pool
area and elegant, Mediterranean-
style pavilion. Double rooms from
$145 (B&B, including service and
tax as well as afternoon tea).

COLOMBO

Due to arrival and departure times
of international flights, a night in
or near the capital may be necessary. Colombo in any case boasts
much fine if decrepit colonial
architecture as well as temples,
markets and gardens. Shopping
has become something of an art-
form at Barefoot (704 Galle Road)
offering homewares and brilliantly
coloured cottons and linens designed by Sri Lankan artist Barbara Sansoni, and at Paradise
Road (213 Dharmapala Mawsha),
a type of upmarket, Sri Lankan
version of Habitat, while designer-
label clothes (Armani, DKNY and
the like) are exceptionally good
value at Arena (338 Darley Road)
and Odell (5 Alexandra Place).

The Galle Face Hotel, 2 Kollupi-
tiya Road (00 94 1 541010; gfh@
diamond.lanka.net; www.galle
facehotel.com) is a splendid
edifice straight out of the British
Raj – oozing atmosphere and in
need of a makeover. Doubles from
US$50 (room only, excluding serv-
ice and tax).

Renting a private villa is a
peaceful alternative to staying in
town. Java Moon, on the banks of
Bolgoda Lake, is about three quar-
ters of an hour from Colombo. The
three-bedroom villa with infinity
pool and beautifully kept grounds
is furnished with antiques, its walls
hung with works by Sri Lankan
artists. (Book through Colours of
Sri Lanka, 020 8343 3446.) £98
per person per night including all
meals.

THE WONDERFUL THING ABOUT TIGERS

by William Gray

Sri Lanka is not far from India, but this article by British freelancer William Gray is worlds away from Harriet O'Brien's piece. This story, written for the UK magazine *Wanderlust*, is designed to yank us out of our comfortable living rooms and drop us in the middle of a tiger-hunting expedition in the Indian jungle. The beginning accomplishes just this, presenting an accumulation of wonderfully rendered sensual details ('shrill snort', 'indignant bark', 'pungent aroma of crushed herbs and freshly bled sap', 'a diffuse patchwork of muted greens and shadows-within-shadows') that root us in the scene and make us accomplices in the effort to decipher the jungle's clues. As you read the piece, note how Gray plays the accordion of time. How many moments does he choose to focus on? How much of his trip has he left on the editing floor? And note, too, how, even though this is a chronologically organised account, Gray ends his piece by looping back to the beginning of the trip, for dramatic purposes. Also note how he modulates his last four paragraphs, culminating in that magical last sentence.

It was almost as if the tiger had flicked a switch in the forest. One moment it was quiet and calm – the trees swathed in webs of early morning mist – the next, the air was charged with tension. Gomati had heard the distant alarm calls – the shrill snort of a spotted deer, the indignant bark of a langur monkey – and her mood suddenly changed. She blasted a trunkful of dust up between her front legs, then shook her head so vigorously that I had to clutch the padded saddle to keep my balance. Gomati's mahout, sitting astride her neck, issued a terse reprimand before urging the elephant into the tangled forest. There was no path; Gomati made her own. Soon the air was infused with the pungent aroma of crushed herbs and freshly-bled sap. Spiders and beetles drizzled from shaken trees; our clothing became wet with dew and stained by moss and lichen. We sounded like a forest fire – crackling, snapping, trailblazing. But through all the noise came a single piercing cry. Gomati stopped and we heard it again – the tell-tale alarm call of a spotted deer.

Manoj Sharma, my guide, leaned towards me. 'When the tiger moves, the deer calls,' he murmured. 'We must be close.' I nodded slowly, my eyes chasing around the shadows of the forest. Sunlight sparked through chinks in the canopy, but the understorey was still a diffuse patchwork of muted greens and shadows-within-shadows – the perfect foil for tiger stripes. Apart from an occasional rumble from Gomati's stomach, the forest was silent. No one spoke or moved.

Gradually, the tension slipped from our bodies. The woodpecker stopped drumming, and Gomati grabbed a nearby branch and stuffed it into her mouth. I reached forward to stroke the elephant's neck; there was a soft patch, free of wrinkles and bristles, behind her ear.

Corbett was always going to be the more challenging of the two Tiger Reserves on my Indian safari. Over 1,300 sq km of forest and grassland tucked into the Himalayan foothills, it's home to about 135 Bengal tigers. But compared with Ranthambhore, further south, the cats in Corbett are shy and elusive. 'Some people have been coming here for years and have never seen a tiger,' Manoj had told me earlier. To expect to see one on my first visit to India, let alone on my first elephant ride in Corbett, was perhaps asking too much. Still, I was happy enough tickling Gomati behind the ear. And at that moment, none of us realised just how close the tigress – or her cubs – really were.

They say tigers make the orchestra of the jungle play and, suddenly, several species seemed to launch into a gusty rendition of 'I can see a tiger!' Sambar and spotted deer began whistling to our left, while langur, babblers and others pitched in with a well-rehearsed repertoire of coughs, grunts and chatters.

Guided by the commotion, Gomati waded into the undergrowth once more. After 50m or so the alarm calls ceased, but now Gomati's trunk was raised and she began to hesitate. The mahout dug his heels in, but she shuffled to a halt. For the first time that morning, the elephant let out a deep, resonating rumble. Clearly, Gomati was going no further.

Moments later we saw why. Less than a dozen metres ahead, the vegetation thrashed from side to side as three tigers burst from cover. The two cubs kept low to the ground, melting into the forest like wisps of smoke. But the tigress paused to glance over her shoulder. For a second or two, she stared straight at us – her eyes locked on ours with the intense scrutiny of a supreme predator. Then she turned and vanished.

It was the briefest of encounters – an exchange of glances that jolted the senses, seared the mind. 'You are very lucky,' Manoj told me as Gomati trundled back to the rest house. 'Not one tiger, but three!' Somehow, though, numbers seemed irrelevant. I began to realise that it wasn't the glimpse of the tigers that had moved me, so much as the supercharged atmosphere of their native forest stronghold. Spotting the tigers had merely reaffirmed their beauty; tracking them had revealed their spirit.

Later, during our afternoon elephant ride, we heard and saw nothing – no alarm calls pulsing through the forest, no pug marks on the sandy tracks that led from the rest house. The following dawn, Manoj took me out in a jeep to explore a wider area of the reserve. But again, no tigers. The forest seemed to be guarding their whereabouts, a silent reminder of their secrecy and rarity.

Leaving the forest, we drove out onto the floodplain of the Ramganga River, where tendrils of mist squirmed in the gathering heat of mid-morning. A large herd of spotted deer, perhaps 200 strong, grazed peacefully, while families of wild boar snuffled amongst them. It was a scene more reminiscent of Africa: a tawny grassland peppered with game; vultures wheeling overhead; a pair of jackals on the lookout for an easy meal. There were even wild elephants, far across the plain, looking for all the world like giant river boulders except for the occasional puff of dust that rose above them.

Quietly and methodically, like a holy man reciting a mantra, Manoj totted up a list of nearly 100 bird species that he had either seen or heard that morning. A huge variety were concentrated around a lake at the heart of the reserve. Herons, plovers and stilts tip-toed around basking gharial crocodiles, while pied kingfishers hovered overhead.

If anything, my next destination should have provided an even greater avian spectacle. Travelling overnight on the sleeper train to Agra, I hired a car and driver to take me the short distance to Bharatpur Bird Sanctuary, a former royal hunting estate. During the breeding season Bharatpur is usually throbbing with painted storks, ducks, pelicans and other waterbirds, but the monsoon had failed in 2002 and the network of lagoons had all but dried up. 'The storks arrived as usual,' said local ornithologist Dilip Saini. 'But they took one look and left again.' With patience, and Dilip's keen eye for birds, we still managed to notch up several dozen species, including a lone pelican squatting dejectedly beside a muddy waterhole that should have been a sparkling lake.

The Rajasthan countryside on the drive between Bharatpur and Ranthambhore was equally arid.

Cattle-drawn ploughs struggled through the hard-baked soil while women, balancing metal water pots on their heads, queued at every village water pump. Numerous camel trains were on the move, their masters leading them, grim-faced, in search of new water and forage. The brick factories lining the roadside only added to the sense of desiccation.

Ranthambhore had not escaped the drought either. In the 400 sq km national park (at the core of the tiger reserve), the lakes were dry and the dhok forest – usually lush after a monsoon soaking – was scantily clad with brittle, golden leaves.

Ironically, the parched conditions boded well for tiger viewing. Ranthambhore's tigers would be more visible in a forest deprived of its seasonal rejuvenation of leaves and grasses – or so I was told.

There are no elephant-back safaris in Ranthambhore. Instead, a controlled number of vehicles is granted access to specific routes on the park's network of tracks. Each vehicle has a driver and guide, and there are strict rules for minimising disturbance to wildlife, such as speed limits and bans on off-road driving or deviations from allotted routes. A sound system, in principle. However, I quickly learned that the route scheme had a drawback. Eager to clinch their 'double tips' for a tiger sighting,

drivers often treated their routes like race tracks. When the park gates opened at 6.30am there was a jostle for pole position – the first jeeps desperate to locate any fresh tiger prints before other traffic obliterated them. By imposing invisible barriers in the wilderness, the route system relied less on fieldcraft and more on chance. You were either lucky enough to have a tiger on your patch or not.

By my fourth game drive in two days, we had seen no tigers. On several occasions we had hurtled at over 60km per hour to beat another jeep to a junction simply so we wouldn't be following in its dust trail. Langurs, peacocks and spotted deer were literally leaping out of our path.

There were, of course, several moments of pure Ranthambhore magic – a wonderful encounter with a lolloping sloth bear and a glimpse of a rare wild dog. We watched ring-necked parakeets raiding a fig tree and witnessed sambar deer stags locking antlers in a rutting contest. But, ultimately, it seemed that the success of our game drives was determined by whether or not we had seen a tiger.

On my fifth and final drive I did see one – a tigress lying in the shade of a narrow gully – but, by then, too much of Ranthambhore's wildness and spirit had been compromised. If I had so desperately wanted to see a tiger,

I could have gone to a zoo. To my mind, the whole essence of tiger reserves like Ranthambhore is that they embody some of the few places left on earth where you can still sense the aura of wild tigers. With its magnificent 12th century fort and ancient chhatris (memorials) and temples, Ranthambhore's importance as a refuge for some of India's last 3000–3500 tigers (believed to be an optimistic estimate) seemed especially poignant. It is a rare place indeed where the crumbling remains of human presence are juxtaposed against a thriving population of one of the world's most endangered species.

Ultimately, the most thrilling tiger encounter of my safari was not actually an encounter at all. It took place several days earlier when Manoj and I were leaving Corbett Tiger Reserve. It was a quiet morning. The sal forest had shrugged off its blanket of morning mist and Manoj was happily scanning the trees for tawny fish owls – one of the few bird species that had eluded us.

When a jeep approached us from the opposite direction we paused to chat to the driver, but he hadn't seen the owls either – so we headed on towards the park gates. A short distance further, Manoj suddenly stiffened and pointed to the dirt track ahead. 'Tigers.' With one word, he transformed our laid-back birding rambling into an edge-of-the-seat drama. There, clearly imprinted over the tyre marks of the jeep we had just passed, were the pug marks of a tigress and her three young cubs. Less than five minutes had elapsed since we saw the other vehicle and, in that time, the cats must have emerged from the forest, strolled along the road a short distance and disappeared into the trees again.

We took a long, hard look around us. A rustle of leaves spun our heads, but it was just a pheasant scrabbling about on the forest floor. Manoj thought he heard the alarm call of a babbler, but whatever it was stopped almost immediately. He signalled to our driver to reverse up the track. About 100m beyond a sharp bend, we found more tiger prints – this time overlaying our own tyre tracks! Again, we stopped and listened. Somewhere, very close, a family of tigers was probably doing the same.

We never did see them. And yet it felt as though we had been directly interacting – pitting our wits and senses against each other. It had been an exhilarating experience – a moment of heightened awareness that stirred some primordial human instinct: part fear, part respect. I had discovered how it feels to fall under the spell of the tiger.

INDIA: FOOTNOTES
Vital Statistics

Capital: New Delhi

Population: Over one billion

Time: GMT+5.5

International dialling code: +91

Visas: British nationals require a visa, which costs £30 and is valid for six months. Contact the High Commission of India, India House, Aldwych, London WC2B 4NA (0906 844 4544, www.hcilondon.net).

Language: Hindi is the most national Indian language, but there are 18 official languages.

Money: Indian rupee (Rs), currently Rs77.4 to the UK£. Take UK£ or US$ travellers cheques. Credit cards are widely accepted in cities and larger towns, and can also be used to get cash advances in rupees.

WHEN TO GO

The dry season begins in November when national parks and reserves reopen after the monsoon. Vegetation is lush and the rain has cleared the air of dust. From February to late April, leaves fall, grasses wither and water sources recede in the tiger reserves, providing the best opportunities for seeing wildlife.

GETTING THERE

Numerous airlines serve Delhi from London, including British Airways (0845 773 3377, www.britishair ways.com) and Air France (0845 0845 111, www.airfrance.com). BA flights from Heathrow to Delhi start at £545 including taxes.

GETTING AROUND

Local transport ranges from auto-rickshaws, cycle-rickshaws and tongas (horse-drawn carriages) to trains, cars and buses. Hiring a car and driver is straightforward and is probably the best option for reaching Corbett Tiger Reserve, an eight-hour bus ride from Delhi. At some stage of your trip, be sure to experience the Indian railway system – a great way to see the country and meet its people. There are several classes with varying degrees of comfort. For overnight journeys, a second-class, four-berth sleeper cabin is a good option.

Sawai Madhopur, on the main Delhi–Mumbai line, is just ten kilometres from Ranthambhore National Park. You'll find numerous taxis and auto-rickshaws at the station, but agree a price before setting off. Elephant rides are available in Corbett for around Rs250 per person. Try to book Ranthambhore 4WD safaris in advance. You have two options: five-passenger 4WDs, which cost around Rs875 for the vehicle (including guide and entrance fee); or 20-seater trucks which enter the park twice a day and cost around Rs110 per person (including entrance fee).

SAFARIS

There are several reserves and sanctuaries in India that can be incorporated into a wildlife safari. Wildlife Worldwide (020 8667 9158, www.wildlifeworldwide .com) offers an 18-day Tiger Tiger itinerary combining the national parks of Kanha, Bandhavgarh and Ranthambhore with a visit to Agra and the Taj Mahal. It costs from £2195 including flights, transfers, guided activities and most meals. Other wildlife hot spots in India include Sasan Gir wildlife sanctuary (the last stronghold of the Asiatic lion), Periyar Wildlife Sanctuary (a beautiful reserve with a lake and forest in southern India) and the Keoladeo Ghana Bharatpur National Park (a world-renowned birdwatching location near Agra).

ACCOMMODATION

Flights from Europe tend to arrive during the early hours of the morning, so it's worth arranging an early check-in at your hotel to freshen up before spending the day sightseeing. Delhi has a wide range of accommodation; try www.india-accommodation.com for details.

Many of the tiger reserves and wildlife sanctuaries also offer a variety of places to stay. In Corbett, Dhikala Rest House (tiger camp@wildquestindia.com) is superbly located in the heart of the reserve with rooms from around Rs1500 and dormitory beds from just Rs200. There is also an excellent value restaurant. Outside the reserve, Ramnagar has several small resorts which charge Rs3500–5000. Ranthambhore also has accommodation to suit most budgets – from modest guesthouses to luxurious tented camps like Sher Bagh (sherbagh@vsnl .com) where the double occupancy rate is US$180 full board.

HEALTH & SAFETY

Malaria is present in India, so you should consult your doctor for advice on an appropriate course of prophylactic tablets, as well as vaccinations against typhoid, tetanus, polio and hepatitis. Many of India's larger cities are highly polluted and travellers with respiratory ailments may wish to take precautionary measures.

FURTHER READING

There are numerous guidebooks to the subcontinent, including *India* (Lonely Planet, 2001) and *India* (Rough Guides, 2001). For wildlife-themed travel guides, try *Indian Wildlife* (Insight Guides, 2001) and *Traveller's Guide: Wildlife of India* (Collins, 2001).

If elephant-riding in Corbett Tiger Reserve inspires you to greater things, be sure to read Mark Shand's *Travels on my Elephant* (Penguin, 1992), which describes his 1000km elephantine journey across India.

For a passionate account of Indian natural history, plus stunning photography, look no further than Valmik Thapar's *Land of the Tiger* (BBC Books, 1997).

FURTHER INFORMATION
For further information, visit the official website of the Indian Ministry of Tourism at www.tourism inindia.com.

GUITAR CENTRAL

by Christopher Reynolds

It may seem a long way from hunting tigers in the Indian jungle to hunting guitars in the Mexican hinterlands, but in fact, this story by Christopher Reynolds – a former travel writer for the *Los Angeles Times*, where this story first appeared – is fundamentally similar to William Gray's 'The Wonderful Thing About Tigers' (p70). Both are essentially 'quest' stories. In each tale, the writer is specifically in search of something – stripes or strings – and that quest frames the resulting narrative. There is much to admire in Reynolds' account. He begins 'Guitar Central' by planting questions in the reader's mind. What is the extra luggage? Why does he need the money? What is this 'guy who knows a guy' trafficking in, anyway? Where are we riding in this rental car? Before we become too frustrated, Reynolds provides the answers and reveals that he is writing to a personal passion. We may not particularly care about Mexico or guitars, but Reynolds does such a masterful job in bringing to life the people and places he encounters on his quest that we are compelled to read on. In particular, note his use of dialogue and character, and his interweaving of fact, history, anecdote and description. By the end of the piece, we have learned more than we had ever imagined we would want to know about guitars and a little town devoted to their creation. Reynolds' story is very personal, but he never drags us into the abyss of egregious self-revelation; he uses himself and his quest as a portal to a deeper understanding and appreciation of Paracho, and Mexico, and finally, of the treasures – both figurative and literal – that he will bring back from that town of guitars.

It is a mild day in the mountains of middle Mexico, a fine day for chasing butterflies or lingering on cobbled side streets, neither of which I'll be doing. I am here to sniff sawdust and engage in arcane conversations with old men in dim, cluttered rooms.

I step down onto the runway of the Morelia airport – the old colonial state capital of Michoacán, midway between Mexico City and Guadalajara – with one less piece of luggage than I expect to take home. In a hidden compartment beneath my belt, I carry a large amount of cash. In my wallet, I carry an address given to me by a guy who knows a guy.

I rent a car and head southwest. As darkness falls on the colonial buildings of Pátzcuaro's main plaza, I corner a wizened man named Raúl, who in a few moments will be singing and playing 'Guadalajara' to a restaurant full of Mexican and American tourists. I nod at his guitar, and in my Spanish, which has been compared with President Bush's English, I say something like: The guitar you are playing, is Paracho from it, that town of guitars in the mountains?

Um, yes, says Raúl in Spanish, half-surprised.

I am going to Paracho this week, to see the festival, and to buy a guitar. Is there a guitar player, no, a guitar-maker, whom you can recommend? The man from your guitar?

'Amezcua,' says Raúl. But he adds that he couldn't afford an Amezcua himself. He's been playing this Velazquez for about eight years now. Anyway, Raúl says, I can find both on the main street. ...

Now it's a Sunday afternoon. The big cities and colonial scenery are behind me, and under a sky full of dramatic clouds, I'm racing along a two-lane highway, passing cornfields, crawling up pine-stubbled slopes, rolling at last into Paracho, guitar-making capital of North America.

Above the town looms a jagged mountain peak, Tare Tzuruan, which in the indigenous Purépecha language might mean Big Hill or Eagle Mountain, depending on whom you ask. But I can't take my eyes off the shop windows: Taller de Guitarras. Barajas Guitarras. Jesús H. Fuerte Guitarras. Casa Amezcua Guitarras...

Inside I see guitars large and small, whole and half-built, hung on hooks, strangled in twine (to hold the wood in place while the glue dries) and cradled in the arms of makers wielding files and hammers and saws and rags and other tools whose purposes I can only guess.

The Morelia airport is about a three-hour drive, perhaps 100 miles, but it seems much farther. Down the street my rental car creeps, past shops advertising guitars, produce, guitars, wooden curiosities (including guitars), gifts (including guitars), food, guitars, toys (including guitars), guitar-making tools, an Internet cafe (hey, this is rural Mexico, not the dark side of the moon), an auto repair garage and more guitars.

Although it's a town whose population wouldn't quite fill Staples Center, Paracho in early August practically seethes. Its annual fair has just begun. In search of a parking spot, I crawl south to north the length of the main drag, which changes names twice in its eight blocks. The buildings are one or two stories, except for the church tower, which looks over the main plaza and a cultural center. At the north end of town, perhaps a five-minute walk from the central plaza, the raw countryside resumes.

'This not just a guitar festival. This is the whole town throwing its summer festival – people all over the streets doing all sorts of stuff,' a Paracho veteran named Kenny Hill told me before I headed south.

Hill, a professional guitar-maker and player who spends most of the year in Santa Cruz, is the only American with a workshop in Paracho. He's been a regular visitor or part-time resident for two decades, and he estimates that there are more guitar-makers in Paracho than in the entire United States. Guesses range from 1200 to 3000.

Paracho's population, including neighboring settlements, was put at 31,003 in the 1999 Mexican census. By some estimates, it produces as many as 80,000 guitars a year.

Search for it on the Internet and you'll find precious little; I only heard of it a few years ago, from a friend who'd wandered through on a backpacking trip in the '80s. But Paracho is not quite invisible. Last year, the National Geographic Society published a children's book on Paracho and its guitars by Peter Laufer and Susan L. Roth. Titled 'Made in Mexico' and filled with wildly colorful paper collages, it features a blurb by singer Linda Ronstadt. Years before she began exploring her Mexican heritage in her 1987 'Canciones de Mi Padre' recordings, Ronstadt recalls, she first learned to play guitar on an instrument from Paracho.

The town's specialty goes back at least 80 years, but beyond that, the history gets hazy. Some local boosters (and some travel guidebooks) would have you believe that the craft of guitar-making was specifically assigned to Paracho by Michoacán's beloved 16th century bishop, Don Vasco de Quiroga. In fact, many sources agree that the bishop did assign specialties to several towns near the banks of Lake Pátzcuaro. But when it comes to Paracho in the mountains, the documentation gets thinner, and some locals take a more skeptical view.

'In the history book, Quiroga never came here,' says Francisco Navarro Garcia, whose workshop is on the north end of Calle Independencia. In those days, neither the town nor the guitar existed in anything like their current form. Though the term 'guitar' apparently originated in 16th century Spain, it then described a four-string instrument with different tuning and shape than most modern guitars.

Either way, the reputation that Paracho developed through the 20th century was for the quantity, not quality, of its guitars. But since the mid-1990s, a handful of workshops have begun concentrating on high-quality instruments, which require more time and costlier materials. While the factories on the edge of town crank out 100 largely machine-made guitars or more a day, a fine craftsman might spend weeks on a single big-ticket instrument. Thus you can spend $50 on a Paracho guitar, or $3000, and it behooves a buyer to visit several shops before making any commitments.

Navarro has been a guitar-maker for 18 of his 38 years. He speaks as bluntly about Paracho's output as he does about its history. 'About 10% of guitars here are of high quality,' he tells me. 'Ten years ago, none were.'

Navarro aims for the high-end market, making about 70 instruments a year and selling most through a dealer in Houston, at prices around $1,800. I linger a long while in his workshop, listening to town gossip and guitar theory, and noodling on one of his instruments. Since we've cut out shipping and the middle man, he might be able to make me a deal.

I'm eager to buy; when I'm home I pick up a guitar nearly every day. But the truth is I don't play particularly well – simple folk and blues songs, no classical compositions. So I hand the guitar back to Navarro and ask him to give it a workout.

He hesitates, picks a few notes, then declines.

'Guitarrero o guitarrista,' he says. 'You either make guitars, or you play guitars. You don't do both.'

A great pink cloud hovers before me: pink cotton candy, carried aloft by a tiny vendor. Like the vendor, everyone on the street seems to be 5-feet-6 or shorter, and a native of Mexico. And the later it gets, the busier the sidewalk becomes.

Campesinos converge from nearby towns – the men in white cowboy hats, the women in their traditional black-and-blue shawls – for their biggest spending binge of the year. Far-flung children, now grown, have come back from their jobs and new lives in el norte to renew their ties.

Technicians are fiddling with a PA system in the plaza, and some of the streets are blocked.

Tonight, brass bands will march and the town pooh-bahs will burn a castle made of sticks. Tomorrow, all the town's craft-makers will march around the plaza, then take the stage and toss special party favors to their neighbors, provoking a scramble no less raucous than the annual skirmishing over Mardi Gras beads in New Orleans.

While this goes on at street level, the town's elite are staging a semi-separate second celebration: the National Guitar Festival. Now nearly 30 years old, it features master classes, competitions among guitar-makers and young guitar players, and free performances by classical guitarists from Cuba, Paraguay, Bosnia, the Czech Republic and Mexico, all in the 150-seat auditorium of the Center for the Investigation and Development of the Guitar (CIDEG, in local language), two blocks from the plaza.

But since the town is so small, the street fun and salon serious-ness end up scrambled, so that the student guitarists, carefully coiffed and clad in black suits to help the judges focus on their performance, find themselves tiptoeing around tuba players and churro vendors on the way to their appointments with destiny in the recital hall. Somewhere amid all this, I know, a guitar waits for me.

Soon I stand before José de Jesús Reyes Alvarez, who is sanding the top of a guitar (the tapa, they say here) while a black-and-white Marilyn Monroe poster peers down over his shoulders. With an ap-prentice boy awaiting orders in the background, Reyes, a slight man of 45 with rolled-up sleeves, drops his tools, pulls up a stool, guides me to it, places an instrument in my hands. I begin the questioning.

You have how many years? When of those did you start the making of guitars? The business is how long?

The questions puzzle him, as if I've asked a dog how long it's been barking.

'All my life,' he says.

The workshop is an oversized Picasso montage. Shaped wood is everywhere in suggestive, incom-plete forms. The walls are pa-pered with Marilyn and carnicería calendars. The air is heavy with sawdust. Against the walls lean stacks of wood from far-off lands. The guitar in my hands feels com-fortable. The top and sides, Reyes says, are palo escrito, a handsome Mexican wood; the bridge, rose-wood from India. This is one of his best, he says, and he's hoping it will sell for 5000 pesos –
that is, around $525. I gulp and change the subject.

Then Reyes barks an order to the apprentice and leads me out of the shop, down the street and into the heart of guitardom: Paracho's cultural center, where the courtyard is festooned with paper decorations cut in guitar shapes, where schoolchildren have made a 15-foot-high guitar out of plywood, cardboard and paint, where a grill full of carne asada smolders.

The courtyard teems with artisans from surrounding villages peddling pottery, textiles and woodwork. Farther back, the mountains jut up beyond the rooftops, and the pines stand in mist like an invading army at attention. Reyes leads me to a door and points inside. Arrayed on tabletop stands is this year's batch of entrants in the guitar-building competition. Precisely joined wood, elaborate inlays. Most are for sale, at prices from $160 to $750.

Looking closely at a guitar is like trying to count all those bones in your inner ear. Most instruments involve more than 100 bits of wood, large and small, which may have come from four continents. To complicate matters, Americans and Mexicans have developed their own intimate terms for types of wood and principal parts.

Americans refer to the neck, where the frets (trastos) are, and head (where the strings are wrapped around the tuning keys). Mexicans refer to el brazo (the arm) and la palma (the palm). On the back of the guitar, where the neck/arm meets the main body, there's a wooden brace that Americans call the heel, and Mexicans call the nariz (nose). Everybody uses 'bridge' (puente) for the crucial strip of hard wood against which the strings are stretched. But while Americans call the opening next to it the 'sound hole,' Mexicans stick with body language. That, they say, is la boca. The mouth.

In the Velazquez shop, I find a broad range of instruments and wooden souvenirs, all the way down to toy mini-guitars priced at about 90 cents each. But nothing speaks to me. In the Amezcua shop nearby, I find Gerónimo Amezcua Gómez, 50 years old and a third-generation guitar-maker, gently pounding trastos into a brazo. Behind him, his late grandfather peers out from a 1923 photo, guitar in hand.

The living Amezcua before me, a gruff, dedicated fellow who could pass for Det. Sipowicz's Mexican twin, made his first guitar at 13. He turns to point out a dusty old instrument mounted on the wall: his first guitar. Amezcua massages the new instrument in hand. 'A guitar like this,' he says, 'I make about four a week.' The price is about $200.

A few more doors down, José Luis Díaz Reyes retreats to a back room and returns with an odd steel-string guitar. Like most of his competitors, Díaz usually makes nylon-string guitars. But this is a one-of-a-kind innovation. The front and sides are bent so that the sound box, where the strings resonate, is extra large. Díaz, 62, says he started out to be a violin-maker but switched to guitars when he was 14.

'You hear the nice tone?' he asks, strumming the extra-large guitar. 'This guitar exists in no other place in Paracho.'

Between shop visits, I duck into the auditorium to hear the students play and wander among artisans under the arches of the cultural center.

The biggest risk in buying a Paracho guitar, I have been told, is making sure that it's not made of newly cut wood. The best guitars are made from the oldest, driest wood, which is less prone to warping and cracking.

Also, certain types of wood, not all of them grown in Mexico, are most suited to certain parts of a guitar. So, as the quality of Paracho's guitars improves, the local specialty takes on a global scope. Even the humdrum $50 guitars around Paracho are likely to feature foreign wood, and probably metal tuning keys from Asia.

In the unadvertised upstairs workshop of Kenny Hill, where a team of builders produces some guitars for his label and some for themselves as side projects, most of the wood arrives by way of the San Diego-Tijuana border. Most finished guitars leave the same way, and the best end up fetching $2000 or more.

That's beyond my budget. But Manuel Hernández, who runs the Hill workshop, is happy to show me around all the same. The machines that dry the wood, the blueprints the makers follow, the rich tone that comes from the low E-string on a well-made instrument.

The low notes, I tell Hernández, they are sounding much pretty.

Most American visitors, if they find their way into Michoacán at all, head straight for the old architecture, craft vendors and lake vistas around the town of Pátzcuaro, about an hour southwest of Morelia, or to Angangueo, at the state's eastern edge, where monarch butterflies cluster in a mountain sanctuary each winter.

Paracho lies on neither path. As the crow flies, it's about 30 miles west of Pátzcuaro, about 20 miles north of Uruapan, on the Mesita Purépecha, a severe but beautiful plateau of forests, cornfields, free-ranging livestock and rugged little towns.

The Purépecha, also known as the Tarascan, are the indigenous people whose ancestors retreated farther and farther into these mountains once the Spanish began their advances here in the 16th century. They raise corn, zucchini, apples and lentils, manage livestock and make crafts for the markets. If Cortez and company had never arrived, the Mesita Purépecha might not look much different today.

Winters can be bitterly cold. Illiteracy is sufficiently widespread that municipal ballots in Paracho offer candidates' photographs instead of names. Unemployment is severe enough that Michoacán rivals Jalisco and Guanajuato among the Mexican states that send the most immigrants to the U.S. In Paracho, skilled guitar-makers might earn as little as $40 per week, perhaps as much as $200.

But in summer, between cloudbursts, the freshly rinsed countryside is something to see. The plateau is more than 7000 feet above sea level, hemmed in by jagged volcanic peaks. Round a corner on one of the roads up here and you may find a pair of Purépecha women ambling along the roadside, shoulders swaddled in black and blue, hands cradling scythes. Twin reapers, their faces and their chores straight out of the 16th century.

Out beyond Angahuan, no more than 20 miles from Paracho on a good blacktop road, you can hire a horse and guide to explore the low slopes of Paricutin, a volcano that rose from a cornfield in 1943, erupted and buried most of the nearest town in lava. On the three-hour horseback trek, you can reach the spot where a buried church tower protrudes like a giant tombstone from a stark black lavascape.

These are illuminating sights – especially for somebody who's never seen beyond those 'I love Michoacán' bumper stickers that turn up so frequently on the freeways of Southern California. (To add a soundtrack to that vision, you need only approach a mariachi guitarist in Los Angeles and ask for 'Caminos de Michoacán.' Part love song, part anthem of homesickness, it tells of a narrator who searches for his lover from town to town throughout the state, from Zitácuaro to Huétamo and Apatzingán to Morelia.) In Paracho itself, there are about 55 hotel rooms, including 16 at the plain and central Hotel Hermelinda, where rates for singles are about $24.

But I want more creature comforts and a bit more distance between me and the revelry on the plaza. So I do my sleeping at the Hotel Mansion del Cupatitzio, a pleasant, river-side hacienda-style hotel at the northern end of Uruapan, right on the road that climbs and winds 20 miles to Paracho. (The hotel's owners, the Monroy family, also control a major guitar factory in Paracho and have thrown their weight behind CIDEG and the guitar festival.)

Summer daytime temperatures hover around 70 degrees. Downpours come mostly in brief bursts, trapping the market vendors under blue tarps with their mangoes and avocados – although one afternoon the pelting continues so long and strong that as I sit outside on a sheltered bench alongside the plaza, I see a 55-gallon drum positioned beneath a faulty rain gutter fill to overflowing in less than an hour.

Monday night. Night of the parade of the torneros, or craftmakers. I stand amid a throng in the plaza, snapping pictures of merrymaking while a master of ceremonies intones the names of Paracho's largest, oldest families. Onstage, the fair's queen and princesses dance with their fathers.

Down in the mosh pit, as I snap away, a boy of about 8 approaches, shyly bearing a wooden toy. For me. A few minutes later, a little girl arrives with a similar trinket. Then a teen-age boy, whose hair is partly dyed blond, singles me out and hands over a handsome pair of maracas.

These gifts are the same party favors that celebrants have been tossing from the stage deep into a surging, hand-waving audience. I keep bowing and saying gracias and passing smaller gifts on to smaller children nearby. But what's up?

Here's what: I am the only readily identifiable foreign tourist. These families are sending their children to make me feel welcome. And now one of the parents approaches. 'My family would like to invite you to join us dancing on the stage,' says Leticia Herrera Bentley, speaking perfect English. 'We would like to show you Paracho's hospitality.'

To the stage we go, and the crowd titters while I attempt to shift my weight rhythmically from foot to foot. Then our party, about 40 people, not counting the 20-piece brass band that will follow us through the evening, lurches to a corner of the plaza. Apparently, I am now an honorary Herrera.

Leticia Bentley, it develops, was born in Paracho, one of 11 children, the only one to leave Mexico. Now she lives in Moab, Utah, with an Irish American husband and three children. She teaches and does social work with Navajo families in connection with the public schools there. But every summer, she comes back for five weeks.

In the last two decades, 'the population has doubled, and you see a lot more professionals,' she says. The week of the Paracho festival, with its reunions and celebrations of roots and community, is so gratifying for her that it's excruciating. 'I told my husband I felt like I wanted to rip up my [return] ticket and never go back,' she says.

Before long, I'm introduced to the rest of the extended family, beginning with Leticia's niece, Carmen Herrera Padilla, a general-practice physician in Zitacuaro.

Then more dancing. Then a bottle of tequila surfaces.

Then it's off to the cultural center, where the bottle makes further rounds. One of my new relatives, in a touching gesture of fraternity, proposes to drink three tequila shots for every one of mine. Grinning loopily, he looks like Diego Rivera, drunk, at 20.

'No,' I tell him. 'You are clearly a professional. I am just a tourist. It is better for me to watch and teach. And learn. To watch and learn. Also, I am working. Must take pictures. Look! Taking pictures now!'

So I have blurry snaps of the plastic cup looming, and my brethren guffawing as another new relative proposes, between shots, to discuss geopolitics. 'El globalismo!' he hollers.

He's in favor of it. I have to agree. From the cultural center, the Herreras and I migrate to a private home, where the wives and mothers serve posole, a hearty stew of pinto beans, hominy, ham hocks and peppers. Fathers and daughters dance, my new friends explain some subtleties of Paracho society, and the tequila is joined by a corn liquor known as charanda. I eat heavily, dance with the doctor and her son, dodge the alcohol and take great secret gulps of mineral water.

Midnight finds me strolling across the town to find my car. Now all the sensitive classical gui-tar types are gone. A band blares in the plaza, fireworks bloom over-head, and bodies lurch merrily on the streets and sidewalks.

But not me. Not only do I have a Herrera retinue to guide me – one social worker, one physician, five teenagers, one 6-year-old and one 3-year-old – I have sobriety on my side. Which is good, not only because of the drive down the hill, but because it wouldn't do to choose a guitar while fighting a hangover.

Tuesday afternoon. Flight home tomorrow. Deal today.

Back in the Kenny Hill work-shop, Manuel Hernández and his guys have finished a side-project guitar that was nearly done when I showed up in town. Its sides and backs are made of gorgeous striped palo escrito. Its neck is cedar; the bridge, rosewood from India; the fingerboard, ebony from Brazil. And, of course, the elbow grease is all Paracho. This, I later learn, is the sort of instrument that Kenny Hill calls 'a concert guitar for the student' and car-ries a $1,200 price tag in music shops. But that's after Hill buys it from Paracho, and Paracho ships it to California, and Hill sells it to a retailer. 'Listen,' says Hernández in Spanish, leaning over the unlabeled instrument. 'This is your guitar.'

He plucks the top and bottom strings, which fill the small room with twin E notes, two octaves apart. You can almost see the sawdust trembling in the air.

We agree on $400 in pesos – a tremendous discount, as long as I don't dwell on the $600 cost of my plane ticket, not to mention hotels and meals. I close the case carefully, shake hands with Hernández and step back out into downtown Paracho, where the rain has mercifully ceased. The fair continues in all its glory, guitarreros and guitarristas eyeing one another's instruments and lazing in the shade.

Now all I have to do is get mine safely home, and then learn some new songs to do it justice. I believe I'll start with 'Caminos de Michoacán.'

GUIDEBOOK: GUITAR HUNTING IN MEXICO

Telephone numbers and prices: The country code for Mexico is 52; the regional code is 4. All prices are approximate and are computed at 9.5 pesos per dollar. Room rates are for a double for one night. Meal prices are for two, food only.

Getting there: Mexicana has direct service to Morelia from Los Angeles. Though often pricier than in the US, rental cars give you flexibility in exploring the countryside, and they can be reserved at the Morelia or Uruapan airport.

Where to stay: In Morelia, Hotel & Suites Villa San José, Patzimba 77, Colonia Vista Bella, Morelia; telephone 315-1738, fax 324-4545, www.villasanjose.com.mx. Forty-three rooms on hillside overlooking the city. Great view from restaurant, with playfully arranged, well-tended grounds. Rate: $128.

In Uruapan, Hotel Mansión del Cupatitzio, Parque Nacional Eduardo Ruiz; tel. 523-2100, fax 524-6772, www.mansiondelcupatitzio .com. Fifty-seven rooms in a hacienda-style setting next to Cupatitzio National Park, a river that runs into the city. Courtyard pool popular with families. Rate: $96.

In Paracho, the Hotel Hermelinda, Ave. 20 de Noviembre, No. 239; tel. 525-0080. Hotel with 16 plain rooms is on the main drag near the center of town; rooms in back may be quieter. Rate: $24.

Where to eat: In Paracho, La Casona, Portal Jesús Díaz, No. 110; tel. 525-0830. A rambling restaurant next to the main square that serves great, hearty Tarascan soup; $20.

In Morelia, La Fonda Santa Mar'a restaurant at the Hotel & Suites Villa San José offers sweeping city views and a few Italian dishes along with a Mexican regional menu. My favorite dish: a cold avocado soup with tomato chunks and a hint of tequila; $25.

When to go: Because of their high-altitude settings, Paracho, Uruapan and environs are cool – and frequently wet – through the summer and chilly in winter. As for Paracho's annual festival, discovering specific dates is like trying to hold water in your hands. But innkeeper Gerónimo Villafán at Hotel Hermelinda says it's always the first two weeks of August, with most festivities (including fireworks and bonfires) on Friday and Saturday nights.

For more information: Mexico Tourism Board, Mexican Consulate, 2401 W. 6th St., Los Angeles, Calif., 90057; tel. (213) 351-2069, fax (213) 351-2074, www.visitmexico.com. Also, Mexico's Ministry of Tourism Office (Mexico City), (800) 482-9832, www.mexico-travel.com.

JUST FOR KICKS
by Stanley Stewart

This article by British freelancer Stanley Stewart, which was first published in the travel section of the *Sunday Times*, is also a kind of quest story, but in this case the quest is less precise and more ethereal. Essentially, Stewart is travelling in search of the American West. We noted earlier how Stewart's vivid beginning introduces the themes of his piece and suggests the mysteries and riches that await the reader on this rodeo ride. There are other qualities to savour in this story. For example, the way Stewart palpably juxtaposes past and present ('To the newcomer, cowboys are the surprise of the American West, like finding Romans in pleated togas waiting for the trolley buses on the Via Appia'), and seamlessly illustrates his opinions ('The West is America's most vibrant sub culture with its own music, its own fashions, its own political orientation and its own folklore') with subsequent information and anecdotes. Stewart also skilfully and coherently develops metaphor (rodeos 'are like church fetes'; 'the Bronco snorted and took off across the plains while I clung weakly to the steering wheel'), interjects humour ('These horses were dangerous and·bad to know, the kind of horses you warn your daughter's pony about') and cleverly uses quotation ('Welcome, laygeezeengenelmen, to the Greatest Show on Dirt'). Also note the way he vividly portrays the cowboys with just a few deft strokes of detail, and where he chooses to place us at the very end of our Wild West ride.

At the rodeo you notice that horses and cowboys are kind of alike. Horses stand around a lot, flicking their tails, breaking wind, doing nothing in particular. Cowboys are like that. They lean on fences, looking at horses. Sometimes they spit, sometimes they don't. With their hats tipped down over their eyes, it is never easy to tell if they are asleep, like horses, on their feet. The similarity disguises a major difference of temperament. Cowboys are soft-spoken mild-mannered fellows. In the West it's the horses that are the outlaws.

To the newcomer, cowboys are the surprise of the American West, like finding Romans in pleated togas waiting for the trolley buses on the Via Appia. Towns like Laramie and Cheyenne and Medicine Bow and Kit Carson are full of people who seem to have wandered off the back lot at MGM. They wear boots and ten gallon hats and leather waistcoats. In town they drink in saloons with swing doors and stand around on street corners in a bowlegged fashion. Back at the ranch their nearest neighbours are miles away. The men are lean laconic figures with lopsided grins. The women look like their idea of a good time would be to rope you and ride you round the corral awhile. The women are rather chatty. With cowboys there is a lot of silence to fill.

The West is America's most vibrant sub culture with its own music, its own fashions, its own political orientation and its own folklore. They care nothing for the suburban world that is the American mainstream. They talk of Washington and back east as if they were part of Red China. It is one of the pleasures of Wyoming to find Americans who are as cantankerous and as sceptical as the regulars of any Yorkshire pub. If the West is the spiritual home of America's ardent individualism, it is the landscape that is to blame.

Between the Missouri River and the Rocky Mountains lies a vast swathe of country that early cartographers called the Great American Desert. They were wrong but you can see where they got the idea. The West is a landscape of skies and infinities. In the loneliness of this place, self-reliance becomes a kind of religion. When the first settlers tried to farm this land, it broke their hearts. The West did not take kindly to the idea of fields. It was a vast sea of grass, a landscape for horses.

The rodeos that are held in small towns all over the West are like church fetes with Budweiser tents and bullriders, a chance to meet the neighbours and complain about the government. They are also the moment for the big show-down between the cowboys and the horses.

In Denver I hired a car called a Bronco, and headed north on

Interstate 28. The road and the landscape emptied and the sky took over. Here and there wooden houses hove into view afloat on the swells of grass. Antelopes bounded away over the brows of hills. I passed four men in an old Chevy, sprawled in the seats, their cowboy hats bumping the windows. The boot of the car, tied down with baler twine, was bulging with saddles. They were rodeo cowboys heading for Caspar. They looked like clean living guys with big chins, ready to tame the wild equine forces of the West.

Rodeo cowboys have taken over from outlaws and bashful sheriffs as the heroes of the modern West, footloose fellows who struggle to make a living from the competitive world of bronco riding and bull wrestling. Lift a handful of their names from the program notes and they seem to describe a way of life: Lance, Cody, Chance, Skeeter, Shane, Chuck, and Rusty. In their pickup trucks and old cars, the cowboys tour the rodeo circuit from Texas to Montana, from Arizona to South Dakota. They often drive a thousand miles between rodeos, compete in the bronco riding for an afternoon, wave at the cheering crowds, then get back in the truck to drive all night to another rodeo in another town in another state. Their only income is the prize money they win. If they do well, it might cover their expenses. It is

the kind of reckless itinerant life I dreamt about when I was fifteen – the American West, the open road, horses and prairie towns miles from nowhere, late-night bars and girls in tight blue jeans.

In Caspar, the banners over Main Street welcomed me to the Central Wyoming Fair and Rodeo. Most of the buildings on Main Street were hardly older than my father. At lunch in a turn of the century hotel I was served by a riverboat gambler with slick hair, a pencil moustache and shiny waistcoat. He looked like he had just stepped off the stage from Carson City. I asked him if he was from Caspar. He said he was just passing through.

In the late afternoon I headed out to the fairgrounds. Pens of horses and steers and a car park of pickup trucks surrounded the open-air grandstand. Just inside the gate I was greeted by one of those tall young men with perfect teeth and day-glow tans who make a living in America on afternoon soap operas. When the romantic leads run out, they turn their hands to running the country.

'Hi, I'm John Thune, and I'm running for Congress.' John gave good handshake. He wore cowboys boots and a T-shirt that said 'Thune!'. 'I want to get government off the peoples' backs,' Thune! said. 'I sure hope I can count on your vote.' I thought Thune! might make a start by getting off my back. But he was already on to the next punter. 'Hi, I'm John Thune!...'

The only people with shinier smiles than Thune! were the rodeo royalty. I was still struggling to gain my seat with a plastic beaker of beery foam and a hot dog the size of Idaho when the Queens arrived.

'We have five visiting Rodeo Queens here today,' the announcer boomed over the loudspeakers. 'And I jes know you're gonna want to give 'em a big Caspar welcome.' The Queens, in spray-on Levis and shiny shirts, galloped in on white horses. They were dazzling figures. There was Miss Country & Western Music, Miss Rodeo Iowa, Miss South-west County Fair and Livestock Show, Miss Rodeo South Dakota. They cantered past in a blur of fixed smiles, big hair and royal waves. The minor royalty tended to out-shine the major players. With high-voltage eyes and a hairstyle with fins, Miss Laramie Feed and Hard-ware Store had more than a little of Princess Michael of Kent about her.

'Welcome, laygeezeengenelmen, to the Greatest Show on Dirt.' The announcers, the D.J.'s of the rodeo, had the honeyed tones of the revivalist tent. They made jingoism an art form. The National Anthem was their big moment.

'We're here for a good time lay-geezeengenelmen. We gonna forget our troubles, let our hair down, go a little wild with the wild west rodeo...[crowd roars]...but first, I'm gonna ask you to pause for a mo-ment. [crowd noise subsides]...I want us to remember just how lucky we are...[crowd is silent] The Good Lord blessed us with this Great Land of Ours, we must never take for granted the Freedoms that We Fought so Hard to Win...I am gonna ask you to stand now, laygeezeen-genelmen, for the most beautiful colours on earth, the red white and blue of Old Glory. God Bless America, laygeezeengenelmen, the Greatest Country on Earth.'

I prided myself in being able to get through these introductions without resort to the sick bag.

Behind the chutes the cowboys were warming up. Some were stretching like ballerinas, others were rocking on saddles on the ground, working the resin into the leather. One was performing a practise mime of bull riding, one hand above his head, snapping his back in slow motion. Another was trying to make his peace with God. He stood with his hat tipped down against the top rail of a corral, praying. A massive bull with a cyn-ic's face and testicles the size of basketballs, eyed him malevolently from the other side of the fence.

I said howdy to Randy, a rancher I knew from the hills back of Kay-cee where the Butch Cassidy gang used to hide out after raiding the Union Pacific railroad. Randy was a bony taciturn cowboy with pale eyes and red cheeks. He was so soft-spoken, in that cowboy way, that conversations became a series of furtive whispers. He had been a bronc rider himself until a horse had thrown him over a wall, breaking his back. He missed the rodeo, and he hung around behind the chutes, chatting to the cowboys, like the ghost of rodeos past.

The bucking horses arrived, snorting and pawing the ground like demons as they were herded into the stalls. A row of cowboys climbed up on the buckboards to set and adjust the saddles. One of the horses snorted and reared in the box, and a tall cowboy in a white hat shot backwards like a cartoon character, coming to rest against the front row of the grandstand. The horse had caught him with a powerful left hook and broken his jaw. It was a sobering moment. These horses were dangerous and bad to know, the kind of horses you warn your daughter's pony about.

When the broncs were saddled and the judges ready, a cowboy lowered himself gingerly onto the first horse. There was a moment of anxiety as he settled himself. Gripping the head rope, the cowboy leaned back, adjusted his hat, stuffed a wad of chewing tobacco in his mouth and nodded to signal he was ready. When the chute gate swung open, all hell broke loose. As the horse charged into the arena, it hardly seemed to touch the ground, and the cowboy, flesh and blood but a moment ago, was whipping back and forth like a rag doll.

The idea is to hang on for just eight seconds, a feat which barely half of the cowboys manage. Hanging on would be enough to occupy most people, but the cowboy must also meet certain criteria to score well, including spurring the bucking horse in the requisite manner, rather like stepping on the accelerator when the car is already out of control. Two of the other rough stock disciplines, bareback bronc riding and bull riding, have the added difficulty of remembering, when you are thrown, to fall off the right side. If you come off the wrong side, opposite to the way your hand grips, your hand is trapped in the rigging with consequences too grim to describe.

For bull riders of course their troubles only just begin when they hit the ground. The bulls make the horses look like teddy bears, and they tend to bear a grudge with people foolish enough to ride on their backs. Part of the job of the rodeo clowns, who entertain the crowd between events, is to distract the bull while the rider makes a hasty escape over the boards. In the world of comedy this is trial by fire; if the bull isn't taken with the clown's stand-up routine, he doesn't just heckle.

I asked Randy why they did it. It is wonderful entertainment but one could understand a young cowboy preferring a quiet career yee-hawing at a herd of docile cows.

'It's a western thing,' Randy whispered. 'They've been around horses all their lives and they like the challenge. They also like the independence, life on the road, no-body telling 'em what to do. Lot of guys when they stop ridin' and get some job somewhere, long for the days when they were a poor young cowboy, driving across Wyoming to the next rodeo.'

I was impressed. I had never heard Randy talk so much. He seemed kind of tuckered out by his monologue, and retired to the beer tent. When I looked round the steer wrestling had begun. Ostensibly this is a more sedate event for cowboys who might have second thoughts about climbing aboard deranged livestock. They chase runaway steers instead, jumping on their backs when they have reached full speed. Participants liken it to driving along a road at about forty miles an hour and then stepping out the passenger door to embrace a passing tree. The cowboy is meant to throw the steer but the fun lies in the fact that it is often the other way round.

The next morning I hit the road in the Bronco. I drove west to Laramie where the rodeo was in a windswept grandstand with a view of the Medicine Bow Mountains. I went north to Belle Fouche in South Dakota where a bronc rider

broke his arm and the post-rodeo street party was washed out by a freak storm out of Nevada. I turned west again into Montana to the night rodeo at Billings where I learnt that the cowboys have their own union, the PRCA, the Professional Rodeo Cowboys Association. Presumably health care is one of the comrades' chief priorities.

Montana has dispensed with speed limits, which are nothing but a Washington conspiracy to deprive the American citizen of his inalienable right to see if he can get his pickup airborne. The Bronco snorted and took off across the plains while I clung weakly to the steering wheel. I was in Idaho before I knew what had happened. The next day I was back in Wyoming, barrelling down the Platte River Valley beneath a huge sky decorated with mare's tail clouds. I was heading for Cheyenne and the 'Daddy of 'Em All', the Cheyenne Frontier Days, the country's biggest and oldest rodeo.

Cheyenne is the product of the Union Pacific Railroad, the Black Hills Gold Rush of the 1870's and the cattle wars of the 1880's. It's an archetypal cowboy town, with wide streets and plain flat-faced buildings. The pawn shop was full of saddles, and the jukeboxes in the bars were devoted to Garth Brooks and Dolly Parton.

Begun in 1896, Frontier Days takes place over ten days in July and attracts almost 20,000 spectators a day. All the best cowboys come here, and all the best riding stock. The bucking horses are wild creatures from a ranch in the Rattlesnake Hills of Colorado and the bulls, part Brahma, are as big and as ornery as you are ever gonna see.

The climax of each day's events were the wild horse races. The idea is simple enough. The cowboys compete in teams of three. A herd of wild horses is released into the arena, and each team runs out to lasso and saddle one. The cowboy who has drawn the short straw then gets to ride the horse round the track. That's the theory anyway.

Few of the teams even get so far as saddling the horses. As the mustangs charged into the arena, white-eyed and wet-muzzled, a blur of dust and horseflesh, the cowgirl behind me became hysterical. She was trying to explain the finer points of the race to a friend. To her it was a simple imbalance in male hormones. 'It's testosterone,' she shrieked. 'It's pure testosterone. It's madness.'

She seemed to be on a first name basis with most of the testosterone-laden competitors. 'Come on Cody. Come on Tuff. Get him Skeeter, get him. Wrassle 'em, Duane,' she cried.

The cowboys were doing their best but the horses were winning.

One took off down the track dragging a hapless cowboy at the end of a rope. It was an impressive burst of speed but sadly he was going the wrong way. The cowboy reappeared, later in the afternoon, limping badly. Another horse head-butted one of the cowboys then swung round and chased the whole team into the grandstands before taking off to terrorise the suburbs. A third simply bit everyone who came near him. Half an hour later when they were all herded back into their corral, they were as frisky as children, whinnying their pleasure at such a jolly outing. The cowboys limped away, their hats crushed, their clothes covered in dust, their levels of testosterone seriously depleted.

That evening at the Hitching Post Inn the car park was full of stretch pickups loaded with saddles and hay. The Hitching Post was the happening place after hours. In the saloon bar it was wall to wall cowboy hats. Cowboys clean up real nice, and they were all turned out in their best shirts. It is said that cowboys have three pairs of jeans. A size too big for practise; the right size for the rodeo itself; and a size too small for the dances afterwards.

The next morning in the western outfitters I bought a handsome Stetson from a sales girl with a mean pair of boots and a serious chewing gum habit. A sign by the till read 'It's Never Too Late to be a Cowboy'. I had already decided it was too late for me. I wasn't sure the testosterone levels were up to it. I put on my hat and went out into the wide streets of Cheyenne. I was happy to walk the walk and talk the talk but there was no way I was going near those horses. They were the real thing, the last remnant of the Wild West.

A NIGHT WITH THE GHOSTS OF GREECE

by Don George

'A Night with the Ghosts of Greece' was the first of my travel stories to be published in a national travel magazine. The magazine was *Signature*, which was subsequently bought by Condé Nast and transformed into *Condé Nast Traveler*. I recently asked the editor who bought the piece why she had liked it. She replied: 'First of all, I liked the uniqueness of the idea – you spent a night on an island where no one was supposed to be. That caught my attention. Second, I liked the way you gave us just the history we needed to know – you didn't weigh the story down with history – and then brought both that past and the present of the place to life with the specific details you chose to describe (and which you described with colour and precision). I liked the small, humanising touches (the lizard slithering over your boot, the cat lapping your cheek in the morning, and of course your encounters with the physicist and the pavilion owner), the humour ('the universal tongue of Loquacious Libation'), the way you imparted a sense of the place's effect on you without overdoing it, and I liked the way you kept a certain sense of mystery throughout the piece. Also, I liked the circular structure of the story, where the end comes back to the beginning – but of course, you (and by extension, we) are part of the island now and so we see it all with new eyes. For *Signature*, this was a very satisfying and unexpected appreciation of a little-ballyhooed Greek island. It fitted our sense of our own style – and of our readers' tastes and interests – perfectly.'

There are no tavernas, no discotheques, no pleasure boats at anchor. Nor are there churches, windmills or goatherds. Delos, three miles long and less than one mile wide, is a parched, rocky island of ruins, only 14 miles from Mykonos, Aegean playground of the international vagabonderie. Once the center of the Panhellenic world, Delos has been uninhabited since the first century AD, fulfilling a proclamation of the Delphic oracle that 'no man or woman shall give birth, fall sick or meet death on the sacred island.'

I chanced on Delos during my first visit to Greece. After three harrowing days of seeing Athens by foot, bus and taxi, my traveling companion and I were ready for open seas and uncrowded beaches. We selected Mykonos on the recommendation of a friend, who suggested that when we tired of the Beautiful People, we should take a side trip to Delos.

On arriving in Mykonos, we learned that for under $3 we could catch a fishing trawler to Delos (where the harbor is too shallow for cruise ships) any morning at eight and return to Mykonos at one the same afternoon. On the morning of our fourth day, we braved choppy seas and ominous clouds to board a rusty, peeling boat that reeked of fish. With a dozen other tourists, we packed ourselves into the ship's tiny cabin, already crowded with anchors, ropes and wooden crates bearing unknown cargo.

At some point during the 45-minute voyage, the toss and turn of the waves became too much for a few of the passengers, and I moved outside into the stinging, salty spray. As we made our way past Renea, the calluslike volcanic island that forms part of the natural breakwater with Delos, the clouds cleared, and the fishermen who had docked their caiques at the Delos jetty greeted us in bright sunlight.

At the end of the dock a white-whiskered man in a navy blue beret and a faded black suit hailed each one of us as we walked by: 'Tour of Delos! Informative guide to the ruins.' A few yards beyond him a young boy ran up to us, all elbows and knees, and confided in hard breaths, 'I give you better tour. Cheaper too.'

I had read the Delphic oracle's proclamation the night before and wondered what these people were doing on the island. I asked the boy, and he pointed to a cluster of houses on a knoll about a thousand yards away. 'I live here. Family.'

At first glance Delos seemed the quintessential ruin: broken bits of statues, stubby pillars, cracking archways and isolated walls. Nothing moved but the sunlight, glinting off the fragments like fish scales scattered over a two-acre basin.

Other movements had once animated the alleys and temples

before us. Legend has it that Delos was originally a roving island when Leto, mistress of Zeus, landed there racked with birth pains. Poseidon anchored the island in its present position while Leto brought forth Artemis and Apollo, the Greek sun god and protector of light and art. Apollo eventually became the most revered of the Greek gods, and religious devotion, coupled with the island's central, protected situation, established Delos as the thriving center of the Mediterranean world, religious and commercial leader of an empire that stretched from Italy to the coast of Asia Minor.

Wandering the ruins of this once-boisterous center, we found temples both plain and elegant, Greek and foreign; massive marketplaces studded with pedestals where statues once stood, now paved with poppies; a theater quarter with vivid mosaics depicting actors and symbolic animals and fish; a dry lake ringed with palm trees; a stadium and a gymnasium; storehouses and quays along the waterfront; and an ancient suburb where merchants and ship captains once lived: the haunting skeleton of a Hellenistic metropolis.

At 12:45 the captain of the trawler appeared at the end of the dock and whistled once, twice, three times, then waved his arms. He repeated this signal at 12:50 and 12:55. My friend left, but

something about those deserted ruins held me, and I decided to spend the night on the island. I watched from the top of Mount Cynthus, the lone hill, as the boat moved away toward the mountains of Mykonos on the northeast horizon. Looking around, I felt at the center of the Cyclades: to the north, Tinos, to the northwest, Andros, then Syros, Siphnos, Paros and Naxos, and beyond them Melos and Ios – all spokes in the sacred chariot of the sun god.

Below me the ruins were absolutely desolate, shimmering silently in the midday sun. A lizard slithered over my boot. The boat crawled farther away. The wind sighed. Droplets of sweat seemed to steam from my forehead.

I walked down the hill to the shade of the tourist pavilion, the one concession to tourism (besides a three-room museum) on the island. I walked inside and asked the owner, a large, jolly man with a Zorba mustache, what he was offering for lunch. He looked surprised to see me. 'You miss the caique?'

'No, I wanted to spend the night here.'

'Ah.' He looked beyond me into the glaring, baked ruins. 'We have rice, meat, vegetables.'

'Do you have any fish?'

'Fish? Yes.' He directed me to a case in the back room, opened it and took out five different fish, each caked with ice. 'Which do you want?' I pointed to one. 'Drink?'

'A beer, please.'

He nodded, pointed out the door to a terrace with tables and chairs scattered at random like dancers at a Mykonos discotheque, and said, 'Sit, please,' motioning me into a chair.

The heat hung in the air, folding like a curtain over the pillars and pedestals, smothering the palms and reeds. Occasionally a dusty-brown lizard would scuttle from one shadow into another. The owner moved from kitchen to terrace like a man who has never waited, never worried about time, wiping off the table, bringing a glass of cold beer, then fish, fried potatoes and a tomato salad.

Eventually, two old men dressed in the same uniform as the man who had greeted us that morning walked up carrying two pails filled with water. One went inside and began to talk animatedly with the owner. The other sat down on the edge of the terrace, dipped his callused hands and pulled out a white and black octopus. He rolled the octopus in a milky white liquid from the other pail, twisting and slapping its tentacles against the cement until he was satisfied it was clean. Then he laid it aside, and dipped in again, pulling out another slippery creature. He cleaned five octopuses in all, leaving them oozing in the sun, their tentacles writhing and their suction cups puckering for water.

At 4 p.m. a cock crowed. What is he doing here? I wondered. And, more important, why is he crowing at 4 p.m.? The sound broke the silence with an eerie premonition. I looked at the bottles, chairs, tables, heard the reassuring murmur of voices inside. Beyond the terrace, in the light and heat, seemed another world.

An hour later I walked into the ruins, following the wide central avenue (the 'Sacred Way') toward the waterfront, the theater district and the hillside temples. On my way I passed columns carved with line after line of intricate symbols with no breaks between the words; sacrificial altars; huge cisterns for storing rainwater and oil; and vast foundations outlining meeting halls and marketplaces by the wharves. I explored the remains of private houses, passing from room to room, trying to imagine where their inhabitants had cooked, eaten and slept, awakened from my reverie only by an occasional spider web or lizard trail. As I walked on and the setting sun cast the halls and walls in an orange-pink light, the ruins seemed to take on a strange life all their own.

What had been eerie desolation became an intense timelessness, a sense of communion with other peoples and other eras. My boots crossed rocks other sandals had crossed; my hands touched marble other hands had touched. When I reached the mosaics, they seemed a living thing, green-eyed tigers and blue dolphins, flowers of every shape and color, the same to me as they were to the countless merchants and artisans who had admired them centuries before. I continued up the hill to the temples of the Syrian and Egyptian – as well as Greek – gods, and reflected how many different cultures had met in that silent hollow below.

While I was sitting in the temple to the Egyptian gods, a figure appeared walking up the hill toward me. It was not the owner of the pavilion, nor any of the fishermen I had seen previously. This was a man in shorts and a Western shirt, with a satchel and a walking stick. We exchanged waves and wary glances until he came up and sat next to me. 'You are English?'

'American.'

'Ah, good.' He stuck out his hand.

He was a physicist from Hungary, on leave from a national research project for two weeks. 'I have been saving my passes for this trip,' he said. 'Isn't this wonderful? Yesterday I examined all the ruins from there' – he waved a finger toward the stadium at the distant end of the basin – 'to here. Today I have walked the circuit of the island.' He paused to catch his breath, his cheeks as grainy as the rocks on which we sat. 'There really isn't that much else to see.'

The mountains were turning purple over the poppy-red water. The ruins were fading into shade. I wanted to explore further before darkness set in, so we agreed to meet for dinner.

When I entered the tourist pavilion, the owner greeted me like a long-lost friend and brought out three glasses and a bottle of ouzo. 'We drink.' The Hungarian appeared through another doorway that, I learned later, led to the pavilion's four 'guest rooms,' distinguished by the presence of a mattress and wash basin. We finished one bottle and began another, talking in Greek, Italian, French, German and English about everything, and soon thereafter about nothing. When one language failed, we tried another, until we were all speaking in the universal tongue of Loquacious Libation.

In another hour or two the owner fixed us a feast of fish, lamb, fried potatoes, rice, tomatoes and cucumbers, with baklava and rice pudding for dessert. While we ate, the physicist and I talked. I learned that the cluster of houses I had seen earlier had been built by the French School of Classical Studies when it was digging on Delos in the 1950s and '60s. When the last archaeologists left, the curator of the museum moved in with his family. It was his son I had met that morning. The old man who had hailed our arrival was a fisherman from a local island who turned to guiding when the fishing was slow.

After finishing our second bottle – compliments of the owner – of sweet, resiny retsina, we drank a good-night toast of thick Greek coffee. Then the physicist retired to his room, preceded by the owner's wife, who had drawn a pitcher of cold water for his use in the morning. I was traveling on a backpack budget, however, and when the owner offered me the use of his roof for 30 drachmas (under $1) – half the cost of the guest rooms – I gladly accepted.

I walked up two flights of cement stairs to a cement roof enclosed like a medieval fortress with a 4-foot-high wall. The stars glinted like a nighttime mirror of the marble ruins. I unrolled my sleeping bag in a protected corner, thankful that the lizards could not reach me at that height, and rummaged in my backpack for soap, toothpaste and a toothbrush.

'Could you use this?' The physicist held out his flashlight. 'I've come to ask you to hurry in preparing your toilet. The owner wants to turn off the electricity.'

After I had washed and brushed and stumbled back up the stairs to my sleeping bag, I heard a scuffling of footsteps; voices thundered back and forth through the blackness, and the lights went out.

The footsteps returned, a door squeaked and banged shut, chairs scraped. Then everything was silent. No machine sounds, no human sounds, no animal sounds. Absolute silence. I lay in my sleeping bag, and the ruins encroached on my dreams – the swish of the lizards scrambling over the rocks, the moist coolness of the marble at sunset, the languid perfume of the poppies dabbed among the fluted white fragments.

Streaming sunlight awakened me. I turned to look at my watch and disturbed a black kitten that had bundled itself at my feet. In so doing, I also disturbed the ouzo and retsina that had bundled itself in my head, and I crawled as close as I could to the shadow of the wall – 6:45. I pulled my towel over my head and tried to imagine the windy dark, but to no avail. The kitten mewed its way under my towel, where it set to lapping at my cheek as if it had discovered a bowl of milk.

I stumbled down the stairs and soaked my head in tepid tap water until at last I felt stable enough to survey the surroundings. Behind the pavilion a clothesline ran to the rusting generator. Chickens strutted inside a coop at the curator's house. Rhenea stirred in the rising mist.

Again I wandered through the ruins, different ruins now, bright with day and the reality of returns: The tourists would return to Delos, and I would return to Mykonos. I ate a solemn breakfast on the terrace with the physicist, then walked past the sacred lake and the marketplace to the Terrace of the Lions. Standing among the five lions of Delos, erected in the seventh century BC to defend the island from invaders, I looked over the crumbing walls and stunted pillars to the temples on the hill. Like priests they presided over the procession of tourists who would surge onto the island, bearing their oblation in cameras and guidebooks. As the trawler approached, a bent figure in a navy blue beret hurried to the dock, and a boy in shorts raced out of the curator's house past the physicist, past me, and into the ruins.

How to get there: The most reliable way to get to Delos is from Mykonos. Caiques depart once each morning (weather permitting) from the pier near the tourist information office, and return once each afternoon to bring visitors back. It is best to inquire on arrival in Mykonos about precise times and also if any other vessels, public or private, are making the trip.

Passage can also sometimes be arranged from other islands in the Cyclades, but such arrangements are subject to the whims of fishermen and sailors.

Where to eat and stay: The Tourist Pavilion offers a small cafeteria and four small and spartan rooms for visitors who want to spend the night. Or, if you prefer to do as I did, you can make arrangements to sleep on the roof. In either case, talk to the pavilion's proprietor.

Guidebooks: A good guidebook is almost essential to understanding the layout and significance of the ruins. My guide of choice was the *Blue Guide: Greece*. Another book that has been highly recommended to me is *Delos: Monuments and Museum*, by P. Zaphiropoulou, which can be purchased on Mykonos.

THE PATH TO SOKKURAM
by Robert Hass

This story by former US Poet Laureate Robert Hass appeared in *Great Escapes*, which was the quarterly travel magazine of the *San Francisco Examiner & Chronicle*. Earlier in this section we discussed the article's effective use of *in medias res*, and the interweaving of themes with indelible portraits of people, places, history and culture. Hass' vivid use of language is striking throughout the piece, but what is most impressive is the way he combines a very personal narrative with a much larger explanation and exploration of the country in which that personal tale is unfolding. We finish this account with a rich, multilayered appreciation of Korea as experienced through Hass' eyes and heart. Even more profoundly, we emerge with a renewed appreciation of the power and potential of travel to heal and restore. We come away with a powerfully personified understanding of how every journey can fling unexpected bridges across cultures and offer life-transforming revelations – both interpersonal and intrapersonal. In this masterful tale Hass evokes a full sense of his connection with Korea. And how does he choose to end? Most appropriately, with one final resonant word, written by Hass but spoken by another: a final embodiment of the intercultural connection the story has described and now become.

'The thing you need to understand about Korea,' said the cheerful, dissolute-looking British shipping agent I had run into at six in the morning at the fish market in the harbor at Pusan – we were drinking coffee at an outdoor table in the reek of fish and the unbelievable choral din of the fish merchants, beside tanks of slack-bodied pale squid and writhing pink and purple octopus – 'is that it's Poland. I mean, as a metaphor it's Poland. Caught between China and Japan for all those centuries like the Poles were stuck between the Russians and the Germans. The Japanese occupied the place from 1910 to the end of the war, and in the '30s they simply tried to eradicate Korea as a nation. Outlawed the language. Everybody in the country over 40 went to school when the teaching of the Korean language was forbidden.'

An old woman pushed past with a cart full of fist-sized reddish-green figs. McEwan, the shipping agent, called her over. 'Try one of these,' he said. 'Damned good.' They were, red-fleshed, packed with seeds. McEwan was waving down a waiter with one hand, clutching a torn-open fig with the other. 'They demand soju, don't they?' Soju is a transparent, fiery, slightly sweet Korean brandy, perfect with figs I was sure, but beyond me at that moment. I had been out the night before with a surprisingly hard-drinking lot of professors from Pusan National University, and wandered afterward rather aimlessly through the night market. Just before leaving America I had come to the end of a long marriage, and I had spent my first few days in Korea, when I did not have to concentrate on a task, in a state of dazed grief. In the night market the families had fascinated me, at one in the morning shutting down their produce stalls, loading up their boxes of fennel and cabbage and bok choy, moving swiftly in and out of the arc of light thrown by a hanging propane lamp, husbands and wives and drowsy children, working easily side by side. I drank beer at a stall and watched the market close down, and then went back to my hotel and couldn't sleep, and so got up again and walked down the hill in the pre-dawn coolness to the wharf.

'A hell of a lot of the Koreans were drafted during the war,' McEwan was saying. The cloud of flies that had risen to reconnoiter the fig cart returned to the gleaming guts of tuna and mackerel that were being eviscerated across the way. 'Either they were pressed into service in factories in Japan or they served in the army. Fellow in my office was conscripted in '44, fought in a Korean unit of the Japanese infantry and ended up in a POW camp in Shanghai, which is where he learned his English.'

I had, so far, only a few definite impressions of Korea: that Koreans were intense, that the country was stunningly, unexpectedly beautiful and that all foreigners who live there and most Koreans had a passion for trying to explain the place. I had liked listening, I noticed, in the way that people made listless by private pain are often stimulated by stories of misfortune. I had particularly liked talking to the students in Seoul who were involved in the demonstrations against the government. They had read the revisionist historians of the Korean War and books on neo-colonialism and 'dependency theory' and were furious at the role the United States had played in the recent history of their country. It isn't always possible to admire what one feels, but like it or not I found the passionate conflicts in Korean politics strangely soothing.

The soju arrived, with a dish of gungju, little charcoal-roasted pond snails that are gathered from the rice field and have a nutty taste. 'The thing is,' McEwan said, 'after the war was over, when they had finally got free of the Japanese, they turned on each other, and they absolutely decimated what was left of their country. Decimated it.' I objected to this interpretation of the Korean War, sipping soju, which I knew was a very bad idea. It was the United States and the Soviet Union that divided the country at the 38th parallel and cut off the possibility of a united and independent state.

McEwan waved me away. 'The Koreans have been lining up foreign help to fight each other since the Chou dynasty. The fact is they lined up the big boys on either side and tore this country the hell apart. In the early '60s, my father-in-law says there wasn't enough food between the used-up winter stores and the summer harvest, and not a cent available to import it. They had "spring hunger," like medieval peasants in wartime. You wouldn't know it now. You know what the average per capita GNP was in 1962? Eighty dollars. Now it's around two thousand.'

I had heard these figures before, quoted by cab drivers, diplomats, bartenders, poets. Koreans seemed to keep track of the per capita GNP as if it were a batting average. When they were not talking about student demonstrations – this was the fall of 1986 – they talked about the 'economic miracle.' And it did seem miraculous. From devastating poverty they had become in twenty years the twelfth most active trading nation in the world, just behind Italy.

McEwan began addressing this subject. 'This wealth was accomplished, of course, with massive infusions of Japanese and American capital, which was attracted by a cheap, hard-working, fairly well educated work force. For which,' he sucked a snail out of its dark blue shell, 'there's going to be hell to pay. The students are pushing political issues, freedom of speech, free elections. Wait,' he said, 'until the workers start demonstrating. They won't offend the generals' sense of order, they'll offend the actual structure of profits, and that's when the civil war inside the civil war begins.'

'By the way,' he had said, as I was leaving, 'if you're going to Kyongju, there's an old temple outside of town that you'll want to see. Up in the mountain behind it there's an eighth-century Buddha in a cave. Quite famous.' And he gave me what turned out to be very good advice. 'Take the hill path to Sokkuram, if you get a chance. There's a road up that takes you most of the way by car, but if you've got time, take the path. It's not a bad climb.'

He waved his long arm and, fortified by coffee, figs, snails, and two or three shots of soju, made his way down the wharf to work. It was almost seven, and Pusan Bay was steaming in the early heat. I felt alive, though slightly wrecked; back at the hotel, the driver from the American consulate with whom I had arranged a ride to Kyongju was waiting.

It was to be a weekend in the countryside and also a journey into the past. Ancient Korea, the green mountainous peninsula jutting out of the land mass of northeast Asia, was probably settled by successive waves of tribal peoples migrating eastward out of the Altai Mountains. From early on, they had some cultural contact – including war, no doubt – with the Yellow River city-states out of which Chinese culture would evolve. Some of the emigrants made their way to the tip of the peninsula and sailed south across the straits to settle in Japan.

At the most only 30 percent of the Korean peninsula is lowland – river valley and coastal plain. Tribal life must have developed at a slow pace in hill villages and isolated valleys. When Athens was flourishing, at about the time of the birth of Confucius, Korea was, in the historical record, silent. By about 200 BC, when the Roman republic was developing, three centers of power were emerging in Korea, one in the northeast, one in the southeast and one in the southwest.

The southwestern dynasty, Silla, eventually unified the country in the latter half of the seventh century. Its capital, Kyongju, sat in a rather remote and extremely beautiful mountain valley some 55 miles east and north of Pusan. It was there in the eighth century, at about the time of Charlemagne in France and of the great Tang dynasty in China, that old Korea, Confucian in its politics, Buddhist in religion, with a strong undercurrent of shamanism – there were religious ceremonies for the sun and the moon and the spirits of the mountains conducted mostly by a caste of sorceresses or priestesses called mudang – a culture of rice cultivation, rich craftsmanship in gold and bronze, and slavery, reached its highest development. It was now, I was told, a market town of about 130,000 people, surrounded by burial mounds, temples and memorial stones, which, as the economy recovered, the government was attempting to restore and preserve. At the height of Silla, Kyongju had been one of the most civilized cities on earth.

I didn't have much time to brood over this fact, nor did I know exactly what to expect. I was out in the Korean countryside. Nothing before I had come had prepared me for the beauty of it, for the soft, intense green of the rice fields, terraces of them carved into the contours of the valleys like the grain in wood, and the dark green pine forest where the rice fields left off, tangled with wild grape and kudzu; red tile roofs in the villages, or thatch occasionally, or corrugated tin; yellow squash blossoms in the gardens beside the houses; black goats; white egrets in the fields; and the mountains climbing up steeply, mist curling about the peaks. Chiri-san, the highest of them, rose in the distance, a pyramidal granite peak, randomly forested. The mountain villages had blue tile roofs. Everywhere the fields look immaculately tended, and there were vegetable patches in every gully.

This was the life, I knew, that all the young in the cities were fleeing. I saw young women stooped over, weeding or cultivating, and remembered the permanently bowed grandmothers I had seen in the parks of Seoul, come to town for the day, quaint in their traditional, Sunday-best dresses – which looked more or less like kimonos. Their backs were badly bent, and their posture seemed to thrust their chins out. Traveling in packs, muttering to each other, they looked rather like the flocks of large Asian magpies, gatchi, that also populated the parks. The old men – whom one saw in the countryside riding bicycles and wearing broad-brimmed straw hats – ambled along in separate groups; they dressed in traditional loose baggy trousers, tight at the ankle. Both the men and the women seemed to have been freed of their teeth, probably by the famine years of the war. They had had hard lives, and seemed at a loss without the habit of labor. In the city, one saw them peering dutifully at the plaques on public antiquities.

Every ancient building in Korea seemed to be a tale of Japanese militarism. This temple or that pavilion was built in 1395, destroyed by a Japanese invasion in 1592, rebuilt in 1867, taken apart by the Japanese occupying force in 1910,

rebuilt as faithfully as possible in 1978. It was a while before I realized that this was ideology. The Japanese had not been the only harriers of Korea. The country had been invaded at one time or another by the Chinese, the Mongols, the Manchurians. But the generation that was rebuilding the temples and palaces and pavilions in Seoul and Kwangju and Pusan had grown up under Japanese domination, so the act of reconstruction was for them at once a celebration of the survival of Korean culture and revenge against the Japanese. It was curious, therefore, to see these old peasants who were being superseded by the new, modernized and vindicated Korea – and who were, to me, far more vivid instances of traditional Korean culture than the buildings they were wandering through bending over to read the solemnly educational public plaques. Which was the historical monument, the old man or the emperor's wife's favorite pagoda?

As the car wound down into the valley of Kyongju – rice fields again, in this milder climate green-going-to-gold, hazy uplands, steep mountains and the town in the distance, which seemed composed mostly of one- and two-story houses with gracefully upward-curving eaves – I thought about the violence of history and the passions of the generations: endless cycles of passion and suffering and response to passion and suffering, division and self-division. The driver pulled up in front of the park that houses the grave barrows of the Silla emperors. A busload of teenagers was filing in; I might be ready to see a statue of Buddha in a cave, I thought, but I wasn't ready for another history lesson.

Still, the park at Kyongju is a haunting place. The tumuli, or royal tombs, whatever they were, are now great grass-covered mounds, which seem, despite the willow trees and gently curving paths that wind among them, much more ancient than the Silla dynasty. The humped-up earth looks like gigantic wasps' nests or like something very archaic, some impulse to burrow against death, rooted in Korean shamanism perhaps, or simply in the appetite for power; some ghost of the insatiable hunger for life and the vanity of it hovers over the old barrows, and the grassy slopes have not tamed it entirely.

There was much more to see. I took in Punhwangsat'ap, the pagoda built by Queen Sondok (Old Silla: her tweezers and a pair of almost miniature scissors were found inside; I thought of her eyelashes, her nubby royal toes), and the tomb of Kim Yu-shin, the most famous Silla general, with its wonderful zodiacal carvings of wild boars and rams with curled horns dressed in the robes of Confucian

scholars. And there was the summer pavilion of P'osokjong, where Silla ended. It was there in 926 that the Silla ruler Kyongae and his family were entertaining when his rival to the east, Kyon Hwon, burst in at the head of an invading army. He had Kyongae butchered on the spot and ordered his men to rape the emperor's wife. But I had had enough of history.

I got a cab to the Kolon Hotel, half an hour outside of Kyongju and within walking distance of Pulguksa, the Buddhist temple that was said to be the crowning achievement of Silla architecture. I took a last look down the valley in the setting sun, had some rice and kimch'i and went to bed. In the morning, I would try to find the path to Sokkuram.

I awoke early, and followed a path that took me to the parking lot where tour buses were unloading schoolchildren to visit Pulguksa. The temple had been built, I knew, in 751 and recently reconstructed. Buddhism came to Korea out of China in the fourth century. It was rich in Mahayana Buddhism with its heavens and hells, its saviors, saints, bodhisattvas and high tolerance for local variation. Pulguksa reflected that tradition. The temple grounds are extensive, built into the hillside and quite peaceful, a rich, complex set of buildings with curving eaves, thickly bracketed, the interlocking, elaborately carved rafters and the wooden pillars painted in bold reds and greens. Inside, tourists were inspecting the weathered pagodas, peering into prayer rooms and the halls where elegant gilt bronze figures sat in the lotus position against brilliantly colored walls. I was not, for some reason, very interested. And neither were the children who began to take turns presenting themselves to me, bowing and saying with great formality, 'Hello, very pleased to meet you.' When I replied, they would run back into their pack of friends, issuing shrill peals of laughter.

I found a guard who spoke some English and he directed me to the hill path, insisting, however, that I should take the bus; it was much too far to walk.

It was, in fact, about five kilometers up the mountain, Tohamsan, with wonderful westerly views of the town and the rice fields and the hills on the other side of the valley. The first two or three hundred yards were paved with small squares of worn granite, grass growing up thickly between, with wildflowers in the gullies and shrubs that looked like mulberry on either side of the trail. Soon, however, I was in the forest and felt a flicker of déjà vu. Korea is on the same latitude as Virginia and North Carolina. The landscape felt at first like hollows I had hiked in the southern part of the Blue Ridge mountains, but the differences were dramatic: soft, deep dust on the trail that had been walked for twelve hundred years; the terraces of rice paddies glimpsed in the distance through spiky pine branches and Japanese maples and gingko-like trees with large palmate leaves; an old gray stone wall on the left side of the trail; and on the steepest parts, granite steps. Lots of wildflowers. A deep forest smell. Tangles of what looked like wild grape in the undergrowth.

I kept seeing birds that looked almost familiar, just as the trees and flowers looked almost familiar. I knew this was the sheer variety and abundance of the gene pool, but it felt as if I were walking in a parallel universe, more ancient than the one I was used to, and more strange: a small woodpecker with a speckled back and a bright yellow head; a chickadee with a black bib and a black stripe down the middle of its white breast; a small finch-like bird, fawn- or copper-colored with delicate black markings over its eye; a lizard with pale blue skin sunning on a rock; everywhere, but rarely visible, a large jay, larger than a magpie, with a buff head, speckled wings and a hoarse cry like the laughing sound a raven makes; and wherever there was water, a wild rose – it looked like a Point Reyes thimbleberry bush but the flowers were a fine, pale lilac.

The shrine itself was an unnerving experience. The trail had taken me over the peak and curved around to the southwest-facing side of the mountain, where it connected with the trail from the parking lot. And then, perhaps fifteen minutes down the road, in a clearing that provided a sudden view of the Sea of Japan glittering in the distance, there was what appeared to be a one-room cottage with sloping eaves wedged into the face of the mountain. It looked like a hermit's shack in an old scroll painting. Sokkuram means Stone Buddha Hermitage, and the little cottage served as an entrance to the grotto. You cannot go all the way in – the main figure having been recently glassed off from the public – but just inside the door, framed by the arch of a short tunnel, this Buddha, Sakyamuni, the young prince, sits, carved out of granite and hugely calm.

The cave is manmade. They must have hollowed out the hillside and then piled up stone slabs until they had fashioned a kind of Norman arch. You walk down the short passageway past guardian figures carved into the wall. They are, I read later in the guidebooks, among the most exquisitely carved bas-reliefs in Asian art, but I hardly noticed them. I was looking at the figure of Buddha, large, about three and a half meters high, eyes closed, right hand resting on his leg, left hand, palm open, in his lap – deeply peaceful, terrifyingly peaceful, so that in the split second of seeing it I had felt my own spirit as a kind of frenetic wind-up toy. I wanted to lay it all down, yearning, grief, anger, operatic sadness, my ragged and insistent passion – the whole idea that something could complete me. I wanted to set it down and leave it there. And I knew that I couldn't do it.

I went outside again. The view across the miles of fields and pine-covered mountains to the sea was hazy, evanescent. There were a few tourists around, all Korean. Most of them stood, like me, silently gazing across the miles toward water. It was intensely quiet. There were slim maples planted against the hermitage and you could hear them rustling against the eaves when the wind came up. My heart hurt. I tried to absorb the information that I was deeply attached to what I was, even if it made me miserable. I had wanted some brilliant, vindicating spiritual experience; my heart leapt toward it like a dog greeting its master. But this master didn't pet you. It sat still, concentrated, turned inward toward unimaginable freedom, scarcely imaginable peace.

Then I did laugh. There was a sign, in Korean, Chinese, English and Japanese, which said that this figure of Buddha, one of the wonders of the world, faced east toward the rising sun to guard the Silla Kingdom against marauding Japanese pirates. It was the older generation at work again, nailing down the political lesson. They had gotten it wrong, just as I had. This Buddha watched marauding pirates, and the rise and fall of empires, and North Koreas and South Koreas, and economic miracles, from some place in which they all seemed old, sorrowing, repetitive. If he faced outward at all, he simply faced toward the sunrise, toward the endless freshness of the coming into being of things.

When I went back to the hermitage from the opposite side, there was a young girl at a table in the entry. She was doing algebra with a turquoise felt pen. I suppose she was a park ranger; she got up, beckoned me into the cave and slid back the glass door. This time I walked up to the Buddha. He seemed immense, a large lotus carved into the dome above his head, a small one, flame-like, on the floor before him. Many bodhisattvas were carved into the surrounding walls, very simple figures, beautifully plain. I looked up at Sakyamuni. I felt sad and tired, happy to be in that presence.

When I left, and walked back down the mountain in the setting sun, the birds active in the last light, the rice fields almost gold, I tried to think what had happened to me. Nothing I could name. I knew I had been in a very powerful place. And I felt as if I had been punched very hard in the chest. It was a sobering, not entirely unpleasant sensation. Going down the mountain in the sunset, listening to the jays cackling in the trees, I felt obscurely cheered up.

It was eight o'clock in the evening when I got back to the hotel. I got in a cab and headed for Kyongju. The cab driver, plump, fleshy, mildly hilarious, spoke no English. I didn't know where I was going. He seemed to think 'anywhere' was a particular place, maybe, since I made gestures of eating, a restaurant, and he tried to indicate that he would take me there if I would only pronounce it more clearly. He also stopped at every country bus stop to negotiate fares with the people waiting for the bus. Two women got in, one with a baby. Then an old man and an old woman. There was much animated talk and laughing. The word 'anywhere' kept coming up in various pronunciations. Finally, in the middle of town, the car stopped. They all piled out and gestured for me to get out. One of the women pointed up the street. 'Is Korean custom,' she said. I got out, paid him, waved them all goodbye and found myself in the middle of the night market.

It looked like an English market day crossed with a flea market crossed with an American carnival or county fair. It was jammed with people. The stands, on either side of the street, sold everything from dried squid to woolen socks and pocket calculators. There were games: bingo, ring toss, shooting galleries. I found my way to the open tents where food was being served, pancakes made from corn flour and roasted baby chicks split in half and soaked in ginger and soy sauce. I ordered two pancakes, one chick and a bottle of rice wine, and sat down at an outdoor table. There were several Korean guys in baseball hats, drinking and singing at the next table. I watched them for a while to see if you ate the bones of the baby chicks. You did. I watched the crowd surge through the narrow alley, Saturday night strollers, buying things, all kinds of things, fish, flesh, fowl, try-their-luck. The food arrived. It looked unbelievably good. I was back in the world, I thought, and remembered the birds in the parallel universe on the path to Sokkuram and the silence and power of the figure in the cave, the purity and the quiet.

The waitress returned with a little paper packet of roast silkworms. On the house. She pointed at a shy boy at the next table and bit her lip before proceeding very deliberately. 'My friend is so exciting only to have this opportunity to speak practical English and having sharing Korean culture.' I understood. He was treating me to the silkworms. We were going to argue about politics. I ordered another bottle of wine and gestured him over. He sat down opposite of me. Two of the waitresses joined us. The silkworms tasted vile, and I smiled gratefully trying to get one down. The girls laughed and the wine came. 'Korea,' the young man began, and shook his head. He said the word as if it were a synonym for life. Then he sighed happily and said it again. 'Korea, Korea, Korea.'

Where to stay: An interesting and inexpensive alternative to hotels are the Korean-style inns or yogwan. At these, guests sleep in the traditional Korean way – on the floor on a thin mattress called a yo, with a quilt-like covering called an ibul. Bathrooms are often shared, and meals can be had in the room for an extra charge. Prices run between $6 and $15 per room. The Korea National Tourism Corporation (address below) can supply a list of yogwan throughout Korea.

In Kyongju, a great place to stay is the Han Jin Hotel, run by a very friendly and helpful host who speaks English. Doubles begin at $8 (2-4097 or 2-9679). Near the Pulguksa temple in Kyongju is Sillajang (2-1004/6) and the Kyongju Youth Hostel (2-991/6). In Kyongju town, try Pulguksa Pyoljang yog-wan (2-9735).

Home-stays can be arranged through the Korea Tourist Bureau, CPO Box 3533, Seoul, Korea; 011-822-585-4461. At least one member of each family participating in this program speaks English, and breakfast is included in the price of your stay.

Where to eat: Restaurants serving Japanese and Chinese food in addition to traditional Korean fare can be found throughout Korea. Korean meals are buffet-style, with the main courses and eight or nine different side dishes all served at once. One of these dishes is invariably kimch'i, pickled cabbage seasoned with chili peppers.

Koreans like to eat outdoors, and all kinds of food can be sampled in the night markets. Popular drinks are makkoli, a rice wine, and soju, a strong brandy. Coffee-shops, or tabangs, are excellent places to relax and chat.

For more information: Contact the Korea National Tourism Corporation, 510 West Sixth Street, Suite 323, Los Angeles, CA 90014-1395; 213-623-1226/7.

AFTERWORD

These seven examples of successful travel articles are widely varied in tone, setting and subject, but united in their ability to bring a place to vivid life within our minds. We hope these pieces serve as rich illustrations of the principles we have been discussing – and of the potential of your own travel writing. We also hope that you took note of how the different service information and fact boxes were tailored to their particular subjects, publications and audiences – these are important parts of the prose package, too.

The possibility of writing for websites and tablet magazines has expanded the publishing playing field considerably. Generally speaking, web articles tend to be shorter and more compact and tightly focused than the stories printed here; they also more often are written in the present tense. Short service pieces of the 'Top 10' variety ('Top 10 Nude Beaches in Spain,' 'Top 10 Sushi Spots in Vancouver') abound on the web. Still, longer form travel writing has also found congenial digital homes in such outlets as WildJunket and Overnight Buses. Where can you find examples of successful digital articles? The traditional advice still applies: To find the best examples of writing that works, thoroughly study the outlets – whether digital or print – that you're most interested in. Immerse yourself in the pieces they've published. Then do your best to write a story that marries your passions with their predilections.

Which leads us to the next step on the travel writer's path: How do you begin to get your writing published? We'll explore this territory in Part II.

INTERVIEW WITH

ANDREW BAIN

Andrew Bain is an Australia-based travel writer, specialising in adventure. His articles appear regularly in publications such as the *Sydney Morning Herald* and *Australian Geographic Outdoor*. His book *Headwinds* describes his 20,000-km cycle journey around Australia, and he is the author of Lonely Planet's *A Year of Adventures*.

How did you start off in your career as a travel writer and journalist?

I studied and received a degree in journalism, then began in the usual journalistic fashion – regional media, city media, branch out. I spent about five years as a sports writer then set off on the standard backpacking tour through Europe. As it is for so many people, travel writing began as a lark to fund more travel, until eventually the writing became the purpose of travel.

What is the best way of establishing yourself if you're just starting out in your career as a freelance travel journalist?

Choose destinations that aren't already clogging the pages of travel sections and magazines. Skip New York, London and Paris, and look for lesser-known places with appealing quirks. If you must stick to the blue-chip destinations, find a different way to look at them. Develop a specialty – food, spas, outdoor adventure – that will gain you a niche market, then supplement it with general stories.

As a freelance travel journalist, how do you get the numbers to add up in terms of an income?

It's a risky business. I determine how much a certain trip will cost me, then calculate how much I'll need to earn to justify the journey. I break this down into the number of stories required from the trip and then scurry about making certain I come up with at least that number of stories. Then comes the problematic bit: selling them. It's difficult at the beginning of your travel-writing career to make accurate forecasts on expenses and profit because you're not sure how much a certain story will bring in, but eventually you get a feel for the markets you're targeting.

What tips would you give to budding travel writers?

Avoid clichés. If the view didn't actually suck the breath from your throat, don't call it 'breathtaking'. Look at places, not the brochures. It's not your job to write a marketing piece but to accurately describe your experience and reaction to a place or activity. Tell them something unique about your particular visit and your interaction with a place.

Good photos are half the battle with selling a story, so bring home a decent selection of images that marry well with the subject in your story.

What are the most common mistakes that travel writers make in their copy?

Not knowing the publication's market or style. Some magazines refuse first-person stories; others are devoted to luxury travel or outdoor adventure. It's pointless sending them something different. Read several issues of a publication and you'll also get a feel for the breadth of its interest. It might cover the world or it might show a preference for local material. Tailor your work to suit the market.

How did you get your first travel literature title published?

Books are a long, slow process... and that's even after the writing's complete. As *Headwinds* was my first book, I completed the manuscript before making any approaches to agents or publishers. It's then a marketing battle – to convince a few people that this book will reap a profit to any publisher. I found an agent who thought the book had potential and she then found it a publisher.

Do you think it's important to have an agent?

I think it's invaluable. Publishers receive so many manuscripts, and the endorsement of an agent may be the only way to get your manuscript read. It tells the publisher that the manuscript has already been considered by somebody whose opinion they hopefully respect.

Are you in a better position as a travel journalist because of your ability to provide photographs?

Photos are crucial. If editors are choosing between a story that requires photos from a library, and a story presented with good photos, they're likely to go for the complete package, especially for writers new to them.

Have you written for genres other than adventure travel? Does having a specialisation help or hinder finding work?

To be too specialist can be a hindrance as it shuts you out of certain markets, so I do range widely in subject matter. Certainly, adventure is my primary focus but I complement this with general travel pieces. If I'm trekking in the Andes, for instance, why not also spend some time in a nearby city and write about it? To have a specialist field is useful for earning respect with a core of publications, but diversity is critical if you're to make a living from travel writing, especially at the outset of a career.

What, in your opinion, constitutes 'good' travel writing?

Good writing is fresh, with observations that are clearly personal. I don't want to read about 'towering skyscrapers' or 'quaint villages'; that's as obvious as calling an elephant 'large'. Good writing incorporates simile and metaphor, and goes easy on adverbs and unnecessary adjectives, to paint pictures of language. Every place on earth has now been written about, so what is it we are trying to achieve by adding to the pool? It can only be our own insight. It was well expressed by Neal Cassady (Jack Kerouac's travel mate): 'I think one should write, as nearly as possible, as if he were the first person on earth and was humbly and sincerely putting on paper that which he saw and experienced and loved and lost...with careful avoidance of common phrases, trite usage of hackneyed words and the like.'

What constitutes 'bad' travel writing?

Too many writers seem to think that they have to be gushing in praise for a place for a story to be marketable. In doing so, they veer dangerously toward writing brochure-style sentences. You get 'sparkling lakes', 'pristine beaches', and how many countries have you read about as having the 'friendliest people on earth'? You can like a place without falling back on lazy language.

What are the rewards of travel writing as a career?

Travel is its own obvious reward, and without being a travel writer I wouldn't have seen half the mountains and deserts from which I draw so much inspiration, both on the page and in life. Equally, while the writing is both a process and a product, it's enormously rewarding. To have a lightning flash of inspiration (until you read the words later in print – they always seem terrible by then)...it's nearly as good as summiting a peak.

What has been the downside for you?

Behind all things glamorous there's the everyday tedium: actors learning their lines, models waxing their backs, and writers spending hours wrestling with a sentence. It happens, and more regularly than we'd all like. And while everybody else at the Grand Canyon is oohing and aahing about the view, you're quietly fretting about how your story is progressing and wondering how you're going to express the scene in words – 'words cannot describe...' will never suffice. Everything you now see and do will be tainted slightly by the knowledge that you'll later be sitting at your computer re-creating what you wish you never had to re-create.

INTERVIEW WITH

TIM CAHILL

Tim Cahill is the author of *Lost in My Own Backyard*, *Jaguars Ripped My Flesh*, *Pecked to Death by Ducks*, *Pass the Butterworms*, *Hold the Enlightenment* and many other books. Based in the US, he writes for *National Geographic Adventure* and *Outside*, among other publications.

How did you start off in your career as an author of travel literature?

I was an editor at *Rolling Stone* magazine. The editor/publisher wanted to create a magazine that would appeal to those who ventured outside. As one of the only two people in the office who ever went outside, which is to say, who backpacked, I was picked to help decide what the future magazine should look, feel, and be like. This was back in 1975. I thought that we should have a travel/adventure story in each issue of the publication that eventually became *Outside* magazine. In fact, I effectively created my own job.

What is the best way of establishing yourself if you're just

starting out in your career as a travel literature author?

My suggestion would be to publish with the local newspaper, in what is generally a weekly travel section. This allows you to travel, to write, to work with professional editors and understand, from the get-go, that travel isn't a high-paying career. Lately, with newspapers laying off journalists right and left, this is a wide-open market for writers.

As a travel writer, how do you get the numbers to add up in terms of an income?

I try to write very good magazine stories. The stories, if I do them right, can then be collected in a hardcover anthology. Then it goes to paper. In effect, I get paid three times for some stories.

What tips would you give to budding travel writers?

I'm not being sarcastic, but the major thing I can say is *write*. No one can give you the magic bullet that, once fired, will make you a writer. Writing is like anything else: the more you do it, the better you get at it. It does help to have someone critique your efforts. Writers' groups are especially good in this respect.

Are there any courses or any training that you'd recommend a budding travel writer to undertake?

I have a Masters degree in English/Creative Writing. I always thought the two years I spent earning that degree were wasted and that I learned a lot more from working with good editors. But who is to say? Did my academic career lay the groundwork for my professional one? I don't know.

If I was starting out today, I believe I'd try to write for a year or two. I'd check such magazines as *Writer's Digest* for appropriate writers' conferences. These are meetings where professional editors lecture and look at your work; where you will meet publishers and agents. Book Passage, a bookstore in Corte Madera, north of San Francisco, hosts a travel writers' conference I attend almost every year.

If, after two years, you haven't sold and are still convinced of your talent, try the academic route.

What are the most common mistakes that travel writers make in their copy?

When I was editing, the most common mistake I saw writers make was submitting their journal. A day-by-day chronicle of events, as seen in a journal, is raw material. One needs to think about that raw material. Hold it to the light and turn it this way and that until you see a prism. When I read a story that begins: 'January 19th: The plane descended over neat cultivated fields that reminded me of a child's blanket...' I can be almost sure that I'm going to read a journal. Which means that this has been submitted by someone who hasn't thought much about what happened. Such manuscripts travel to the circular file, post-haste.

What, in your opinion, constitutes 'good' travel writing?

Good writing is good travel writing. Travel is a forgiving medium – as soon as you walk out the front door, you're travelling.

At *Outside*, we discovered early on that the world's best ice climber may not be the person you want to write about ice climbing. He or she will be consumed by their passion for ice, not writing. They will tend to address their (very few) peers, not a general audience. No, you want someone who can write.

Do you need to do extreme things?

Naw. Lots of people do extreme things and are never published because they can't write. Writing is the key. Better a well-written travel story about a picnic in the backyard than a tedious story on someone who did cartwheels up Everest.

What constitutes 'bad' travel writing?

A chronological recounting of events is usually not good. (There are exceptions, of course.) People who can't find the story and hope description will carry them.

What are the rewards of travel writing as a career?

Obviously, travel. I get to go wherever I want to go, do what I want to do. Because much of what I do is physical, I have to stay in some kind of shape, which is good. I never spend money on a foreign vacation. My idea of a vacation is staying home.

What has been the downside for you?

Poor pay, a little too much travel early on that wasn't good for my social life or my love life.

How did you get your first book published?

In 1984 I published a book about a serial killer that became a best-seller. That gave me the clout to publish what I wanted next, which was a collection of my outdoor travel pieces.

How long does it take to write your books?

A book takes anywhere from one to three years, depending on the research involved and how scared I am.

Do you have an agent, and how important do you think they are?

I have an agent. They are important for books. You can get one by submitting a query and/or manuscript to the list of agents who accept manuscripts found in the back of *Writer's Market 2013* (or whatever year it is: the book, as you may have guessed, comes out yearly).

An agent is familiar with contracts (which are, in my case, 80 pages, single spaced). In the contract, the publisher takes everything. An agent knows what can be crossed out without a fight, how much of a fight this deletion will entail, and what clauses the publisher will not delete under any circumstances. You need this expertise. Otherwise, believe it or not, a publisher will screw you.

INTERVIEW WITH

PAUL CLAMMER

Based in Wiltshire, England, Paul Clammer abandoned a career in molecular biology for the more precarious existences of a tour guide and, later, travel guidebook writer. He is the author of Lonely Planet's *Afghanistan* and the Bradt travel guide *Sudan*, as well as contributing to many other guidebooks, mostly to countries in the Islamic world.

How did you start off in your career as a guidebook writer?

Purely by accident! I'd travelled in Taliban-era Afghanistan and written a website about it. After their ouster I added more travel information, so it evolved into a guide. In 2003, Lonely Planet was looking to send an author to Afghanistan for the first time since the 1970s, had seen my site, and got in touch. Guidebooks have been paying the bills ever since.

What is the best way of establishing yourself if you're just starting out in your career as a freelance guidebook writer now?

Well, I didn't plan my career, but building my website clearly put my profile out there, so people could read examples of my work. Getting that profile and portfolio has to be a vital starting point.

How do you think guidebook writers get the numbers to add up in terms of an income?

Well, no one gets into travel writing to make it rich. A lot depends on the type of guide and publisher. If your fees cover the research costs on top of actual income, fantastic. Books that pay royalties are more of a long-term investment, taking a lot longer to recoup your costs and turn a profit. In some cases you can defray costs by arranging freebies, but that's dependent on the publisher – some encourage it, for others it's forbidden.

How do you get the numbers to add up?

My guidebook income is supported by selling articles, doing consulting work on my areas of expertise, occasionally bits of media. I never really know how much I've earned in a year until I file my taxes.

What advice would you give to budding guidebook writers?

Develop an area of expertise, so you can really sell your skill set to editors. My foot in the door was Afghanistan, but it could equally be something like trekking or regional food. You need something on your résumé to help you stand out against the competition.

Are there any courses or any training that you'd recommend a budding guidebook writer to undertake?

The best training is simply to read lots and write lots. Develop your observational skills – looking at your own hometown through the eyes of a visitor can change your perception of the place. Tie that fresh look to your deeper insight on the place and you're halfway there.

What are the most common mistakes that guidebook writers make – in their research and in their writing?

The biggest mistakes are to do with accuracy. It doesn't matter how beautiful your prose is, no reader will forgive you if you put down the train station on the opposite side of town. Everything else flows from the accuracy of those facts you collect in the field.

What are the main differences between guidebook writing and writing for a newspaper, magazine, or website?

Those other mediums allow you to tell a broader narrative, and be a lot more subjective about your own personal experience of the place. As a guidebook writer you're primarily an information provider, often writing in a very structured way – first the introductions, then the sights, then the hotel listings and so on.

What, in your opinion, constitutes 'good' guidebook writing?

Writing that's insightful, that tells it like it is, and teaches me something I wouldn't necessarily be able to discover just by breezing through on a trip. Hopefully the author will be demonstrating not just their knowledge, but also their passion for the destination.

What constitutes 'bad' guidebook writing?

Guidebooks that send me down the wrong street, looking for a restaurant that closed five years ago!

What are the rewards of guidebook writing as a career?

Finding a great new place to visit or stay, and then getting to share that with a wider travelling public. It's like being a journalist – you're going out there to get the story, and that's fantastic fun. And of course, all authors get a big kick out of seeing people reading their books. What's not to love about that?

What has been the downside for you?

Work-life balance takes on a new meaning when you're away for months on the road. Throw in the financial uncertainty of never knowing where your money is coming from in a few months' time, and it's not always a bed of roses.

What's the role of the internet in the landscape of contemporary guidebook/travel writing?

As a research tool the internet is a big help, especially with pre-trip research so you can hit the ground running when you're in the field. But objectivity and accuracy aren't always happy bedfellows online, so it's very much a case of being careful with your sources. The same applies equally to user-generated content – whether that's hotel reviews or travel tips – which is providing a healthy challenge to traditional guidebooks.

How can would-be guidebook writers best utilise the web for their own professional development?

Well, as someone who got their start by putting out his own website, I'd say that's not a bad place to start. The web constantly demands new content, and those articles don't write themselves. You won't get paid initially, but it will get your profile started.

Where do you see guidebook publishing going in the next five years?

Guidebook publishers are going to be providing more content online, with faster turnarounds than traditional print product, and users of books are probably going to get more involved in content providing. But I don't think we'll see the death of the guidebook – in a world with such information overload, there'll still be a premium on accurate, objective reporting, from people with real expertise and insights on the destinations.

Any other tips or reflections you would offer would-be guidebook writers?

It's rewarding in so many ways, but it's not a job that really has a career ladder. You're always hustling, so if you get in, make sure you enjoy it. Oh, and never try to buy a house when you're in the middle of a research trip in the Indian Himalaya.

INTERVIEW WITH

GEORGE DUNFORD

Based in Melbourne, George Dunford is a freelancer writer for *Wanderlust*, the *Big Issue* and several other publications. He's also a podcaster, blogger and sometime fiction writer. Read his blog at http://hackpacker.blogspot.com.

How did you start off in your career as a guidebook writer?

I've always been writing something for somewhere, whether it was freelance restaurant reviews or short stories. I got into Lonely Planet by working in-house as a writer/editor and then later on the website.

What is the best way of establishing yourself if you're just starting

out in your career as a freelance guidebook writer now?

Get writing. Any way to get your name out there can be good, so start out with street press, your own blog or self-publishing. They are all great ways to build your skills and get a publication record that you can show to editors.

Online is a different environment because the challenge isn't to get published – anyone can do that with a blogging platform. The real goal is to get traffic and get people to read what you're writing in a busy media space. I heard one blogger liken posting a blog to throwing a message in a bottle into a sea which consists entirely of messages in bottles. You have to be doing something exceptional to be noticed.

How do you think guidebook writers get the numbers to add up in terms of an income?

I know Lonely Planet writers who make money from being able to write articles or create other content about places they visit. After a while you get a sense for stories that might not be right for a guidebook but could make a great magazine article or blog post. Some do corporate jobs like copywriting and there are a few who act as location scouts for films.

How do you get the numbers to add up?

I've done it by diversifying. I teach travel writing and writing for the web, which is a great way to get you out of the office. I write journalism and reviews for newspapers and magazines, plus I try not to get tagged as the 'travel writing guy'. The market in Australia is just too small to be that specialised, but I also think that a professional writer should be able to write to a variety of briefs. These days I work more in content strategy – looking at how websites can get better at talking to their audience.

What advice would you give to budding guidebook writers?

Get out there and write – don't just talk about ideas you have for articles because that wastes energy you should put into the keyboard. Writing for a market is a good discipline but write for yourself at first, that way your piece will have a genuine passion without trying to work out how to be published. Most importantly, don't work for nothing for long. Everyone takes a job as a CV builder, but if your CV is heavier than your bank balance then you won't be able to do this for long. I've worked on books where the previous author got diddled on a fee and it comes out in the quality of the writing – there's a lot of mentions of budget places to eat, scrimping on accommodation and generally having a bad time. If you're not paid properly you won't enjoy it and you won't be able to write about it with that excitement.

Are there any courses or any training that you'd recommend a budding guidebook writer to undertake?

I did a Diploma in Professional Writing and Editing at RMIT (Royal Melbourne Institute of Technology).

It was useful as it gave me a sample of all sorts of writing from corporate writing to novel, plus the school has a really strong tie to industry so it felt very practical. Aside from the skills, it was also about being in a culture of writing with people talking about the publishing industry alongside artistic ambitions. Doing a short course at your local writer's centre can be a great way to get a taste.

What are the most common mistakes that guidebook writers make – in their research and in their writing?

In research it's probably knowing how much to do. You can kill yourself by tracking down every last detail from bus timetables to restaurant opening hours, but at some point you develop a sense of how much you actually have to do.

The other extreme is too little where you return to your office after being on the road and realise that you needed those bus timetables. The key is balance and I'm still working it out myself sometimes. I've come home with 80kg of excess baggage, most of which is pamphlets or books – which comes from all those times I've been in my office thinking, 'I swear I had a brochure about that somewhere.'

The other tip is fight the cliché. Your voice must be new to be heard.

What are the main differences between guidebook writing and writing for a newspaper, magazine, or website?

Guidebooks have a bigger focus on hard information while magazines have more room for literary playfulness. The web is a combination of both with the added problem of currency – people have an expectation that information on the web is up-to-date. With Lonely Planet they also have an expectation that it will be correct as well.

The other obvious difference is size. A guidebook project will take anything up to six months while a newspaper article won't take more than a week. You can do a lot of little newspaper and magazine articles but a career in them can be difficult to sustain because you need to be constantly finding the next article, the next big thing. Web content is even trickier, because there's still a fair amount of unpaid content out there, which just means the quality is variable.

What, in your opinion, constitutes 'good' guidebook writing?

Good writing hits that balance between inspiration and information perfectly. It should be exciting enough to get you to book a ticket but also be able to deliver the goods when you get there.

The value of independence is also crucial. There's a lot of

information out on the web, but a lot of it is dubious or sponsored by tour companies. It's fine if you know that what your reading is trying to sell you something, but it's like the difference between a press release and news story. One is about what a company wants you to know and the other should be about what a journalist has found out beyond that.

What constitutes 'bad' guidebook writing?

I'm not a fan of writing that showcases the verbal gymnastics of the writer over actual information about the place they're visiting. I think as a guidebook writer you owe it to your audience to give them a fair perspective of a destination, not just your amazing vocabulary or hilarious in-jokes. I've written reviews where it was about being clever, not informative, and I think I ripped off the reader by doing that. Anything that becomes more about showing off than what the reader wants is bad.

What are the rewards of guidebook writing as a career?

You get to do some cool things and meet some interesting people. I've been to Finnish music festivals, remote Scottish islands and Cambodian spider markets – mostly as part of this job. Because you're working on a story, you can ask 'Why do people do that?'

What has been the downside for you?

Distance from family and friends. I was working in Singapore when my aunt died and missed her funeral, which is impossible to replace. You spend a lot of time away and it can be hard to stay in touch with people as their lives change.

What's the role of the internet in the landscape of contemporary guidebook/travel writing?

Superficially it seems as though the internet is making it possible for anyone to research their own travel. But there's a lot of material out there – much of it confusing and some misleading – so I think guidebooks have a value in being able to put readers in the right direction. Curating the right information to readers is becoming more valuable as there is so much information out there. People are looking for trusted guides.

In terms of travel writing the emphasis is on writing that has personality. If anyone can go places then the destination isn't fascinating – it's the voice that's telling you about it that's interesting. There was a review of Colin Thubron that warned against taking his books with you because they were more engaging than the scenery around you. That's writing with a future.

How can would-be guidebook writers best utilise the web for their own professional development?

Start with a blog. You won't make a fortune out of it but you'll get feedback from your audience and you'll get practice writing. Plus you never know who will read it if it's out there rather than bundled in your notebook. You should look to write content that will build an audience around your blog.

While making your fortune off a blog is tough, you can make a little extra beer money if your blog is getting reasonable traffic. Services such as Google Adsense (www.google.com/adsense) plug contextual advertisements into your blog based on your entries, so if you're blogging about Turkey it will include promotions for hotels in Istanbul. They work based on click-through so if your friends click every time they visit, it can help your bank balance.

Another option is to get affiliate programs with people such as Amazon (www.amazon.com), so if you mention a book, you can send people to a place where they can buy and you'll get a share.

Finally, if you think you're going to be bigger than a rock band, think about getting some merchandise with sites like Cafe Press (www.cafepress.com), which will slap your logo on a T-shirt, cap etc.

I created an app for Melbourne that I update regularly. That's meant I share the revenue with the iTunes store which is a great way to DIY. The web has so many ways to get your content out there, so look at all the social networking sites for the ones that suit you.

Another way to utilise the web is to use social networking as a research tool. Throw out a call on Twitter for an interview subject and you'll get some suggestions back.

Where do you see guidebook publishing going in the next five years?

There will be more online, but I hope readers still look for content that's independently researched. Lonely Planet is looking beyond writing and thinking about content on various devices and channels, so we're becoming content producers, not just writers. Creating an app was a great way to explore new ways of distributing content.

It's a challenge facing all print media, with newspapers getting rid of reviewers in favour of links to blogs, but I think there's opportunity there as well. Going online gives you access to a bigger audience.

Any other tips or reflections to offer would-be guidebook writers?

A guidebook writer colleague said something smart to me: 'If you don't enjoy it, you can't write about it.'

INTERVIEW WITH
PICO IYER

Pico Iyer is the author of *Video Night in Kathmandu*, *The Lady and the Monk*, *Falling off the Map*, *The Global Soul* and numerous other books. He writes for *Time*, *Harper's* and *Condé Nast Traveler*, among other magazines. Born and raised in England, Pico has long been based in Japan.

How did you start off in your career as an author of travel literature?

I was lucky to be a traveller from birth, more or less, and I quickly found *that* whenever I went on vacation, I started keeping voluminous diaries – as I never did at home. Clearly, I was so quickened and filled up by what I was seeing and experiencing that I needed to get it out in some form. And after I began noticing the pages begin to fill up – I would routinely write 200 pages after a two-week trip – I decided that if I were writing all this for myself, I might as well inflict it on someone else, in something more than just letter form.

So I began looking for practical ways to get my records out into the world – the best, because most strenuous, of which was working for two summers while at grad school for the Let's Go series of guidebooks for young travellers in Europe. I wrote parts of seven of those books, travelling through 60 cities in 70 days, having to visit every site and hotel and restaurant in every one (theoretically) and then having to reel back to my resting place and copy them all down on carbon paper. The opposite of a vacation – and an ideal training for the living-by travelling I tried to do later.

What is the best way of establishing yourself if you're just starting out in your career as a travel literature author?

Just write, write, write – and if you're trying to write for a living, you have to believe that quality will show, that what you have to offer fills a niche and meets a need (if you don't believe that, it's hard even to begin). For me, the great advantage was that I was always writing as a way to travel – writing simply in order to sponsor and give shape and meaning to the journeys I wanted to take in any case; which meant that the writing was a means to an end and not an end in itself.

There's no substitute for writing, if you want to be a writer. In travel writing, the main thing you have to address is what you can say – how you can approach Kyoto or the Pyramids or Machu Picchu – as no one has ever done before, and as few could do today. What do you bring to the dialogue you conduct with these immortal places?

But the main thing is just writing – for the free website run by your friend, for the non-paying alternative newspaper in town (as I did), for magazines that may never dream of hiring you, or even for just friends and family.

As a travel writer, how do you get the numbers to add up in terms of an income?

Quite simply, you don't – and you never will. If you're going to try to write about place, I think you have to surrender at the outset any idea of doing it for the money; all the rewards will be internal ones. There was a boom in the publishing of 'travel literature' twenty years ago, and there will always be a market for travel pieces in magazines and newspapers, but really it can only be something you do on the side. To take an example, I have to write 10 pieces a month (on subjects other than travel) just to pay the bills; and although I've published ten books now, I can still only afford to live in a two-room flat in the countryside in Japan, paying rent as when I was a student, without bicycle or car or printer or almost anything. And I will get as much income from four days of visiting a university as from writing a book that almost kills me over a period of several years.

Even the most distinguished writers have trouble finding a publisher, more and more – most of the writers of travel I know and read do it only as a sideline, a vacation, as it were, from the real business of life. Jan Morris is an inexhaustible journalist; Paul Theroux is a full-time writer of fiction who publishes five or more novels every decade; Bruce Chatwin worked at Sotheby's before he took to the road. For me, part of the beauty of travel and writing about travel is that it forces you to see all material things inwardly: you're not going to get rich and comfortable doing it, but you are going to have experiences and memories and challenges that could put Bill Gates to shame.

What tips would you give to budding travel writers?

Do it for the love of it, and always begin by asking yourself what you have to bring to the Taj Mahal or the Grand Canyon or Venice that no one has brought before. What is particular about your experience and background and interests that will allow you to see and describe things that most of the rest of us could never see?

Maybe you're a jeweller, and so can read meanings into the lapis and coral of the inlay work at the Taj that few of the rest of us could discern; maybe you're of Islamic descent and so can see how the gardens outside the Taj reproduce the outline of an Islamic paradise; maybe you're an architect, and so can explain to the rest of us how science and craft can produce wonder. But you have to begin with something more arresting than just the place and the emotions it arouses in you.

And having chosen a focus – as specific as possible – and decided what will be your angle and your structure, having asked questions of both the place and yourself, and having taken down all the details you could want and more, then you have to work out how to shape the piece and how to find a voice that will make it compelling and fresh to a reader who has no interest in you and never wants to see another piece about the Taj Mahal. Tell your experience and observations as if you were trying to convey them to a friend with whom you long to share your passion; but do so as if you had to win that friend over every time, with your enthusiasm, your clarity and your specificity.

And write it all up even if there's going to be no guaranteed publication, and no reader other than your mother, your partner or your best friend, at the end of it. You won't regret it.

Are there any courses or any training that you would recommend a budding travel writer to undertake?

None whatsoever. The only training for writing is writing – and reading and reading and writing some more. Writing can't be taught, it can only be done; and reading the masters of the trade is a good way of seeing how it can be done in myriad voices and contexts. All the worthwhile training I've done is private, and at my desk; by contrast, I studied literature and nothing but literature for eight years, and feel that that has only hindered and encumbered me as a would-be writer.

What are the most common mistakes that travel writers make in their manuscript?

I don't think you can presuppose that the reader is interested either in you or in the subject matter; and I think you have to remember that your enthusiasm can only be conveyed through specifics. You have to take the reader by the hand and lead her into the place you're describing, and then lead her into the wonder or terror or mixture of the two it evokes in you.

Which is a way of saying that the easiest mistake, especially when you're starting out, is to forget that there's a reader at the other end, and that your first obligation is to him. And it's wise, I think, to read much that's already been written on the subject so you know what *not* to do, what's been done already.

The question I always ask myself before undertaking a project is, 'How can I ever begin to justify the time and heartache and effort I am going to put into this, and tell myself it's bringing something new into the world, or at least into a friend's apartment?' There is a justification, always, but it's often a rigorous or subtle one.

What, in your opinion, constitutes 'good' travel writing?

Travel writing, more than any other kind of writing, has to transport you, has to teach you about the world, has to inform you, and,

ideally, has to take you into deeper and deeper questions about yourself and the world. The writer's job, as Milan Kundera once told Philip Roth, I think, is to get the reader to see the world as a question. And travel writing has to hold your attention, first, and then take you into a dialogue between yourself and the world that tells you something new about both and grips you more powerfully than any other dialogue around.

It hardly matters what you call it or what impels the writing – much of the best travel writing is offered by Graham Greene and D. H. Lawrence and, these days, John le Carré or David Mitchell, in their novels just because they are driven by a curiosity about the world – other cultures and other people – and because they have refined and developed that curiosity so that they can seize other places and people quickly; they have trained their instincts. These are travellers who are consistently eloquent and perceptive on place, as opposed to those, like Heinrich Harrer in *Seven Years in Tibet*, who stumble into an experience so transcendent and moving that they give voice to what they know is a once-in-a-lifetime adventure.

What constitutes 'bad' travel writing?

Something that doesn't hold the reader.

What are the rewards of travel writing as a career?

All the rewards are inner. They have to do with coming to a better understanding of the world and of oneself, of learning more sharply what one can appreciate about home, and what one is lacking there, of being able to see life as a pilgrimage and journey in which no answer is ever final and one is really moving from mystery into deeper mystery, from one way station to the next.

Writing of any kind is a way of making a clearing so as to make sense and shape out of the world, and to take all the rubble of one's experiences and emotions and observations and piece them together into a kind of stained-glass whole. It is a way of removing oneself from the world, and sometimes from the self, so as to see both more clearly. But travel writing is different because it engages with the world in a very urgent and specific way, keeps (ideally) one's eyes constantly fresh, confers on life the sense of an adventure and reminds you that every moment is provisional, every perception, local, ready to be thrown over by the next epiphany.

It keeps you on the move, teaches you (enforces) alertness and makes you more attentive than when you are at home, or blurred by the familiar. As Thoreau famously said, it doesn't matter where or how far you go – the farther commonly the worse – the important thing is how alive you are. Writing of every kind is a way to wake oneself up and keep as alive as when one has just fallen in love.

What has been the downside for you?

The drawback of travel writing comes when the travelling seems part of a job – something to get done rather than something to do – and one cannot embark on it with the freshness and excitement of a possibly life-changing adventure. Then, often, it's time to stay home, or write about things closer to home. (Thoreau, after all, did all his travelling and travel-writing at Walden while staying still, and these days our hometowns are often more exotic and full of new curiosity than Timbuktu or Easter Island.)

Travelling is about freshness and going out into the unknown; if it starts to become known, if you begin to have too clear a sense of where you're going, or if it even begins to resemble a routine, then you have to rethink what you mean by 'travelling'.

How did you get your first book published?

I started taking holidays from my otherwise all-consuming job in Rockefeller Center in New York, and as soon as I did, I found I was so quickened, so stimulated and engaged, by what and whom I had met, that all I wanted to do was return to them, in person or in memory and imagination. So I started writing out my travels, on the basis of the exhaustive notes – or diary entries, really – I would keep while on the road.

And then, determined to spend even longer travelling, I made up a three-page proposal – asking myself, again, what was special about my background and perspective that would allow me to bring something new to Japan and China and India and elsewhere – and, not knowing better, just sent it out to 'Nonfiction Editor, Random House', 'Nonfiction Editor, Simon & Schuster', and eight other unsuspecting nobodies in the 10 biggest New York publishing houses I could think of.

Seven never replied to me; but at three houses I got letters from editors who said that I might be onto something interesting, and asked me to send them a sample chapter. I did that, and they were sufficiently intrigued – though not persuaded – to ask for another sample chapter, and then for me to start revising what I'd sent them.

I should stress that this was all hard work, as hard as the work that followed. My regular job often kept me in the office till 4am, and then had me back again at dawn even on Saturday mornings,

so it hardly seemed as if I had time to write anything on the side. But I kept on hammering away, using all my free time for six months, every weekend and slow morning, till I had two sample chapters done, and, at the end of that, with much skepticism but a touching leap of faith, one editor offered me the lowest advance then available – but enough for me to take a six-month leave of absence to write my first book.

Once I took those six months off, I still had to find a way to support myself, of course, so while I was travelling around 10 countries in Asia, writing my first book, *Video Night in Kathmandu*, I holed up in a tiny hotel in Manila, and wrote a long article on the 12th-century Assassin sect of Persia and Syria in order to finance my travels beyond the small advance.

My first book found a few readers and friends, but nonetheless, when I went to my editor to suggest a second, he did not recommend an advance and told me he couldn't begin to guarantee that he would have a place for it.

How long does it take to write your books?

It generally takes me two years, though to say that is to make it sound easier than it is. My last book really consumed me for nine years, even though the writing of it took two. And during one of those years of writing, I was so preoccupied with it that I barely slept, and was staggering through life like an insomniac madman.

Before I began writing – and when I wrote that first book in the second half of a six-month leave from work – I figured it would be easy to do since I had no trouble covering space when writing my diary or knocking off letters to friends. But writing, when I began to do it properly, seems very different from that. One of the chapters in my first book went through 300 drafts – and that was the book I wrote most quickly! And many passages in every book go through 30 drafts or more, to catch the right feeling or slant of light.

My sense is that the longer you put into a book, the longer it will stay with a reader. A book that takes six months to write is often forgotten six months later; one that claims a decade of your life has a greater solidity to it, and feels more durable.

Do you have an agent, and how important do you think they are?

I do have a wonderful and brilliant agent, though even she, being a wonderful and brilliant agent, often tells me that she can't begin to send out the manuscripts I give her, and they are best kept to myself.

When I wrote my first book, I didn't have an agent – and the advance was so small, and so welcome, I was more than happy to accept it just as an act of faith, in both directions. And I was well-embarked on my second book before an agent or two approached me, through recommendations or pieces of mine they had seen in magazines.

These days it does seem more and more imperative to find an agent, to the point where it can be harder to find an agent than an editor and, when you've got the former, you can often suppose that the hard part is behind you.

But, alas, no agent can work wonders if the quality isn't there. A good book sells itself, with no intermediaries needed; even the best agent in the world can't sell a weak book.

I always tell my friends not to worry about agents, or editors, let alone publication, until they have truly made their work as good as possible. In any case, the joy and adventure all come in the writing; everything thereafter can sometimes feel like sales tax.

INTERVIEW WITH

RORY MACLEAN

Canadian Rory MacLean (www.rorymaclean.com), long resident in the UK and now living in Berlin, is the author of 10 books, including the UK best sellers *Stalin's Nose* and *Under the Dragon* as well as *Magic Bus*, *Falling for Icarus*, *Gift of Time* and *Berlin: Imagine a City*.

How did you start off in your career as an author of travel literature?

I'd always dreamed of being a film director. To that end I wrote dozens of movie scripts, following every trend, choosing 'saleable' subjects rather than stories that moved me. The result was a series of flops, tame thrillers and busted blockbusters. But after each movie, to regain my sense of self, I went travelling. And soon I realised that I loved journeying into territory unknown (to me) and writing about the people and places met along the way.

What is the best way of establishing yourself if you're just starting out in your career as a travel literature author?

Win a prize. I'm not being flippant. There are dozens of travel writing competitions run by newspapers and magazines. Researching and writing a travel article forces you to focus. Winning a competition opens the door to agents and publishers. Alternatively, marry the son or daughter of a newspaper baron.

As a travel writer, how do you get the numbers to add up in terms of an income?

To be honest, for the first book they rarely add up. But if you're serious about writing, you just have to take the risk. I was lucky. My first book, *Stalin's Nose*, made the UK top 10. It meant that the advances paid for my second and subsequent books have been enough to survive on.

What tips would you give to budding travel writers?

Write. Write. Write. Then write some more. And if you feel you've had enough, it'd probably be a better idea to do something sensible like becoming a dentist or raising rabbits.

Are there any courses or any training that you'd recommend a budding travel writer to undertake?

In the UK, the Arvon Foundation (www.arvonfoundation.org) offers writing weeks tutored by experienced, professional authors. I also co-tutor shorter courses in London, Dublin and Paris (www.travelworkshops.co.uk).

What are the most common mistakes that travel writers make in their manuscript?

First, many first-time travel writers choose subjects because of their perceived popularity. Second, some of them don't engage their imagination or sense of wonder. Third, many don't check their spelling.

What, in your opinion, constitutes 'good' travel writing?

A book that is written from the heart. As a reader, I want to know how a journey affected the writer, what he or she learned through the trip, and how he or she was changed by the experience.

What constitutes 'bad' travel writing?

Writing to catch – or cash in on – a trend.

What are the rewards of travel writing as a career?

The opportunity to try to understand peoples, societies and histories. Then to communicate that passion with others.

What has been the downside for you?

No office Christmas parties.

How did you get your first book published?

I won the *Independent* newspaper's first travel writing competition. That enabled me to approach publishers with an idea for a book on Eastern Europe. Then Gorbachev was kind enough to knock down the Berlin Wall, making the subject-matter of my book highly topical.

How long does it take to write your books?

Usually just under two years: three months' preparation, three months' travel and about 15 months bent over my MacBook.

Do you have an agent, and how important do you think they are?

An agent is vital. To find one, scan the *Writers' & Artists' Yearbook* or look up the name of your favourite travel writer's agent and approach him or her. Books submitted directly to big publishers often go unread.

INTERVIEW WITH

DAISANN MCLANE

Daisann McLane is the author of *Cheap Hotels* and *Living in Asia*. Based in Hong Kong and the US, she wrote the 'Frugal Traveler' column for the *New York Times* travel section and writes regularly for *National Geographic Traveler* magazine. She has also written for *Rolling Stone*, *Vogue*, the *Village Voice* and *Harper's Bazaar*.

How did you start off in your career as a travel writer?

I've been working at writing and journalism since before I graduated from college. I began as a rock critic and feature writer, working for *Crawdaddy* magazine and later for *Rolling Stone* and the *Village Voice*. *Rolling Stone* sent me all over the world to go on the road with rock bands like Fleetwood Mac, Cheap Trick and Peter Frampton. When I look back on some of those old stories, like the one I wrote about Cheap Trick's phenomenal tour in Japan (where they were greeted as if they were the second coming of the Beatles, with young shy Japanese girls suddenly screaming and throwing themselves over the band's motorcade cars!), I realise that I'd started to write about travel way back then and I didn't even know it.

Later I went to live on the island of Trinidad for a while, and got interested in the great musical culture there (calypso and soca). I eventually became a calypso singer myself, and made a couple of records. The incredible experience of participating in someone else's culture really launched my career in a different direction. When I went back to New York, I wasn't very interested in rock and roll or celebrity culture anymore. I started writing about the music I loved, from the Caribbean, from Latin America and from Africa. The term 'world music' hadn't been coined yet.

Articles about such things were a hard sell back then, even in New York, where so much of the action was going on in the ethnic enclaves of Brooklyn and Queens. So I stumbled onto a strategy to finance my travels – when I wanted to go, say, to the Dominican Republic to learn more about the local music, I'd call up some of the travel magazines and ask if they wanted a story on the destination. In this way, I built up a portfolio of travel articles, although I wasn't really thinking of travel as my main interest as a writer; it was a sideline to writing about music. (Selling those music stories did get easier after a while – I became world music columnist for the *Village Voice*, then for *Rolling Stone*, and did articles for *Vogue*, *Harper's Bazaar*, *US Weekly*, the *New York Times Magazine* and the Sunday Arts and Leisure section.)

I was in graduate school at Yale, studying Caribbean culture and freelancing on the side, when quite by chance, an opportunity came up to try out to write the 'Frugal Traveler' column at the *New York Times*. The editor of the column had worked with me before as a music writer, and so she already knew my work. They sent me to Budapest, liked what I came back with, and thus began a frantic merry-go-round of travelling that has pretty much taken over my life for the past five and a half years.

As you can see, I've poked around at a lot of things in my life, following what interested me at the moment. I don't recommend this approach to others! But it somehow has worked out for me. And in a wacky way, every stage I have passed through, from rock to world music to cultural studies at the university, seems to have been a terrific preparation for what I do now.

To me it's funny that now people think of me as a 'travel writer' since for most of my career I was doing something else.

What is the best way of establishing yourself if you're just starting out in your career as a freelance travel writer?

This is a question that I don't really have an answer for, since 'travel writing' is truly something I stumbled into. I've never been good at selecting career goals and then aiming for them, and I never set out to do what I'm doing today. I still don't think of myself as a 'travel writer', but as a writer with an overdose of curiosity about other people's cultures and how they live. The other day Keith Bellows, my wonderful editor at *National Geographic Traveler*, said to me: 'You aren't a travel writer, you are a writer who travels.'

I'm very lucky that I started out as a writer more than 20 years ago. I've had a lot of practice, and many years in which to make contacts and establish a professional reputation. That makes things easier for me than for someone just starting out. If I were just starting out today, and certain that travel writing was my biggest interest, I'd probably try one of two things – getting an editorial job with a travel-related magazine to get my foot in the door, or moving to another country that totally fascinated me from top to toe, while writing a book that I'd hope would blow everyone away.

How have you managed to get your name known as a freelance travel writer?

I'm terrible at self-promotion, so I mostly just do my work and hope for the best. I'm not the sort of personality who will send 150 emails out to my dearest 'friends' every time I have a piece coming out somewhere. I don't maintain a website or do Letterman. But I did notice that there was a jump in my career when I put out my book *Cheap Hotels* in 2002. Having a book out in the market makes a big difference to magazine and newspaper editors, I think. It gives you more heft, more presence. It also makes a great hostess gift.

As a freelance travel writer, how do you get the numbers to add up in terms of an income?

It never really adds up. Some years are good, others are disasters. I know that just about every writer has a similarly discouraging tale, so I'll just leave it at that.

What tips would you give to budding travel writers?

Besides marry an investment banker? Seriously, I think that if you want to do this, you should be prepared to cut yourself loose and go on adventures. Go to places you adore, and immerse yourself in the people and their culture. Be open and humble. If someone invites you to come home with them and sleep on their floor, go. Put yourself in vulnerable situations and then come back home (or stay out there) and write marvellous stories. Do it because you love it, not because you see it as a way to make a fortune or be famous. Do it because you want to look back in 30 or 40 years on an amazing life lived.

Are there any courses or any training that you'd recommend a budding travel writer to undertake?

Absolutely. Learn another language. Two would be even better! Learning a foreign language is the best way to break through the wall between you and the place you are writing about. There's a quantum difference between a piece that is written by a writer fluent in the language and culture, and a piece written by someone who's just dropped in.

Living abroad for a spell is another great way of stretching your imagination, and acquiring a different point of view that will set you apart from the rest of the would-be travel writers pitching stories. Although I have to admit that if I read another article by a travel writer about teaching English in Asia or working in the Peace Corps, my eyes will glaze over. Both those activities are fantastic living-abroad experiences, but don't fall into the cliché of writing only that story – find a way to make other connections with the place you're in.

Studying and becoming expert at something that is identified or connected with another culture or place – say, for example, martial arts, or yoga, or French cooking – will give you an insider's edge for an article about India, China or France.

What are the main differences between travel writing for a newspaper as opposed to a magazine?

I think it's very hard to generalise the differences between magazines and newspapers. I think that the editor is more crucial than the format. Some newspaper travel sections allow writers to use their own voice freely, others will slice and dice your copy until it fits their mould. Some travel magazines are very tightly formatted, and print mainly service features that are edited and focus-grouped and worried to death so much that by the time the thing gets printed you don't even want to have your name on the piece. Other magazines

love it when you dance and dazzle, and give you all the freedom you could want.

Over 20 years of writing, I've had four, maybe five editors who really clicked with me and understood and supported my writing. The editor makes all the difference in this work. When you find a good one, keep them in your life by any means possible. Remember their birthdays. Send chocolates from Belgium, silks from Vietnam. Offer them the name of your favourite massage therapist in Thailand.

What, in your opinion, constitutes 'good' travel writing?

This is really a matter of personal taste. Off the top of my head, here are some books that I love: *The Middle Passage*, by V. S. Naipaul; *Miami*, by Joan Didion; *Iron and Silk*, by Mark Salzman; everything by Ryszard Kapuscinski. Oh, my old buddy Mikal Gilmore's *Shot in the Heart*, and as long as we're talking memoir, the first 200 pages or so of Gabriel Garcia Marquez' *Vivir Para Contarla*. None of these writers is specifically a 'travel writer', yet each takes the reader on amazing journeys to other places, from a village in China to Mormon Utah; decodes other ways of life with great authority, empathy and understanding; makes other cultures, other belief systems accessible to the general reader. All of these writers have fascinating minds, strong points of view, and great passion – whether positive or negative – for the cultures they are travelling in. This is what turns me on about them.

Of the old-school travel writers, I adore Norman Lewis, and have a soft spot for Patrick Leigh Fermor.

What constitutes 'bad' travel writing?

Again, this is very personal. I am not particularly interested in 'light' travel writing – you know, those 'I spent a year with the wife and kids in a Mediterranean village and look at all the wacky and tender things that happened' kind of books. There's a market for such books and they have their place, but it isn't on my bookshelf. I'm also put off by the travel genre I'd call 'Cynic on the Road' – I see a lot of stuff out in the market these days that is witty, but doesn't really have much to say, except that the author thinks that he (and it is nearly always a 'he') is cleverer and sharper than the people he is using as material.

What has been the downside of travel writing as a career?

There's no security in this career, and that can be really scary. On the other hand, when you travel to so many different places, and you see how people live outside of your little bubble, you realise how ridiculous the very idea of security is, from a global perspective. Empires come and go, personal fortunes rise and fall, the river waters flood and recede, and people somehow keep going. When I catch myself freaking out about my lack of a 401(k) plan, I slap myself back with a reality check: most people in the world don't have anything to catch them if they fall except their will and their determination to press on.

The other downside, at least in the last couple of years, has been witnessing first-hand and close-up the disintegration of America's image in the rest of the world. It's depressing to know that so many people around the world think my country's government is foolish at best, warmongers at worst – and even more depressing that I have to agree with them. When George W. Bush was running for president, my biggest objection to him wasn't his position on taxes or abortion – it was that he was a man who had almost never travelled abroad. Spending time in a different place watching the world from an unfamiliar (and, perhaps, uncomfortable) perspective should be a requirement for all our leaders.

What is the greatest challenge facing travel writing?

Just as travel itself is threatened by mass tourism and unsustainable tourism practices, travel writing is facing an ecological crisis. When the world was larger and more inaccessible, the role of the travel writer was to go out and bring back stories of the marvellous, the wondrous, the things and people that readers might not ever see in their lifetimes. As the world shrunk, the travel writer's role transformed: he or she was the confident insider, ready to whisper in your ear to steer you 'off the beaten track' to more rarefied, or let's say 'authentic' experiences.

But in this era of globalisation, where – thanks to the internet – I can surf and easily find information as arcane and specific as the 10 best hawkers of *char keow tow* noodles in Kuala Lumpur – who needs that kind of travel writer? So travel writers have to come up with another reason to be doing what we do, another approach or mode. Some of us have opted to specialise in extreme or adventure travel, searching for material in those (very very few) remaining corners of the globe that are beyond the reach of average travellers. Others have decided to specialise in telling stories about the clashes of culture and modernity in the globalising world.

Both approaches, though, are tapping out. Firstly, because there are very few places left on earth nowadays that are truly inaccessible, and secondly, because globalisation has been so thorough and pervasive that the contrast between tradition and modernity has become almost a given, it is no longer a big deal. Now every traveller *expects* to attend video nights in Kathmandu. What's more, in response to escalating numbers of tourists and the pressures of economic development, travel destinations themselves are becoming more and more faux (for example, in China, they tear down their traditional neighbourhoods and move the vendors to new, Disney-like 'Old Streets').

So what exactly is a postmodern travel writer to do? It's going to be very interesting to see where the next generation of travel writers will find its subject in a world where, increasingly, all the urban centres are beginning to match each other – starchitect for starchitect – and where everything once marvellous has turned to faux.

Here's a thought: as economies shrink, oil diminishes, and travel becomes more costly and difficult, we travel writers may end up back in our 19th-century role as the eyes and ears of the armchair wanderer.

INTERVIEW WITH
DANNY PALMERLEE

Danny Palmerlee is a freelance writer and photographer based in Portland, Oregon. He is the main author of numerous Lonely Planet travel guides, including *Argentina*, *Buenos Aires*, *South America*, *Ecuador*, *Baja California* and *Yosemite, Sequoia & Kings Canyon National Parks*. His blog can be viewed at www.travelburro.com.

How did you start off in your career as a guidebook writer?

I submitted a sample chapter to Lonely Planet after meeting a friendly LP editor in a bar. She pointed me to the right person, who assessed my sample chapter, clips and résumé and gave me the thumbs up. A month or so later I received my first assignment.

What is the best way of establishing yourself if you're just starting out in your career as a freelance guidebook writer now?

Two things: networking and clips. If you're starting from scratch and lack clips, fork up the cash for things like writing workshops – *established* writing workshops – led by people in the industry. Aside from learning, you'll meet editors who will help you out if they like your work. It'll cost you

some money, but think of it as an investment. Good writers who network are the most successful. Then you can build your clips.

Guidebook writing is sort of a breed of its own, and becoming an expert on something helps you stand out from the rest. Start a blog about something, anything: surfing in South America, California taco stands, wild mushrooms, the city you live in – whatever. In doing this you can show an editor, alongside your application and clips, something that makes you unique.

How do you think guidebook writers get the numbers to add up in terms of an income?

By padding it with other writing work, piggybacking and working like a maniac. The only way to make it financially viable is to take back-to-back guidebook assignments (which can be exhausting) or to pad the guidebook writing with other freelance work. You also have to get stories out of your guidebook work, which is tough because you're travelling so fast. After finishing the guidebook, you have to pitch stories like crazy to publications about the place you went.

How do you get the numbers to add up?

With a credit card! Honestly, it can be tough. But it's definitely doable, especially if you avoid living in expensive cities. I lived in Buenos Aires for a while when it was cheaper than it is today, and that helped me save money.

What advice would you give to budding guidebook writers?

Again, build your clips and network like crazy.

Are there any courses or any training that you'd recommend a budding guidebook writer to undertake?

If you've never taken writing classes, do so now – unless you *know* you're a good writer. Even then, classes never hurt. Workshops can teach you things and be a good way to network. If you have access to independent publishing resource centres, take classes on self-promotion.

Successful writers know how to promote themselves.

Also, taking classes in a subject that will help you specialise or become an expert in something might also help.

What are the most common mistakes that guidebook writers make – in their research and in their writing?

During research, saying 'I'll come back for that' is a huge mistake. You never do. There's never time. Maybe that sounds trite, but look at it this way: when you have 25 businesses to visit in a section of town and it's starting to get dark and you're hungry for dinner, it's easy to say, 'I'll come back for those last three hotels tomorrow.' Forget it, you won't. The next day you'll be in the same situation on the other side of town.

Another huge mistake, especially in small towns that rely heavily on tourism for money, is letting it leak that you write for a major guidebook. Before you know it, you have people knocking on your door asking you to do this and visit that and it can be a real headache.

A big mistake during write-up is delaying your start date. It's easy to research and research until you think you have everything, but then you're jammed when it comes to write-up time. Make a schedule before you start researching and stick to it. If you don't have enough write-up time, you'll never make your deadline – and missing your deadline is one of the hugest mistakes you can make, period. (Aside, of course, from obvious mistakes like providing incorrect information.)

What are the main differences between guidebook writing and writing for a newspaper, magazine, or website?

Guidebook writing is macro. Writing a story for a newspaper or magazine is micro. When you're writing a guidebook, you're in a destination covering as much as you can as fast as you can. When you're writing a (good) travel story, you have to focus on the experience more, and dig in deeper. And you only have room for a few lodging and eating options (although that varies depending on the topic of your piece).

In guidebooks, you rarely have to tell a story, and you rarely need a hook. When you're writing an article, you have to have a hook and a good story.

What, in your opinion, constitutes 'good' guidebook writing?

Accuracy is key, obviously. Then comes making text interesting and fun to read without being cute. When a writer tries too hard to be funny or witty it's painfully

obvious to the reader, and the reader, I think, quickly loses faith in the writer. And a good writer can capture the feel of a place – whether it's a country, city, village, hotel, restaurant – in *very* few words. Good writers always keep the old admonition 'Show, don't tell' in the back of their minds.

What constitutes 'bad' guidebook writing?

Being too cute. Being funny for funniness' sake. If it's not helping the reader make a decision, it probably shouldn't be in there.

What are the rewards of guidebook writing as a career?

People. The folks I've met during 10 years of guidebook writing are by far the greatest reward. The beaches and mountains start to run together in my mind, but my memories of the people I've met, most of whom helped me out in some way or another, are crystal clear. But that simply mirrors travel itself. Travellers see people's generosity every day, and guidebook writers get to experience this all the time, even when they're travelling undercover.

For all of its challenges, guidebook writing is extremely exhilarating; I never ever wake up and think, 'Oh crap, I don't want to go to work today' (OK, except around deadline time, when I'm going on day 20 in a row).

What has been the downside for you?

Years without having a home. Not having plants or long-term relationships, although I was eventually able to work all of these into my life. Eating in too many restaurants: after your 99th restaurant meal in a row, you really, really just want to eat at home. And struggling to make ends meet.

What's the role of the internet in the landscape of contemporary guidebook/travel writing?

The pretravel research you can do before setting out is an incredible help. And you can get the opinions of other travellers. For example, if I go to a supposedly good restaurant and have a lousy experience, I might go online to see if others had an equally bad experience before I cut the place out of the book. But no matter how much information is online, it can never, ever replace the need to actually visit a place. Websites regularly have incorrect information. It's an outstanding secondary tool.

How can would-be guidebook writers best utilise the web for their own professional development?

Start a blog, and make it specific (don't look at mine for inspiration).

Make it specific about a country or a city or a cuisine and you'll build credibility. It shows that you have a passion and a knowledge about something, and editors like to see that when screening potential authors. Do all the Web 2.0 social-networking websites you can possibly do. The more your name is out there, the better. And once you assemble some clips, build yourself a website. It shows that you're serious.

Where do you see guidebook publishing going in the next five years?

Everything is going online, and more and more guidebook material will be accessible via handheld devices, which, obviously, are a lot easier to carry than guidebooks. However, I think the (guide)book format will be around longer than five years. But I imagine publishers will invest more and more in digital material and water down their print material because it's more expensive to produce. I think authors, unfortunately, will increasingly get the short end of the stick in this world as publishers continue to squeeze as much out of their material as possible. I also see independent publishers/writers/experts, via the internet, playing an increasingly significant role. With the rise of Web 2.0 and blogs, travellers can get content that's up-to-the-minute fresh, and, although the quality control that goes into guidebooks isn't there, people love it.

Any other tips you would offer would-be guidebook writers?
Pack your Strunk & White [*The Elements of Style*] and never miss a deadline.

INTERVIEW WITH
MARGO PFEIFF

Canadian travel writer Margo Pfeiff writes for the *Los Angeles Times*, the *San Francisco Chronicle*, *Doctor's Review* and Canada's two national daily newspapers – the *National Post* and the *Globe & Mail*. She has won gold at the SATW Lowell Thomas Awards as well as eight Northern Lights Awards from the Canadian Tourism Commission and the Travel Media Award at the 2002 British Columbia Tourism Awards for travel stories on the region.

How did you start off in your career as a travel journalist?
I actually started out as a photographer trying to sell my photos to magazines in Southeast Asia in the late 1970s. Editors were often enthusiastic about the slides, but didn't have the budget to send out a writer for an accompanying text. They asked if I could write something to go with the photos. I have been doing both travel writing and photography ever since and am glad of the joint right brain/left brain exercise.

What is the best way of establishing yourself if you're just starting out in your career as a freelance travel journalist?
Write, write, write, write, then pitch your best stuff to get enough tear sheets from local newspapers and magazines to allow entry into an established travel writers' organisation. If you are good you will get published eventually; editors are always on the lookout for new talent as more-established travel writers move on to books or scriptwriting.

How have you managed to get your name known as a freelance travel journalist?

As I tend not to be a joiner when it comes to writers' associations, it's been mostly by the volume of material I've written and the volume of years I've been in the business. Journalist friends have also been very kind in helping me gain access into the markets for which they have been writing.

As a freelance travel journalist, how do you get the numbers to add up in terms of an income?

I sell stories before deciding on a trip so that I know I will make a reasonable return for my time spent on the road. Then I syndicate my travel stories to a number of newspapers and magazines that do not have overlapping circulations. My photos increase the size of my pay checks and I also write for non-travel publications that pay higher word rates than most newspaper and magazine travel sections.

What tips would you give to budding travel writers?

Study the style and content of the publication you're aiming at until you're very familiar with it. Make sure your idea or destination hasn't recently been covered by that publication. Editors are very busy, so if you can make their jobs easier in any way you'll make a positive impression. Be professional: meet deadlines, pay attention to details. That can mean anything from supplying photos that complement your story to doing a fact box/sidebar that includes all the details the publication requires. Do your homework.

Are there any courses or any training that you'd recommend a budding travel writer to undertake?

The best travel-writing courses I've seen offered were at the Book Passage travel writers' conference in the San Francisco area.

What are the most common mistakes that travel writers make in their copy?

Writing first-person journals rather than travel stories. Stories are best told through the writer's eyes, and the writer's perspective and personality should come through in the telling, but the writer should not be the focus of the article.

What are the main differences between travel writing for a newspaper as opposed to a magazine?

Magazine stories generally allow the luxury of a longer word count. For me that means the space to develop anecdotes and build a narrative to better put the reader in my shoes. There is less emphasis on the service aspect of travel writing in magazines, more emphasis on literary writing.

147

What, in your opinion, constitutes 'good' travel writing?

Using anecdotes, characterisations of people you meet, setting scenes to put the reader into the location rather than telling about a place. Dialogue and humour are, for me, good indicators of fine travel writing – and they are too rare in most travel stories.

What constitutes 'bad' travel writing?

Clichés of every sort. Gushing about how wonderful a place is.

What are the rewards of travel writing as a career?

The countries I've had the good fortune to visit and the doors that were opened before and after hours that allowed me such memorable experiences as watching the sun rise as I sat all alone on the Acropolis. The behind-the-scenes glimpses of what makes a Zambian safari camp run. The amazing people I've had the privilege to meet and talk with who probably wouldn't have given me the time of day if I was a tourist. Being paid to do something I love more than anything else in the world.

What has been the downside for you?

Pay rates that have often not changed in two decades. Being treated – primarily by media outside of travel writing – as a hack in a field that is often perceived only as a haven for freebie-seekers.

INTERVIEW WITH

ROLF POTTS

Rolf Potts is the author of *Vagabonding*: *An Uncommon Guide to the Art of Long-Term World Travel*, and *Marco Polo Didn't Go There: Stories and Revelations From One Decade as a Postmodern Travel Writer*. Based in the US, he has written for Salon.com, *National Geographic Traveler* and the *New York Times Magazine*, as well as public radio and the Travel Channel.

How did you start off in your career as a travel writer?

My career started, as most do, with failure. Right after university, I saved up and spent eight months travelling around North America. When I got back, I decided I was going to write a book about the experience, and that this book would be the biggest thing since Kerouac's On the Road. The problem, of course, is that I hadn't considered my audience. What was interesting to me was not always interesting to the people who read these travel tales. After months of writing and unfruitful attempts to attract agents and editors, I came to the difficult realisation that I would have to learn how to tell a story and evoke a place and an experience through the details.

A couple of years after I quit that failed book, I was able to rewrite one of its chapters (a story about Las Vegas) and sell it to the online magazine Salon.com. I was living and teaching English in Korea at the time, so I began to write Korea travel tales for Salon as well. Eventually, I built up a working relationship with the editor, after proving my ability to work hard and write well. When I left on a two-year trip around Asia (funded by my years of teaching in Korea), I was able to talk the editor into making me a travel columnist for Salon.com. That exposure led to being published in other magazines, and my career took off from there.

What is the best way of establishing yourself if you're just starting out in your career as a freelance travel writer?

There are several things you can do to get your name out there. One is to write a lot, and to write well. Another is to market yourself with a website that selectively showcases your stories and photos and publications. But, as much as anything, the best way to get your name out there is to write in a very distinctive way. Some people do this by writing stories that are funny. Other writers are good at evoking the human essence of the travel experience. Other travel writers become experts on certain countries, or on travel planning, or on certain types of travel, like adventure travel or food-oriented travel. If you can combine a talent for more than one of these elements, of course, you will do well.

In recent years beginning travel writers have grown increasingly savvy at using online and social media to help build their careers. Even if your career isn't to the point where you're selling a lot of articles to formal publications, you can write stories and advice for your personal travel blog, and interact with your readership through Twitter and Facebook. This allows you to develop your writing and travel expertise while building an audience for your work. (The key, of course, is to be disciplined and strategic with the online self-promotion, since constant connectedness on the road can compromise the quality of your travels.)

How have you managed to get your name known as a freelance travel writer?

My website (www.rolfpotts.com) has been a big help. It was an integral part of my initial pitch as a columnist at Salon.com, and has showcased my writing ever since. It includes links to online stories and radio pieces, as well as photos and interviews and essays. For the past several years I have also maintained a daily blog containing travel-related information, inspiration, and advice. In this way, if you provide people with new and interesting travel information and stories, they will come back again and again to see what you are saying.

My books, *Vagabonding* and *Marco Polo Didn't Go There* have also been key in establishing me as a person with something to say about independent travel and travel writing. To use a business term, books are a "platform" that help draw attention to your writing voice and travel expertise.

As a freelance travel writer, how do you get the numbers to add up in terms of an income?

Through simplicity, and not spending very much. That allows me to get by just fine on a minimum of money. It also allows me to concentrate on the kind of stories I like, the kind of stories I excel at. I mean, I could supplement my income by writing a lot of travel news and service articles for newspapers and magazines, but these kinds of stories don't interest me as much as more involved, in-depth features. Thus, I write fewer stories in a given year than your average travel journalist, but I enjoy them more, and I think my writing benefits from this kind of focus.

As for keeping things simple and saving money, I've found the easiest way to do this is to live overseas, preferably in a less-expensive region, like Asia or Latin America. Not only does this save me money on day-to-day living, but it also increases my chances of getting work writing about those regions for newspapers and magazines.

What tips would you give to budding travel writers?

Travel a lot. Write a lot. Read a lot. Don't do it for the money, because there are better ways to make money. Don't even do it for the travel, because there are better ways to fund and facilitate travel. Do it because you love to write, and you love to write about travel. Do it because it is your passion and obsession. Don't ever do it just because you think it will make you seem cool or sexy, because it will never match your expectations.

Another thing to keep in mind is that, while writing well is key, travel writing also involves a degree of business savvy. You have to familiarize yourself with the kinds of publications that are out there, develop working relationships with editors, promote your work through online and social media, and stay attuned to trends in an ever-changing travel-writing market. These business aspects of the profession sound less romantic than the travel and writing parts of travel writing, but they're important skills to develop.

Are there any courses or any training that you'd recommend a budding travel writer to undertake?

I think the most important thing as a writer is to read well. Be familiar with good writing (not just travel writing, but creative nonfiction, novels and poetry), and try to recognise what makes it work.

Also, don't be afraid to fail, so long as you learn from your mistakes and always work at getting better. The best training in the world is the school of hard knocks. Of course, for a little extra guidance and inspiration, you can always check out my creative nonfiction writing course each July at the Paris American Academy (www.pariswritingworkshop.com).

What are the most common mistakes that travel writers make in their copy?

First, they assume the reader will be as interested in their travels as they are. Second, they stick too hard to chronology, without ever telling a story. All the worst stories are just a bland recounting of events.

Thus, while travel writing should never be fictional, it *should* emulate the best techniques of fiction, such as character, action, plot, foreshadowing, dialogue and payoff. Character and dialogue are especially important, since they bring the story to life. Think about it: do we enjoy *Seinfeld* or *Cannery Row* or *American Pie* for the setting and descriptions? Of course not – we are drawn to their *characters* and what the characters do and say. Thus, be an extrovert as you travel, and colour your story with the people you meet. Provide action and dialogue, setup and payoff. Draw the reader into the story with these elements.

What are the main differences between travel writing for a newspaper as opposed to a magazine, or for the web versus print?

Newspaper features tend to be shorter and more service-oriented, though this often depends on the taste of the editor. Newspapers are more likely to exclusively publish 'destination' pieces. Magazines like a bigger theme or news hook to the story, and rarely take a standard piece about a 'place'. Web writing is harder to pin down. As a rule, web writing is short – but then some of my longest pieces have appeared online. The web is very flexible and often allows for the kind of storytelling that you couldn't get away with in magazines and newspapers. Recently I've noticed that more and more people are using apps like Instapaper to do their reading on phones and tablets, and if this trend continues I'd reckon it will blur the distinctions between those different kinds of media.

What, in your opinion, constitutes 'good' travel writing?

Engaging stories and essays that evoke people and places around the world in a personal way. Naturally, they must also be well-informed and well-researched.

What constitutes 'bad' travel writing?

Bad writing often comes from bad travelling – and bad travel is unimaginative, uninformed and unoriginal. Thus, to write well, you have to get into adventures and meet people. You have to try new things, or experience old things in new ways. Of course, people can have good adventures and still write poorly, if they don't tell a story (with a beginning, middle and end), evoke characters, and put themselves in the shoes of their readers.

What are the rewards of travel writing as a career?

The ability to see the world, live creatively, and express yourself through the written word. Each new day is an adventure.

What has been the downside for you?

Travel writing doesn't pay well, if at all, and it is often a solitary pursuit that your friends and families and lovers don't understand. I have personally come to terms with all of this, of course; I'm just mentioning these factors to those who think there is some way around the bad pay, frequent solitude, and lack of life consistency. There isn't. But I love it just the same.

Where do you see travel publishing going in the next five years?

In the business sense, I have no clue where travel writing is headed, though if I did, I could make a fortune as a media consultant. Consumer travel writing is paired quite closely with the travel industry, and thus is likely to wind up wherever the most readers are tuning in – be it websites, or magazines, or whatever media technology is invented next week. Literary travel writing will continue to appear wherever it is championed by individual editors and publishers, and its more specialised readership will follow accordingly.

In artistic terms, I think travel writing will always be the product of its age. As recently as 100 years ago, for example, travel writing was characterised by detailed cultural and topographical descriptions.

In an age of mass information, however, description is no longer enough; writers need to make connections and actively interpret the texture of places that can retain their distinct character even as they change rapidly. This applies to American flyover country as much as it applies to Yemen or Botswana.

It has been said that travel literature was crucial to the evolution of the modern novel, that Victorian Romanticism emerged from a 19th-century travel boom that created a fascination with faraway places. I'd like to think that travel literature in coming decades will champion a kind of Postmodern Realism – a measured-yet-optimistic sensibility that cuts through the fantasies of tourism and the alarmist hue of international news reporting to leave us with something that is essentially human and true about the rest of the world.

INTERVIEW WITH

ALISON RICE

Alison Rice is a UK-based freelance travel writer, broadcaster and presenter. She was Editor of *BBC Holidays* magazine (1992–95), and Director of Programmes for Travel Channel (1995–2000).

How did you start off in your career as a travel writer?

I was a magazine editor and had a weekly BBC Radio 1 program and got fed up with being an editor. I went freelance and was advised to have a specialty. I had written some travel pieces as an editor (editors get the pick of travel trips and I'd done some travels around the East off my own bat) and I thought there was a gap in the market (this was 1983) for a specialist on mass-market travel. A bloke who liked my writing and radio stuff offered me a gig as travel editor on TV-am. The bloke was Greg Dyke (ex Director-General of the BBC).

What is the best way of establishing yourself if you're just starting out in your career as a freelance travel writer?

Be very knowledgeable in a certain type of travel. You can't be all things to all people.

If at all possible, don't freelance until you've spent time as a staffer in some form of publishing/media and developed your own network of editors. Do your homework about the publication before offering ideas to the editor.

How have you managed to get your name known as a freelance travel writer?

Because I started when I was already known – as an editor and broadcaster. Because I worked bloody hard for the first 15 years and really got to know the travel industry. Because after about the first five years I found a style that was mine and that suited me and that people seemed to want.

As a freelance travel writer, how do you get the numbers to add up in terms of an income?

I don't. You have to work very hard and be very well established to make a decent living just from travel writing, and I think only a very few achieve this – all well-established and knowledgeable gurus.

After 20 years in the field I don't want to produce the number of features I'd need to write for what I think is a decent living, so I use my experience and expertise in other ways to produce the sort of income I want.

What tips would you give to budding travel writers?

If you want to be a travel journalist, get a job in the media first. If you want to produce travel literature à la Thubron, Lewis etc, get a private income or downsize from taxi to bus, high mortgage to bedsit. Develop your own fresh, unclichéd look on the world.

Are there any courses or any training that you'd recommend a budding travel writer to undertake?

It might be worth trying a summer school or evening class to see if you really have that fresh look on the world, or whether you should keep the day job and stick to writing great emails on your holidays.

What are the most common mistakes that travel writers make in their copy?

Clichés. Tired stereotyping. No spirit. Kowtowing to tourist boards, PRs. Believing the hype they're offered. Never checking facts...shall I go on?

What are the main differences between travel writing for a newspaper as opposed to a magazine?

Deadlines. News. Some magazines treat travel pages as no more than payback for free staff holidays. Dire.

What, in your opinion, constitutes 'good' travel writing?

Something that so conjures up the spirit of the place I can smell it. Some of the best travel writing makes me know I'd never want to go to the place. Something unexpected that's sharp and fresh and might make me laugh or cry.

What constitutes 'bad' travel writing?

Much easier to answer – clichéd, lazy, 'what I did on my holidays' stuff and the belief that because the destination is 'exotic' the feature must be good. They rarely are. Trying to cover everything about a place in one feature.

What are the rewards of travel writing as a career?

The reward of travel journalism is that sometimes you really can make a tiny difference – for the better – to the way that the extraordinary travel industry conducts itself.

And sometimes your advice really can mean some family has a better holiday. The reward for travel writing is that around the world you get to peep through doors that are locked to most nonwriting travellers and holidaymakers.

What has been the downside for you?

The downside of freelancing is occasionally having some of what I thought was good work 'changed' by staffers. Still, I've learned to try not to fret too much as long as they get my name on the cheque right.

INTERVIEW WITH

ANTHONY SATTIN

Anthony Sattin is the author of many books, including *The Pharaoh's Shadow*, *Shooting the Breeze*, *The Gates of Africa* and *A Winter on the Nile*. Based in the UK, he contributes regularly to the *Sunday Times*, *Financial Times* and *Conde Nast Traveller*.

How did you start off in your career as a travel writer?

Writing other things. I spent years in London writing fiction (and publishing some of it), but then had the urge to see and do and write about something new. I went to live in Cairo, lured by love. Before I departed, I persuaded my editor to commission a book about a novelist's eye on the city.

What is the best way of establishing yourself if you're just starting out in your career as a travel writer?

It may seem obvious, but writing is the best way forward. Get your book commissioned, written and into production. Once it is on its way, then try getting your name about in other ways – travel features for newspapers or magazines, book reviews and radio features all help. There are now many online avenues to pursue.

As a travel writer, how do you get the numbers to add up in terms of an income?

You don't, unless you are one of a very select band of best sellers. If you want to make money, take some advice and try your hand at banking. Travel writing has other rewards. Having said that, it is possible to make some sort of a living writing books and contributing to newspapers and magazines.

What tips would you give to budding travel writers?

Be original and be true to yourself. Only write what you really want to write, not what you think will sell.

Are there any courses or any training that you'd recommend a budding travel writer to undertake?

The nearest I got to training was taking a Masters in Creative Writing. My only thoughts were for fiction in those days, but the novel I was working on was set abroad. It must have started something. Travel writing courses have flourished in recent years. I teach some courses for Travellers' Tales (www.travellerstales.org).

What do you think are the most common mistakes that travel writers make in their manuscripts?

Although there are more travel books being published these days, very few stand out. Often this is because few progress beyond telling us what happened on the journey. The best books have their own distinct angles, or characters, or motives. In the age of TV and online maps, when we all know so much about even the most remote places on earth, there needs to be something beyond the journey that makes the story unique and involving.

What, in your opinion, constitutes 'good' travel writing?

Something that moves and amazes me. I want to feel the wonder – or the horror – of the world. And I want to have a sense that the writer has looked for the universal in the particular story they have told.

What constitutes 'bad' travel writing?

I don't need to read about what you did on your holiday. Or how macho you are.

What are the rewards of travel writing as a career?

Not often financial (see above). One of the biggest rewards is having the opportunity to see the world, and often in a way of your choosing, whether through the filter of a historical character or while floating along a river. I have also been fortunate to return to some countries over a long period, have made friends in far places, and have seen them and their countries develop.

What has been the downside for you?

Travel writing is too easily dismissed by some editors, booksellers and readers as a lesser form of writing. I find that frustrating. Like the best novels, histories or any other sort of writing, the best travel writing has the power to cast light on the essential things in life and to move us.

How did you get your first book published?

The usual route: I had already published short stories and reviews. I wrote a proposal and my agent hawked it around the likely editors.

How long does it take to write your books?

How long is a piece of string? I tend to write quickly and can get a story down in a few months. But I let the story gestate, sometimes for years before I begin writing. And I believe in thorough rewriting and that can take a lot, lot longer. One book took more than 10 years from gestation to print but definitely benefited from the wait.

Do you have an agent, and how important do you think they are?

Agents have become increasingly necessary in the time I have been writing. I have always had one, simply by getting them to read my work. Some publishers will now not consider a manuscript or proposal unless it comes through an agent. As agents have become more powerful, so they too have put up more barriers. It helps if you are approaching an agent who handles the sort of writing you want to produce. A good agent can be a big help and can do everything from helping to shape

a proposal, providing encouragement when things are going bad,
to being there at publication
celebrations.

What would you say have been the major changes in travel publishing in the UK in the past four years?

We are living through a moment
of transition. The traditional
models of publication have been
made redundant by a shrinking
market and the arrival of internet
publishing in all its many forms,
from blogging to book downloads.
No one can etll how long this
transition will last, nor what the
process and market will look like
when it has been remade. But I
think there are new and exciting
possibilities ahead, just as there
are big problems at the moment,
the lack of funding for writing
being one of the greatest.

Are the travel magazines still relatively robust and good outlets for travel writers?

The UK travel magazine market
has expanded in the past decade
and none of the titles has folded,
so it must still be viable. The variety of titles presents writers with a
range of outlets.

How about the newspaper travel sections?

All newspaper travel sections have
suffered budget cuts as newspaper
sales and advertising revenues
shrink. As a result most have cut
the rates they pay writers. But
they are still there and they do still
need copy.

INTERVIEW WITH
STANLEY STEWART

Stanley Stewart is the author of *Old Serpent Nile*, *Frontiers of Heaven* and *In the Empire of Genghis Khan*. Based in the UK, he has twice been winner of the prestigious Thomas Cook Travel Book of the Year Award.

How did you start off in your career as a travel writer?

My own start was unusual. I began with a book. I set off up the Nile for nine months, without a publishing contract, wrote an account of the journey and sold it to a publisher when it was complete. The success of the book opened doors for travel journalism which helped to feed, financially, more books.

What is the best way of establishing yourself if you're just starting out in your career as a freelance travel journalist?

Try to find an area in which you can specialise, or to which you bring unique experience, like cycling in the Alps or conservation in Africa. Try as well to master the more mundane nuts and bolts of travel journalism – how to get a cheap air-fare or good hotel package. The best way to get started is to land a job on a newspaper, however junior – answering the phone, opening the post. You will then be on hand to pick up those assignments that someone else has just dropped on Thursday afternoon when copy is due for the Sunday paper. They will be so desperate to have someone cover it, they won't notice you haven't written before. You'll also learn how it all works from the inside, where the decisions are made. When you go freelance, you will not only have the inside dope,

but you will have the best kind of contacts – personal ones.

As a freelance travel journalist, how do you get the numbers to add up in terms of an income?

With difficulty. At the beginning, you are likely to be working for a pittance. But hang in there. As you become better known, and as your polished prose becomes more admired, rates will go up and you will be able to pitch to higher-paying journals. Travel writers need to be able to double up – so when you are in Rome doing a story about riding a Vespa along the Appian Way for newspaper X, you are also getting the info together for a restaurant story for magazine Y and a piece on the Coliseum for newspaper Z. And think about other markets, different ways to use the same material for other journals, as well as selling the same story to different newspapers abroad.

What tips would you give to budding travel writers?

Be persistent. Don't be put off by rejection. In the end, landing a junior job at a paper, or a commission for your first story, will largely be a matter of luck and timing. Keep at it until you call or knock at just the moment when the editor is at their wits' end trying to find someone to do that piece on Greek island ferries or that feature on shopping in Milan.

Are there any courses or any training that you'd recommend a budding travel writer to undertake?

I am not aware of any. Better to travel, and to read. It may sound blazingly obvious, but the best preparation for a career in travel writing is travel. Take a year off and travel round the world. When you come to pitching a story about the hot springs of Iceland, you will have the advantage of sounding like someone who knows what they are talking about. But remember that you must be able to write. And the best education for a writer is to read, as widely as possible.

What are the most common mistakes that travel writers make in their copy?

They forget that travel stories must be stories, not merely descriptions of a destination. It is not enough to enthuse about the blue seas or the difficulties of the hike or the charm of the old quarter. What you write must be able to stand as a good story when all the 'colour' and atmosphere are stripped away.

What are the differences between travel writing for a newspaper as opposed to a magazine?

Length. A magazine will often allow you to write to a much longer length, up to 3000 or 4000 words, and that allows you to write a piece with greater depth and complexity. At least that is the theory. In practice, economy can give birth to some wonderful writing.

What, in your opinion, constitutes 'good' travel writing?

Good travel writing is done by good writers who travel. It is not enough to have swum through piranha-infested waters to the source of the Amazon. You must be able to write well to convey that experience. When you have learned the craft of writing, you can a make a stroll through your own suburban neighbourhood interesting, even exciting. Good travel writing needs much the same ingredients as any good story – narrative drive, characters, dialogue, atmosphere, revelation. Make it personal. Let the reader know how the place and the experience are affecting you.

Good travel writing is just good writing. It must have literary merit. The most important journey you will make as a travel writer is the journey of a good sentence. Without that, your close encounter with the piranhas is wasted.

What constitutes 'bad' travel writing?

Bad travel writing is done by travellers who mistakenly believe they can write. There seems to be a lot of them about. Their prose is littered with clichés, their sense of narrative timing is inept and their characters, whether themselves or people they encounter, are clumsily portrayed. Too many travel writers seem to believe that the journey 'makes' the story. It doesn't. In the end, anyone can travel to Timbuktu, but only a few people will write about the journey well. Bad travel writing is just bad writing.

What are the rewards of travel writing as a career?
To travel the world and get paid for it. And hopefully along the way to understand a little more about other peoples and other cultures, and thus about yourself.

And the downside?
Too much travelling can put a strain on relationships.

INTERVIEW WITH

MARA VORHEES

Mara Vorhees is a travel writer, mother of twins and de facto expert on family travel. She has written guidebooks about Belize, Brazil, Costa Rica, Morocco, New England and Russia for Lonely Planet. Follow her adventures and misadventures traveling with twin in tow at www.havetwinswilltravel.com.

How did you start off in your career as a guidebook writer?
I was living in Yekaterinburg, Russia, in the late 1990s, working on a US-government sponsored foreign aid project. I was becoming increasingly disillusioned with the field of international development in general and increasingly frustrated with my job in particular.

But I was doing a lot of writing, which I enjoyed.

Living and travelling in Russia, I always used the Lonely Planet guide, but I felt like I probably knew more about that country – or at least the region where I was living – than the authors did. On a whim, I wrote a letter to Lonely Planet, sent some writing samples, and offered to work on the next update. I was completely floored when somebody actually responded. As it turned out, that was the start of a new career.

What is the best way of establishing yourself if you're just starting out in your career as a freelance guidebook writer now?

Develop a regional expertise: travel, learn the language, develop a network of contacts. Learn as much as you can about that place, so you can demonstrate that you are an expert. And by the way, you'll probably do better if your regional expertise is not France.

How do you think guidebook writers get the numbers to add up in terms of an income?

Guidebook writers get the numbers to add up by spending a lot of time on the road, doing back-to-back and overlapping assignments. It's also useful to supplement with other writing gigs and even other jobs (teaching, temping, waiting tables, whatever it takes).

How do you get the numbers to add up?

When I started working for Lonely Planet, I had a full-time 'real job' that paid my bills quite nicely. I had a great relationship with my boss, who allowed me to take a leave of absence once a year to work on a

guidebook. Eventually, I got laid off from that job, and that was the kick in the pants I needed to transition to being a full-time writer. Now I usually do two or three full-fledged guidebook writing projects a year, and a slew of articles and other smaller pieces. Also, it helps that my husband is gainfully employed.

What advice would you give to budding guidebook writers?

Take every opportunity to travel and be sure to write about it along the way. Stay abreast of the latest technology (do as I say, not as I do) There are always new tools that are bound to make your job a little easier. You can also use technology to develop and promote your personal 'brand'. Becoming known as an expert in your field can open doors for bigger and better opportunities.

Are there any courses or any training that you'd recommend a budding guidebook writer to undertake?

Learn the language! You don't need to be fluent, but being able to communicate in your country will make your job hundreds of times easier. And you'll have a lot more fun along the way.

What are the most common mistakes that guidebook writers make – in their research and in their writing?

The most common mistake in research is not allowing enough time to cover the destination. It's inevitable that you will discover some new unexpected place that you want to explore, and there is never enough time to do everything. I still make this mistake, even after writing guidebooks for almost a decade!

The most common mistake in guidebook writing is using the book as a soapbox to spout one's opinions. Writers should certainly not be shy about expressing their opinions, but readers get turned off by a preachy, snide or sarcastic tone in the text. They want to learn from the guidebook, but not be lectured by it.

What are the main differences between guidebook writing and writing for a newspaper, magazine, or website?

Guidebook writing comes in relatively big chunks, meaning that one assignment will keep you busy (and pay the bills) for several months. Assignments from newspapers, magazines and websites are usually much smaller, occupying a couple of days or perhaps a week. Compensation for these smaller assignments is usually commensurate with the amount of time required, but it does not account for travel and research or – the bane of my existence – sending out pitches.

The writing itself is also different. Guidebook writing is very structured, although there are plenty of opportunities to get creative within the confines of that structure. Depending on the demands of the publication, newspaper and magazine writing often allows for more creativity, writing from personal experience, crafting a story.

What, in your opinion, constitutes 'good' guidebook writing?

'Good' guidebook writing is accurate and informative, but it is also entertaining. It is insightful, funny and inspiring. It allows readers to make informed decisions about how they will spend their valuable travel time.

What constitutes 'bad' guidebook writing?

The obvious example of 'bad' guidebook writing is factual inaccuracy. But guidebook writing is also bad when it states the obvious instead of providing an insightful or informed perspective.

What are the rewards of guidebook writing as a career?

The biggest and best reward of a travel-writing career is seeing the world. Travel always inspires learning – even more so for guidebook writers, who must become experts about their destinations. We go everywhere, we see everything, we have incredible adventures; then we come home with a suitcase full of notes and a head full of stories and histories to share with others.

What has been the downside for you?

Being away from family, friends, cats etc. It's very important for me to have a stable home, but it's hard to keep it stable when I am travelling all the time. Now that I have children, I am not willing to leave them for long periods of time. Balancing work life and family life is challenging!

What's the role of the internet in the landscape of contemporary guidebook/travel writing?

With the proliferation of travel websites on the internet, there are more outlets for travel writing than ever before. There are also more sources of information than ever before. The web can be a very useful resource when it comes to verifying information for inclusion in guidebooks, but it's no substitute for first-hand experience!

How can would-be guidebook writers best utilise the web for their own professional development?

Get yourself a blog. Write for your friends at home, your parents, your own amusement. You'll get in the habit of writing for other people's consumption and will amass a good selection of travel-writing samples. Also promote your blog. Use social media. Read other blogs and interact with them. Don't be shy. This is not something I am adept at, but it's going to become more and more important as the internet expands.

Where do you see guidebook publishing going in the next five years?

Because of the widespread availability of free information, the publishing industry is going to have to refine its products so they offer an added value that people are willing to pay for. I think technology will play a huge role, with digital guidebooks and apps that incorporate audio, video and other elements that we can't even imagine. For example, it won't be long until guidebooks include virtual tours of Ancient Rome or Machu Picchu that allow travellers to experience the place as it was in its heyday. Technology will also make it easier for publishers to put together customised products that fit individual traveller's needs: customised itineraries, thematic walking tours, one-stop trip-planning tools. I also see more interaction between publishers, writers and readers. The industry needs to find a way to take advantage of the increased opportunities to get feedback from readers.

Any other tips or reflections you would offer would-be guidebook writers?

Remember that life is trade-offs. This is not an easy job. The hours are long, the pay is short and the benefits (capital B benefits like healthcare and retirement plans) are non-existent. But the small-b benefits are infinite. We guideebook authors definitely have more than our fair share of once-in-a-lifetime experiences, and that's what makes it all worthwhile.

That, and meeting our fellow travellers, who lug those books around, trust our opinions, share our adventures, forgive our oversights (hopefully) and make the planet a little less lonely.

~ *Part 2* ~

THE CRAFT
OF TRAVEL
WRITING

THE BRAVE NEW WORLD OF TRAVEL PUBLISHING
OFFERS A WIDER-THAN-EVER RANGE OF POSSIBILITIES
FOR YOUR WRITING, FROM SIMPLY SHARING YOUR
EXPERIENCES AND THOUGHTS TO TRYING TO MAKE
TRAVEL WRITING A FULL-TIME PROFESSION. LET'S
EXPLORE YOUR OPTIONS.

WHAT TO DO WITH YOUR WRITING

The first thing you need to determine is your goal as a travel writer – what you want to do with your travel writing, and what you want your travel writing to do for you.

If your principal goal is to share your travel experiences with others, without necessarily receiving compensation, you have more opportunities now than ever before. The internet has evolved to the point where virtually anyone with access to a computer can create a website where they can post their writings and photographs. There are now literally thousands of self-created blogs where everyday travellers are sharing their wanderings with the world. There are also third-party websites where you can post your experiences and opinions. If you just want to create and communicate, these options are for you.

If you want to combine communication and compensation, you'll want to target websites that pay, as well as newspapers and magazines. Writing books, whether guidebooks or travel literature titles, is another option. Writers dedicated to making a living from their travel writing will consider all of these and aim for a mix that makes best use of their knowledge and experience to maximize exposure and earnings.

The travel-writing trail is long, and there are numerous goal-destinations along the way, from Just-Posting-My-Journal and Writing-as-a-Hobby to Trying-to-Make-a-Living and Want-to-be-the-Next-Bill-Bryson. We'll talk about appropriate strategies and outlets for these later in this section. First, to give you some sense of where your desired destination on that trail should be, let's talk about what it takes to be a travel writer.

WHAT IT TAKES TO BE A TRAVEL WRITER

THE QUINTESSENTIAL QUALITIES

While travel writing can be one of the most agreeable professions on the planet, it's not for everyone. In fact, trying to make a living as a travel writer can be extremely demanding and daunting, requiring a particular temperament and setting limits on your lifestyle.

What are some of the qualities you need?

Flexibility

One of the hallmarks of the travel writer's life is its general instability and spontaneity. This is equally true both at home and on the road. At home, you have to be able to drop everything and take off for a far-flung destination at a moment's notice. Your life is dictated by the whims of editors and printer deadlines. To a certain extent, you can negotiate timelines with editors, but often their deadlines just cannot be adjusted – and then, if you're not flexible, you risk losing the commission (or assignment, as it is called in the US). You might also risk building yourself a reputation for saying 'No', which you definitely don't want to have in the close-knit travel editorial world.

On the road you also need to leave room for the unexpected. You may need to alter your itinerary to take in a once-every-seven-years festival you hadn't known about, or to spend an impromptu afternoon with the wine-maker who promises to make a fascinating subject for your article.

The moral is this: the more flexible you are, the better.

Adaptability

The second quality is a corollary to the first. If you want to maximise your chances as a travel writer, you have to be equally ready to explore the heart of Paris and the heart of Papua New Guinea. This means that you have to have a closet full of suitable clothing and accoutrements but, even more important, you have to have a head full of suitable attitudes. Are you equally at home on high seas and low roads? Can you keep your cool in hot situations? Is your stomach strong or are you susceptible to illness? Could you hop from an expedition ship in the Antarctic to a $15-a-night hut on an isolated South Pacific island and then to a five-star hotel in London? To take the maximum advantage of such opportunities, you have to be adaptable.

Frugality

Let's get this out of the way right now: it's not likely that you're going to get rich as a travel writer. Not in terms of money, anyway. You will certainly accumulate an uncommon wealth of experience, but to be a travel writer, you need to be able to live on a precarious income. If you are a freelancer you never know how much you're going to earn in a year, and you don't know when the money you *have* earned is going to come in. Some publications will pay you on acceptance of a piece, while others may not pay you until your piece has been published – and that could be many months or even years after your initial outlay. Some publications will pay automatically and on time; others will have to be reminded many times before you finally receive your payment. As a result, the commitment of significant, regular, ongoing expenses – a mortgage or school fees, for example – does not fit well with the freelance travel writer's life. If you are lucky enough to get a staff job as a travel writer, you will at least have a regular income you can count on but, generally speaking, the travel writer's lifestyle is a frugal one – and you need to be content with that. We'll talk in more detail about money matters later in this section (see p174).

An Understanding Family

The 'here today, gone tomorrow' nature of the travel writer's life takes a significant toll on friendships, and of course on more permanent and intimate relationships. You have to have an extraordinarily understanding and supportive partner who is able to carry on without you virtually at the drop of a hat, for uncertain – and sometimes prolonged – periods of time. If you have children, the situation is further compounded. This complaint by a UK travel journalist's wife (who wishes to remain anonymous) is telling:

> In one year my husband managed to be away for my 40th birthday, our sixth wedding anniversary (he was also away for our fifth), our first daughter's third birthday and my brother's wedding. These are all dates he'd had in his diary for months and months, but we just can't afford to turn down work due to prior family commitments.

Even friends can become irritated by your comings and goings, and feel that they can't rely on you – they'll complain that they just don't know if you'll be there for them. In addition, when you *are* there you seem to be working all the time – working long hours is one of the only ways you can make travel writing pay. All in all, in committing yourself to the travel writer's lifestyle, you relinquish a certain amount of control over your own life – and the people in your life have to be satisfied with that.

Curiosity

Curiosity is one of the prime characteristics common to all great travel writers – they are constantly studying the world around them, asking how things work and why they appear the way they do. They always observe and absorb, and they always talk to people – waiters, taxi drivers, sales assistants, fellow travellers. It is essential to have a passionate and insatiable curiosity about the world, and it is equally essential to keep recharging this curiosity so that you bring a fresh eye and enthusiasm to each new place and story. It will set your research, reporting and writing apart from the pack.

Pluck

Travel isn't easy, especially when you're on a mission to track down information and experiences that will make good travel stories. No matter how exhausted and overwhelmed you may be, you have to keep plugging on, overcoming cultural differences, leaping over language barriers, smoothly swallowing stomach-tumbling foods. You have to find the courage to talk with people you've never met, and to learn to trust the kindness of strangers. Time after time, place after place, you can't give up until you've got your story and then you can't give up until you've written it down and the editor has accepted it. And then it's time to start the next story.

Self-Motivation & Discipline

If you are a freelancer, you are your own and only boss, and procrastination is your enemy. You have to make yourself sit down at your desk every day, organise your material, plan your story and write. You need the self-motivation to repeatedly rework and resubmit your articles, and the organisational skills to manage travel schedules, workloads, deadlines, finances and networking. On the road you need the discipline to be continually researching, interviewing, taking notes and gathering information. Wherever you are, travel writing can be a relentless, ongoing, time-consuming balancing act that requires unstinting dedication.

Perseverance

Think of your favourite travel writer. Whoever they are, at some time in their life they were unknown, struggling to get a foothold in the writing world, just as you are today. They faced rejection, probably many times, but they always persevered, continuing to send in their proposals and stories to editors. To survive as a travel writer, you too need the confidence, ability and just plain thick skin to bounce back from rejection after rejection. You need a tenacious faith in yourself and an inventive perseverance. The same applies for temporary setbacks on the road. If an avalanche has closed the route to your destination, you hire a horse. If the local tourism office doesn't have the information you need, you track down the long-time resident who is happy to spend an hour telling you neighbourhood tales. Somehow you find a way to accomplish what you need to do.

Passion

Finally, and fundamentally, you have to have passion – passion for people, passion for the world, passion for the whole business of travelling and for exploring and integrating your discoveries into precise and palpable prose. Travel writing is essentially a lonely profession, and it is your passion that will sustain and reward you.

THE GLAMOUR VERSUS THE HARD WORK

So there you are on the African savannah, notebook in hand, camera around your neck, bouncing through the bush in hot pursuit of the king of beasts. Later on you'll be sitting around the campfire recounting the day's exploits while sampling the local beer.

Sounds wonderful, doesn't it? But to get there, you had to fly for a day and a half, squeezed into an economy-class seat between an apprentice sumo wrestler and a man whose personal beliefs forbid bathing. You spent a skin-slapping night on a flea-infested mattress, then had your bones rearranged on a bus bounding over a potholed highway. Your stomach hadn't adjusted well to all the time and temperature changes, so you subsisted on bottled water and biscuits.

And now, while others snore blissfully away, you sit in your tent scribbling into your notebook by lamplight, having cursed the flat battery in your laptop. The following afternoon, while others nap, you interview the driver and the cook. And on the day when everyone sleeps in after the late-night bush trek, you get up before sunrise to photograph the tawny dawn light. Now, is that glamour tarnishing just a bit?

While travel writing certainly has the reputation of being an alluring profession, 95 per cent of the job involves a lot of hard work. It's gathering minute details on hotels, bus timetables, restaurants and walking tours. It's researching which god did what, which ruler took over from whom and when, and what is signified by the curious ceremony that's performed every third Friday in May. It's waiting for planes and trains, buses and ferries, *tuk-tuks* and trishaws. It's swatting mosquitoes and squatting over hole-in-the-floor toilets. It's eating alone night after night, while whispering couples glance piteously your way. It's enviously eyeing all the people languorously sunning themselves on the beach and realising that you've got six more beaches to check out before lunch.

Being a travel writer can be lonely, exhausting and depressing. You're always on the lookout for a useful anecdote or scoping an angle. You can't ever let up, because you're always working. And that's just the travelling part. After the trip you have to sell your piece – and that can be a very time-consuming and energy-draining process. Even if your work has been commissioned beforehand, you have to be patient until the editor finds time to read it, and you may have to rewrite your article substantially after they've read it.

BURNOUT

Burnout is a major factor in the travel writer's life. You grow tired of gruelling travel schedules; of airports, train stations and bus depots; of late departures and late arrivals; of packing and unpacking; of trying to drum up the enthusiasm to explore some new uncomfortable corner of the world; of juggling home life and road life. You have to strive constantly to balance fickle earnings with fixed expenses in order to pay your bills and maintain ongoing accounts. You have to set aside money for unexpected expenses and, in the US, take care of your own health care. Both personally and practically, it can feel like you're always playing catch-up.

It's important to heed the warning signals, and to structure your life accordingly. One antidote is to take a purely pleasure trip at least once a year. If you find yourself burning out in the middle of a trip, try to turn off your mental note-taking machine for a morning and just wander at will, for pleasure, or laze on the beach. Most successful travel writers ground themselves by building in a certain number of months at home between trips; they catch up on relationships and bills, write the pieces they've researched, and recharge their batteries.

OVERCOMING WRITER'S BLOCK

Sometimes I get up in the morning and just can't think of anything to write, or what I do write comes out all wrong. In my early writing days when this happened, I would while away an hour staring into the void – or clean the refrigerator for the 10th time or check yet again to see if the mail had come – but over the years I've found two techniques that help get the words flowing. The first is to write about my writer's block: 'Today, for some reason, I just can't get started writing. I'm not sure why. I wonder if it's because of the pizza I ate last night, or maybe it's just because I don't know how to get where I know I need to be in my story today. The problem is bringing that village back to life. Here's what I remember...' Suddenly, I've forgotten about my writer's block and started writing my piece again.

The second technique follows the model that John Steinbeck used when he wrote *East of Eden*. He kept a notebook. In the left-hand pages of the notebook he wrote a daily diary – this was his way of warming up his writing engine. In the right-hand pages of the same book he wrote the novel itself. I have adapted a version of this. If I simply can't get going on my story, I start writing about whatever comes to mind – the Yosemite hike we did over the weekend, the Borges story I read the night before, the glistening cheesecake in the refrigerator, the Polynesian beach I wish I were lying on... I just start writing about whatever is occupying my mind, and somehow this unlocks me and liberates my imagination to get back into the story again.

SOME STRAIGHT TALK ABOUT EARNINGS

If all the people on the planet who make a living solely from their travel writing (excluding travel guidebook writers) were brought together in one room, they would number only around three dozen. Most of the guests at this globe-girdling gathering would write books for a living, and their income would be a mix of advance payments for their new books and royalties from their old ones, supplemented by a few travel magazine or newspaper pieces a year. Only a very few would make a living exclusively from writing articles for magazines, newspapers and websites – there simply isn't enough work to go around, and it just isn't well paid enough.

In today's publishing world, many travel writers outlay their own time and money upfront without any guarantee that they'll ever see any money. Even if and when their article is finally published, if they were to calculate the hours that went into the travel, research and writing of the piece, they'd need a microscope to see their hourly wage.

Others who choose the self-publishing route pour hours, energies and dollars into creating a beautiful, bountiful blog, only to realize they have no strategy and no means for monetizing it.

Another reality to consider in the earnings picture is the lack of any Freelancers Retirement Fund Limited that will squirrel money away for you and dole it out after you've stopped wandering and scribbling. You have to do that yourself. Many travel writers in their fifties and sixties are only thinking about this now, and realising that they should have started saving for this phase of life decades ago.

The fundamental caveat is that you must be realistic about the amount of money you can earn as a travel writer – but if you are able and willing to try to make travel writing your primary source of income, more power to you. And good luck!

Earnings in the UK

Pay varies enormously in the UK, and how much you can earn in a year will depend on who you write for, how often your pieces are published, and how hard you work. As the quality newspapers have a weekly or biweekly travel section, freelance travel writers often find themselves writing more pieces for newspapers than for magazines, which are normally published monthly. Pay for newspaper articles varies from £200 to £500 per 1000 words; for travel magazines the rate ranges between £150 and £400 per 1000 words (of course, well-known writers or regular contributors are paid more). However, the length of a standard destination piece in the UK is around 1000 to 2000 words, so this needs to be factored in when you're calculating how many articles you need to write to make a living. Sometimes you might be commissioned to write 3000 words or more, especially for a magazine, but it's rare.

Expenses are rarely paid on top of your article fee, because it is assumed you'll be negotiating 'freebies' – trips arranged for low or no cost with airlines, hotels and other travel providers in return for coverage in the article you write, usually in the fact box (or sidebar, as it is called in the US) accompanying your story. (The attitude towards freebies is very different in the US, and is discussed on p197.) Procuring such deals with airlines and hotels can take up a prodigious amount of your precious time. Of course, travelling also takes up a lot of your time, and days when you're travelling are days when you are not earning – in effect, you are paid to write, not travel. This is why you need to write as many articles as you can from one trip. Another point to consider is that many articles are commissioned 'on spec' – this means that a travel editor has said they like the idea of what you might write but will only agree to run it (and pay you) once they have seen your copy. It is also much more difficult to negotiate free travel or accommodation with an 'on spec' piece as there are no guarantees of coverage for the service provider.

Earnings in the US

Very few US-based freelance writers make more than $100,000 a year; the vast majority earn in the vicinity of $15,000 to $40,000 a year. A very good scenario would see you being lucky enough to receive six assignments from major magazines in one year. If each assignment was for an article of 3000 words, and the magazines paid an average of $1.50 a word, that would come to $4500 per story and a grand total of $27,000. That would be it, and you'd still have all your life expenses to cover, from housing and food to medical costs and phone bills. Unlike the situation in the UK, you would at least be compensated for any expenses incurred, but could you possibly survive on this amount?

To be even more realistic, few US magazines would pay $1.50 a word to a new writer. Top magazines would most likely start you at $1 a word for articles ranging from short pieces (250 words) published at the beginning of the magazine to longer features (4000 words) in the middle sections. And some magazines pay dramatically less than this, down to 10 cents a word.

Major newspapers pay considerably less than major magazines, with most of them paying between $200 and $500 for articles of 1000 to 2000 words. Rates do vary, however; for example, in March 2013 the *Los Angeles Times* paid $750 for cover features and $500 for inside stories, the *Chicago Tribune* and *San Francisco Chronicle* paid $500 for a lead story and from $200 to $350 for inside stories, and the *Miami Herald* paid $250 to $300 for a cover story and $100 to $250 for inside stories.

Earnings in Australia

Most Australian newspapers pay a rate of 50 cents a word, rising to perhaps 70 cents if you're very lucky. Features range from 1500 to 2000 words, and inside pieces vary between 700 and 1000 words. Metropolitan and smaller regional newspapers can pay a set fee of as little as AU$50. Magazines vary wildly, from a set fee of AU$350 to as much as AU$1 per word from the majors. As in the UK, expenses are rarely paid, reviewers for publications such as restaurant guides being the fortunate exception. Making a living solely from travel writing is tough in a relatively small market such as Australia, and most writers end up looking for staff jobs.

Travel Literature

If you are writing a literary travel book on contract you will at least get some money up front from the publishers – this is called an 'advance' and the publishers award it in the hope that sales of your book will recoup that sum and more. An advance for your first book from a major publisher will probably be in the region of £10,000 in the UK, $15,000 in the US or AU$20,000 in Australia, though there are plenty of first-time writers who have published a book for much less, and smaller publishers will pay correspondingly smaller advances. Unless you have a supplemental income, this advance will have to fund your travels and your general living expenses for the length of time it takes to research and write your book – generally one to two years. Of course, if your first book is a success and you want to write a second, the financial picture can brighten considerably.

Travel Guidebooks

Many travel guidebook authors write full-time, either for one publisher or for a variety of companies, with only one- or two-day gaps in between assignments (for more detailed information on earnings for guidebook authors see p229). The formula for paying guidebook writers depends on where you are researching (for example, whether it is a cheap or expensive destination), how well the publisher calculates the book is going to sell (the author of a guide to Thailand will be paid more than the author of a book on Vanuatu), and on your reputation to deliver a sparkling manuscript to length and on time. As with newspapers and magazines, some guidebook publishers pay better than others, and some take expenses into consideration while others don't. Very roughly, a full-time guidebook writer can expect to earn between £10,000 and £25,000 per year in the UK, from $20,000 to $45,000 in the US, and approximately AU$30,000 to AU$50,000 in Australia.

IN-HOUSE VERSUS FREELANCING

There are two main avenues for making travel writing your career: either working as a salaried staff member for a newspaper or magazine, or working as a freelancer.

Working as a Staff Writer

To be brutally realistic, staff-writing jobs are as elusive as the creature Peter Matthiessen seeks and never quite finds in his classic work of travel literature, *The Snow Leopard.*

There are in total perhaps three dozen full-time travel writer jobs at newspapers in the US, the UK and Australia, and these positions are usually occupied by long-time staffers who have cut their teeth on the city desk and the business beat, for example, before being offered the plum of travel (and as newspapers tighten their belts in tough economic times, these jobs are becoming even rarer and more precarious). Even the best of these jobs require a good deal of decidedly unglamorous desk-bound work making telephone calls and internet expeditions to research car-rental rates and single-traveller supplements for the kinds of practical pieces the staff writer is frequently called on to produce.

The picture is the same for the very few staff-writing jobs on travel magazines: the staff writers for the most part fill in the holes in the magazine's editorial picture-puzzle, writing news-oriented pieces, industry stories, book and product reviews and the like. Occasionally a staff writer may be allowed to take a long weekend to some nearby or far-flung locale, but those meaty middle-of-the-book stories are usually written by freelance writers. In terms of travel and writing, probably the best gig you can hope for is to become a contributing editor (despite the name, this means someone who writes regularly for one publication; it actually has nothing to do with editing) – but these coveted spots go to people who already have a reputation (and who actually enhance the magazine's reputation by appearing on its masthead and in its pages). And while the contributing editors may be guaranteed some kind of annual stipend from a publication (usually in exchange for a specified number of articles or for enhanced rates of pay for what they do write), they do not enjoy the perks of full-time employment.

An added complication is that in-house travel writing jobs or travel desk jobs at newspapers and magazines are rarely advertised. Travel publishing is a very small world and most jobs go to internal candidates or are advertised by word of mouth to colleagues in the industry. The plain truth is that if you are just starting out as a travel writer it will be extremely difficult for you to score a staff writing job. Even if you have a few published articles under your

THE FINE ART OF REPURPOSING

Repurposing is one of the greatest tools – and challenges – of the travel writer's job. The aim is to make as many different publishable articles as possible from one trip. The key here is having a good sense of the different markets you want to write for, and the different kinds of stories, or angles, that appeal to those markets. Think this way, and even in the planning process, you can divide your trip into likely story subjects. Your aim should be to get three or four articles from each trip.

Let's plan a one-week stay in Kyoto, Japan. With the proper planning and execution, here are four stories that could be written from that one trip.

Cultural

Let's say you arrange to spend two nights on a homestay with a Japanese family. Your first piece, based on this stay, describes the riches and revelations of overnighting with a family and seeing Kyoto through their eyes, living it through their lives. You sell this to a general-interest travel magazine that appreciates the different perspective on an oft-described destination.

Destination/Quest

Before you went to Kyoto, a friend told you about a particular shop that sells old *ukiyo-e* woodblock prints. He vaguely remembered that it was in the covered shopping area near the river, and said once you got there anyone could tell you the way. So you spent a day in search of the shop – and as it turned out, your search led to all kinds of revealing detours and delights before, at the end of the day, a kindly kimono shopkeeper went a half-hour out of her way to walk you to the tiny woodblock print wonderland. Your second piece describing this odyssey would capture Kyoto's venerable neighbourhoods, spirit and artistic – and personal – treasures. You sell this to a high-culture magazine that specialises in coverage of the arts.

Service

On the third and fourth nights of your visit, you stayed at a traditional Japanese inn, or *ryokan*. There are many riches to this experience, but one of the most memorable is taking a bath the traditional Japanese way, first soaping yourself off outside the tub, then sinking slowly into the steaming water and letting the cares of the day ease away. Your third piece would be a straightforward 'service' guide to taking a Japanese bath – what to do and what not to do, with recommendations on places to enjoy this unique experience, and some contextual reflections on the deep value of a good Japanese soak. You sell this to the in-flight magazine of an airline that has just recently inaugurated service to Japan.

Personal Essay

The rock garden at Ryoanji Temple is one of Kyoto's most famous and sacred sites. On your second morning you went there to see what all the fuss was about. Inexplicably, unexpectedly, you felt a deep connection with the place. You returned at noon on the third day and in the late afternoon on the fifth day. Your fourth piece would be a personal essay describing the history and appearance of the rock garden, and then evoking and reflecting on the hold the place exerted on you – and the lessons in attentiveness, impermanence and wholeness that it bestowed. You sell this to a literary travel website.

In the age of the internet, repurposing has taken on another potential as well: you can make creations in multiple media from one trip. To take the subject examples above, you could keep a blog describing your homestay, augmented with a video of the family's children showing you how to put on a kimono; you could do a video or a photo portfolio recording your quest to find the *ukiyo-e* shop and the discoveries you made on the way; you could produce a video on how to take a traditional Japanese bath; and you could post a photo gallery accompanied by a podcast reading of your reflections on the rock garden at Ryoanji.

The key to this kind of multimedia repurposing is to think imaginatively about the different ways of evoking a subject and the lessons of that subject, and the medium that is most appropriate to the particular qualities of the place or experience that you want to evoke. For centuries the writer's traditional tools were words, then some travel writers added images to their repertoire. For the 21st-century travel writer – perhaps more accurately if less felicitously called 'content producer' – the quiver of artistic arrows has expanded even further.

belt, the same applies. However, if you start off as a freelance writer, become known, get a good reputation and move in the right circles, then you may hear of a job on offer or be tapped on the shoulder.

Another way of breaking into salaried employment – and occasionally to get your name in print – at a newspaper or magazine is to apply for unpaid work experience on the travel desk. In the US such work experience is called an internship and is usually offered in affiliation with an academic program. Working on a travel desk means that you are the office anchor, doing all the administration that goes along with the travel pages – answering the phone, dealing with reader queries, organising travel arrangements etc. It may also include some commissioning, editing and a little writing. Although a work experience intern on the travel desk is often at everyone's beck and call, it's a wonderful training ground for any would-be travel writer. If you show initiative and flair, you might be asked to do some research on a piece and to write it up – and suddenly, *voilà!*, your name's in print. Doing unpaid work for a busy travel desk also gives you a foot in the door and means that you could be 'in the right place at the right time' when a suitable position comes along. From here the only way is up, heading toward your long-term goal of becoming a staff travel writer.

The benefits of a staff job, as opposed to freelance travel writing, are a steady income, health coverage (in the US at least), the camaraderie of office life and regular publication of your work. Writing as a staffer means you avoid the frustration, uncertainty and general agony of freelance life – continually pitching to editors for work, never knowing where or if your articles will be published, never knowing when your money will come in, and hardly ever taking a holiday because it is unpaid. In some ways, having a reliable outlet for your work is even more valuable than having the steady income.

So what could possibly be the downside of working in-house? There are the problems and pitfalls – the Machiavellian minutiae – of office politics, for one thing. Also, like all other office workers, you essentially have to go to work every day (when you're not travelling for work), and you don't have a lot of control over what you do. If you're told to write 1000 words on the history and highlights of consumer taxes, you do it.

However, as an in-house writer you'll have access to some fantastic travel opportunities. And more importantly, working in-house, even if it is only for a short period of time, is an invaluable way of building up your contacts if you later want to go freelance. The bottom line is that as a novice travel writer you'd be crazy to turn down a staff job if you were offered one. Take it, learn everything you possibly can, network like mad and then decide if you want to remain on staff or go freelance.

Working as a Freelancer

For most writers who choose the freelance life, the freedom of setting their own schedule far outweighs the benefits and perks of a salaried position. As a freelancer you can work when you want, on what you want; you usually have the freedom to write for several publications (as long as they are noncompeting), as opposed to only one; you can write all night and sleep all day if you wish. You are your own boss, and in control – and this is a rarity in the working world.

On the other hand, unless you have some sort of independent income, you're always wondering where your next payment is coming from. That is the hardest truth of the freelancer's life: the lack of certainty, stability and regularity. Even the most famous freelancers cannot assume a steady income. When Paul Theroux, perhaps the best-known travel writer in the US, was researching his book on Africa, *Dark Star Safari*, he proposed Africa-related articles to virtually all the major magazines in the US – and did not get one commission.

One thing you'll definitely need to develop as a full-time freelancer is fiscal discipline. You may receive one big sum in January and not get another until July, so you need to develop a system to make your money stretch through the lean periods. If you're writing a travel literature book, there's the problem of making an advance last until your royalties kick in – which they will only do if your book sells well. Similarly, if you're working on a guidebook, payments normally come in three instalments, months apart: there's an up-front fee for signing the contract, a payment upon acceptance of your work and the final cheque upon publication.

If you're writing for newspapers, magazines and websites, smaller amounts of money will be coming in on a very ad hoc basis and you'll never know from one day to the next whether you'll be rich or poor that week. Some outlets pay at the end of the month after the month of publication – so if your story appears in the first week of July, you won't see the cheque until September. The bottom line is that as a freelancer you need to set up an efficient article- and payment-tracking system to ensure you don't fall into a financial crevasse.

Part-Time Travel Writing

Using travel writing as an additional occupation to supplement your earnings and career is much more common than depending on full-time travel writing work. Some part-timers teach (those long school holidays can be spent on the road) or work as tour guides or cruise-ship lecturers; others expand their specialty by writing restaurant or book reviews, personality profiles or feature stories on the arts and culture. Some write corporate copy – year-end reports, catalogue texts, corporate brochures or press releases, for example. Some of them work as editors, copy editors or fact-checkers; some as flight attendants or booksellers.

In many ways, it makes a lot of sense to try to make travel writing a complement to the job that you depend on for your livelihood. You can research travel articles during holiday periods and on weekends. This takes the pressure off your travel writing and allows you to ease into it. It also gives you more flexibility to pursue and write the stories you really want to do, knowing that you're not dependent on their sale to put bread on the table and a roof over your head.

Whether your travel writing is a full-time profession or a part-time passion, publishing is the professional pathway you'll want to follow. How do you begin to get your travel writing published? We'll explore this territory straight ahead.

GETTING PUBLISHED

We've talked about knowing your goals and about the riches and requisites of the travel writer's life. Now let's focus on the different markets that publish travel writing, and on how to begin to get published in those markets.

Whether you are writing for newspapers, magazines or the web, you will follow one of two approaches: you can pitch an idea or proposal to an editor before you write the actual piece, or you can write the piece in its entirety and then submit it. (The other option, of course, is self-publishing. We'll discuss the pros and cons of this in our section on the web, starting on page 216.) Generally speaking, if you are a beginning writer, it's unlikely that a publication or website will commit to publishing a piece by you based on the idea alone, without reading the finished piece. So if you are starting out, the best advice is

HINTS & TIPS
There are a number of different strategies you can follow to get started in your travel writing career but, in essence, they come down to this progression of points: know your goals; know your markets; start local and start small; build up your clips, your confidence and your contacts; hone your craft and your expertise; keep your eyes – and your door – open for opportunities; keep your focus on your goals.

to write your story first, with a particular publication (and so story angle) in mind, and then submit it.

The key to success in this process – and it merits repeating, because it is so important – is to know your market intimately and thoroughly. So now we'll look closely at the different media markets in different regions.

NEWSPAPERS & MAGAZINES

The three main print outlets for travel stories are newspaper travel sections, travel magazines and lifestyle magazines with a travel component.

Get a feel for the types of stories they publish. Are the destinations mostly short-haul, long-haul or a mix of the two? Is family travel an important element, or do most stories target the adventurous, independent traveller? Are articles tailored to bare-bones, mainstream or luxury budgets, or do they cover a spectrum of destinations and options? What is the tone, the approach and the length of the stories? Are most of the articles service pieces, round-ups or destination based? Are there any regular formats that appear each week?

In the UK, for example, the *Independent on Saturday* always features a stopover destination piece called '48 Hours in...' If you have a good idea that fits this format, you'll be offering copy that you know the travel editor needs each week. Conversely, if you offer a city-break piece that is not in the '48 Hours' format, it is not likely to be considered. Similarly, in Australia the travel pages of papers such as the *Age* and the *Sydney Morning Herald* regularly feature a mix of news and destination pieces, following a clearly identifiable editorial template.

In the US, a good example of regular formatting is *National Geographic Traveler* magazine's three round-up sections that appear at the front of the magazine every month: Hotel Central, Cutting Loose, and City Life. These cover the globe with a wide mix of short pieces grouped under the same sub-categories each issue. Study these and you'll vastly improve your chances for publication by proposing an 'On the Road' story for the Cutting Loose section, or an 'On Foot' guide for City Life.

Detailed research will pay off. Keep brief notes about the stories your targeted publication has printed. Also make use of the publication's online archives – you can search by topic and destination to find any stories similar to the one you're planning to pitch. Such research will enable you to begin a proposal for a piece on Swiss chocolatiers, for example, by saying, 'I'm aware that you published a story on Belgian chocolates a year ago, but...' At the very least, this research will help you tailor your articles to a particular publication. In addition, you will never commit the cardinal sin of offering

SPECIALISATION

As mentioned in Part I, one of the best ways to advance professionally is to develop a particular specialty or focus. This might be a geographical focus, such as Eastern Europe, Southeast Asia or Hawaii; a focus on a particular mode of travel, such as hiking, budget travel or the luxury beat; a specific subject niche, such as food or culture; or a stylistic niche, such as humour.

Food

Food is a favourite: whether our on-the-road interests tend toward biking, Bach-ing or beachcombing, we all have to eat. Writing about food isn't as easy as devouring it, of course, but newspapers and magazines do publish a wide range of food writing, from quick 'brights' – short, front-of-the-book articles – to feature-length pieces.

Here is an example of a bright from *Gourmet* magazine, written by Jonathan Gold, that vividly brings a see-worthy site in Seoul to life:

Tsukiji in Tokyo and New York's late Fulton Fish Market may have more of a hold on the popular imagination, but the Noryangjin Marine Products Market is one of the greatest food spectacles on earth. A yawning structure in central Seoul, as large as several football stadiums laid end to end, it's crammed snout-to-elbow with exotic sea creatures from every conceivable aquatic locale: acres of stingrays aligned precisely as roof tiles; gilt lengths of ribbonfish; regiments of pike; oceans of halibut; endless trays of pickled clams; and more kinds of jacks and mackerels and anchovies than could be identified with a libraryful of reference books. As you weave through the 700-odd stalls, dodging the blasts of frigid water that the merchants occasionally sluice through the aisles, and the very small men charging through bearing very large bags of ice, you may notice the absence of anything resembling a fishy reek, replaced instead by the fresh smell of the sea.

Koreans favor species toward the bottom rungs of the food chain, so while you will see the occasional bluefin or salmon at Noryangjin, they are far outnumbered by croaker and corvina, bubbling clams and giant octopus whose arms extend farther than Shaquille O'Neal's. You will also pass miles of live-seafood tanks, many of them filled with the usual lobsters, prawns, and crabs, but also finfish of every description, and a disconcerting array of bottom-of-the-sea stuff whose uses are difficult to contemplate. (It's hard to know which sea squirts are more alarming – the ones that look a little like warty, pulsing pineapples, or the pink ones resembling throbbing uncircumcised phalluses, right down to the undulating slit at the business end.)

There is a big auction area on the second floor of the 24-hour market, but almost all of the downstairs stalls are prepared to slice any one of their fish into sashimi for you on the spot – or better yet, to put your purchases into plastic bags and point you toward one of the cavelike seafood restaurants that line the north end of the complex, where they will serve up your sashimi in the traditional Korean style with sesame leaves, bean paste, sliced chiles, and raw garlic, and transform the rest of the creature into a seething cauldron of spicy, bright-red fish soup. Throw in some steamed Korean blue crabs, a few grilled prawns, some kimchi, and a bottle or two of soju, and you've got the greatest Korean breakfast in the world.

The stalls are unnumbered and unnamed, but I like the crab stall toward the extreme northwest corner of the market run by Robert, who spent much of his life in Wichita, Kansas – you will spot the phone number 813-9780 above his stall.

This piece is lively, quick, picturesque, and to the point. Without wasting a word, Gold captures the look, feel and smell of the place for the armchair traveller and conveys the essential information for anyone visiting Seoul who might be moved to stop by. With fishy pith, his bright serves up a tasty combination of food, culture and practical advice.

Now consider this can't-stop-reading lead from a *Guardian* piece by Jane Dunford on mushroom-hunting:

Sitting at a table in an antique-filled dining room in the New Forest, I'm trying to identify a series of objects laid out before me. On one plate sits what looks like a dried human liver. It's big and red, but underneath it's the pale colour of naan bread.

'When it's really fresh there's jelly on top and it seems to drip blood if you cut into it,' says Jackie, my host.

This is a beefsteak mushroom, she reveals, very popular with London chefs and delicious when thinly sliced and fried with garlic. The large, fluffy-looking ball turns out to be a Chicken of the Woods – which does indeed have a headless hen-like appearance – and then there's a plate of more mushroomy-shaped mushrooms, 'spongy underneath' boletes and dimpled chanterelles.

I'm on a seminar at Gorse Meadow Guest House near Lymington with 10 other fungi fans, delving into the fascinating world of mushrooms. There are, I learn, around 3000 types in the New Forest alone, but we're only interested in identifying about 10 edible varieties.

This is a good example of a story that uses food as a portal to a deeper understanding of a place. Dunford's mysterious mushroom lead immediately draws us into her subject and sets us up for an entertaining and illuminating introduction to a corner of England through its fungi.

Culture

Culture can take many forms. You might take readers deep into the soul of Bali by exploring its local dances, evoke Aboriginal values and beliefs on an Australian outback odyssey, or illuminate one side of the New York aesthetic by investigating its booming gallery scene.

Here's how Tahir Shah, in the *Guardian*, introduces us to the soul of Morocco through the city of Fes:

Abdul-Lateef sits in the shade at the front of his shop, a glint in his eye and a week's growth of beard on his cheeks. With care, he weighs out half a dozen dried chameleons, wraps them in a twist of newspaper, and passes the packet to a young woman dressed in black.

'She will give birth to a handsome boy child,' says the shopkeeper when the woman has gone.

'Are you sure?'

Abdul-Lateef stashes the money into a pouch under his shirt. He scans the assortment of wares – mysterious pink powders, snake skins, live turtles, bundles of aromatic bark, and he smiles.

> 'We have been helping women like her for five centuries,' he says slowly, 'And never has a customer come to complain. Believe me, I speak the truth.'
>
> Walk through the bustle of Fes's medina and it's impossible not to be catapulted back in time. It is as if the old city is on a frequency of its own, set apart from the frenzied world of internet and iPods and all the techno clutter that fills our daily lives. Abdul-Lateef and his magic-medicinal stall are a fragment of a healing system that stretches back through centuries, to a time when Fes was itself at the cutting edge of science, linked by the pilgrimage routes to Cairo, Damascus and Samarkand.
>
> These days the low-cost airlines shuttle the curious back and forth to Europe. And everyone they bring is tantalised by what they find. Fes is the only medieval Arab city that's still absolutely intact. It's as if a shroud has covered it for centuries, the corner now lifted a little so we can peek in. Once the capital of Morocco, Fes is one of those rare destinations that's bigger than mass tourism, a city that's so self-assured, so grounded in its own identity, that it hardly seems to care whether the tourists come or not. Moroccans will tell you that it's the dark heart of their kingdom, that its medina has a kind of sacred soul.

Doesn't this make you want to wander into the very heart of Fes, with Shah as your guide?

Humour

Humour is exceedingly tricky because it is so subjective and often so culture-bound, but humorous travel pieces are always in demand. Travel humour tends to work best when it contains at least a dose of self-deprecation; making fun of others is not nearly as engaging or entertaining as making fun of yourself. Some great humorists whose work merits and rewards close scrutiny include Mark Twain, Bill Bryson, David Sedaris and Dave Barry.

Here are a couple of examples from the last two. First, David Sedaris writing in the *New Yorker* about an unfortunate incident on a plane:

> On the flight to Raleigh, I sneezed, and the cough drop I'd been sucking on shot from my mouth, ricocheted off my folded tray

*table, and landed, as I remember it, in the lap of the woman
beside me, who was asleep and had her arms folded across her
chest. I'm surprised that the force didn't wake her – that's how
hard it hit – but all she did was flutter her eyelids and let out a
tiny sigh, the kind you might hear from a baby.*

*Under normal circumstances, I'd have had three choices, the
first being to do nothing. The woman would wake up in her own
time, and notice what looked like a shiny new button sewn to
the crotch of her jeans. This was a small plane, with one seat
per row on Aisle A, and two seats per row on Aisle B. We were
on B, so should she go searching for answers I would be the first
person on her list. 'Is this yours?' she'd ask, and I'd look dumbly
into her lap.*

'Is what mine?'

*Option No. 2 was to reach over and pluck it from her pants,
and No. 3 was to wake her up and turn the tables, saying, 'I'm
sorry, but I think you have something that belongs to me.' Then
she'd hand the lozenge back and maybe even apologize, confused
into thinking that she'd somehow stolen it.*

*These circumstances, however, were not normal, as before
she'd fallen asleep the woman and I had had a fight. I'd known
her for only an hour, yet I felt her hatred just as strongly as I
felt the stream of cold air blowing into my face – this after she'd
repositioned the nozzle above her head, a final fuck-you before
settling down for her nap.*

And here's Dave Barry managing to make fun of himself and a venerable
Japanese art form without really offending anyone:

*When it comes to the classical arts, I'm basically an
unsophisticated low-rent Neanderthal philistine kind of guy,
which is why I'm probably just revealing my own intellectual
limitations and cultural myopia when I tell you that Kabuki is
the silliest thing I have ever seen onstage, and I have seen a man
juggle two rubber chickens and a birthday cake.*

*For one thing, all the actors were wearing costumes that
made them look like John Belushi on* Saturday Night Live
*playing the part of the samurai delicatessen clerk, only with
funnier haircuts. For another thing, since all Kabuki actors
are male, a man was playing the role of the heroine. According*

to the program notes, he was a famous Kabuki actor who was extremely skilled at portraying the feminine character by using subtle gestures and vocal nuances perfected over generations. What he looked like, to the untutored Western eye, was a man with a four-year supply of white make-up, mincing around the stage and whining. It was Belushi playing the samurai whining transvestite.

In fact, everybody seemed to whine a lot. It was all that happened for minutes on end. Kabuki has the same dramatic pacing as bridge construction. It's not at all unusual for a play to last ten hours. And bear in mind that one hour of watching Kabuki is the equivalent of seventeen hours spent in a more enjoyable activity, such as eye surgery.

From time to time, a member of the audience would yell something. This is also part of the Kabuki tradition; at key moments, audience members, sometimes paid by the performers, yell out a performer's family name, or words of appreciation. Our guide, Mr. Sato, had cautioned us that this yelling had to be done in a certain traditional way, and that we should not attempt it. It was a good warning – although I'm not sure what I would have yelled anyway. Maybe something like: 'NICE HAIRCUT!' Or: 'WAY TO MINCE!'

While gently poking fun at his subject and at himself, Barry also manages to slip in some key facts about Kabuki.

The advantages of specialisation are that it cultivates expertise in a particular area, subject or style, and that it can accordingly help establish you as the 'go-to' expert for editors and producers who are looking for content on your specialty. The disadvantage is that you might work yourself into a professional pigeonhole; if you get known for writing about Southeast Asia, for example, your editor may scoff when you propose a piece on Paris. Or if you establish yourself as a consummate humorist, you may have difficulty getting outlets to publish a serious essay or destination piece. As with most things in travel writing and life, specialisation is a question of balance. Developing a specialty in one area may be your springboard to articles on the wide world; your success will ultimately depend on your flexibility, imagination, perseverance and skill.

a travel editor a story that they have just run, and so risk taking a giant step backward in this tricky relationship.

Whether you are targeting a newspaper or a magazine, your first step should be to look on the publication's website for contributor guidelines or a style guide. If this information isn't available online, ring or email and request that a copy be sent to you; in the case of US newspapers, mail a self-addressed stamped envelope (an 'SASE') to the travel editor with a note requesting the guidelines. These guidelines will usually spell out what the editors are looking for in an article and how they prefer to deal with freelance writers. They should also advise on how your submission should be presented, and whether they require accompanying photographs (this is less likely in the UK). Having these contributor guidelines will help to maximise your chances of giving the editors what they want. As examples of these guidelines, we have reproduced the contributor guidelines for the UK's *Wanderlust* magazine and for *National Geographic Traveler* magazine and the Sunday travel section of the Los Angeles Times newspaper in the US; see p000.

There are broad differences in the ways writers need to approach and work with newspapers and magazines. There are also significant differences in practice between the UK and the US, while Australian and UK working methods are generally similar.

The UK Newspaper Scene

The UK newspaper scene has been in flux as free publications replace paid-for ones across the media spectrum. One such free publication is *Metro*, the nationwide free newspaper, which runs travel stories through the week. Free weekly magazines that compete with the newspapers for readers, including London's *Evening Standard* and *Time Out*, and the nationally distributed *Stylist* (aimed at women) and *Shortlist*, its masculine counterpart, also cover travel. Given this new scene, writers need to cast a wide net when looking for commissions and publishing opportunities.

Across the country there are more than 70 local and regional newspapers – daily or weekly – which are likely to carry travel stories. Often these papers will be syndicated, but they are always interested in local people doing interesting things, so travel writing opportunities shouldn't be discounted. While pay is lower with these publications, they're the best bet, so they're especially good options if you're starting out as a travel writer.

The highest circulation newspapers, and those with the highest profile and (usually) rates of pay, are the 'nationals'. These are split into three categories:

The 'red-top' tabloids: the *Daily Mirror*, the *Star* and the *Sun*, and their Sunday counterparts, the *Sunday Mirror*, the *People* and the *Sunday Sun*. Distinguished by their traditionally red-coloured mastheads and comparatively down-market sensibilities, these papers offer relatively slim travel coverage, and that coverage is usually handled in-house or by regular freelancers.

Middle-market tabloids: the *Daily Mail*, the *Mail on Sunday*, the *Daily Express* and the *Sunday Express*. These papers have larger travel sections, but again are usually written in-house or by regular freelancers – or by celebrities.

'Quality' newspapers (previously more commonly called 'broadsheets' because of their larger format, until they began downsizing in 2003): the *Guardian*, the *Independent*, the *Daily Telegraph* and the *Times*, plus the *Financial Times*. These papers publish their main travel issue on Saturday, sometimes adding a minor travel section during the week. Their Sunday equivalents – the *Independent on Sunday*, the *Sunday Telegraph* and the *Sunday Times* – also have substantial travel sections (except for the Financial Times, which has a single weekend edition).

A daily paper and its Sunday equivalent are usually compiled by totally different staff; this means that the *Times* and the *Sunday Times*, for example, have separate travel teams and travel editors for you to target. The size of these travel pages or pull-out supplements ranges from four to 24 pages.

Wales, Northern Ireland and Scotland also have national newspapers that publish travel stories tailored to their readers' interests.

The US Newspaper Scene

An enormous variety of US newspapers carry some form of travel content; these range from small-town dailies and free weekly city broadsheets to major metropolitan papers. Travel content in the small-town dailies and city broadsheets tends to focus on local getaways; the pay for these pieces is usually minimal, but they do offer writers the chance to get their bylines in print and to hone their skills.

All major urban newspapers publish travel content on Sunday. The best publishing opportunities are to be found in papers with the largest circulations, which also tend to have the largest travel sections. Such majors include the *New York Times*, the *Los Angeles Times*, the *Washington Post* and the *Chicago Tribune*. Although these papers publish the largest number of freelance articles every week, and so offer writers the best opportunities to be published, the competition with other freelance submissions is intense. Other newspapers that feature travel sections include the *Boston Globe*, the *San Francisco Chronicle*, the *Dallas Morning News*, the *Miami Herald* and the *Philadelphia Inquirer*.

As in the UK, the size of these travel sections runs anywhere from four to 20 pages, depending on the publication, the time of year and the number of advertisements it contains. Opportunities for freelancers vary greatly from paper to paper, and indeed from year to year. It's good practice to regularly analyse how much space is open to freelancers and what kinds of freelance stories are being published. Especially given the turbulence of the newspaper publishing world in recent years, would-be contributors should check to see the current status of a newspaper's travel section – Are they currently buying freelance articles? What kinds of articles are they particularly looking for? – before submitting articles for consideration.

The Australian Newspaper Scene

Australia has 20 national and metropolitan newspapers, and more than 120 regional and community papers. In general, you'll find the best travel content in the *Australian*, the Adelaide *Advertiser*, the Melbourne *Age*, the *Sydney Morning Herald*, the Brisbane *Courier Mail* and the *West Australian*. Travel is a feature of Sunday editions such as the *Sun-Herald*, the *Sunday Herald Sun*, the *Sunday Mail* in Brisbane and the *Sunday Mail* in Adelaide, the *Sunday Telegraph* and the *Sunday Times*. Travel sections range from four to 24 pages; see below for details of various papers' travel 'special section' schedules.

Special Sections

Most travel sections feature half a dozen to a dozen 'special' or 'theme' sections a year, presenting an exceptional opportunity for freelancers.

In the UK, special sections often concentrate on a particular part of the world – more often than not it's somewhere in Europe – and are produced in conjunction with the local tourist board. Typical special sections in the US include Cruising, Mexico, Hawaii, Family Travel, Europe and the Caribbean. In Australia the sections focus on regional and seasonal fare such as snow- or other activity-based holidays, mid-winter breaks and European, Asian and domestic destinations.

The themed sections are planned a year in advance, in conjunction with

HINTS & TIPS
Travel editors should include a calendar of special sections in their contributor guidelines; if not, ask the editor to send you a copy. It's a good idea to request special-section calendars from all the newspapers you're interested in and take full advantage of the expanded editorial possibilities they offer.

the papers' advertising sales staff – if the sales team knows that a specific section will be devoted to Hawaii, for example, they will have extra leverage to try to persuade a Hawaiian hotel owner to buy an ad in that section. The editorial content in these sections is not directly linked to the specific advertisers (that is, if a particular resort purchases an ad, this does not oblige the editor to publish a story about it), but the editor is obliged to put together a package of stories around that section's theme.

This is where your opportunity comes in. If you know that a particular newspaper will be publishing a special section on a particular date, you'll also know that the travel editor will be sourcing content specific to that destination or theme. In the UK you would contact the travel desk two to three months before publication with a proposal for a couple of articles; in the US you would send in two or three of your best relevant stories three months before the section's publication date.

Themed sections offer particularly good opportunities to publish niche, off-the-beaten-track or reflective essay pieces – an article on studying the hula, for example, or hiking a remote but rewarding trail.

Pitching to Newspapers

Travel editors are very busy people. In addition to travelling and writing (they often provide a weekly column and/or a few big stories each month), they also commission, edit and select the content for the weekly travel section; attend weekly editorial meetings; deal with advertising departments; process paperwork; read manuscripts (and return them if they have time); liaise with art and photography departments; and much more. The result of this busy schedule is that although travel editors might like to deal in a humane way with freelance writers, they don't always have the time. The hard truth is that they are not going to call you up and offer advice on how to improve your submission. Basically, if you submit a story to them, they'll read what you've written and if it is a good fit, they'll take it; otherwise, they'll reject it. Do not expect more than that.

A decade ago, snail mail was the standard method of contacting a travel editor with an unsolicited submission or a proposal. These days, however, email is so ubiquitous that most editors expect to receive submissions and proposals by email. Still, it is wise to read the contributor guidelines to see if there is a preferred method for submissions – some editors still want to be contacted by post – or a particular editor to whom your article or proposal should be directed. One preference all travel editors share: They do not want to be contacted by telephone (unless you have already built up a relationship with them).

PITCHING TO UK NEWSPAPERS
In the UK there are three main ways of pitching a story or a proposal to a newspaper.

Unsolicited Submission
This is when you send a completed article to a travel editor or travel desk out of the blue, on the off chance that they'll publish it. You have little idea whether your story is of interest, whether it fits with future publishing schedules, or if a similar article is due to be run this week or is in the pipeline. For all these reasons, this method offers the least likelihood of publication. For you it is also the least financially astute because you've incurred all your costs upfront with absolutely no idea if you'll be able to sell what you have written. In addition, you can send that article to only one newspaper at a time, unless you make it absolutely clear that you are offering it to more than one, and let the other(s) know once it has been accepted; this kind of multiple submission is usually only advisable for a time-sensitive story. Complicating matters further is the fact that travel editors often sit on submissions for months before you learn that it will never be used, or you open up the paper one day and discover that it has been published. On the other hand, there is always the extremely slight chance that your unsolicited article is just what the editor needs to fill an unexpected gap in the travel pages next weekend.

HINTS & TIPS
No travel editor wants to be contacted with vague proposals that haven't been thought through. If you tell them that you're off to Finland, for instance, and ask them if they want a story, you're likely to be told that Finland is a country, not an article. If you are going to Finland, think of a few angles or ways to treat a story that would suit the newspaper you're targeting.

On Spec
To avoid many of the unknowns in the first scenario, you could submit your article 'on spec'. To do this, you need to contact the travel editor or travel desk before you travel (or at least before you write) with some story ideas. If the editor likes one of your angles, and can see where it might fit in their paper, they'll ask to see the article when it's finished, but with no obligation. If they like the finished article, they'll publish it. This is a good deal for you and a good deal for them. You know that the editor is interested in publishing your article, assuming your writing is up to scratch. They know that they'll

get a story, and if it isn't what they want they won't have to pay you for it. Many freelance travel writers work this way until they've built up a relationship with a travel editor. Of course, after you've written a few articles on this basis, you become more of a known quantity and the travel editor will have enough faith in your abilities to give you a paid commission.

Commission

This is the goal of every travel writer: you come up with an idea that the travel editor likes enough to guarantee that they will publish your story and pay you for it. A paid commission also means that you will have little trouble arranging free facilities such as flights, rental cars and hotels, because the paper's travel desk will usually give you a letter outlining the arrangement (for more information see p212). Sometimes, particularly if you have proved your reliability, the desk will contact you and ask you to write a specific piece, though this tends to happen only with the most regular contributors.

PITCHING TO US NEWSPAPERS

For the vast majority of US newspaper travel editors, there is only one way to pitch your story: write it and send it in. The only newspaper travel section in the US that welcomes query letters rather than complete submissions is the *New York Times*. When you submit your story to a newspaper, enclose or email a cover letter pithily describing what the story covers and any special experience or expertise you may have that makes you better qualified to write this story than any other writer (e.g., 'The enclosed article about where to find and buy the best Japanese pottery synthesises what I learned in the past five years living in Kyoto...'). If you have other writing credits, you should mention those in your cover letter as well. Some travel editors in the US still prefer to receive submissions by post rather than email;

HINTS & TIPS

When submitting an article by post, some writers put three options on a self-addressed postcard which the editor can simply check, minimising their work even further. For example:

Article: 'Exploring Korea'
☐ I plan to use this article on _____.
☐ I am holding this article for further consideration.
☐ I cannot use this article.

others refuse to accept anything other than emailed submissions. Check the contributors guidelines.

Many writers submitting by post enclose a self-addressed envelope or postcard with their submissions. This is a courtesy for overworked editors, saving them the time of copying the writer's address; the editor can write a quick note on the postcard or stuff a pre-printed note into the envelope.

Such time-saving gestures may seem trivial, but when you consider that many travel editors receive more than a hundred unsolicited submissions a week, you realise that the amount of time required to scribble all those addresses and notes adds up very quickly. Editors appreciate the gesture and the professionalism it embodies.

In the US, the phrase 'on spec' does not carry the same weight as it does in the UK. If a US travel editor says, 'I'll be happy to consider your story on spec',

SAMPLE UK NEWSPAPER PROPOSAL

Here is a successful proposal addressed to the travel editor of the *Times* from freelance travel writer Lee Karen Stow, a regular contributor to the paper. Her subject is Timisoara in Romania:

Timisoara

December 2004 is the 15th Anniversary of the Romanian Revolution, dubbed the 'Christmas Revolution of 1989', which led to the downfall of dictator Nicolae Ceausescu. Timisoara is where the uprising began, when demonstrations by hungry citizens calling for bread swelled into mass protests of angry men and women screaming 'down with Ceausescu!'.

On anniversary days, Timisoara remembers its bloody, short period of rebellion and the shooting dead of up to a hundred of its people. A member of the town is honoured to stand guard at the cemetery of the unknown soldiers. A 'forever flame', a gas flame, burns continually, in rain, snow and sunshine. Candlelit church services are held in the town and a guided tour takes in the revolution black spots, winding through streets where, encrusted in the walls, are numerous memorial slabs to those who fell. Here also is Ceausescu's villa, being refurbished for visiting and paying guests.

Tour: With Transylvania Uncovered (ABTA, etc.) set up by husband and wife team. Wife was born in Timisoara and has family still there.

it does not necessarily mean that they think your story has a good chance of being published. It means: 'If you send it to me, I'll read it, no strings attached.' Period. Also, note that policies and practices regarding press trips and freebies in the US are extremely different from those in the UK; see below.

How long should you wait to hear about your submission? If you haven't heard back within three months, send a follow-up postcard or email checking to make sure that the editor received your piece and inquiring about its status. If you don't hear anything for another month or so, consider that the piece has fallen into the vortex of travel editor hell, and move on.

Press Trips & Freebies

Journalists will sometimes be offered an all-expenses-paid trip to a particular destination arranged by travel companies such as tour operators or government

Cath Urquhart, the editor who received this pitch, points out why this query is appealing to a busy commissioning editor:

1. An anniversary is often a useful device to peg a piece around. Giving plenty of notice of the anniversary, as Lee Karen did, is also important – in this case she gave six months to make this work.
2. The pitch demonstrates the writer knows the subject matter/ history well.
3. It shows she understands that travel editors are always on the lookout for interesting/new things that visitors can do; for example, the references to guided tours and the refurbished villa. In other words, this is something our readers can do, not just something set up for a writer.
4. The note about the tour operator at the end of the proposal shows she has researched how to get out there and found a specialist company. Again, this is good planning/research.
5. The proposal is brief and to the point.

Cath discussed this proposal with Lee and commissioned it. She also asked her to visit Bucharest, as she felt visitors would likely transit through the capital. Cath had one suggestion about how this proposal could have been improved. Lee had visited Romania twice before – a fact that gave her a huge advantage when pitching this story – and Cath thinks it would have been good to include this in her proposal.

tourism organisations, usually in association with an airline. Such press trips can involve travelling with three to 15 journalists and a PR consultant: you all fly out together, you all stay in the same hotel, and you are all expected to follow the same pre-arranged itinerary (lunches, dinners, museum and carpet-shop visits etc). A good press trip will build in plenty of free time for journalists to explore the destination independently, so that any ensuing articles won't be based on exactly the same experiences (but not all press trip organisers are so imaginative or enlightened). The sponsors will be hoping that the writers will write favourable stories about the destination or tour for their various publications.

PRESS TRIPS IN THE UK
The press trip has long been an integral part of the UK travel journalism scene, and most travel editors receive a dozen or so such invitations each week, asking them to nominate a writer.

Many publications prefer not to use pieces based on press trips because they want their writers to take a more independent approach than is often possible on such a subsidised trip. Also, they don't want to run the risk that another publication – whose writer also accepted the press trip – might publish the story ahead of them. Regardless, hundreds of press trips are taken by staffers or freelance journalists each year.

Before a journalist agrees to go on a press trip, it is important for every party – the writer, the publication and the benefactor – to agree on the credit that will be given to the organisations that are providing facilities. This is often less of an issue for tourist boards (who are generally happy simply to see their country/region/city in print), but is of considerable concern to commercial firms. Some publications will mention that 'Joe Bloggs travelled as a guest of Soaraway Vacations, which has holidays to the Costa Brava from £299', but will then go on to suggest other companies. It is very unlikely that an editor will agree to an 'exclusive' mention, although some airlines issue formal contracts to this effect.

FREE FACILITIES
While UK publications rarely pay travel expenses, it's also true to say that very few UK travel writers pay for their own travel. When travel journalists receive a commission from a newspaper or a magazine, it is commonplace for them to negotiate free facilities with tourist boards, airlines, hotels, tour operators and car rental companies, on the understanding that some sort of credit will be given in print.

These freebies exist because travel organisations believe they will gain more of an impact from money spent on a journalist than if they were to spend the cash on advertising – there is even an industry term, 'equivalent advertising spend', which means an estimate of what it would cost in advertisements to procure the same level of media coverage. The effect is to help the journalist make a living.

PRESS TRIPS IN THE US

This is a very hot issue among newspaper and magazine travel editors and writers in the US these days. (For more about online editors' and writers' perspectives on this issue, see below.) Thirty years ago press trips were an accepted part of the business of travel writing. They were seen as ways to broaden editorial horizons at minimal expense, and as excellent perks for otherwise under-rewarded staffers.

Since then, however, acceptance of subsidised travel of this kind has changed dramatically because of the issue of impartiality. Most publications do not allow their own staffers to take press trips or to accept freebies, and many do not accept freelance articles that have resulted from accepting such perks.

The development of a special discount rate called a press rate has further complicated matters. This is a reduced rate that sponsors will often offer to writers who want to participate in a trip but who have to show that they have paid for the trip. Essentially, it was developed as a way to get around prohibitions on press trips. Press rates can make an absurdity of the whole situation. For example, if you pay $25 or even $250 for a $2500 trip, is that more valid than getting it for free? It's a tremendously delicate and complicated issue – but the best thing is to be as honest and upfront with your editor as possible, and to be clear about the publication's guidelines and policies. Sometimes the publication's policies on press trips and freebies will be spelled out in their contributor guidelines, but if you are in any doubt whatsoever, be open and honest about the situation before you find yourself in a predicament you could later regret. A few publications still rely on press trips to supplement their own meagre travel budgets, so it is essential to know a publication's position on this issue before you accept any travel offers.

Sometimes sponsors will insist on reviewing any articles that result from the press trip, prior to publication. This is absurd and you should never agree to any such conditions. If a sponsor wants you to go on their trip, they need to give you editorial freedom. Equally, although you need to write your story based on your observations, you also need to ensure that your description isn't coloured by any special treatment you have received. In most cases, it's futile to report experiences that would not be available to the general traveller.

OBJECTIVITY

Both press trips and freebies introduce the thorny issues of objectivity and impartiality. If a hotel has given you a free room, how objective can you be in assessing it and writing about it? If an airline has flown you across the ocean in business class, won't that prejudice the way you think about the company? Integrity is the editorial bedrock. If you take a press trip, or negotiate free or discounted accommodation or services, you must not feel obliged to write a favourable piece just because someone else is paying your way. Your story will be judged – and your reputation as a travel writer will be based – on your integrity; your primary obligation is to the reader.

Rights & Syndicating Your Stories

In order to augment their earnings, many freelance writers syndicate their stories, selling one article or story multiple times. This happy scenario is much more likely to occur in the US than elsewhere.

SYNDICATION IN THE UK

It is normal for a freelance writer to offer an article to a UK newspaper with First British Serial Rights; this is also true for UK magazine submissions. This means that the writer is giving the publication the right to be first to publish their article in the UK. In theory this allows the writer to resell the piece later to someone else, either in the UK or abroad, in which case they might be selling Second British Serial Rights or Second EU Serial Rights.

In reality, however, if a newspaper or magazine publishes your piece, it will usually expect to retain syndication rights to your article for a specified period. Some publications will ask writers to sign a contract; others will either verbally, or merely on their website, say that you are bound by their conditions of acceptance. This means that they reserve the right to sell your article on to other publications in Britain or overseas and keep a percentage of the fee (typically 50 per cent). The prospect of earning more cash for no extra work in this way sounds attractive – but the arrangement is unlikely to be as lucrative as it sounds. Very often your article isn't resold by the original publication, and you are powerless to sell it yourself.

It is very rare for writers to resell their own travel articles in the UK. This is not only because of the rights situation described above but also for the following reasons:

- Most UK newspapers and magazines are national, and so their readership overlaps. You would not be able to sell a travel piece to more than one of them.
- As most freelance travel writers tailor an article for a specific slot in a specific publication and its readership, the article simply wouldn't be appropriate for another newspaper, magazine or journal.
- In reality it is only regional newspapers that might be interested in a syndicated travel piece. However, this will only be worth your while in terms of payment if you have a regular, nonregionally focused column to sell. Reselling individual

pieces just won't be worth the time it takes to do so. Plus there'd be few takers because international travel isn't usually a topic of interest to a regional newspaper, and local travel would be written by a staffer.

SYNDICATION IN THE US

The US has five 'national' newspapers, to the extent that they buy first national rights to the stories they publish: the *New York Times*, the *Washington Post*, the *Los Angeles Times*, the *Boston Globe* and the *Christian Science Monitor*. All of the nation's other newspapers buy local rights, which means that they want exclusivity within their circulation area but do not care if your piece appears in a paper outside their area. You would be ill-advised, therefore, to submit your story at the same time to the *Chicago Tribune* and the *Chicago Sun-Times*, or the *Sacramento Bee* and the *San Francisco Chronicle*, because their circulation areas overlap. However, you would have no problems sending the same piece at the same time to the *Miami Herald* and the *San Francisco Chronicle*. This is called simultaneous submission and most newspaper travel editors in the US recognise that, given the low fees they pay, simultaneous submission is a necessity of freelance life. It is a courtesy but not a necessity to inform an editor in your cover letter if you are simultaneously submitting a story.

The vast majority of freelance writers who sell their stories more than once practise self-syndication. That is, they develop a list of travel editors –anywhere from five to 20 – to whom they routinely submit their stories. A timely, well-written story may be published by 10 papers, or sometimes even more. Preparing and keeping track of these submissions is both time- and energy-consuming for the writer, and for every story that gets picked up by 10 papers, there are two dozen that may get published by one paper or by none at all. Still, writers who make significant earnings from their newspaper writing all practise some form of self-syndication.

The other syndication option that tempts freelancers is the notion of selling their work through one of the national syndication agencies. The top agencies include King Features Syndicate, Scripps Howard, Tribune Media Services, New York Times Syndicate, Hearst News Service, Creators Syndicate, United Media, Universal Press Syndicate, and Gannett. If you peruse newspaper travel sections, you will often see these agencies credited under the bylines of different writers. The truth, however, is that most of these agencies do not accept submissions from freelancers. When you see an agency credited, this usually means that the writer works for a newspaper that belongs to this syndication group.

The only syndicate even considering freelance travel stories at the time of this writing is Creators Syndicate (www.creators.com). If this syndicate accepts one of your stories, they will submit it to all of the newspapers that subscribe to their service. If any papers publish your story, you will receive a percentage – often 50 percent, though terms may vary – of the money the syndicate has been paid for your story. This arrangement will be specified in the contract you will have signed with the syndicate. The hard truth is that this option is hardly viable for the vast majority of freelancers.

The Newspaper Production Process

THE UK PRODUCTION PROCESS

In the UK, the production process followed by most newspapers resembles a sausage factory. As soon as one issue has been sent to bed, production begins on the next, but many of the ingredients will have been chosen months ahead.

Most newspapers have an editorial schedule that can sometimes extend a year or more in advance. There will be certain topics coming up that the editors know they will want to cover – for example, a trip to Liverpool in 2010 to celebrate the half-century since the Beatles were formed – and these pegs are the building blocks around which each issue's contents are structured. In March, for example, a newspaper may well include a city guide to Dublin for St Patrick's Day, plus a look ahead to Easter breaks in Britain. In addition to these 'time-sensitive' stories, most publications will also carry a range of articles that complement them: a long-haul beach holiday, for example, or an overland expedition in Africa. Space can always be made for late-breaking stories, however. If a dengue fever epidemic threatens travellers to Indo-China, or an airline fares war creates incredible bargains for city breaks, many editors will want to replace a planned story with a fresh article. This is one reason why you may not be told that your piece is definitely being used; weary travel editors try to manage expectations, and a good way to avoid having to call a freelance contributor to say their story has been postponed is by never having made any promises in the first place.

Most of an issue's 'raw' copy will not be read in detail until the previous issue has been finished. Press day, when electronic images of all the pages are transmitted to the print site, is Thursday for travel sections published in national newspapers on a Saturday. For the Sunday travel sections, it can be anything from Thursday to Saturday, depending on how the newspaper prints its different components. Typically, the travel editor will start to look at the stories for the following weekend on Friday morning. They will probably begin with the longer and more prominent articles: the lead story; the comprehensive round-up (for example, a guide to the best Greek islands or beach destinations for young families); the city-break page. Even at this relatively late stage (as it will seem if you submitted your story months ago), you may be contacted for clarifications, embellishments or even a rewrite. If the editorial team cannot contact you, it is possible that your story will be replaced by someone else's – this is why it is essential to provide contact details (ideally your mobile phone number and an email address that you check regularly). If you plan to be away on a long trip, say so – and call the editor a few days before you leave to remind them that they have a limited window if they need any changes, so perhaps they should look at the story ahead of time.

Some editors merely tidy things up a little; others will restructure a story to their liking. But often they will have to cut back a story to fit the available space, and rarely will you get a chance to review their edit – this is a good reason to make sure you don't overwrite.

Most national newspapers have staff (or, increasingly, interns on work experience) who check telephone numbers and websites – and possibly hotel rates, admission prices and hours. Every writer is allowed a little leeway in getting the odd figure wrong, but if a check turns up more than a few errors your reputation could be jeopardised.

Once the editorial staff are confident that the story is in good shape, it is passed to the designers and sub-editors. They are professionals who are concerned with getting the story to look good and to match the house style. They will lay out the page, 'flow in' the story (usually a simple copy-and-paste job), apply the house fonts and add the 'furniture': the headline, 'standfirst' (sub-heading), captions etc.

When their work is done, a proof copy of the page is printed out. The travel editor, features editor and editor will usually look at it, though only the travel editor is likely to study it in detail. Last-minute changes are made, the issue is transmitted, and the whole circus begins again.

THE US PRODUCTION PROCESS

If an editor in the US decides to use your story, you will most likely receive a phone call notifying you one or two weeks before the piece is scheduled to appear. The editor will tell you when your story is going to be published and how much you'll be paid. Depending on the subject, the editor may also ask if you have any photographs to go with the piece (for which you will be paid an extra fee). Do not expect a lengthy style discussion. Newspaper travel editors do not have the luxury of time or staff to go over minute editing changes; in the case of some especially overworked editors, you'll be lucky if you get the opportunity to go over editing changes at all. If editors want to make substantial changes to your story or have serious questions about the content, they'll tell you.

Many newspapers require freelancers to sign a contract, so you should be notified – and you should sign a contract – before a paper publishes your piece.

But not all papers require contracts, and at many of those that do, signing a contract once a year is sufficient, meaning that you may not be notified about your second or third published piece. Still, most editors make a great effort to notify writers before their pieces are printed. In the worst case, you will find out when you're paid. (Such 'worst cases' are rare; many newspapers now require writers to send in an invoice before they are paid, so at the very least, the editor or someone from the paper's staff will contact you to request an invoice.)

In general, weekend travel sections are edited on Monday and Tuesday and 'put to bed' by Wednesday or Thursday. Editing will be sharp, quick and usually minimal; fact-checking of only the most potentially troublesome facts – such as phone numbers and prices – will be performed. This is an important detail to note: travel editors in the US rely absolutely on writers to get their facts straight. And if a writer's false 'facts' bring on a deluge of complaining phone calls and emails on Monday morning, you can be sure the editor will not be overly enthusiastic about using that writer's work again.

The Magazine Scene

Magazines with a market for travel stories fall into four basic categories.

SPECIALIST TRAVEL MAGAZINES

These include *Wanderlust*, *Traveller* (the Wexas magazine), *Condé Nast Traveller*, *Lonely Planet Traveller*, *Real Travel* and *Sunday Times Travel* in the UK; *Travel + Leisure*, *National Geographic Traveler*, *Condé Nast Traveler*, *Afar* and *Islands* in the US; and *Vacations and Travel*, *Luxury Travel*, *Travel + Leisure Australia*, *Australian Traveller*, *Get Lost!* and *Coast and Country* in Australia.

TRADE MAGAZINES

These include the UK and US versions of *Travel Weekly*, Australia's *Travel Week* and the UK's *Travel Trade Gazette*.

CORPORATE MAGAZINES

The majority of corporate magazines aimed at consumers of travel are inflight magazines such as British Airways' *High Life*, Virgin Atlantic's *Hot Air*, United Airlines' *Hemispheres*, Delta's *Sky*, American Airlines' *American Way* and Qantas' *Australian Way*. Leading hotel chains also publish lavishly produced magazines for their customers, as do most train operators, ferry companies and car-rental companies. A number of cruise lines – including Princess, Holland America, Royal Caribbean, Norwegian and Carnival – also publish magazines for their on-board and 'preferred' clientele.

LIFESTYLE MAGAZINES

The core focus of lifestyle and niche magazines may not be travel, but their content includes a travel element. Examples in the UK include *TNT Magazine*, *Travel Africa*, *Harpers & Queen* and even *Dogs Monthly*. In the US this spectrum includes high-brow publications such as the *Atlantic* and *Harper's*; men's/adventure magazines such as *Outside* and *Men's Journal*; regional and city magazines such as *Caribbean Travel and Life*, *Coastal Living* and *New York*; bridal and women's magazines such as *Modern Bride* and *Elle*; and subject-focused publications such as *Preservation*, *Saveur*, *Smithsonian* and *Organic Style*. Australian lifestyle magazines with travel content include *TNT Magazine*, *Inside Out* and *Australian Gourmet Traveller*.

The editorial requirements of these aforementioned publications will differ sharply, and your approach should, as always, be clearly targeted. Specialist travel magazines provide the most promising opportunities, because of their robust appetites for travel stories. Trade magazines are much less useful, unless you have an inside knowledge of the workings of the industry; they would be far more interested in a story on new developments in Cuban resorts, for example, than in pursuing the trail of Che Guevara. Corporate airline magazines provide more encouraging opportunities, particularly for features on the destinations they serve – whether Asian beaches for an international airline, American festivals for a domestic US carrier or British cities located along a main railway line. Numerically, lifestyle and niche magazines take up the most space on the shelves, but they can be tricky to sell to – often their modest travel needs are looked after by a small team of regular freelancers or in-house contributors. However, the range of these publications does offer some alluring possibilities for freelancers, especially in the US; as always, the better you know the publication, the better your chances of pitching the perfect article.

MAGAZINE SECTIONS

In the trade, the three parts of a magazine are called the 'front-of-the-book', the 'well' or 'middle-of-the-book', and the 'back-of-the-book'.

The front-of-the-book refers to the section of the magazine that appears between the table of contents and the feature stories. In this section, along with all the advertisements, you'll find snappy reports of hot hotels, spas, restaurants, bars or boutiques that are just opening in a major city; new galleries or museums; inventive and useful new travel products; and noteworthy news such as a major museum moving to a new location or a change in a venue's status – a new owner, new chef or multimillion-dollar renovation. Slightly longer pieces might include destination news updates or issues-oriented reports.

The well, or middle-of-the-book, is where you'll find the juicy 2500- to 4000-word feature articles illustrated by lavish photographs. These are the high-profile stories that sell the magazine each month.

The back-of-the-book is reserved for promotions, a few round-up pieces and classified advertisements.

The best way to break into magazines is to start off by writing front-of-the-book stories. Some publications require proposals for these; others are happy to read the entire piece (after all, the proposal may be as long as the piece) – usually this will be spelled out in the contributor guidelines. These days the path to magazine writing success most often proceeds this way: you write a few of these front-of-the-book pieces, get your name published in the magazine, establish a relationship with an editor at the publication and lay the groundwork for further, possibly larger, commissions. You do these well and, after a year or two, you start working on a 'favoured-writer' basis, which eventually results in a big middle-of-the-book feature. You do that well, and you're on your way. Many successful writers have followed this exact path to develop working relationships with different magazines. Never underestimate the power of the front-of-the-book story.

As front-of-the-book stories generally run from only 150 to 300 words, it's important to remember that the subject has to be just right. You have to hit the bullseye with your proposal or story, so it's essential to study the front-of-the-book pieces closely to see what the editor is looking for. Unfortunately, it's harder to write 250 words than 2500 words. Every single word has to pull its own weight, yet you need to use zingy language and precise colourful details to convey some feeling for your subject and still get the essential information across. The answer is to edit, edit and edit some more.

Another point to keep in mind is that it's never too early to pitch a story to a national magazine. Editors know about most significant tourism developments before they even break ground. Don't wait until that great new

HINTS & TIPS

Front-of-the-book stories offer an excellent opportunity to write about your local area. Keep your eyes and ears open, and join a few local travel industry–related mailing lists to ensure that you know what's coming up in your region. And remember, a story that seems well known to you may be intriguing news to an editor at a publication in another part of the country or world.

resort or museum opens to propose a story on it; pitch your piece as soon as the plans are announced. Otherwise you're likely to be told, 'Oh yes, we know all about that. We've already commissioned it.'

Pitching to Magazines

As with newspapers, the traditional way of contacting magazines in the past was by snail mail, but today preferences vary from publication to publication and even from editor to editor. Check the magazine's contributor guidelines, and if you're in doubt, use the mail.

PITCHING TO UK MAGAZINES

In the UK, pitching a story to a magazine is a very similar process to pitching to a newspaper (see p194). However, there are some critical differences between the two types of publications to bear in mind before shaping and submitting a proposal or story.

Lead Times

Magazines work much further in advance than newspapers. Printers' and distributors' deadlines often dictate that the final page proofs are signed off a month before the edition hits the streets. As a result, most magazines have a much longer planning horizon than newspapers – some editors know the main ingredients of their magazines up to 12 months in advance. If you want to write an article with a Christmas angle, for example, you'll need to submit your proposal in February or March.

Because of these long lead times, it isn't a good idea to base an article around a subject that is highly topical and potentially time-sensitive, as it won't be current when the magazine appears on the shelves. The reason that some magazines appear to be up to date when we buy them is because their writers have become adept at predicting and anticipating travel trends. For example, when Romania and Bulgaria joined the European Union on 1 January 2007, there was a corresponding surge of articles on these countries – the staffs had prepared those pieces in advance so the publications would look timely.

Photography

Magazine publishing has a strong photographic component. At its most extreme this could mean that a magazine might turn down your examination of the best choices for changing money because it just isn't interesting visually. They might also reject a good story because the photography will be too expensive (words are cheap in comparison with the photo shoots that are needed for magazines such as *Condé Nast Traveller*).

Editions

Magazines are usually published monthly, which means there are far fewer pages to fill each year in comparison with newspapers. However, there are literally thousands of magazines out there, so that has to be good news.

PITCHING TO US MAGAZINES

Pitching a story to a US magazine is done by writing a query letter. The query letter is your foot in the door, and as such it's your chance to impress the editor with your perceptiveness and your prose.

Your query letter should be no longer than one page and should propose no more than three article ideas. It should be a pithy, provocative and compelling condensation of your story, illustrating how well you know the magazine you're pitching to, how vividly you can bring your particular idea to life, and why you are particularly suited to writing the best story on this topic. Your letter should always include details of any experience or expertise you might have that distinguishes you from other writers. It can also help to enclose copies of your previously published articles (known as 'clips') – especially

PRESENTATION

Professional presentation is all-important when sending in proposals and submissions, whether by mail or email.

The content must be logically set out, legible and neatly presented. It sounds obvious, but it's important to spell the editor's name correctly. It's also vital to ensure that your grammar, spelling and punctuation are correct throughout, as obvious errors and sloppy presentation can lead to a knee-jerk rejection.

Don't try to use fancy fonts or fussy design elements; just present your story in a simple, clean manner, with ample margins (one inch is fine unless otherwise specified in the contributor guidelines). Some magazines prefer that you double-space your article submissions; check the contributor guidelines.

If submitting a completed story, include on the first page: the title (which in most cases will not be the title used if the story is published), your name and contact information (address, home and mobile phone numbers, and email address), and word count. On subsequent pages, type your surname, one word identifying your story and the page number (e.g., George/Delos – 2) in the upper right-hand corner of each page. For the sake of clarity, write 'The End' at the conclusion of the story.

articles that are similar in style, subject or tone to the one you're proposing, and that have appeared in reputable publications.

When writing your pitch, it's vital to keep in mind everything you have learned about the publication you are targeting. What kind of tone, angle and subject do they prefer? In addition, think about what might actually help to *sell* the magazine – most editors will tell you that writers rarely give this all-important aspect any consideration, proposing stories that interest *them* rather than stories that will interest a particular publication's readership.

Simultaneous Submissions

It is virtually impossible – and definitely not recommended – to send simultaneous queries (that is, copies of exactly the same query letter) to more than one magazine. Your proposal should be closely tailored to fit an individual magazine, and if you are successful, the magazine will be buying exclusive North American Rights. It is absolutely fine to propose quite different stories from the same trip to noncompeting publications (a story on open-air markets for *Saveur*, a hotel review for *Travel + Leisure* and an adventure narrative for *Outside*, for example), but you should not propose the same or similar stories to editorially competing publications.

Timing

Most magazines close their editorial pages three months before the date on the cover; for example, the contents of the April issue will have been finished in December/January. Editors plan their editorial content at least six months – and in many cases 12 months – in advance. Keep this in mind when proposing time-sensitive stories, and don't be late with your proposal. The best rule of thumb is to send in your proposal as soon as it is finished; if you're writing about a once-a-year festival, the editor will determine when they want to publish it. Many magazines produce an annual editorial calendar that outlines the specific themes they will be focusing on, month by month; for example, March might be the Cruise issue, June the America issue, and November the Island issue. As with newspapers, this schedule helps advertising salespeople target potential advertisers. This doesn't mean that an entire issue will be given over to a designated subject, but it does mean that the editors will be producing a substantial package of articles based on that theme. If a magazine you're interested in has such an editorial calendar (and most of them do), request a copy and propose stories based on the relevant monthly themes as far in advance as possible.

SAMPLE US MAGAZINE QUERY LETTER

Here is a query letter I sent to the articles editor of the US magazine *Signature*, which resulted in a feature assignment:

Dear Ms Shipman

Every month Signature *presents a mix of stories that takes readers beneath the surface and behind the scenes of countries and cultures around the world. One subject that I have not yet seen covered in your magazine – and that I think would intrigue and enrich* Signature's *readers – is a new travel option in Kyoto, Japan: Travelers can now spend the night at a Buddhist temple in the heart of the city. In marked contrast to staying at a hotel, spending the night in a temple can open up entirely new aspects – and bestow an entirely new appreciation – of this ancient capital.*

I know this firsthand because I recently spent an exhilarating night at Myokenji Temple, about 20 minutes from Kyoto's main train station. This night was the highlight of my two-week journey through Japan this spring, and I would like to write about it for Signature.

The article I have in mind would focus on my own experience at the temple: I would describe first impressions of the clean, serene space; a meeting with the koan-quoting, baseball-loving head monk; a glorious evening encounter on the temple's grounds, when the past seemed to spring to life; and an enlightening immersion in incense and chants at a pre-dawn service the following morning.

This little-known alternative is open to all travellers, and I would detail the practicalities as well as the poetry of a temple stay, telling readers exactly how to arrange such a visit, and how to behave at the temple itself.

My own experience in Japan is extensive. I lived in Tokyo from 1977–79 and have visited the country every two years since. I have written about Japan for a variety of publications, including the San Francisco Examiner & Chronicle *and* Winds *magazine, and I speak Japanese fluently. (This is not necessary to enjoy the temple experience, however.)*

Thank you for considering this article proposal. I look forward to hearing from you.

Addressing Your Proposal

You'll find a listing of a magazine's editorial staff on the publication's masthead, usually a couple of pages into the magazine. The best practice is to write to an editor three or four rungs from the top of the editorial ladder – this person's title will usually be articles editor, features editor, senior editor or travel editor. If you are unsure which editor to write to, address your submission to the editor-in-chief or managing editor, who will in turn pass it on to their assistant to assess.

HINTS & TIPS
Another strategy for addressing your proposal is to find an editor at the magazine who also writes, and whose articles you admire. Send in your article to them, with a note saying how much you enjoyed the piece they wrote for a recent issue – any writer who has struggled to produce a good story will be happy to hear that at least one reader enjoyed it, and this strategy will help get you noticed and read.

After the Pitch

If you haven't heard back from a magazine after two months, send a follow-up note to check that the editor received your piece, and ask about its status. In as nice a way as possible, mention that if you don't hear something in the next month you'll assume that the editor is not interested and you'll send your proposal elsewhere. If you don't hear anything in the next month, just move on to the next publication. (Of course, you will probably have to rework your proposal to fit that next publication.)

When you do hear back, the response will bear one of two messages: rejection or acceptance.

PROVISIONAL ACCEPTANCE

A magazine acceptance will take one of two forms: a provisional acceptance or a commission. In the UK provisional acceptances are rare, as British magazines usually use writers who are known to them and who are respected in the industry to write their big stories – which is why it is recommended that you break into magazine publishing by writing front-of-the-book pieces.

In the US, if an editor is unfamiliar with your work but intrigued by your idea – or familiar with your work and tempted by but not quite convinced about your idea – they may ask you to write the article without a guarantee that it will be published. The editor will go over the approach, length and deadline of the story with you, but will not offer you a firm contract. This is still an excellent opportunity and you should follow through on it.

COMMISSION

This is what every writer hopes for. If an editor is convinced that they want to buy your story, they'll contact you by phone or email and discuss the story with you, then send you a contract with a cover or commissioning letter. If the editor doesn't send you a follow-up letter, it's a good idea to request one. The letter will reiterate what the editor went over with you: the angle and approach your story should take, the length, your deadline and your fee. Make sure that your deadline is reasonable, given the amount of research and writing you'll need to do and any other dictates of your personal schedule; it's far better to negotiate the deadline at the beginning of the process than to have to ask for an extension at the end. The contract will reconfirm the subject, length and deadline, the rights the magazine is purchasing, the fee to be paid for the article, the amount of expenses (if any) you will be reimbursed for, and the kill fee you will be paid if the article is not published.

KILL FEE

'Kill fee' is the rather aggressive expression used by the industry to denote compensation that is given when a commissioned article is submitted (or an

WORKING ON COMMISSION

When you score a commission, the real work has just begun. Your obligation and goal is to give the magazine what the editor wants. Every article is a compromise between the writer and the editor, but remember that in this relationship, the editor holds the final power to publish or reject your piece. So take the editor's guidance very seriously.

If you find that your story is deviating from what you had agreed upon, call the editor and talk it over. Don't surprise the editor by turning in a story that is completely different from the one they are expecting. The editing process may go smoothly or bumpily, but either way, your job is to work with the editor to make it as smooth as possible. If an editor asks for a major rewrite, make sure you understand why, and what changes the editor is looking for. Occasionally, an editor may ask for so many changes or so drastic a rewrite that you simply can't agree. In this situation you have the right to say you're not going to do the story after all, but this should be a truly last-case scenario. You'll forfeit the money you were supposed to be paid (including the kill fee and any expenses you may have been promised) and also effectively squander any chance of working with that editor again.

article sent on spec is formally accepted) and the editor eventually decides not to publish it – that is, to 'kill' it. There can be many reasons for this. It could be because the subject has been overtaken by events – for example, the destination you wrote about has been devastated by an earthquake or disrupted by internal social upheaval. More often it is because of a change in personnel or policy, which means your story is no longer required. The kill fee is usually between 25 and 50 per cent of the fee agreed upon for your story. If you receive a kill fee, you are free to sell the story to another publication; you may sell the story just as it is or rewrite it to suit a different editor and readership.

RIGHTS

In the UK, magazine and newspaper rights are handled in a similar fashion; see the section on newspaper syndication on p200.

When you sell a story to a US magazine, you're generally selling First North American Rights – meaning your story is appearing for the first time in a North American publication. Your contract will usually give you the right to resell the story after a certain amount of time has passed – often 90 days after publication – but you'll need to read the contract carefully to make sure of this. These days most magazines also include the purchase of Internet Rights in their contracts (meaning they can publish your work online in addition to in print), and many also buy foreign rights (often indicated with the phrase 'worldwide license'), usually stating that they will pay you a percentage of your original fee if the piece is published by one of their foreign siblings. In theory this means that they will try to sell your story to all of their overseas equivalents, but in practice this rarely results in further publications. If possible, you'll want to retain the right to republish your work in another magazine, in any future book of your own or in an anthology. You'll want to sign away as few rights as possible. The bottom line: Read each contract carefully before signing, so that you know exactly what rights your're signing away, and what you're allowed to do with your work and when.

The Magazine Production Process

When a magazine editor accepts a story, they will call you to discuss

HINTS & TIPS
Always read the contract you're signing. Don't get so overwhelmed or flattered by acceptance that you neglect to read the fine print or decide not to negotiate on points that make you uncomfortable. You may well regret this later. And if you breach your contract, even unwittingly, you will be legally vulnerable.

your article. Sometimes the editor will want a substantial rewrite, and will go over the article in great detail with you, paragraph by paragraph and even sentence by sentence, as necessary. At other times the editing changes will be minimal but, again, the editor will discuss them with you in detail. When your story has been reworked and edited to the editor's satisfaction, you will often be sent a copy of the edited version. This is a final opportunity for you to approve the changes or to raise any final concerns, because you will most likely not be sent a final proof of your story as it will appear on the page.

DEALING WITH REJECTION

Rejection is part of the freelancer's life. To survive, you need to adopt a certain Zen attitude, and accept that your stories or proposals will often be rejected. Above all, don't be derailed by the notion that a rejection is somehow personal, a fundamental rejection of you as a writer or, worse, as a human being. Editors are inundated with stories, the vast majority of which they cannot use; they choose the very few that happen to fit into the particular edition they are currently working on. Becoming a published writer is a job, and you have to approach it with a certain steely professionalism. Prepare your work by following the tips in this book, and persevere by continuing to write and submit your proposals and stories.

If you ever do find yourself sinking into the slough of depression, remember that virtually every writer, even the most legendary, has been rejected at some point in their professional life. For example, when he was starting out as a writer, the National Book Award–winning US writer John McPhee submitted dozens of story ideas to the *New Yorker*; each one was rejected. He persevered until they finally accepted one. A few years later he was a staff writer for that renowned magazine – one of the most coveted writing jobs in the US. Rejection is simply part of the process.

In the UK, many newspapers and magazines don't have the time or staff to send you a rejection note and so you're often left in limbo, not knowing what to do next with your unsolicited submission or proposal. To avoid this situation, it's a good idea to send a covering letter with your article or proposal saying that if you haven't received a response within one month for newspapers, or two to three months for magazines, you intend to submit it elsewhere. If you haven't heard

At some point in the editing process, depending on the publication, you may be contacted by a fact-checker or sub-editor. In the US, the fact-checker will ask you to supply materials that corroborate your information – maps, brochures and pamphlets, pages from guidebooks and other source materials, tapes of quoted conversations and the like. The fact-checker or sub-editor will also contact all of the places mentioned in your story – every hotel, restaurant, shop and museum – and will use independent resources to verify every cultural, historical and geographical fact in your story. So, to avoid humiliation and to cultivate an ongoing relationship with the magazine, be sure to do your

from the publication after this amount of time, write a courtesy letter or email telling them that you will now be submitting your story or proposal to other outlets.

In the US, rejection notes, whether from newspapers or magazines, usually come in the form of either a form rejection or a personal rejection. A form rejection is a preprinted note or templated email, thanking you for your proposal, but letting you know that it can't be used. While this method may seem very cold and impersonal, it's just a practicality for most editors. Much as they might want to add a personal note, they simply don't have the time.

A personal rejection is an email or note clearly addressed personally to you. The editor may write that, while they cannot use your submission, you should feel free to send in other articles, or that they liked your article but just published a piece on the same subject. Consider this to be a major victory, and follow up immediately with another submission or proposal, thanking the editor in your cover letter for the encouraging note they just sent you. If the editor opens the door a crack in this way, you need to keep pushing and open it further. Rejections can and do lead to acceptances. You just have to keep knocking – politely but persistently – on the door.

Form rejection letters are often used by book publishers, but if an editor does include any comments, you should review them carefully. Don't bury your manuscript away after the first rejection. Bear in mind that most of literature's greatest success stories were rejected by at least one publisher – and sometimes dozens – before making it into print.

own scrupulous fact-checking before you deliver your story. The more errors the editors find in your story, the less likely they will be to use you again.

Magazines have a much more elastic publishing timeline than newspapers. For example, your article could be accepted in May and a photographer sent to shoot photos to accompany your piece in June (photographic conditions permitting); the editor would then contact you about editorial changes in the piece in August, and then work on it with you until the end of September. The magazine would go into production in October, close in November – and hit the newsstands in February or March. Because of the lengthy printing process, magazines work on issues many months in advance – and often on three editions simultaneously.

In another scenario, a piece may sit at a magazine for a year – or much longer – before it appears in print. This might be because the magazine is waiting for the appropriate season to publish your article or because the photographs needed to accompany your piece can't be shot until the following year – or quite simply because space is limited and other stories have higher priority due to the volatility of their subject matter or the celebrity of their author. If this is the case, you won't be contacted to fine-tune your work for many more months. In such cases it is wise to maintain a cordial relationship with your editor, periodically checking on the status of your story and pitching new ideas. Above all, don't be precious about your work – once you've submitted your piece, allow the magazine staff to get on with what they need to do to make it publishable without interference. If the wait is sometimes great with magazine publishing, the rewards are usually great, too.

THE WEB

Surveying the scene of online publishing right now is a little like trying to describe a landscape that's in the middle of a prolonged earthquake. We know there's a whole lot of shaking going on that's rearranging a whole lot of features, but we don't know what the place will look like when the shaking stops.

The essential overview is this: As the internet continues to evolve, the world around the internet evolves as well – the readers, the travelers, the travel industry providers, the advertisers and sponsors, the technology tool makers. And these multiple overlapping evolutions create more and more opportunities for travel writers/content creators.

What does all this mean for the world of travel publishing and for you as a content creator? One thing it means is that there are many more ways to get published than ever before. It also means that there are many more ways to make money than ever before. And these two developments mean that there are many more people who are inspired to try to make money through travel writing/content creation than ever before. All of which adds up to one pithy truth: More people are making less money than ever before in the history of travel writing. (Barkeep, make that a double!) Let's focus on the most important areas in this ever-shifting landscape of possibilities.

Self-Publishing & Social Media

CREATING A PERSONAL WEBSITE

The web allows you to present yourself – and your travels and creations – to the world in a way that was impossible in the benighted pre-internet age. If you want to launch yourself as a travel writer today, unless you already have some other established platform, it's essential to seize this opportunity and create at least a portfolio website: This is a digital billboard where you can showcase your biography, your published articles, essays and books, your photos, your videos, your past and upcoming travels, your social media feeds, your world-bettering deeds, your speaking appearances and awards, your adorable dog – well, ok, probably not your adorable dog (unless you're a traveling-with-pets specialist!), but certainly your adorable blog.

In the ever-more-congested world of travel content creators, the portfolio site is a great place for readers/viewers – and editors – to find you. Put your URL – and ideally you've been able to use your name or some phrase associated with you in registering your domain name – in your email signature and on your business card. This site is your multi-layered, multimedia portal to the wide world you're trying to reach. (And it can become the foundation for a deeper, richer site where you can begin to develop a niche and build a community. More on that below.) So – build your portfolio platform now!

How? There's a wealth of information and advice online about which web hosts and platforms to use. And there are dozens and dozens of tools to choose from, from simple and free to sophisticated and pricey. First you need to decide what you want to include on your site and what you want your site to do for you, then you can choose the website-creation tool that will best showcase you, your wanderings and your work. (To get you started, Wix.com, Weebly.com and Yola.com are all worth investigating.) The best advice is to start out simple and uncluttered. Make it as easy as possible for the reader to grasp almost instantaneously who you are and what you offer. Make your visuals enticing and your prose inviting.

WEAVING A WIDER WEB

Over time, if you decide that it's consistent with your goals and energies, you can expand your website by adding layers of content, including the work of other writers/creators, and incorporating a variety of sophisticated, money-making tools and features. We'll talk more about this later.

TO BLOG OR NOT TO BLOG

A blog is a regular, diary-like posting of words and often photos, published as a chronological scroll with the newest content at the top. A blog can be published as a separate stand-alone site on the web or as part of a larger website. A personal blog is a wonderful way to communicate your experiences to the world. But it isn't for everyone. Unless you're making money from your blog, every minute you spend creating unpaid content for it is a minute you've not spent creating content someone else might pay you for. If you have limited time, energy and resources, you have to decide where to invest them. Creating and maintaining a blog can help you build confidence, skills and recognition – and can connect you with a larger living network of people who share your passion. You just have to weigh the pros – communicating with an audience, building a platform and a community, potentially becoming recognized as an expert on a particular subject, relishing the sheer joy of creating something just the way you want it – with the cons, which might include exhausting yourself with minimal returns, a depleted bank account, and fraying personal relationships.

If you decide you want to create a blog, there are dozens of helpful blog-creating tools and hundreds of articles and forums online evaluating their usefulness. Some of these tools are free and some require a monthly subscription fee. Again, as with websites, your first step should be to decide exactly what con-

USING THE WEB TO EXPAND YOUR OPTIONS

As a resource, the web's potential usefulness is staggering. A recent Google search I did for 'writers guidelines', for example, brought up www.freelancewriting.com/guidelines/pages/Travel, which turned out to be a very helpful site. It has the writers' guidelines for some 30 magazines and websites, including *National Geographic Traveler*, *Travel + Leisure* and Perceptive Travel. Freelance Writing (www .freelancewriting.com) also has a database of online travel writing jobs, with new job listings posted virtually every day.

Again, you're not going to live lavishly based on the money you earn from these jobs, but if you're serious about making money from your travel writing, sites such as this show that numerous opportunities exist online; you just have to be diligent in your searching, meticulous in your execution and prudent in your choices.

tent and features you want to incorporate in your blog; then you can choose the blog-creating tool that's best suited for you. Some of the more popular tools/services include WordPress (www.wordpress.org), Movable Type (www.movabletype.org), Blogger (www.blogger.com) and TypePad (www.typepad.com); the first three are free, the fourth requires a nominal monthly fee. For encouragement and advice, you can find helpful communities at TravelBlog (www.travelblog.org), BootsnAll (www.bootsnall.com) and Matador Network (www.matadortravel.com).

What makes a blog successful? Compelling prose, eye-catching visuals, illuminating information, an engaging voice and subject, humor, thoughtfulness, compassion. Expertise is often critical to the success of a blog. If you know more than anyone else about a specific area or activity, and can present that knowledge in an engaging way, you have a good chance of becoming successful on a small scale, and then you can build on that success. With a mind-boggling 150 million-plus blogs in existence, it's a challenge to stand out – but with more people online than ever before, you have the widest potential audience in history, and even if you reach only the slimmest sliver of them, that can still be a substantial readership.

So, blog about what you know and love, whether it's birding in Costa Rica or beaching in Greece, pilgrimaging on Shikoku or partying in San Francisco. You may blog about your around-the-world adventures or your backyard's budget bounties, camping with your kids or cruising with your grandparents. Whatever you blog about, always keep the Bloggers' Rules of Engagement in mind: Embrace your readers in your conversation, giving them information they can use and inspiration that will excite them. If you do this right, your passion and insight will draw people to your site. And then you can promote this passion through social media channels, drawing a wider network of similarly impassioned people to you too. (One corollary point to remember: While it's engaging to develop a personality and a presence through your blog, if you want to expand your audience, your blog should ultimately shine a spotlight on the world, not on you: as in most great first-person writing for any medium, you should use yourself as a portal to a place.)

SOCIAL MEDIA

One extraordinary byproduct of the explosion of the internet as a whole has been the quantum-leap of social media sites into the global media mainstream. In the same way that the web has allowed content creators to communicate directly with an audience (rather than going through the Old World Curators once known as editors and publishers), networking and microblogging services/sites such as Facebook, Twitter, Google+, Pinterest, Instagram and Tumblr (and undoubtedly new iterations have sprung up in the time it took you to read this sentence) present new channels for communication and community-building, and new resources for information- and advice-gathering. The possibilities for direct personal connection – and instantaneous interactivity, a key feature that differentiates these new media from the old – are now almost limitless.

These social media channels are really hybrids of publishing and marketing, and the content posted on them runs the spectrum from pure ideas and information to blatant promotion. What's the best way for you as a content creator to use social media? Engage, connect and construct. While your ultimate goal is to use Facebook, Twitter and their social siblings to entice an audience to your blog or website and thereby to your work, you will quickly drive people in the other direction if you relentlessly promote only your own content. A much better idea is to become a valued source of information and inspiration by curating the content you find on the web and elsewhere and pointing your readers – your 'followers' and 'friends' – to it. If you're an expert on family travel, for example, share the helpful tips you discovered on your last trip and on your wide-ranging print readings and web wanderings. You can also pose questions of common interest and build up a community as the host/home for stimulating and value-bestowing conversations. Join forums. Respond to other people's tweets and Facebook posts. In all these ways your goal is to engage your audience, connect with them on an ongoing basis and construct something of value through that connection. Be an informed, empathetic and enthusiastic participant in the community of tips and tales around the subject that impassions you. As people find your information valuable, they will tell their friends, who will tell their friends, and your network of readers will grow and grow.

One more way to use Facebook and Twitter is as a forum to gather information. In the course of creating this third edition of Travel Writing, for example, I posted on Twitter and my own Facebook page, as well as on the pages of a number of bloggers' organizations, soliciting ideas for topics and tools I should be sure to cover. The response was inspiring and helpful and provided new information and examples for this book. In addition, these very postings act like pebbles dropped in a pool, creating concentric rings of connection as more and more people comment on and post responses to my original post, then others respond to those responses – thereby reaching ever wider circles of fans and followers.

In a similar way, many travel journalists use Twitter and Facebook to find sources for stories they are researching. If a cruise ship has been in an accident, for example, they may ask online if anyone on the ship is available to be interviewed or to write dispatches from the ship. Or if they're writing a story on lost luggage, they may pose a general question asking if anyone has a luggage horror story they would like to share. In this way, social media have expanded the journalist's reach.

Writing for Other Publications

What if you want to make money writing about travel for the web? Many sites have sprung up in recent years that pay for travel content. The catch is that they don't pay much, often $10 for a post of 250-750 words. So, yes, you can make money writing for the web, but you will have to live extremely frugally – more bean casserole, please! – if this is your primary source of income.

WEBSITES

Some stable sites that regularly publish and pay for high-quality travel writing include Gadling (www.gadling.com), World Hum (www.worldhum.com), Perceptive Travel (www.perceptivetravel.com), Transitions Abroad (www.transitionsabroad.com), GoNomad (www.gonomad.com) and The Smart Set (www.thesmartset.com). Payments generally range from $50 to $500 for articles of 250 to 1000 words. Most of these sites have their contributor guidelines posted; study these carefully so that you know how to approach each site and what each editor is looking for. Vela magazine (www.velamag.com), founded by a team of worldly women and featuring female contributors exclusively, is a high-quality site well worth reading – and worth trying to write for if you're a woman. (Check the site's About page for contributor guidelines; they ask for 'writer recommendations' rather than proposals or stories.) Another site worth reading for the quality of its articles is Travelmag (www.travelmag.co.uk); unfortunately, it does not compensate contributors.

TABLET MAGAZINES

One heartening area of the ever-changing digital publishing landscape is the oasis of tablet magazines. In the past few years astonishing and delightful blooms have appeared here. Some of the most rewarding and promising include: Overnight Buses, WildJunket, Nowhere Magazine, TRVL, Travel by Handstand, Jetpac, Fotopedia Magazine and Departful.

As symbolized by these indie tablet magazines (the traditional magazines also publish tablet versions, but these consist mostly of repurposed and reformatted print content, sometimes with an added photo gallery or video), the digital publishing landscape is constantly expanding and permutating. If this were a tablet book, I'd encourage you to momentrarily suspend your reading here and Google 'travel sites that pay for content' and 'travel tablet magazines.' Undoubtedly dozens of articles listing a whole new set of publications would appear. In other words, to maximise your understanding of the opportunities the digital landscape currently presents, it's essential to continually survey the scene. See what the new and renewed travel websites and tablet zines are and what kinds of content they're posting; research what they pay and how they like to receive submissions. Do they want text only, or do they want photos and/or videos with submissions? How long are the stories they publish? Do they prefer service pieces or narrative stories?

The best practice really is to follow the same principles as with newspapers and magazines: study the publications you're interested in and learn as much as you can about how they prefer to deal with writers. All submissions are via email, of course, but you still need to get to know the length and type of articles that different editors or producers are looking for. Choose the sites you like the best and target some stories for them. Send your story to the editor, and if you don't get a response within a month, email them again to check on the status of your piece. Writing for digital publications won't make you rich, but it can be a great way to build those three Cs – Confidence, Contacts and Clips – digitally.

What do you need to be successful producing content for digital publication? What are digital editors looking for? In terms of writing, what they're looking for is not so different from what print editors have long sought: crisp, compelling prose that's exactly as long as the subject merits and not a word longer. Like their print counterparts, digital editors want useful, informed service pieces written with style and passion, on subjects appropriate for their target audience. For narratives, they want stories that vividly transport a reader into the author's experience and ideally bestow some larger truth or lesson. One counterintuitive wrinkle worth noting here: While the ascent of the web was widely seen as portending the demise of long-form writing, a number of websites and publications have emerged – including many of the ones mentioned just above – that specialize in publishing pieces of 3,000 words and more. So there is still hope for great long-form narrative storytelling in the digital domain! (Let us pause and raise a nice glass of virtual Champagne!)

There are some general differences between print and digital writing/content. The online medium has an immediacy that encourages writing in the present tense and in a more conversational tone. And the relative compactness of digital screens favors punchy headlines, shorter paragraphs and long texts divided into two- or three-paragraph sub-sections with bold subheds. Another big difference from print is that increasingly, in addition to producing excellent writing, digital content creators need to be multimedia talents – taking their own photos, filming their own videos. As technology and digital media evolve, these skills are becoming more and more essential.

One fundamental question to ask yourself is the same question we asked earlier in the print section: How can you set yourself apart from the crowd? How do you travel? What do you gravitate towards? What do you know best? What do you love? You can write about babies or bagels or bargains, barebones hostels or bodacious hideaways. And don't limit your considerations simply to subject matter. Wandering American writer-artist Candace Rose Rardon has traced a different trail to differentiation: An artist since childhood, Rardon has incorporated her charming, colorful on-the-road sketches into her creative portfolio. Combining these with short, evocative prose descriptions and reflections, she creates signature 'sketch-stories' that occupy a distinctive place on the web and stamp her work with an immediately identifiable character and a singular appeal. How can you set yourself apart?

ONLINE RESOURCES

The web is such a fecund wilderness, it's exhilarating and exhausting. Doing a Google search for 'travel writing' will start you off on a magical mystery tour that will turn up some truly illuminating and excellent sites you'll want to regularly read, some sites you'll never visit again, and some sites you'll occasionally revisit to glean helpful information or inspiration.

Some excellent websites that merit multiple visits include Written Road (www.writtenroad.com), Write to Travel (writetotravel.blogspot.com), ProBlogger (www.problogger.net), Travelwriters.com (www.travelwriters.com), mediabistro.com (www.mediabistro.com) and Media Kitty (www.mediakitty.com) for professional advice and inspiration; Iloho (www.iloho.com), Real Travel (www.realtravel.com), Gusto.com (www.gusto.com) and Virtual Tourist (www.virtualtourist.com), as well as the aforementioned BootsnAll (www.bootsnall.com) and Matador Network (www.matadortravel.com), to connect with travel communities; and Conde Nast Traveler (www.cntraveler.com), Travel + Leisure online (www.travelandleisure.com), National Geographic (www.nationalgeographic.com), jaunted (www.jaunted.com), HotelChatter (www.hotelchatter.com), Gridskipper (www.gridskipper.com), and Gadling (www.gadling.com) for information, entertainment and illumination. For a somewhat overwhelming but handy all-in-one compilation of useful online travel articles and outlets, visit Alltop (http://travel.alltop.com). Also see Part III for listings of other useful websites.

A FINAL NOTE ABOUT DIGITAL PUBLISHING
As already expressed above, you're not going to finance a lavish lifestyle writing for digital publications. But your chances of getting published digitally are hugely better than in print, so your goal should be to build a substantial portfolio, establish your credibility as an author and as an expert, build an audience, and attract the attention of editors who can pay you what you deserve (or at least more than what you're getting now).

There's also another financial path that more and more content creators have begun to follow, and we'll talk about that in the next section.

The Rise of the Internet Entrepreneur

The old model for content creators was: You write something; you send it to a third party publisher; they pay you; then they publish, promote and distribute your work and keep whatever profits ensue. The internet has enabled an entirely new model: You create something; you publish, promote, and distribute it yourself; and you reap all the profits that ensue. In this model, your content becomes just one part of a much larger entrepreneurial package, and you control the tools of production, promotion and profit.

Sounds great, doesn't it? But how do those profits ensue? This is the challenge of the internet entrepreneur. Successfully monetizing your site – and yourself – requires a prodigious amount of work, energy and expertise. The easiest starting step is probably to publish third-party ads on your site, from Google Adsense text ads to affiliate ads with relevant companies such as Expedia, Patagonia and Amazon, to broader sponsorships. Farther down the road, you could become a spokesperson for a travel service provider or clothing manufacturer, host online discussions underwritten by a tour company or preside at real world presentations organized by a hotel chain. Eventually you could even become a New Media Mogul: You could publish a suite of other writers on your site, post a totem pole of display ads, sell third-party products (from airline tickets and hotel rooms to world-girdling vests and inflatable brooms), and develop deep-rooted relationships with deep-pocketed partners. As Dr. Seuss might have said: 'There's really no limit to what you can do; your limiting limits are only in you.'

To learn more about these entrepreneurial opportunities, you should plunder the web's treasure trove of articles and studies, actively participate in forums on Facebook and various travel-blogger websites, and consider attending conferences such as the TBEX (Travel Bloggers Exchange: www.travelblogexchange.com) and Travel Bloggers Unite (www.travelbloggersunite.com) gatherings in North America and Europe. These offer rich and raucous settings for learning and networking. While some attention is paid to the ancient and evolving art of storytelling, speakers and panels tend to focus on the more modern art of monetizing, and especially for beginners, a semester's worth of hard-won, hands-on experience in the business of blogging can be vicariously absorbed. Another notable source for a wide range of practical information and advice on making money in new media is Tim Leffel's informed and helpful book Travel Writing 2.0.

In the new world of the internet entrepreneur, creating high-quality content does not automatically ensure success. In fact, one could argue that success – financial success, at least – in this brave new world has much more to do with high-quality marketing and self-promotion. For the content creator, this duality raises some fundamental questions: What's your definition of success? What's your goal? Do you want to make a living from your digital efforts? Do you just want to get cool new gear and satiate your wanderlust with free press trips? Or do you want to share your world-wandering quests and lessons with an engaged audience?

Just as the first fundamental step in writing a successful travel story is knowing your point, the first step in being a successful content creator is knowing your goal. Once you decide that, the stepping stones of the unfolding story become much clearer.

As you ponder these preeminent questions, a few additional observations and thoughts may provide some useful perspective:

Your ultimate goal may well be to have it all: a whizbang website, oodles of money from advertisers and sponsors, a year's worth of press trips, and acclaim for the quality of your work from the judges of prestigious competitions and everyday adoring readers who believe you have singlehandedly enriched their lives.... That sounds good, doesn't it?

Now let's get serious. You can't achieve all these things at once. You need to decide where your priorities lie, and focus your energies there. If you want to be a storyteller, work on your storytelling and make it as transporting as it can be. If you want to be a moveable talk show host, hone your skills, cultivate your contacts and study the secrets of your most successful predecessors. And if you want to raise your Google and Alexa rankings and ratings, and universalize your audience of fans and followers, push your SEO-ization and social

WRITING FOR OTHER OUTLETS

Anthologies

One more editorial print outlet that deserves mention is travel anthologies, compilations of a mix of previously published and original stories by a variety of writers. San Francisco–based Travelers' Tales specialises in anthologies that are focused either geographically or thematically (women's travel tales, food, humour etc.). Seattle-based Seal Press publishes themed travel anthologies that feature women contributors. Lonely Planet also produces anthologies that draw on a wide range of contributors, from best-selling travel writers to never-before-published writers.

Most publishers of anthologies announce their upcoming projects on their websites, and post guidelines on the theme and length of the stories they require. While the monetary prospects are underwhelming – most anthologies pay in the range of £50 to £150 for an original story – they do offer good publishing opportunities, especially for narrative pieces. It's good practice to periodically check the websites of the aforementioned companies – and other websites dedicated to writing opportunities – for updated information on forthcoming anthologies.

Brochures, Catalogues & Newsletters

Travel-related print materials are not restricted to newspapers, magazines and books. Virtually every travel-related company promotes its products in some kind of printed format. Travel agencies and tour operators, airlines and cruise lines, global hotel chains and family-run guesthouses, urban museums and rural galleries, government tourism organisations and regional visitor information offices – all of these organisations produce brochures, catalogues and newsletters, and all of these products need at least one writer and/or editor. It may not be the Sunday Times or Travel + Leisure, but it's an excellent way to put baguettes and brie on the table while you're waiting for the big editors to discover you.

You may want to try to find work as a freelancer with one of these companies to maximise your free time and flexibility, or you may want to try to get a staff job to give yourself some financial stability and security. If you discover a travel company of any kind that intrigues you, contact them and see if they need anyone with your experience and abilities, particularly in the areas of public relations, marketing or advertising. Whatever your professional goal, stay alive to the possibilities all around you. Think out of the proverbial box.

Apps

The opportunities for apps writing – creating text content for applications, programs that can be downloaded onto mobile devices – are growing all the time. As with other forms of digital publishing, pay in this area is low, but the experience and expertise you gain can often be used in other ways. Most of these opportunities involve research and writing for guidebook-style destination apps, where precise practical content is king. Most of these apps are highly templated, meaning you'll have few chances to spread your literary wings. But while you're waiting to soar, apps-writing is one more option for your content quiver.

TV & Radio

The markets for radio and TV writing are much more specialised than the print and web markets. One spin-off option is to produce your own 'radio' and 'TV' spots in the form of podcasts and videos which can be posted on the internet. There are numerous third-party forums where you can post your creations, or you can upload them along with your blog entries and photo galleries on your own website. As with print and photography, the web offers a new medium and opportunity to create, refine and showcase your audio and video work – and can lead to professional assignments.

If you're looking for a staff job in radio or TV, an internship is the usually recommended way to start out. Getting a job at a local radio or TV station often provides the best opportunities for on-the-job training. When you do land that internship, be energetic and helpful. Observe and when you can, ask questions – not just what but why. Volunteer to help out on special projects or after-hours assignments. Learn as much as you can by observation and osmosis – and then, when a chance arises to fill in, you'll be ready to leap at it. The vast majority of major-market reporters got started in this way at local stations, gradually working up the broadcasting totem pole through a combination of diligence, vigilance, flexibility and skill.

media-fication to the limits. If your efforts make you happy, wonderful! And if they don't, then it's time to press reset and ask yourself: What's my definition of success? What's my goal?

Corollary consideration #1: In navigating the plazas and alleys of the social media-blogosphere, it's easy to get seduced by the competition to see who can score the sweetest swag or the poshest press trip. The reader can easily get lost in all this. And if your goal primarily is to communicate, that's a problem – for your reader, of course, but more fundamentally for you.

Corollary consideration #2: As alluringly immutable as numbers are, sheer figures – whether eyeballs, followers or friends – do not ensure engagement. If you put all your energy into marketizing your travel writing and optimizing your rankings to extend your reach, you may one day find that all you're holding is air. To put this another way: If your dreams extend beyond the financial to the influential, whether your goal is to teach travelers how to thrive on Ha Long Bay for $5 day, savor Chateau Margaux in Old Bordeaux or fund a waterless loo in Timbuktu, putting your efforts into quality in thought and creation will seed engagement, and that engagement will bloom into inspiration and action. Numbers alone do not engagement make.

Corollary consideration #3: A word about press trips in the blogosphere: The range of press trips offered to bloggers runs the full spectrum. At one end are professionally organized trips where the participants come from a variety of media and the hosts impose no editorial restrictions but simply facilitate the opportunity for the writers to connect personally with the people and the place. At the other end are glorified public relations junkets wherein a bevy of bloggerati descends upon a place under the careful control of a sponsoring host and posts pretty much the same vapid succession of beach-tweets and dinner-pics, sometimes even choreographed by contract. While most savvy public relations professionals realize that the best stories come from independent in-depth research, some PR people love the latter variety of press trips because they essentially control the information about their clients; one blogger told me she was kicked off such a trip when she said she couldn't guarantee how her editors might edit her dispatches.

As the press-trip-osphere tilts in this direction and as ever more intricate and opaque (and potentially insidious) iterations of the blogger/creator-sponsor/partner/provider relationship evolve, we need to reiterate what we wrote above about press trips and readers, 'Your story will be judged – and your reputation as a travel writer will be based – on your integrity; your primary obligation is to the reader.' This equation doesn't change just because you're posting on Facebook, Twitter, Instagram-land or your own blog rather than writing for Conde Nast or National Geographic. Your primary obligation is still to your reader, not to your host. You need to have the freedom to describe things as they are – and you need to describe things as they are. If you don't, and you mislead your audience, you risk losing your base – metaphorically and literally. And in the intimate world of travel editors, if you develop a reputation as a press trip player who posts pretty much whatever a host dictates, don't expect any plumb professional assignments to come your way. For public relations professionals too, it seems worth wondering if it isn't ultimately a disservice to your client to have a flock of Tweeters posting essentially the same #hashtag #heaven content. (A hashtag – # – is used on Twitter to denote a searchable keyword or topic term. Blogger press trips have become somewhat infamous for their hellbent hastagery, accompanying every tweet with the hashtagged name of the destination. If Lonely Planet were in fact a planet and you were a blogger on a press trip there, you would hashtag your tweets as #LonelyPlanet – or more likely a custom hashtag created for that trip. For example, you might write: 'Awesome Travel Writing tutorial w/Veuve Clicquot. Amazing Melbourne-berry pie. Next: 5-star spa massage! Best. Planet. Ever. #LPblogplanet')

The bottom line: Readers – everyday travelers – want and deserve reliable information and real passion: This is the combination that will inspire action.

BOOK PUBLISHING
Guidebooks

The two fundamental truths about writing for guidebooks seem contradictory. The first is that the pay you'll receive as a guidebook contributor, especially when you're starting out, will be dauntingly and even depressingly incommensurate with the energies and hours you put into your work. The second truth is that every year a number of people make a decent living as full-time guidebook writers. The bridge between these two seemingly contradictory truths is built out of experience. The more you hone your craft as a guidebook researcher and writer, the higher the fees you'll receive and the more efficient you'll become. At some point, the ascending graph-line of your payments received will intersect the descending line of your hours expended – and you'll be making money!

Of course, that's assuming you persevere through the early years of little pay for lots of work.

What qualities do you need to be a good guidebook writer? First of all, you have to love to travel and, in particular, you should have a passion for exhaustive exploration of the logistical minutiae that undergird travel – where to stay, where (and what) to eat, how to get there, what to see and do. You should be obsessed with accuracy. And you should be able to write with poetic precision and concision.

Guidebook writing is probably the most demanding branch of the travel writing tree. To make it work, you have to investigate multiple attractions, restaurants and hotels every day. You have to juggle your budget, your assignment and your deadline – making sure that you cover everything you need to cover as economically as possible (so that you maximise your earnings) but also as efficiently as possible (so that you have enough time to write up all your findings).

But if you're fascinated with a particular country and culture – or even better, if you're already living in a fascinating country and culture – guidebook writing can be just the ticket for you.

How do you get started as a guidebook writer? The vast majority of work for guidebook writers involves updating already existing guides. A much slimmer slice of the guidebook pie is devoted to writing first editions – guides to an area or on a theme that the publisher hasn't covered before.

Whichever kind of work you're hoping for, the way to get started is the same as with writing for print and the web: study the markets. In this case, that means study all the different guidebook publishers' products closely. What areas do they cover? What audiences are they targeting? Study where the publications intersect your passions. Do you hike in the Himalaya every year? See if there's a Himalayan hiking guide that you can update, or a publisher who has covered hiking in Europe but hasn't yet expanded to Asia. Have you honed the fine art of surviving on five rupees a day? Perhaps there's a bare-bones guidebook line perfectly synched to your practice.

When you've determined the subject you want to pitch and the publisher you want to pitch it to, do further research to discover how that publisher works with first-time contributors. Follow their guidelines, and briefly but evocatively describe your writing and travel background, being sure to cover any particularly relevant experience and expertise you have. The unasked question you need to answer: what can you (the writer) bring to me (the publisher) that I don't already have? The answer may be your deep personal knowledge, your fresh perspective, your extraordinary writing skills or some combination of all these. Your job is to show the publisher that you understand their books intimately and that you can provide exactly what they need.

If you're pitching an entirely new idea, you'll need to sell the publisher on the value of the idea itself as well as your unique ability to realise that idea. In this case, you can bolster your argument with figures on the number of visitors to the area you propose to cover, or the growing popularity of the theme you're presenting. You need to make the business case that the book is worth publishing, that a sufficient audience exists to make the publication profitable.

What happens next? You may receive a rejection – in which case, move on to the next publisher and the next project. You may not receive any reply at all; in this case, after a couple of months, contact the publisher to inquire about the status of your application, noting the date of your original inquiry. If you still don't hear from them, it's time to move on.

A happier scenario is that you receive a response asking for more detailed information. In the case of Lonely Planet, you'll be asked to create a writing sample that shows your ability to write lively prose in the Lonely Planet style, and to pass a mapping test. If your submissions are accepted, you'll be made part of Lonely Planet's author pool, from which virtually all the company's guidebook contributors are drawn. Typically, your first assignment will be small – covering a section of a city for a city guide, for example, or a second-tier city for a regional guide. If that's successful, you'll be given a larger assignment – more areas of the city you originally covered, or a major city for that regional guide. If all goes well with this assignment, you'll be given more responsibility with your next assignment, and in this way both your area of coverage and your remuneration will grow. Most other major guidebook publishers work in this same way.

Some smaller and more specialised publishers offer greater opportunities for beginning contributors. Depending on your experience and expertise, you may be asked to cover an entire city or region. The downside is that because sales tend to be fewer with smaller publishers, your remuneration will probably be lower as well. As always, you need to balance the opportunity for valuable travel and writing experience with financial reality.

Whether you're working for large or smaller publishers, your work should be based on an assignment or commission that clearly details the scope and content (including tone, style, audience and number of words) of your coverage, the deadline, and the pay and payment schedule. It is absolutely essential that you have a contract before you begin your work (unless you have so much money that you don't mind spending a few months and thousands of pounds researching a destination with no firm commitment that your efforts will be published).

Your assignment – or 'brief', as it's often called – is your roadmap. Make sure that you cover all the content requested, write it up in the required style, and submit it on time and to the commissioned word count. After this, you'll likely work through a number of drafts with your editor; the editor's goal is to make the book as lively and useful as possible, but also to make sure it conforms to the company's or the series' style. Making this as smooth a process as possible will help ensure that you continue to move toward the front of the author pool.

Now, about payment: guidebook publishers work on one of two payment models, the flat fee and the royalty. In the flat-fee model, which most major publishers have adopted, the writer receives one set fee for their work; this fee covers all the travel and research expenses incurred and the writer's 'salary' for the weeks or months spent on the book. This fee is usually paid out in instalments – for example, one-third on signing of the contract, one-third on acceptance of the manuscript, and one-third on publication of the book. These fees will vary tremendously based on the writer's assigned focus and area (not just the geographical expanse but also the cost of living and travelling there). The most important thing to remember is that this fee is your total compensation for the book and so has to cover *everything* – your expenses on the road and your rent and meals at home – for the duration of your work on the book.

In the royalty model, the writer receives a percentage of the sales of every book. If you're receiving a royalty of 5 per cent for your guide to Costa Rica, for example, and the cover price of the book is $20, you'll receive $1 per sale. If the book sells 15,000 copies, you'll receive $15,000. When this royalty model is used, the writer usually receives what's called an advance. Like the flat fee, this advance is often paid in instalments – for example, half on signing the contract and half on acceptance of the manuscript. Remember that the advance is just that – money *advanced* to you based on the publisher's notion of how many copies the book will sell; it's not an 'extra' payment. So, if you received an advance of $10,000 for your Costa Rica book and the book sells 15,000 copies, you'll receive an additional $5,000 in royalties.

Does all this add up? It's a complicated equation. You have to balance the amount of money you can make, the amount of money and time you'll have to expend on the road and at home, and the experience and knowledge you'll gain. Other factors complicate the equation even more: as you're researching, can you write articles for newspapers, magazines or websites to supplement your guidebook fee? If your subject is a country where living expenses are low, can you base yourself there and so double or quadruple the cost-of-living coverage of your payment? Ultimately, the decision comes down to you and how this piece fits into the picture-puzzle of your life. If it's not right for you, don't take it. But if it is, make the most of every day, and look on the assignment as a pathway to more travel – and travel writing – adventures.

Travel Literature

If you want to publish a book-length work of travel literature, in the vein of Bill Bryson or Paul Theroux, there are two possible scenarios to follow: you can write the entire manuscript and send it to an agent or publisher, or you can pitch the idea for your book to an agent or publisher and, if you're among the lucky few with just the right proposal, get a publishing house on board from the start. (A third and increasingly popular option, of course, is to publish your book yourself. We'll talk about self-publishing later.)

The first option is full of uncertainties: you don't know if a publisher (approached directly or through an agent) will be interested in what you've written and you'll have to fund all the research and writing yourself. Pitching an idea seems a better choice, but it is extremely rare for a writer, especially a beginning writer, to pitch a book idea directly to a publisher and have it accepted. The most common – and desirable – path is to pitch your book idea to an agent, who will then aim to rouse the interest of a publisher.

Travel literature payments work on the royalty model. If your proposal is accepted by a publisher, they should pay you an advance, which will be deducted from your subsequent royalties. The advance will go some way toward keeping you financially afloat while you're working on your book, but as discussed earlier, this might not amount to much: roughly up to £10,000 in the UK, $15,000 in the US or AU$20,000 in Australia. For listings of publishers who produce travel literature, see Part III.

A proposal for a book-length travel narrative is a much more ambitious package than a simple proposal letter to a newspaper or magazine. You will need to send a short covering letter and include a two- to three-page synopsis summarising your book's themes and structure, a table of contents, a sample chapter or two (usually of around 5000 words) and a little biographical information. Your covering letter will need to establish why you believe your topic and perspective are compelling, why the particular company you've targeted should publish your book and why you think your book will sell. An analysis of any recently published books on a similar theme or covering a similar area is also essential, as is your own best indication of the potential audience for your book. You'll also need to send an SASE if you want to have your work returned. Your whole package should look as professional as possible.

The Role of an Agent

Only a very few publishers will consider book proposals and unsolicited manuscripts sent directly from an author. Most book publishers, particularly the larger ones, will only deal with an agent.

Initially, if an agent likes your book and agrees to represent you, they may work with you to strengthen your book editorially, identifying any narrative weaknesses or suggesting ways to smooth out rough spots in your story and prose. Once your manuscript is finished, your agent will target appropriate publishers. Agents know what interests different publishing houses, and also what different editors within those houses are hoping to find, as they develop relationships with editors over time. Rather than blindly sending your

HINTS & TIPS

Do you need an agent or do you have the skills and knowledge to do all of this yourself? The answer is up to you, of course, but you will most likely save yourself a great deal of hassle and heartache if you can find a sympathetic and enthusiastic agent.

proposal into the vast editorial slush pile, an agent will send your book directly to the person who is most likely to be interested in it.

If a publisher is interested in publishing your book, your agent's next task is to represent you and make sure the publisher's contractual terms are as fair and favourable as possible. If your book attracts interest among multiple publishers, your agent will oversee an auction, with a number of publishers bidding for the right to publish your work.

They will also advise you as to which publisher is likely to promote your book the most robustly and generally treat you well. As any published writer knows, getting your book published is only half the battle. If the publisher doesn't allocate any resources to promote it, your beloved tome can quickly sink into literary oblivion.

An important part of negotiating your contractual terms concerns the split of foreign-language publication or screen and other media rights. If you're lucky enough to attract the attention of a film production company, for example, an agent will help navigate you through the tricky waters of rights and fees negotiations.

If you do enter into an agreement with an agent, you will sign a contract. The agent will agree to represent you and your work and you will agree not to seek representation with any other agent and to pay the agent a commission (anything up to 15 per cent) if they find a publisher for your work. Usually, the contract will also spell out circumstances under which one or both parties may terminate the agreement and may include the time period of the mutual commitment.

These days, however, finding an agent can be as hard as finding a publisher. Lizzy Kremer, an agent for David Higham Associates Ltd in the UK, comments:

> *Although agencies often indicate that they don't pay any attention to the manuscripts that are sent to them on an unsolicited basis, my experience is that good writing stands out a mile and will be read. If an agent is not interested in representing travel writing, they might not read past the letter. However, you might have to make some of those submissions in order to find the right agent for you. You can call*

before sending your work but you probably won't gain anything by it. Make sure your submissions are well presented, professional (no long chatty letters) and always enclose a two- to three-page book outline, the first few chapters and a self-addressed envelope. Work hard at getting yourself published in other ways. If you have had articles printed in papers, magazines or websites, enclose those with your book. When choosing your representation, trust your instincts. Go with the agent who seems passionate about your writing. Make sure the agency has a good reputation within the industry by reading up on them in the various writers' handbooks available. You should take as much care as possible when choosing an agent. If you have written something wonderful, the power is in your hands. I take on new clients when two things fall into place: when I love their writing and when I think I can sell the ideas they have. Apart from that I just have to get a sense we would work well together.

Dealing with Book Publishers

If your book is accepted by a publisher, either as a completed manuscript or as a substantially fleshed-out proposal, your authorial job from that point on is to give the company what they want – just as with a commissioned magazine article, only on a bigger scale. Your agent will stay in touch with you to monitor your progress, but in effect, once the contract is signed, they will hand you and your book over to the publisher's commissioning editor. This editor is your bridge to the publishing house, the internal champion for your work, as well as the person charged with making sure you deliver a publishable and marketable manuscript on time. Deal with your editor judiciously. Fight for what you believe in, but be as professional and easy to deal with as possible. In the long run, you both share the same goal of bringing out the best – and most successful – book possible.

The Book Publishing Process

Depending upon their location and culture, publishing houses are apt to call their production processes and personnel by different names, but the following is a general overview of the book production process.

Once you have delivered your manuscript, meeting contractual obligations such as length, format and delivery date, your work will be assessed, usually by the commissioning editor or publisher. They will either return the manuscript for further work, discussing any problems in detail and setting a later delivery date, or they'll accept it for publication and authorise the disbursement of any payment-on-acceptance monies. On acceptance, your manuscript will enter the publishing company's editorial and design production process. You will be assigned an editor, who in some situations will be the commissioning editor you've already been dealing with, and it is part of your contractual obligation to work cooperatively with them, responding to suggestions and criticisms in an open and understanding manner. As Bill Bryson has said, 'Even the most experienced writers need an editor.' Your book may be your baby, but the editor is the midwife, delivering it to your readers.

The editing process includes a structural edit, which reviews your book's themes and narrative, chapter by chapter. The editor will work directly with you to fix major editorial issues that may arise at this stage. Copy editing is sometimes handled by a different editor, who will ensure that all grammar, punctuation and spelling are consistent and correct.

Once the book has been edited, you will be provided with a copy of the revised manuscript, usually delivered by email or couriered parcel. This version will usually be submitted as draft 'page proofs', meaning that the book has been laid out by a designer: design specifications such as fonts and heading weights will have been imposed, and each page of the printout will contain a double-page spread (emulating the final printed book). Any major alterations, queries or problems should already have been discussed with you, and any remaining minor issues will be clearly indicated for your attention in the edited text. At this point you will have a last chance to make corrections and changes, in consultation with your editor. Once you have returned your author corrections to your editor, and your comments and changes have been taken in, the work will be proofread by a second editor.

You may be able to review the manuscript one more time at final proof stage, shortly before the book heads off to the printer, but any changes made at this stage are expensive and strictly limited. You should also be involved in the cover design process and be shown the back-cover text, summarising your book for the reader – but do not expect that you will have final approval; that usually lies with the publisher.

Self-Publishing

Once upon a not-very-long-ago time, publishing your own book was seen as an admission that no reputable publisher wanted to touch it. Today, how-ever, self-publishing has gained a new credibility and even, in some circles, a certain cachet. Rather than 'vanity' publishing, it's seen as pushing a new frontier, forging a new trail, taking control of your destiny, and a handful of spectacular success stories have propelled this new image.

Perhaps the most heartening of these is the tale of Australian Torre De-Roche, author of an originally self-published book about falling in love with an Argentinian in San Francisco and the adventures that ensued when she accepted his offer to sail her to Australia. DeRoche self-published the book in September 2011 under the title Swept. In just over two months, she had sold publishing rights to major publishers in the US, UK, and Australia/New Zealand (who retitled it Love with a Chance of Drowning), and the film rights to a Hollywood studio. How inspiring is that?!

For now, the primary self-publishing options can be divided into three categories. The website WritersSite.com offers this compact assessment:

'Today's self-publishers generally come in three different flavors - traditional self-publishing, full-service self-publishing, and free self-publishing. Traditional self-publishers will print your book on an offset press in mass quantities. The benefit is that if you print enough copies, you can drive your per book cost down below $2-3. Most bookstores will also agree to stock books that are published in this way.

'Full-service self-publishers print a book on demand as a copy is ordered. This results in less upfront cost but a higher per book price. Print-on-demand (POD) books can cost anywhere from $3-$30 per copy depending on length, images, etc. Bookstores generally don't carry the books because they are too expensive. It is called full-service because the self-publisher can provide editing, format the manuscript, design the jacket cover, and distribute the book for an upfront fee that usually ranges from $200-$5,500 depending on the level of services.

'Free, or self-service, self-publishing has no upfront cost to publish. The writer only pays to purchase a copy of the book. But the writer must have the resources or ability to edit their own manuscript, or get it edited, format the manuscript, design a jacket cover, upload it according to the self-publisher specs and get it listed on Amazon and other channels.'

Which is right for you? Terms and features vary from category to category and service to service, so it's essential to compare what they offer with your goals for your book. A few key questions to consider include: Are you content with just a digital e-book or do you want to be able to heft it, thumb its pages and present it as an inscribed gift to friends? How important is the book's look and feel? Do you want it to be sold in bookstores? How important is reaching as wide an audience as possible? Are you willing to package and prepare it yourself or do you want a professional to do that? How important is making money from it? While new services and innovations continue to pop up, some prominent self-publishing sites to check out include xlibris, iUniverse, Lulu, createspace, Smashwords, BookBaby, Blurb, Scribd and Kindle Direct Publishing.

Of course, if you decide to go the self-publishing route, you become your entire publishing team: designer, editor, CFO and head of marketing and public relations. While this sounds daunting, and is, the truth is that even with traditional publishers these days, unless you're a celebrated author or your work has a blockbuster hook to it, your book is likely to be accorded such a meager marketing budget that you'll end up being your own major marketing and pr person anyway. One other factor to consider is that it's still very difficult to get a self-published book reviewed by serious literary review publications. But even the importance of this is diminishing with the rising influence of book review bloggers, sites such as Goodreads, crowd-sourced star rating systems as on Amazon, and services such as Kirkus Indie and PW Select, where you can pay to have your book reviewed objectively.

Where is all this going? The landscape is still a-shaking, but here are some fascinating and provocative thoughts on the future of self-publishing from English storyteller and blogger Mike Sowden: 'I think a travel blog is a thing of immense, largely untapped value for the travel writing profession. We're still in the foothills of a self-publishing revolution. Crowd-funded successes are still few and far between, although gaining in popularity and exposure every single month. I think the first travel blogger who finds a way to self-publish his or her work on a platform like Kindle or Nook, using a cleverly marketed micropayment model, perhaps even a serialised one, is going to change everything. I think when that happens, when a travel writer manages to reach the truly vast general public out there that doesn't think twice about buying something on the Kindle Store for a couple of bucks *just to find out if it's any good or not*, I think amazing things will happen and a lot of people will jump for their laptops. I've been following the micropayment revolution very closely, both in video-gaming (in relation to a game delivery system called Steam) and at Amazon, and the power of getting enormous amounts of people to hand over a sum of money they consider to be piddling in order to get something they want – something that has no physical limit, no print run and no overheads to cover – is colossal.

'So that's where I hope a lot of quality narrative travel writing will go – the extended long-reads, the brilliant 40-pagers that would struggle to find a traditional publisher, and the full-sized books broken up into chapters and serialised, Dickens-like. I hope that will turn into the sustainable commercial model travel writers have been hoping for, to complement traditional publishing. I hope that turns into a way for excellent travel writers with a web presence to be financially sustained, in part or in full, by their readers.'

Sowden posits a very intriguing possible new iteration of a traditional trail, one that future travel writers may well forge. For now, one conclusion seems clear: While there are still numerous pros and cons to weigh, self-publishing is a more viable pathway for travel writers to ponder than ever before.

THE TOOLS OF THE TRADE

Most serious travel journalists carry three items with them wherever they go: a journal or notebook, an audio recorder and a camera. Depending on the circumstances of the trip, they also usually carry a laptop. And many add a video recorder as well. In the bad old days, this could require lugging a Sherpa-worthy load of equipment wherever you went – but today, most of these features are magically combined in the hold-in-your-handable Smartphone.

JOURNAL

Don't go anywhere without your journal. It's where you record your first-hand experiences, impressions and reflections. Sometimes you will just need to jot down a word or phrase that will help you remember an experience; at other times it will be whole paragraphs of description. This is also where you'll feverishly copy down all the practical information you'll need for your travel pieces, such as restaurant or museum opening and closing times, costs and transport timetables. It's best to write down everything you want to remember while you're right there. You may think that you won't forget, but you will, and your notes will be especially important if you want to draw out a memory at a much later date. (Don't forget to pack an ample supply of pens and/or pencils, too.)

AUDIO RECORDER

As technology has evolved, microcassette recorders have been replaced by minidisc recorders or MP3s, which have been supplanted for many content creators now by Smartphones. In choosing your audio recording tool, the most important considerations are size, weight, sound quality and simplicity. Their relative significance will vary of course with your needs and goals, but for most travel writers, unless you're planning to produce broadcast-quality audio, a Smartphone or its equivalent should suffice.

The traditional downside of using an audio recorder as a note-taking device was that you had to play back everything you'd recorded and manually transcribe all the notes you needed for your article. Happily, new advancements allow you to download your audio files to your computer and then use voice-

MY JOURNAL

I've been using the same particular style of journal since I discovered it in Tokyo in the late 1970s. It measures about 10 inches by seven inches and has a durable but soft cover so that I can roll it up and stuff it in a pocket when I need to. At the same time, it's stitched so that the pages don't fall out and there's no awkward metal spine. Many travel writers use a standard reporter's notebook, roughly five inches by three inches, but their rigid cardboard covers aren't as adaptable as my soft-cover version, although it is a handy, stuff-in-your-shirt-pocket size.

Notebook entries are very powerful portals that transport you back to a place and to your experience there. Try to make time at least every other day to sit in a café or other suitable place and write about the world around you for an hour. The peripatetic Pico Iyer has told me that when he is travelling, he sets aside time every night before going to bed to record the most important experiences and impressions of the day. There is absolutely no substitute for words written on the day, in the place, as close to the experience as possible, so the details and your reactions and thoughts are fresh.

Use your journal as a friend and confidant, sounding board and *aide-mémoire*, all in one. Number your notebooks and, whatever you do, make sure you don't lose them. I always write a big note on the first page of each notebook: 'If found, please return to:...', and then my name and address. When I finish a notebook, I note the dates of the first and last entries, and put it in storage with all my other notebooks.

recognition software to transcribe them. Voila – instant notes! Well, it's not exactly that simple: You still need to read, correct and edit the transcription closely. But unless you enjoy pressing Pause and Play, Pause and Play, over and over again, you should investigate these options. While they're not flawless, they're getting better all the time.

Interviews

An audio recorder is vital when carrying out interviews, whether informal or with officials such as museum curators or hoteliers. You might also want to record what locals or fellow travellers think of a certain situation, be it their reaction to a new restaurant or a new travel advisory. In the trade, these short interviews are called 'vox pops'. It's good practice to get the names of the people you interview on tape, together with any tricky spellings; you may not end up using the person's name even if you do quote them – depending on the context, it may be fine to write simply, 'A tourist from London told me that…' – but it's good to have the name in case you do need it. Recorded interviews are very helpful when you're writing up your story, and indispensable when publications ask to fact-check quotes; see the section on interviewing techniques on p20.

Too Much, Too Soon

It's also useful to start recording if you find yourself in a situation where someone is dispensing valuable information too quickly for you to take notes. This can be especially handy in a museum, for example, where a guide is talking about the history and technique of a particular painting or sculpture. Another situation where an audio recorder comes in handy is on the guided city walks which many tourist offices or private individuals run these days. Using a recorder will help you capture important details that you might need later on when you're writing up – there is nothing worse than coming to a crucial spot in your writing and realising that you've missed a particular piece of information.

Replacing Written Notes

Audio recorders are a useful way to record what's happening in a situation where taking notes is impractical – such as bumping through the African bush on a safari, for example, when your written notes are likely to start

SOUND MEMORIES

Sound is a powerful key that can open up all kinds of stored-away memories, and bring a place back to life.

Twenty years ago, I accompanied a tour group on a three-week journey along Pakistan's Karakoram Highway. When we stopped in Hunza, we were visited by an impromptu band of musicians. I don't know how it happened that they materialised at the moment we entered the village, but there they were, and they began to play. I quickly got out my tape recorder and stuck it into the air to capture their spontaneous performance. Even now, two decades years later, when I begin to play that tape, I am transported back to that scene: the marvellous musicians, the snow on the peaks around us, the crisp sunshine, the muddy fields, the neat stone walls and the rows of poplars all around.

looking like the profile of Mt Kilimanjaro. You can orally jot down words or phrases just as you normally would in your notebook – 'vast golden savannah', 'elephants running, ears flapping', 'gurgling roar of lion' – and they'll help re-create the scene when you're back in front of your computer. You may also want to use on-the-spot sounds to augment a web presentation. It's a good idea to record evocative background noise, if appropriate.

CAMERA

On the most basic level, a camera can be used to make a visual record of a place you want to write about later. Use it to take photographs of particular features you may want to remember in detail, and which might figure in an article or story. When writing your piece, you can surround yourself with images of your destination or journey to help transport you back to a situation or place. Photos can also be used to record information you may want to use in your story, such as details provided in a historical plaque, temple marker or store sign, or in the printed explanatory text hung beside a work of art in a museum or gallery.

These 'memory snaps' can be taken on any camera, but ideally you want to be taking photos of publishable quality, so that if the opportunity arises you can sell both your words and your pictures to a publication or website – or post them on your own site. This is a very different enterprise and demands rather more sophistication in terms of equipment and photography skills.

Adding Photography to Your Skills

Photography and writing are two very different arts, requiring completely different skills. However, it does make sense to think about developing your photography skills if you are a travel writer. You are there, in situ; you know what you're going to write about and you're in a unique position to illustrate your words.

If you're writing for a newspaper, photos could help you get published. Your story might be good but not so great that the editor simply has to run it; having compelling photos can sometimes push the editor into deciding to publish your package. Photographs taken by guidebook authors are sometimes published in the guidebook they're writing, particularly if they're researching a remote location or have pictures of unusual or infrequent events (festivals or rituals, for instance). Glossy travel magazines are very photo-led, and employ a stable of professional photographers who are sent into the field to illustrate middle-of-the-book feature stories. The glossies might occasionally be interested in competent photos for front-of-the-book or back-of-the-book stories, but you have a better chance with more down-to-earth travel magazines. In fact, many tighter-budget magazines actually rely on their writers to provide photos. The better your photos, the better your chances of getting published. Every magazine, large or small, needs a cover shot – if you work on your skills and study the kinds of shots that feature on magazine covers, this coveted slot might someday be within your reach. For web publications, having high-quality photos can definitely help you sell your story – and some web editors will require that your story be accompanied with a photo gallery.

With the phenomenal growth of photo-sharing sites such as Flickr, Pinterest and Instagram, photography can also become an essential tool for expanding your social media presence and influence. Consistently posting attention-getting photos can become the nucleus for a growing community of followers.

Photographic Rates

While good photos may sometimes help your story get published, or enhance your visibility in the online jungle, another incentive to add photography to your CV or repertoire is, to put it plainly, money. Selling both a story and photos to a publication can be much more lucrative than selling the story alone.

In the UK, most newspapers and magazines have arrangements with picture agencies and tend to favour these sources (not least because they have attractive commercial arrangements with them). If your picture is used it will probably be paid at 'space rates', which might be in the region of £40 to £65 for a small 'drop in' photo and £150 to £180 for a half-page shot. Rates also depend on the circulation (and budget) of the newspaper or magazine, and where your photo is being placed; cover shots for a travel supplement or magazine cover would obviously attract a greater fee. A UK magazine with a circulation of around 10,000 would pay around £80 for half a page and in the region of £200 for a front cover; a magazine with a circulation of 150,000 might pay anything from £100 for a half-page and £325 for a cover shot. US newspapers generally pay from $25 to $50 for a black-and-white shot, and $50 to $100 for a colour photo. As in the UK, glossy magazines tend to assign favoured photographers to shoot stories, but they occasionally publish noncommissioned photos, and pay from $200 to $1000 for a single shot. In Australia, words and photos are often commissioned as a package. For photographs alone, based on a print run of 50,000, newspapers pay AU$50-$100 for images; magazine rates vary considerably, going up to AU$338 for a full page.

As advances in technology enable more and more photographers to take publishable-quality photographs, photography payments are in flux – and in some corners, one might even say they're in free fall. In particular, many web publications now pay one set fee – and not the kind of fee that will fund your next photo safari – for a package of text and photos. Whatever the medium you're publishing in, if an editor requests photos, it's essential to ask if you'll be paid extra (and if so, how much) for any of your photos that are used.

Photographic Equipment

If you're going to get serious about trying to shoot for publication, you'll need to learn about digital photography, and you may want to invest in more sophisticated equipment. Check the photography submission guidelines before approaching a publisher; they will usually have a preference regarding file formats and how to submit images. To offer pictures that are up to the highest professional standards, you'll need a digital SLR (single lens reflex) camera capable of capturing at least 8 megapixels of data. Oftentimes the standard, low-cost, 'kit' zoom lens offered with the digital SLR provides a useful range of focal lengths in one lightweight package. Typically these zoom lenses range from the equivalent of around 28mm, used for a wide-angle 'overview' shot, to around 105mm, used for a tight portrait shot. As you get more ambitious, consider adding better quality and faster lenses with a wider range of focal lengths to your repertoire. A light tripod is also very useful when shooting landscapes or low-light situations.

For considerably more information on digital photography – and traditional photography as well – see the new edition of Lonely Planet's *Guide to Travel Photography* by Richard I'Anson.

Taking Shots

As a travel photographer, what kinds of photos should you be taking? Try to think like an editor, and take photos that will help readers to see your story, complementing and enhancing your words. Your photos should illustrate the highlights and main points of your story – the landscapes or cafés, people or animals, ferries or tuk-tuks, fossils or flowers. To maximise your chances, submit a wide variety of photos, from close-up details to expansive vistas, and shoot a robust mixture of horizontal and vertical images, because you never know what size space will be available in a publication. If you're photographing a building, event or landscape that is absolutely crucial to your story, be sure to take both vertical and horizontal shots.

When composing your photos, look for interesting angles and perspectives to give a twist on the standard view of a particular scene or subject. Also, make sure that your shot has a clear visual focus – a central element that the eye is drawn to and that helps centre the image. Be aware of the full frame of your picture, and of the elements you are using to frame the scene. Frame

THE SUPER SMARTPHONE

The Smartphone is a super-powerful toolkit in a super-sleek package. In addition to being a camera, audio and video recorder, and note-taker, it's also a phone, a currency converter and calculator, an address book, a translator, a GPS and a computer, providing access to a wealth of online destination information and the ability for you to publish your work from the road.

The only drawbacks, of course, are that your Smartphone does require regular access to electricity to continue to operate, and that even with that access, it doesn't work everywhere on the planet – yet. And so if your wanderings are taking you off the grid, you'll need to plan ahead and bring old-school versions of all the aforementioned items that you think you might need.

Like the Smartphone, as technology evolves, more and more products will emerge that may have uses for the travel writer's lifestyle. As you assess these products, keep in mind the equation of convenience and cost. What do you absolutely need to do your job? Is that particular new product suitable for the kinds of travelling you will be doing? Hi-tech products are great when they do more work for us – but not when we end up doing more work for them.

your shot so that the entire photo is the tableau you want the editor to publish but, if this is not possible, include too much in your photo rather than too little, as the image can always be cropped.

Light is the most important element of any photo, and in order to capture the best effects some professional photographers shoot only in the early morning, just after sunrise, and in the late afternoon, just before sunset (the so-called 'golden hours'). The harsh light of midday tends to wash out or drain the colour and definition in photos. If you are serious about your photographs, plan to shoot in the early morning and late afternoon, and use the middle of the day for your article research or for interior shots. Photos that include local people are important to an article portfolio, but these can be tricky because if the person can be identified, you may need them to sign a model release form; see p349 for an example form. How do you decide if you need to ask someone to sign a release form? This is an ambiguous area, but if you want your shot to appear on a magazine cover or to be used for advertising purposes, or you want your work to be represented by a photo agency, you've got to have a model release form. You won't need permission to publish photographs for editorial purposes.

Beyond this, the issue is a combination of legal, practical and contextual concerns. On the legal front, you can be sued for defamation or invasion of privacy if you publish a photo of a person who can convincingly claim that they have been damaged by that publication. Let's say you take a shot of a Parisian café scene; the photo appears in a major national magazine, and the couple romantically clasping hands and looking deeply into each other's eyes in the lefthand corner of the frame catches a woman's eye – because the man in the photo is clearly her husband and the woman is clearly not herself. Bring on the lawyers! To complicate matters even further, it isn't just people who pose potential legal liabilities – publishing unauthorised photos of certain buildings and logos can cause problems, too. For detailed information about the intricacies of this issue, consult Lonely Planet's *Guide to Travel Photography.*

Ultimately, you can take photography as far as your resources and energies permit you. You can add to your income if your photos are published, but you have to weigh the costs of equipment, preparation of digital files and time involved – particularly the time it takes to sort and label your images – against the income and exposure you garner from your photos. The important thing is to decide what you want your photography to do for you, and then to work toward that goal.

LAPTOPS, NETBOOKS AND TABLETS

Most travel writers today take their laptops, netbooks or tablet/keyboard combos with them on the majority of their trips, but there are still cons as well as pros. If you decide to leave these devices safe at home, bear in mind the sometimes life-saving ubiquity of internet cafés and the multiple talents of your super Smartphone. You can still use these options to write on the road, post your content on the web and/or email it to yourself or to your editor.

The Advantages

The biggest advantage of traveling with these devices is the most obvious: you can easily and efficiently write your article while you're travelling. This may sound pretty basic, but there's nothing like writing your article while you're in situ, or working on chapters of your guidebook while you're actually staying in the particular city you're updating. If you've already sent in your article by email, you can answer any questions that may arise or gaps that may appear in your research right on the spot – plus it's a wonderful feeling to walk in your front door at the end of a trip knowing that your story is already done.

The Disadvantages

Sometimes a laptop, netbook or tablet can be a significant impediment to the kind of travelling you plan to do. Hard travel, difficult environments and long periods away from electricity supplies pose sometimes insurmountable – or at least, frustrating and exhausting – challenges. Especially on rigorous adventure trips, taking care of your precious device can become more of a hindrance than it's worth. Before you embark on such a journey, it's best to anticipate and balance the pros and cons. It's also worth remembering that if you carry these devices around the streets with you, they can make you an enticing target for muggers. Then again, if you leave them in your hotel room or car, there is also a chance that they will be stolen, taking all your notes (and your story!) with them.

In addition, laptot-toting travel journalists must always search for places to recharge their devices, whether it be in hotel lobbies, restaurants or airport lounges. You need to carry suitable plugs or adapters with you at all times, and keep track of how much time your battery has left so you don't lose any priceless prose if your device abruptly shuts down. Finally, even under favourable conditions, these devices can be a literal pain in the neck to lug around. Even the most lightweight device doesn't feel so light after you've been carrying it around all day.

VIDEO RECORDER

Video recorders have evolved tremendously in both size and sophistication over the past few years, and the options for both beginner and veteran are greater now than ever before. Whether you're interested in focusing on videos of your travels, or simply in incorporating video coverage into your overall travel content package, do some online and in-store research before you buy. Consider the types of conditions in which you'll be shooting, and the uses you want to make of the videos you produce. Though prices are more reasonable now than ever, the highest-quality recorders are still pricey – and may offer much more in terms of quality and function than you can realistically use. For many travel writers, the Smartphone may be all that's needed.

You can find numerous articles online that compare the advantages and disadvantages of different makers and types. As always with any kind of technical equipment, your goal should be to get the recorder whose ease of use and quality of image best match your need. If your precious recorder has bells and whistles that just befuddle you, it's a hindrance, not a help. And the last thing you want is to be on an Antarctic ice floe or African savannah, video recorder poised, only to discover that some hi-tech geegaw has malfunctioned and that the only image you'll have of the penguins plopping or wildebeest galloping is the one in your mind's eye. In such a situation, you want to have simple equipment that you're comfortable with and know exactly how to use; less is more.

CAREER MAINTENANCE

Whatever stage you're at in your writing journey, it's always helpful to refine your art, re-evaluate your craft, and restoke your passion. Writing courses, workshops and conferences, author readings and lectures, and literary festivals are all excellent ways to meet fellow writer-travellers, swap tales, make connections and broaden your perspectives.

COURSES
Writing Courses & Workshops
Writing courses, workshops and conferences are often overlooked as tools of the trade, but they can be an invaluable means of recharging your professional batteries and refining and expanding your expertise and skills. The attendees usually comprise a good mix of professional and amateur writers.

The majority of courses in the UK and Australia are for creative writing, but they shouldn't be discounted, as travel writers old and new can learn a lot from courses such as these. Some courses offer travel writing as a component of a more general course, while others, such as those run in the UK by the Arvon Foundation, TNT or London's Mary Ward Centre, specialise exclusively in the genre of travel writing. Learndirect (www.learndirect.co.uk) is an invaluable resource for finding out what courses are available in the UK. For part-time and full-time study opportunities in the Greater London area, consult Floodlight (www.floodlight.co.uk). Grants are sometimes available to help less-privileged students cover costs, so it is always worth asking the course organisers about funding opportunities. In Australia, Good Guides (www.thegoodguides.com.au) publishes a print and online guide to every university and college course available in the country.

In the US a good resource for classes (especially for freelancers) is mediabistro.com (www.mediabistro.com), a professional journalists' organisation that offers writing classes around the country. Magazines like *Writer's Digest* (www.writersdigest.com), the *Writer* (www.writermag.com), and *Poets & Writers* (www.pw.org/magazine) are also good sources of information on classes. The Book Passage Travel Writers & Photographers

Conference is a four-day conference that focuses exclusively on travel writing and photography, and is held every August in the San Francisco area; conference faculty regularly features prominent travel writers and editors, including such luminaries as Tim Cahill, Isabel Allende, Simon Winchester, Jan Morris and Pico Iyer. Numerous other summer writers' conferences offer nonfiction writing classes and workshops that can include travel writing.

Travel writing classes are offered across the globe through community colleges, universities, writers' centres and independent learning organisations; they can also be held in conjunction with bookstores. See Part III for more details on courses offered in the UK (p297), the US (p313) and Australia (p328). For information on writing courses available worldwide, take a look at ShawGuides (www.shawguides.com), which lists almost 1500 writers' conferences and workshops, and is searchable by country, state, date and genre. The internet offers virtually inexhaustible information about writing classes – including some virtual courses that take place entirely through online classes, submissions and critiques. Don't just consider courses on writing; learning how to edit, how to find and work with an agent, and how to work with editors can also be very beneficial in helping you understand the pressures and requirements of the publishing world.

When you're considering a particular workshop, course or conference, find out as much as you can about the presentations and course structure. What topics are covered? Who are the guest speakers? What are their credentials? How much interaction is there between lecturers and students? What kinds of opportunities are there for close critiquing of your work, and for one-on-one or small-group contact? Do the topics correspond to your interests? Ask for feedback from past students, and find out what former students have gone on to achieve.

SETTING UP YOUR HOME OFFICE

One of the essentials for a writer is a comfortable and compatible place to work, and ideally one that is a dedicated work space. In the UK it is best to have your work space as part of a room that's used for another purpose – for example, a bedroom or living room; if you set up your home work space in a separate room, you could become liable for business tax rates (that is, nondomestic rates). In the US and Australia it is actually a tax advantage if you can set aside a separate room as your workplace.

Wherever your work space is, you want it to be truly your office. When you go there, even if you are simply stepping from one part of a room into another, you have to have the mindset that you are now entering your workplace. You are there to work and not to watch TV, listen to music or chat with friends by email, IM or phone. If at all possible, it should be free of all such distractions – except the telephone, of course, which you may be using to check travel information for fact boxes and the like. Of course, you have to set up a schedule that works best for you, and if that means periodic TV, music or phone calls to friends, that's up to you. But to get the most out of your workplace, wherever it may be, you need to adopt it in your mind as the place where you focus on your work.

In terms of equipment, you will need:

- a reasonably powerful and up-to-date computer and computing software
- a phone and voicemail (or an answering machine)
- a letter-quality printer
- at least one filing cabinet
- broadband internet connection (you'll be doing a lot of research online, so you need a fast connection that allows you to be online and make phone calls at the same time)
- a scanner (useful for emailing contracts, fast-checking materials etc)
- a fax machine (this technological dinosaur is still important for chasing invoices)
- a world atlas
- English and foreign-language dictionaries
- a thesaurus
- a small library of guidebooks, travel literature books and other editorial and reference works: for example, an up-to-date copy of the *Writers' & Artists' Yearbook* in the UK; a copy of *Writer's Market* or *Literary Market Place* in the US; or *The Australian Writer's Marketplace* in Australia. For listings of other useful reference tools, see Part III.

BASIC ADMINISTRATION

Once you start earning money as a freelance travel writer there are certain administrative and legal steps that you will need to take, such as filing taxes, keeping careful records and taking out insurance.

Taxes

TAXES IN THE UK

Whether you start writing full time, part time or on weekends and evenings after your 'proper' job, you will need to register with the Inland Revenue as being self-employed. You need to register within three months of receiving your first cheque (regardless of how small it might be), as otherwise you'll incur a fine of £100. Once you become self-employed, you will have to pay your own National Insurance contributions, but only when your net travel writing income is more than £4825 a year. While you're earning less than this, you can apply for a Certificate of Small Earnings Exception. To register with the Inland Revenue and talk through all your options, ring the Newly Self-Employed Helpline on 08459-15 45 15. You should also be sent a useful leaflet called 'Thinking of working for yourself?' (P/SE/1). The Inland Revenue publishes another helpful booklet called 'Working for yourself – The Guide'; ask for this to be sent, too, or download it at www.inlandrevenue.gov. uk/startingup.As a self-employed writer, you will also have to pay your own tax (see www.inlandrevenue.gov.uk for more information). Each April, at the end of the tax year, the Inland Revenue will send you a Self-Assessment Tax Return; if you return it to them before 30 September, the Inland Revenue will work out your tax bill. You will be required to pay your tax and National Insurance contributions in two instalments, on 31 January and 31 July. If you haven't given up your day job, you will be required to pay tax on any travel writing income from the outset because your tax-free allowance of £6035 will already have been used up. The tax rate of either 22 or 40 per cent will be worked out on your total earnings. If your travel writing income reaches £67,000, you'll have to register for VAT. (Note that all figures quoted above are for the tax year 2008–09, and usually change annually.)

TAXES IN THE US
The situation is a bit less formalised in the US. If freelance writing is a source of income, in addition to the 1040 standard tax form, you'll need to fill out the Schedule C tax form for self-employed individuals, 'Profit or Loss from Business'. For your freelance income, you'll use the 1099 forms you have received from all the publications that have paid you to fill out the Schedule C form's earnings information.

If you are filing as a freelancer, you should also fill out a Schedule SE Self-Employment Tax form. The SE tax is a Social Security and Medicare tax primarily for people who work for themselves; it is similar to the Social Security and Medicare taxes withheld from salaried employees. Regulations and rates vary from year to year, so the best advice is to research the current rules and requirements by reading the IRS' concise and helpful Publication 334, 'Tax Guide for Small Business (For Individuals Who Use Schedule C or C-EZ)'. You can download this publication and peruse a wealth of other tax-related information on the IRS website (www.irs.gov).

TAXES IN AUSTRALIA
In Australia freelance writers need to apply for an Australian Business Number (ABN), which must be included on all business-related invoices and stationery. If you do not have an ABN, any payments you receive may be

subject to a Pay As You Go (PAYG) withholding tax of 48.5 per cent. If your annual income reaches or exceeds AU$75,000 you'll also need to be registered for GST, and will be required to lodge quarterly Business Activity Statements (BAS) specifying the GST payable or refund receivable, and any income tax payable or receivable.

If you keep a separate office in your residence, you can claim a proportion of heating and lighting, rates, insurance and interest payable on your home loan. You can also claim for stationery, plus depreciation on your computer, printer, modem, desk and library etc. You need to be rigorous about keeping documentation such as invoices, fees, contractual agreements, purchase contracts and receipts. It's also a good idea to keep a running diary of your expenses and income, detailing your working hours and time spent using your computer for private use, and to keep track of business phone calls, emails and faxes. For more information, go to the Australian Tax Office website (www.ato.gov.au).

HIRING AN ACCOUNTANT

It's highly recommended that you engage an accountant to prepare your taxes. An accountant can handle (and educate you about) the intricacies of your tax return, give you up-to-date advice and ensure you are not over- or underpaying income tax. A possible alternative to hiring an accountant is to use one of the popular tax software programs, such as Quicken or TurboTax, to prepare and file your returns. The best of these feature a step-by-step 'interview' process that will record and analyse your answers and then generate the required tax forms.

However you choose to prepare your taxes, it is very important to bear in mind that you may be able to deduct many of your business-related expenses. These include your office expenses (stationery supplies, postage, phone calls, internet connection etc.) and a portion of your heating, lighting and other home expenses. You may also be able to deduct expenses for books, newspapers and magazines, as long as they are genuinely for research purposes, and of course research-related travel expenses such as transportation, accommodation, meals and some work-related entertainment expenses. As each individual's circumstances and options are different, hiring an experienced tax accountant is a good idea to ensure that you take full advantage of your qualifying deductions.

Record-Keeping

Clearly, all of this means that you have to be a meticulous record-keeper. As a travel writer you'll incur a wide range of expenses – air tickets, hotel bills, car mileage, meals, equipment, entrance fees – and virtually all of these may be tax deductible. From the outset you need to make sure you understand what is an allowable expense and what isn't. In the UK, for example, you can claim travel expenses only on a work trip and not for a holiday which may also result in your writing a travel piece. In order to prove your legitimate business expenses, you need to keep all your receipts, and to have a thorough, well-organised calendar of your travels and other work-related activities during the year. You must keep all your records for six years in the UK, for seven years in the US and for five years in Australia.

With regard to expenses and deductions, you should be aware that the government will expect your business to become profitable at some stage. If you are incurring a business loss year after year, you should consult with a tax accountant because you will be permitted to lose money for only a certain number of years in a row. In the US and Australia, for example, you must make money in any three out of five years or your travel writing will be classified as a hobby rather than a livelihood, and your travel-related expenses will be disallowed (but any travel-related earnings, of course, will still be taxable).

Record-keeping is important not only when it comes to taxes, of course. If you are travelling on assignment for a US publication, and that publication is paying your expenses, you will have to turn in a record of your expenses with related receipts in order to be reimbursed. Keep all your receipts in a safe place, and carry a blank receipt book so you can supply your own receipts in situations where the local establishment doesn't have a form. To avoid the nightmare of sorting through dozens of scraps of paper days or even weeks after a trip, try to record all your expenses at the end of each day – you'll then have the date, the place, the reason for the expense and the amount, all ready to be categorised and submitted when you get home. It's also a good idea to keep a running tab of your expenses, because if you go over your expense limit, you'll be responsible for the difference.

Record-keeping is also fundamental when it comes to income. Having a story published doesn't automatically guarantee that a cheque will appear in the mail. These days most publications expect or require you to submit an invoice after your piece has been published; the invoice should include the subject of the article, the date of publication, the agreed-upon payment for the piece, your address, and your social security number (if in the US) or ABN (if in Australia). It is also a good idea to include your phone number and/or email address so you can be contacted if necessary. And even after you've submitted your invoice, it isn't the editor's responsibility to keep track of whether you've been paid for your piece; they have far too many other balls to juggle. You are the only person who will be watching out for *you* – and you can be sure that at some point your payment will slip through the cracks. Keep track of your publications and payments rigorously, and follow up on any outstanding invoices. The best practice is to create a table or spreadsheet that tracks all of your proposals and story submissions – where and when you submitted them and what responses you received, plus any commissions and deadlines, expenses submitted (if in the US), dates of publication and payments received.

As a freelancer you have to be a businessperson, too. Your writing is your livelihood and you need to keep your business records up to date, as if your life depended on them – and it usually does. If you are absolutely hopeless at record-keeping but sufficiently successful, consider taking on an intern or hiring a well-organised friend to keep your records for you.

Travel Insurance
It's also extremely important to make sure you are covered by insurance when you travel. In the UK and Australia, you will need business travel insurance if you are travelling to research and write. Most travel writers take out annual policies so they don't have to worry about this aspect of their trip each time they travel. In the US, writers should check to see what kind of coverage they already have through their personal insurance and what kind of supplemental travel coverage they may need. Consult with your insurance agent to make sure you have protection for all the potential hazards of your professional world-wanderings, from trip disruption or cancellation to loss of business equipment and medical emergencies.

LEGAL MATTERS
As a professional, you also need to be aware of the legal protections and issues pertinent to your work.

Copyright
Any original text that you write as a freelancer is your intellectual property and is automatically protected by copyright; you don't need to register or apply for it. As the writer, you can grant certain rights or licences to publish your work. Copyright lasts for 70 years after your death. For more information about copyright, contact the British Copyright Council (www.britishcopyright.org), the US Copyright Office (www.copyright.gov) or the Australian Copyright Council (www.copyright.org.au).

Electronic Rights
Electronic rights are an extremely thorny issue. When a newspaper, magazine or journal agrees to publish your article in print, they usually expect to have the right to publish your article on their website, without any further payment. These issues should be spelled out clearly in your contract. Writers'

groups have tried to make the argument that if a print outlet posts an article on its website, it effectively takes away the writer's ability to sell that article to a web-only outlet, and that therefore the writer should be paid separately for the web posting. But for the most part, wrapping electronic rights with print rights has become standard practice.

Beware the inverted principle, however, as manifest in this example recounted by American travel writer-blogger Pam Mandel: "A certain large brand really got my hackles up by presenting me a contract that paid digital rates (typically lower) but included purchase of print rights. Um, no. It's important to understand the distinction and to negotiate each separately. If a site wants to use my work for their print publication, I expect them to compensate me the same as their print writers."

If you decide to negotiate over rights issues, enter into those negotiations with a clear sense of what you think your work is worth, what conditions you will accept and what offers are simply unacceptable – but you should also consider whether you are hindering your career more than helping it. Each case will be different, depending on the article, the publication and the pay, but it is always best to have a good idea of your priorities and options in advance, and to know exactly what you want to get out of a negotiation.

Contracts

Most contracts, whether for newspaper or magazine articles or for books, are forbidding. They're written by lawyers and in tiny type. Your mind goes numb when you read them. But they spell out your legal obligations and opportunities, so it is extremely worth your while to plough through them slowly and to make sure you understand every clause. If it is a book publishing contract and you have an agent, they'll explain everything to you and endeavour to negotiate the best possible deal. Otherwise, you may want to consult a friend who has dealt with contracts before or, in extreme cases, a lawyer who can explain the fine print. You can also ask your editor to explain points you don't understand.

In theory at least, most UK newspapers and magazines will email you a contract before you start writing for them. Sometimes this contract will last a year or longer. If you write several articles for the same newspaper or magazine, it is rare that you'll receive a contract for each piece you produce. However, there will be times when you won't receive anything at all because staff on the travel desk are just too busy. In the US, magazines send contracts with each article, while most newspapers send annual contracts.

Most newspaper and magazine contracts are standard, and editors are usually extremely unwilling to deviate from the template. The most crucial considera-

NETWORKING

The world of travel is small, and knowing the right people is key to establishing yourself as a travel writer. A contact at a tourist board or PR company can be invaluable in helping you get the information or the interview you require. You also need to meet the travel editors or the publishers who might run your articles or be interested in your book.

A feast of launches, parties, dinners and lunches are held regularly by tourist boards, airlines, bookshops, publishers, travel fairs, hotel chains, travel agents and tour operators to promote anything from countries to new airline routes. It is the aim of these companies to invite as many travel editors and travel journalists along to their event as possible in order to generate coverage. To begin with, you should try to attend as many of these functions as you can, as they all offer opportunities for networking. As you become better known, you'll become more discriminating and probably only attend one a month or less. You can receive invitations to these events by joining a company's press mailing list or by ringing up the marketing department or PR agency handling the event. Networking is exhausting, and there's a real skill to working a room, but making the right contacts, putting a face to a name and establishing a good relationship with a wide range of travel professionals is central to building a successful travel writing career.

If a prominent travel writer comes to town, the odds are good that members of the local travel writing community will turn out to hear them speak; you can make good connections at such events. Other excellent ways to network include joining a writers' organisation, taking a writing class or attending a writers' conference; for more information on courses etc., see Part III.

tions are your fee (and whether it will be paid on acceptance or on publication), your deadline, the rights they are buying and the rights you retain, and whether a kill fee will be paid if they do not publish your work. Book publishers send their authors very detailed contracts. One detail you'll want to make sure your contract specifies is the percentage of compensation you will receive if excerpts from your book are published in a newspaper, magazine or anthology.

In the UK and Australia you can ask the Society of Authors (www.society ofauthors.org in the UK; www.asauthors.org in Australia) or the Writers' Guild (www.writersguild.org.uk in the UK; www.awg.com.au in Australia)

I have taught at a number of writing conferences over the past two decades and have always come away with some helpful new piece of information and a life-enriching new contact or two. In 1991 I co-founded the Book Passage Travel Writers & Photographers Conference in Corte Madera, California. Every August this conference brings together approximately 120 students and two dozen faculty members – prominent newspaper and magazine editors, book publishers, literary agents, travel writers and travel photographers – for four days of workshops, panels and events devoted exclusively to travel writing and photography. This gathering has proven to be an extraordinary launching pad for travel writers and photographers, dozens of whom have emerged from those intensive four days with magazine assignments and book contracts; a number of these alumni have later returned to the conference as faculty members, with numerous published articles and books to their credit. Such conferences can provide an unparalleled opportunity to interact with top-flight writers, editors and publishers – and to meet like-minded travel lovers from around the world.

Finally, when you are on the road, you should consider virtually everything you do as an opportunity for networking, fact-finding and story-generating. If you're flying somewhere, talk to the ticket agents about how business is doing, and with the flight attendants about great places to see and things to do in the city you're visiting. Taxi drivers are an endless source of anecdotal entertainment and illumination. Hotel concierges and desk clerks can often give you valuable tips about special places in the neighbourhood. All of these opportunities can enhance your life professionally and personally. And one way or another, they can help you distinguish and develop stories that get published.

to check a contract, provided you are a member. A useful book to consult in the UK is Michael Legat's *Understanding Publishers' Contracts*, where you can compare what you've been offered with a Minimum Terms Agreement and learn more about those clauses which should be questioned. *Australian Book Contracts* by Barbara Jefferis is a helpful resource for Australian writers.

In the US, contact the Authors Guild (www.authorsguild.org) and the National Writers Union (www.nwu.org). The resource book *Writer's Market* also has very helpful chapters on contracts, rights and other aspects of the business of writing.

INTERVIEW WITH

KEITH BELLOWS

Based in the US, Keith Bellows is Editor-in-Chief of *National Geographic Traveler* magazine.

How did you start off in your career as a travel editor?

By staying away from writing about travel. One of the lucky things was that I was never a travel writer. I had done a lot of actual travel and I had made a living as a writer, but I had never really put the two together. When I was asked to interview for this job, I leapt at the chance, because I'm experienced at putting magazines together and I thought there was an opportunity to apply those skills to making *Traveler* better. Add to that a lifetime of travel and a love of writing and, to me, it added up to the perfect job. Or to the perfect storm, depending on your perspective. But what's important about all this is that I never set out to be a travel journalist. Some people have done that – and succeeded. But not many. Because it's not a job. It's a passion. And, as we all know, if you pursue your passion – and you're good at what comes from that – then you will succeed.

What is the best way of establishing yourself if you're just starting out in your career as a freelance travel writer?

First of all, I would beg the question a bit. I would say: do you want to be known as a travel writer or do you want to be known as a writer? The really great writers in our genre – Peter Matthiessen, Paul Theroux, Jonathan Raban, Jan Morris – I don't think any of them said, I want to become a freelance travel writer; this is my goal in life. No. They wanted to write, they happened to go to places, places inspired thought and reaction, and that's what they went after. One of the things that gives me the heebie-jeebies is hearing someone say, 'I am a travel writer.' Uh-uh. You're a writer who loves to travel. You're a writer who is very good at getting on the ground, quickly canvassing the territory, surveying the folks and figuring out what the take is, what your angle on the place is and then being able to channel the place to your readers.

What I think is so important is not telling people about the place, it's channeling. And what I mean by that is when you look at a documentary, it channels the place. It's what do the people say about themselves, what do they say about the place they're living in, how do they feel about things, where do they go, and how do you live like the locals. That's the important thing, this sort of packaging, which, by the way, we do in our magazine. In some respects we tend to do the 'Insider's Guide to Boston', but at the same time we make sure that everybody who says anything about the place is not the writer but the person who lives there.

How do you think freelance travel journalists get the numbers to add up in terms of an income?
First of all, let's define travel journalists. There are two kinds. There are those people who decide they're going to go into this business and work for the *Podunk Times*. They're going to take the press trips. They're going to take the freebies. They're going to do whatever they can, and they're going to write for whoever will take their copy because they really just want to travel. They're not so much interested in becoming celebrated as a writer. That's one class. The other class of people

want to write. I am a writer. That's what I do, and I really want to write about places. And they have some passion, and they also have some self-respect in terms of the fact that they want to be proud of what they do.

So back to your question, how do you do this? Lord knows how you do it. I think the number-one thing is you have to be a good writer. You have to be a good writer and you really have to have a sense of story. If you come to us or you come to any magazine and you say, I want to do Paris, they're going to say, well, you know, we do too. They all know about Paris.

We have a little thing we say to writers. Why now? Why *Traveler*? Why you? And that's all about how you can make yourself stand out from the pack. And standing out from the pack is how you make a living. I also would say that a lot of the really interesting writers that write for us do a lot of other stuff. They may be covering business in Paris. They may be working for *Wired*. Whatever it is, they're not monosyllabic. They don't just do travel. They're curious about the world. They want to get to other fields. They'll say to me, I'm going to Ethiopia to trace the trail of my daughter. We adopted my daughter. She was found in this place. She was brought to us here. I want to go back and do that. That particular story is a potentially terrific travel story because it's not one note. It's not: I'm going to tell you about the architecture, the food, the hotels, the location, the specialties and the attractions. It's about: I want to put you here through my eyes and set an experience in a place.

What tips would you give to budding travel writers?

I guess I get back to that question of do you want to be a travel writer or do you want to be a traveller and turn your adventures into prose. If you want to get up in the morning and say my goal in life is to be a travel writer, I think first of all you need a second job. I won't say there's nobody – I'm sure there are people – but it gets very difficult to be able to say I'm going to go out and hit home runs where it takes people with 20 and 30 years of experience and with a great deal of tenacity and talent to hit those home runs.

So I think it's wise to start on three fronts. The first thing is to say I'm going to do this as an experiment, but I'm going to have something that roots me, something that's going to put bread on the table. The second thing is that I'm going to really, really, really study what I think is good travel writing. Who are the writers I like? And don't be afraid to mimic them for a while. If you like Tim Cahill or Paul Theroux, look at how they write, and try to imagine yourself writing that way. Then the third thing I think is important is to think about why you love to travel and what personally connects you with a place. You can start to mine those areas. If in fact you have a sub-genre – if you're really, really passionate about the issues that surround sustainable tourism, let's say – become an expert in that. If you really want to mine the travel industry, there are so many sub-genres. There's business travel. There's health travel. There's children and family travel. There's singles travel. There's European travel and Asian travel and so forth. If you can focus on an area where you can become an expert, that expertise will really, really help.

Are there any courses or any training that you'd recommend a budding travel writer to undertake?

Nope. I think the best diploma is to travel.

What are the most common mistakes that travel writers make in their copy?

Trying to mimic guidebooks, or thinking that what editors want is I went there, I saw this, I ate this, I slept here, that kind of stuff. Not paying attention to the basics of writing – writing bad leads, bad transitions, poor grammar, just bad writing. We see that a lot in queries. We have three curses in a query. Hi, I'm really good, and I notice in your index that you haven't done Tucson lately. I'd like to do it for you. That's number one. Number two is: hi, I'd like to write about Tucson, and I live here, and here are the great things about Tucson – wide open boulevards, great buildings, fabulous museums, yada, yada, yada. But no angle. The third is: I happen to be going to Tucson; I've never been before but thought you might like an article. There's no: I'm from Tucson, I grew up there for 30 years, I've been on the East Coast for 20, I'm going back to find blah blah blah – where there's a real angle so you really get a sense. It's really hard to find a writer underneath all the banalities of what you see in the query.

What are the most common mistakes that travel writers make when pitching to you?

The first is pitching by phone. The second is pitching by email. I get jillions of emails, so please send me a note and include published clips. That's the third thing; they don't include published clips. We have a wonderful phenomenon among our British brethren which is…I'm going out for the next six months and here are the 37 stories that I'm pursuing. Which one would you like? I want one story that you're passionate about. I

want it in one page. I want to get a sense of your writing on that page. And I want to know, once again, Why me? Why *Traveler*? Why now?

Also, I really invite people to think cinematically. And what I mean by that is, when you see a movie there are some central characters and lots of dialogue. You know immediately in the first 10 or 15 minutes of the movie either exactly what the movie is about or if there's a hook. What am I going to find out? What's the quest? What's the mystery? And you're pulled into it. There's a beginning, middle and end, and you're satisfied, we hope, at the end of the movie. It's all scene setting, dialogue, character and, in terms of magazines or stories, anecdote. You want to see stuff. You don't want to be told about the artesian well that dates back to 1500. You want a story. Most folks don't really realise that. They send manuscripts. We can't take manuscripts because we send people out, and we send photographers with them or pretty much coincident with their trip. So it's not much good to have a manuscript after the fact.

Then of course the cardinal sin is that they don't read the magazine. They don't understand that we're different from our competitors, that we have a very specific mission and a very specific way of expressing our take on travel, and they don't really give us a sense that they know the magazine. That's death.

What are the main differences between travel writing for a newspaper as opposed to a magazine?

Money is probably the biggest difference. And to put that in very crass terms, when we do a story on Africa, we're sending a writer and a photographer into the field collectively for about a month. The writer's going to come back with a manuscript, and the photographer is going to come back with anywhere from 300 to 500 rolls of film. That trip could cost us $40K. We're not going to say, Hey Betty, we loved your lead, and we're going to send you off on a $40K goose chase. We've got to be darn sure of what we're doing. We define everything from the get go. We're very clear about what we're looking for. I don't mean that from the point of view that we say here's what we want the story to be. But we certainly want to point an angle that the writer can work around. We plan from the inside out, which is to say that before you leave we're trying to nail down all the details. The photographer is going to be there for eight days between these dates for this amount of money. The writer is going to be...same kind of thing. The contract says, in general terms, this is what the story is about.

A newspaper, which has far less resources, will say you're going to Berlin. Let us know what's going on when you get back. Or they'll say it's the 50th anniversary of the bratwurst, and we want you to do a bratwurst piece. And of course we hope you know that we can't afford to pay you to go there, so you're going to have to figure out how to get there on your own. The really good newspapers are very imaginative. They try to tap a very far-flung resource pool of writers and so forth. They don't have the budgets. The smaller newspapers really don't have the budgets.

What, in your opinion, constitutes 'good' travel writing?

First of all, a sense that you're in sure hands, that the person on the ground who's writing the piece is a writer – not an observer, but a writer who can filter things out.

The second thing is that I want to meet the people. I want to smell the place. I want to hear the place. I want to taste the place. I want a sense of place, of atmospherics. I'm much less interested in the litany of wonderful things to see and do in a place, unless it's a service piece. But in a narrative story, I want a slice of the place. I want you to make me understand the place, not by telling me everything you know about it, but by showing me some aspect of it that makes me excited about wanting to know more. And that's about meeting the people, hearing their voices, listening to the cadence of their voices, getting a sense of what they eat, getting a sense of how they conduct their day. This is the wonderful thing about the slice of life approach, which is where I want to move the magazine. I don't want a piece that says: Well, I got off the plane, and I got in the taxi, and I went into London, and I checked into my hotel, and the hotel room was blah, blah, blah, and then I went downstairs and had a meal, and I went to...You just don't do it that way. You say: The most amazing thing that happened to me was this gypsy woman who came up to me in Piccadilly. And she said, death be on your soul, and you went, what? And you sat down with her, and she told you this story, and you bonded with her, and she took you to this place, and you had an experience. That's the essence of travel. It's the surprise, the unpredictable.

What constitutes 'bad' travel writing?
Paint by numbers. What you really want is a story. I went to Dubai because 20 years ago I had lost a watch there in a market, and I wanted to go back and find out what that market was like. Whatever you're doing, it's a quest. Travel is all about a quest, and when the quest is to find that next 400-thread-sheet bed linen set,

it just doesn't work. So what it's about, I think, is what's the movie? What's the story? The bad stuff is the predictable stuff: these are the markets we visited, this is what we did during the day, this is the shopping district, this is the hotel, these are the restaurants. It's just like paint by numbers.

What are the rewards of travel writing as a career?
I don't think you can make a career of travel writing. I think you can make a career of travelling and then doing things around that passion. The people that I have the most respect for are people who just figure out how to build their lives around the process of travelling. The good ones express themselves through writing. It's not so much I want to be a travel writer because I want to make a bunch of money, because that's a very difficult proposition. What it is is I'm travelling. How do I take that passion that I have and mutate it into bank funds? One of the things that has astounded me from Rangoon to Hong Kong to Sydney to Vancouver is the amazing people in the travel business. They got into the business because they're passionate about travelling, and they figured out how to take that passion and make a living out of it.

Writers can do it too. Maybe not just writing...I just spent some time doing research online, and I was looking at all the websites that are directed to expats. There are a lot of them. I found at least 30 in just an hour. What that told me is that a lot of people have a lust for life, love wanderlust, want to get out there, and they're figuring out how to live in places other than the US and sort of leverage that lust for the other, for the foreign. And writing is just a part of it. So I think that if you just think about how you're going to make a living off of writing about travel, that might be a little one-dimensional.

How can I make a living off travel and then, the sidebar is, can I write about it? If I'm living in Paris and I'm a banker, but I'm having extraordinary experiences and feeling some sort of simpatico with the local community, then I start to look overseas (i.e. the States), and say how can I sell my experience to markets there? So, in other words, if I'm from Pittsburgh and living in Paris, is there a way to connect those two places because of who I am and the fact that I'm living in Paris? I'm not a travel writer; I'm a banker. But maybe I can make people in Pittsburgh understand the foreignness of France.

What is the downside of travel writing as a career?

I think the problem with travel writing as a career is, first of all, you get a lot of competition.

Second, sometimes travel writing gets tough in the way of travelling. You're so caught up in taking notes and interviewing people and taking pictures and looking at things because you've got to learn how to turn them into saleable prose or saleable pictures that you miss the place. I've had this happen to myself where I've been so fanatically looking at some particular thing, because I wanted to get the take, that I missed something that I should've gotten.

I think the best way to become a travel writer is to travel and let the experiences accumulate and aggregate in your notebook. In a way you almost have to be just experiencing and not constantly documenting.

The other thing that's really interesting to me is that we're getting more and more queries from people who have what I would call international connectivity. I mentioned the guy from Ethiopia who's going back there to trace the trail from where his daughter was born to where he picked her up. And there's another one that we got which is really terrifically crafted about a guy who met his wife in Hue in Vietnam about 20 years ago. Magical descriptions of the place then. Two kids now, going back. That idea of the foreignness seen through the eyes of the domestic. I think that's what's going to happen now, that more and more people are really interested in this multicultural mix. And I think that's an important thing for writers to mine. When I get a query that says I lived in Country X for 20 years, and this is something that happened to me, and this is what I want to investigate – there's a connectivity there which I think is very, very important and which I gravitate toward. I think that what we all gravitate toward is people. Travel is about people. It's not just about place. I think we all tend to fixate on explaining the place and not experiencing the people.

INTERVIEW WITH

JIM BENNING

Jim Benning is the co-founder and Co-Editor of the online travel magazine World Hum (www.worldhum.com). His writing has appeared in many publications, including *National Geographic Adventure*, *Outside* and the *Washington Post*.

How did you start off in your career as a travel editor?

I majored in English literature and worked as a newspaper reporter for a few years, then as a freelance magazine writer. In 2001, while earning a living as a freelance writer, I launched World Hum with fellow writer and editor Michael Yessis. Our goal was simply to publish great travel writing, especially after Salon (www.salon.com) shuttered its terrific Wanderlust travel section. We worked on World Hum in our spare time for six years. It was a labor of love – we didn't make more than a few pennies from the site until the Travel Channel acquired it in 2007 and hired us to be the editors. From a financial standpoint, my career as a travel editor didn't begin until then.

What is the best way of establishing yourself if you're just starting out in your career as a freelance travel journalist?

There's no substitute for publishing the best stories you can in the best publications you can get your stories into. That's as true at the beginning of your career as it is later on. Starting out, you may be writing for small newspapers or websites, or on your own blog. Do your best work, regardless of the publication, and pitch to more established and respected publications. Beyond that, read – a lot. Read travel websites, magazines and literature, including travel literature.

How do you think freelance writers get the numbers to add up in terms of income?

It's challenging, to say the least. Keeping expenses down is important. It's very difficult to live in Manhattan or support a family as a full-time travel writer. Many travel writers make the bulk of their livings writing about other topics – technology, business, you name it. Travel writing may be only one aspect of their work. You have to be creative.

What tips would you give budding travel writers?

Travel is easy. Writing great stories takes a lot of skill and hard work. So work on improving your writing. Get critical feedback. It's hard to get that from friends and family, so reach out to others. Join a writers' group. Write multiple drafts. Revise, revise, revise. Avoid clichés. Narrow the focus of your stories. Rather than writing a general story about Paris, write about an aspect that's often overlooked.

Or better yet, venture to places few others are writing about.

Are there any courses or any training that you'd recommend a budding travel writer to undertake?

Everyone learns in different ways, but if you're inclined, take writing classes and workshops: travel writing, feature writing, essay writing, fiction. Anything you can do to hone your writing will benefit your travel writing. Beyond that, learn a foreign language or two. Take classes in history, literature, architecture – any topic that interests you. Or simply read about these things on your own. You can draw on all of this knowledge for your travel writing. That's the beauty of travel writing: You can indulge your quirks and passions, and doing so can make for great stories.

What are the most common mistakes that travel writers make when pitching to you?

They don't read the site carefully and they pitch stories we'd never publish. Or they send a generic pitch to us and dozens of other editors, hoping one might bite. That approach never works for us. We want to work with writers who are familiar with our site and have a specific idea about how and where their story might fit.

What are the main differences among travel writing for a website,

travel writing for a magazine and travel writing for a newspaper?

It's hard to generalise, but I would say that newspaper writing generally involves writing first-person stories that have a strong service element – details about where you stayed, what you ate. On the web, you're more likely to write top-10 lists (top ski resorts, Caribbean islands, etc.), or short blog posts, or personal travel essays. In glossy magazines, few writers get the prized assignments of crafting long, descriptive narrative stories. You're more likely to write short, punchy articles about new attractions, the latest travel gear or how to spend a weekend somewhere. From a financial standpoint, glossy magazines still generally pay the best.

What, in your opinion, constitutes 'good' travel writing?

Writing that has a strong point of view, that feels fresh and true; writing that transports the reader through great description and strong storytelling.

What constitutes 'bad' travel writing?

Cliché-ridden writing – does every cottage have to be 'quaint', every inn 'charming', every small town a 'hidden gem'? – and writing that doesn't feel true and authentic. Too much travel writing feels as though it was written by a public relations agency trying to sell the reader on a place.

What are the rewards of travel writing as a career?

Travelling far and wide, meeting people from other walks of life, then stepping back to consider what those experiences mean. Getting paid to learn about the world and, in Thoreau's words, to 'live deep and suck out all the marrow of life', to discover the 'mean' and the 'sublime'. And the pleasure and satisfaction that come from crafting a story that has the capacity to move or even inspire others. I love that travel writing requires action in the world – getting out beyond your backyard – and then retreating to your desk for reflection. They're two very different ways of being, and yet I think both are necessary for a rich life, as well as to make great travel writing.

What is the downside?

For most writers, money. It's just a tough way to make a good living.

What's the role of the internet in the landscape of contemporary travel writing?

It's increasingly important, particularly as more newspaper travel sections fold and magazines devote more space to practical tips at the expense of narrative writing. For top writers, it's an outlet for publishing great writing (though to date they're generally not being paid magazine rates) and a place to experiment with new kinds of travel storytelling. For beginning travel writers, it's where many are now getting their first publishing credits and establishing themselves.

How can would-be travel writers best utilise the web for their own professional development?

If they're serious about developing a career, they should create a personal website where they can showcase their work and highlight their accomplishments and areas of expertise. If they're drawn to blogging, they can start a blog that reflects their point of view or specialties, or contribute to an existing blog network. On sites like Facebook and Twitter, they can meet other writers and participate in a growing online travel-writing community.

Where do you see travel publishing going in the next five years?

More newspaper travel sections will shrink or disappear, sadly. Magazine stories will continue to get shorter. Travel websites and blogs will evolve in new and different ways. Online, we'll see more writers experiment with audio slideshows, video and new forms of storytelling. One thing, thankfully, won't change: a good travel story will always be a good travel story.

INTERVIEW WITH

SIMON CALDER

Based in the UK, Simon Calder is the Senior Travel Editor of the *Independent* and a radio and TV travel broadcaster.

How did you start off in your career as a travel writer and journalist?

I have always loved travelling but for many years I had no disposable funds so I used to hitchhike a great deal. I had a pretty miserable time going to new destinations, mostly because I'd spend hours beside a motorway outside Leicester only to find out too late that one mile away there was a service station where I would have got a ride within minutes. So I began to compile a hitchhikers' manual to Britain.

I did things completely the wrong way around and began to

look for a publisher only after I'd completed the book. I was put in contact with a radio reporter who interviewed me about the book, or rather manuscript, as it was then. Charles James from Vacation Work heard the interview and invited me to send him the manuscript. He published it, and it was the first of half a dozen guidebooks that I wrote for him. As a spin-off from the research I did, I offered a couple of stories to newspapers.

What is the best way of establishing yourself if you're just starting out in your career as a freelance travel journalist?

Get a reputation for being available and reliable. Don't try to be brilliant – try to be competent and deliver clean copy on time. It is surprising how elusive these apparently simple requirements appear to be to a lot of writers.

How have you managed to get your name known as a freelance travel journalist?

You have to remember that no one reads newspaper bylines, except possibly the writer's mum, and travel editors scouting for talent. But there is no real substitute for basic competency in delivering clean copy. Once you have demonstrated you can do that, your name will be remembered.

In general, less is more. Targeting a few publications with a single well-thought-out idea that you can see will work perfectly in their pages is a hundred times better and more likely to succeed than coming up with a dozen stories and sending them to dozens of travel editors.

How do you think freelance travel journalists get the numbers to add up in terms of an income?

Very tricky and becoming trickier; all publications are under pressure to reduce costs and boost productivity while maintaining quality. And sometimes the only way those conflicting aims can be resolved is by reducing the amount of work available to freelance writers. Don't give up the day job, always have another source of income. Often you have to work 15 hours a day and have lots of ideas which come from one trip.

What tips would you give to budding travel writers?

Bear in mind that almost any trip you can think of has already been written about, so instead think about how to cover familiar topics in a fresh way. For example, if you are visiting New York, keep your watch on British time and do everything at the 'wrong' time of day; e.g. finding somewhere to eat breakfast at 2.30 a.m. Or walk the length of Broadway – scary neighbourhoods and all.

Are there any courses or any training that you'd recommend a budding travel writer to undertake?

Competence in written English is the most important quality – if your apostrophes are all over the place, it doesn't bestow a sense of trust in your getting the facts right. But clearly the more training you have in crisp, clear writing, the better.

What are the most common mistakes that travel writers make in their copy?

Simple errors of fact. Of course, we're all human and I make as many mistakes as anybody, but if I read a piece where two or three 'facts' turn out to be wrong, then I will not be inclined to provide that writer with a great deal of work – especially if I recognise the original source as a guidebook that got its facts wrong.

What are the most common mistakes that travel writers make when pitching to you?

Not reading a number of the *Independent's* travel sections thoroughly in a row to see the regular categories that we have and offering stories that for a range of reasons do not fit any of the possible segments. I am by no means rigid in the format of the *Independent's* travel pages, but a 5000-word diary of a trip to Kyrgyzstan is not likely to appear in the near future.

What are the main differences between travel writing for a newspaper as opposed to a magazine?

In both cases you should be writing for the specific publication. That sounds obvious, but a story that works well for *Lonely Planet Magazine* would not necessarily work for the *Independent.* You can assume that readers of the magazine are intensely interested in travel, and most have probably had more experience than you. But people don't usually buy the *Independent* purely on the strength of its travel section. Therefore you can take nothing for granted about the readership.

What, in your opinion, constitutes 'good' travel writing?

The *Independent* strives constantly for imaginative, informative and inspirational travel pages, demystifying the world – and the travel industry. Usually this means bringing the place and its people to life, and leaving yourself, as the writer, in the background.

What constitutes 'bad' travel writing?

Anything that contains clichés or inaccuracies.

What are the rewards of travel writing as a career?

You have the immense good fortune to travel the world and meet all kinds of fascinating people, while working (or pretending to work).

And the downside for you?
Long, stressful hours and time away from my young family.

How did you break into travel radio/TV from travel writing?

After many years of writing about travel you acquire a certain amount of expertise that is sometimes appealing to broadcasters, who may then get in touch.

INTERVIEW WITH
ANTHONY DENNIS

Anthony Dennis is the Editor of *Travel + Leisure Australia & New Zealand*.

How did you start off in your career as a travel editor?
I'd been in various roles at the *Sydney Morning Herald* over many years, one of which involved travel writing and covering tourism issues. When I heard that Fairfax Media and American Express were planning to launch an Australian edition of *Travel + Leisure*, I said I'd be interested and, happily, I got the role of founding editor. I'd been a long-time reader of the US *Travel + Leisure* so I had a reasonable understanding of its ethos.

What is the best way of establishing yourself if you're just starting out in your career as a freelance travel journalist?

T+L operates a policy of not accepting free or sponsored trips. This eliminates most freelance writers from the *T+L* equation. Additionally, the Australian edition of *T+L* is able to republish material from the US parent edition which means our needs aren't great in terms of freelance material, aside from that we proactively commission. I find that the majority of the unsolicited pieces we receive at *T+L* are far too conventional and indicate that the writer does not understand the magazine or hasn't bothered to read it.

How do you think freelance travel writers get the numbers to add up in terms of an income?

It's difficult with the per-word rates that magazines, and particularly newspapers, pay for stories. My advice would be to develop your skills base beyond travel writing to travel photography, travel book authorships, speaking engagements, even specialist tour guiding.

What tips would you give to budding travel writers?

Read as much good travel literature as you can, including the classics; read the best travel magazines from here and around the world; and travel, travel, travel.

Are there any courses or any training that you'd recommend a budding travel writer to undertake?

I don't believe you can teach travel writing.

What are the most common mistakes that travel writers make in their copy?

They fail to tell a story or provide a strong narrative and their stories are too predictable. This is partly due to the lack of imagination of those who compile itineraries for sponsored trips, or junkets, rather than allowing input from the writers. And too many travel stories talk about the elements of a trip that you can now research easily on the web. At *T+L* we operate on the 'why here, why now?' philosophy – this means that we don't cover a destination unless there is a real imperative or story

angle. We try not to publish general stories of the sort you see in newspaper travel sections.

What are the main differences among travel writing for a magazine, for a newspaper and for a website?

Some of our main features can run to 3500 words, a word length you're unlikely to see in a newspaper travel section or on the web. If you write one of those longer pieces for *T+L* you will need to have done your research in depth and also be able to sustain a narrative.

What are the rewards of travel writing as a career?

The best reward is to hear from a reader who has followed in your footsteps, as is often the case on *T+L*, and hear that you got it right.

What is the downside?

A colleague once said, 'Anyone can write a travel story', to which I replied, 'True, but not everyone can write a good travel story'. A good travel story can take at least a few drafts and, as editor of *T+L Australia & New Zealand*, a lot of my writing has to be done after work and at weekends. There is no such thing as a free trip – the hard work is at the other end, when you sit down to write the piece and make it work.

How can would-be travel writers best utilise the internet for their own professional development?

The web has been a boon for research, especially for checking information on hotels and airlines, before and after travel. It's also a great tool for the consumer but it's not often inspiring, independent or reliable – that's where a magazine like *Travel + Leisure* comes in.

Where do you see travel publishing going in the next five years?

I don't feel that the travel industry, at least in Australia, in general supports quality travel publications. They're happy to keep handing out the free trips, and getting a fairly mediocre outcome, and not engaging and educating the media about travel. That said, I expect the enthusiasm for travel will continue to grow because it's a life passion for a lot of us, and we won't give it up easily.

INTERVIEW WITH

ED GRENBY

Ed Grenby is the Editor of the *Sunday Times Travel Magazine* (www .sundaytimestravel.co.uk).

How did you start off in your career as a travel editor?

Laziness, luck, cowardice and the kindness of others. I'd started off in men's magazines (first job was through work experience), met the travel editor of a proper respectable national newspaper on a group press trip somewhere; was too feckless to pester him for work (which I now realise must have been a refreshing change); stayed in touch; ended up doing some stuff for him after all; was too chicken to go freelance as a full-time travel writer; leapt at the chance when he offered me two days a week on his travel desk, which gave me just enough financial security to freelance the other three days; then, after a year, was offered my current job.

What is the best way of establishing yourself if you're just starting out in your career as a freelance travel journalist?

Write the less glamorous stuff that the bigshots wouldn't deign to. Magazines (and, to some extent, newspaper travel sections too) carry maybe one or two big 2000-word destination features every issue – but dozens of smaller news or advice or round-up pieces. And guess which everyone always pitches for.

Don't worry, either, that these little stories won't give you the opportunity to demonstrate your dazzling talent; if you file to deadline, to length, to style, to required standards of accuracy and to the brief, you're definitely in with a shot when it comes to getting a chunkier commission.

How do you think freelance travel writers get the numbers to add up in terms of an income?

See previous answer. You're paid for words, not for travel – so the more copy you can generate without leaving your desk, the more money you'll make. One of those big 2000-worders might take you 12 days including research, pitching, organising, travel and writing – and you can earn the same money in three days if you're doing a couple of round-up features. So if you want to make a living, you need to sell two or three stories from each trip, and take enough notes (on the destination, the food, the hotel, the bars, how good it would be for kids – everything), so that, two years later, you could still be using that trip in round-ups or when a panicky editor sends round

a circular 'anyone know the foodie scene in Christchurch?' email.

What tips would you give to budding travel writers?

See previous answer. And if a career in travel writing doesn't sound quite so much fun anymore, then bear in mind that many travel writers don't make a living from it, treating the whole thing as a lovely sideline to a more lucrative career, either in journalism or even outside it altogether.

Are there any courses or any training that you'd recommend a budding travel writer to undertake?

I would advise reading a lot – and not just the good stuff. Bad stuff will teach you what to avoid, and will remind you that there are probably worse writers than you out there who are still getting published.

What are the most common mistakes that travel writers make in their copy?

Not having a story. And 'person goes to place, has a look around, comes back' is not a story.

What are the most common mistakes that travel writers make when pitching to you?

See previous answer. And, at the risk of sounding facetious, pitching to me is a mistake in the first place: a cursory glance at my magazine will reveal the names of our Commissioning Editor, Features Editor, Deputy Editor and other section editors, who are the people who do all the real (commissioning) work. Not bothering to find out stuff like this – just like not knowing that we're monthly, or what our price bracket is, or what kind of destinations we cover, or what our regular slots are – means you're likely to be wasting your own time (as well as ours) by pitching inappropriate ideas.

What are the main differences among travel writing for a magazine, for a newspaper and for a website?

I only really know about specialist travel magazines, but I think mags are the most exacting. Papers (and websites?) start every week with blank pages they need to fill, devour copy, need a relentless supply of it, generally want to say yes to it, and don't have much time to mess around with rewriting it. Magazines are the opposite: they only have 12 (or even six) opportunities each year to do their thing, are constantly asking themselves 'is this brilliant enough to make someone hand over £3.50 for it?', generally want to say no to it, and will whiffle away at something for days or weeks before they're happy with it.

What, in your opinion, constitutes 'good' travel writing?

Above all, it just has to make you keep reading till you get to the end. Beyond that, if it tells you what the place is like, and leaves you with a strong sense of either wanting to go there or definitely not wanting to go there, even better.

What constitutes 'bad' travel writing?

See previous answer and reverse it. And if the first sentence doesn't make you want to read the second, forget it.

What are the rewards of travel writing as a career?

That would be the travel and the writing. But beware: if it really is your career, and your sole source of income, both the travel and the writing lose their appeal a bit – the former because it's not a holiday anymore, it's a rush to see as much and get as many stories as possible; and the latter because you probably won't be writing the features you want about the places you want, you'll be writing the pieces editors want about the places their readers might like to visit.

That said, it's definitely better than a real job.

What is the downside?

It's difficult to find the balance. As a freelancer, you envy the salary and sociability and security of the staffer who doesn't have to travel three times a bloody month; as a staffer, you envy the carefree, be-your-own-boss, get-away-as-often-as-you-like lifestyle of the freelancer who isn't stuck in the office rewriting other people's copy all bloody month.

What's the role of the internet in the landscape of contemporary travel writing?

The internet means all the information holidaymakers could ever possibly need is out there somewhere – but they still want a trusted publication (and at this stage that seems to mean a newspaper or magazine) to filter it for them. Magazines, meanwhile, with their big, gorgeous, glossy, beautifully photographed pages remain a tactile pleasure as yet unmatched by any more modern technology.

How can would-be travel writers best utilise the web for their own professional development?

Having a blog would be a good way of demonstrating your commitment, your savvy and your writing style. And being able to include a link to your work (even if it's self-published online) in your pitch emails might make an editor more inclined to check out your work than if they had to find it for themselves.

Where do you see travel publishing going in the next five years?

I expect to receive an email, any day now, from a PR announcing the moon's first boutique hotel opening.

INTERVIEW WITH

CATHARINE HAMM

Based in the US, Catharine Hamm is the Travel Editor of the *Los Angeles Times*.

How did you start off in your career as a travel editor?

I don't really know how this career happened. I think it's because I can recite all 50 states in alphabetical order in less than 30 seconds. I also have a lot of varied experience: reporter, copy-editor, travel editor, assistant city editor, assistant managing editor, managing editor and the editor at various newspapers. About 10 years ago, I realized my years in news and features had taught me some lessons, the most important of which was this: do something that makes you happy. I looked back at all the jobs I'd had and realized that travel made me very happy, so I applied for the job as deputy travel editor at the LA Times and was lucky enough to be selected and eventually became travel editor.

What is the best way of establishing yourself if you're just starting out in your career as a freelance travel journalist?

Be fresh and bold. And learn to work in multiple platforms, especially the visual ones.

How do you think freelance travel journalists get the numbers to add up in terms of an income?

They don't. The math doesn't add up, unless you can take a story that runs in one newspaper and resell it a gazillion times. It's a tough way to make a living.

What tips would you give to budding travel writers?

1. Good writing begins with good reporting.
2. There is no good writing. There is only good rewriting.
3. As Winston Churchill famously said: 'Never, never, never, never, never give up.'

Are there any courses or any training that you'd recommend a budding travel writer to undertake?

For a long time, I thought a liberal arts foreign language degree was about the most ridiculous thing I could have done. Now I think it's the best preparation I could have had for this job. Take classes, too, to update skills. For instance, if you're not web conversant, look for classes that can help.

What are the most common mistakes that travel writers make in their copy?

Not fact-checking, especially dates. Using too many adjectives and adverbs. Telling the reader, not showing them. Forgetting that it's really good reporting that's the foundation of every story.

What are the most common mistakes that travel writers make when pitching to you?

'I'm going to Rome. Would you like a story?'

What are the main differences between travel writing for a newspaper as opposed to a magazine?

About 1500 words. I think we can be a bit more writerly in a magazine piece, particularly if it's a novel approach to a place that's well known. We can paint word pictures with that extra space that we sometimes can't do in the [newspaper travel] section. But the basics of both are the same: take me along for the ride.

What, in your opinion, constitutes 'good' travel writing?

The same thing that constitutes any good writing: a good foundation of facts; a commitment to truth and fairness; a desire to educate and entertain and, yes, even amuse.

What constitutes 'bad' travel writing?

When there's no 'there' there. Sometimes, as editors, we get seduced by the lovely phrase and the well-crafted paragraph, and when we sit down to edit, we realise it's cotton candy. You know you have a problem when you try to write a headline with an active verb and nothing comes to mind. That's a trick all writers might try to make sure they have a nut graf [nutshell paragraph]; use it to try to write a headline with a verb.

What are the rewards of travel writing as a career?

There are many, but the most important is a kinder heart. To know the world makes me a better, more understanding person.

What has been the downside for you?

It is hard to sit still. That might be the travel bug or it might be Adult Attention Deficit Disorder. Either way, the world sings its siren song, and I can hear it so clearly.

What's the role of the internet in the landscape of contemporary travel writing?

It's hugely important as a source of information, but it also requires a different kind of writing and it needs to make us re-evaluate when and where we write long-form narrative.

How is writing for the web different from writing for magazines and newspapers?

All writing should be fact based, but long-form narrative tries to weave those facts into a rich fabric for the sheer pleasure of the read. The internet, meanwhile, is the tool for people who are seeking information instantly. Indeed, some studies suggest that the web ultimately will change not just what we read but the way we read, which makes our task as writers and purveyors of information much more, um, complex.

How can would-be travel writers best utilise the internet for their own professional development?

It's a goldmine of writing opportunities, but the key is to learn how to adapt what you've already reported to a form that works for the web as well.

Where do you see travel publishing going in the next five years?

We are going to have many more tools in our toolkit for readers. It's not just print; it's not just internet; it's not just video; it's not just electronic newsletters; it's all these things plus stuff we haven't even envisioned yet. Check back with me in five years. I can't predict next week, never mind half a decade from now. I do know this: it's exciting and offers all of us an opportunity to play to our strengths.

INTERVIEW WITH

LYN HUGHES

Based in the UK, Lyn Hughes is the Editor-in-Chief and co-founder of *Wanderlust* magazine.

How did you start off in your career as a travel editor?

I started my own magazine! Back in late 1992, my partner, Paul Morrison, and I were frustrated by the lack of travel magazines. We were heading off to South America for the winter, and on the flight were bored so started scheming out our ideal magazine. The idea stuck, so despite having no previous publishing experience, we launched *Wanderlust* in our spare bedroom a few months after we returned.

What is the best way of establishing yourself if you're just starting out in your career as a freelance travel journalist?

Be as professional as possible, sending editors well-thought-out proposals that demonstrate that you understand their publication and what makes their readers tick. This might sound basic, but it's surprising how many people fall down at this first hurdle.

How do you think freelance travel writers get the numbers to add up in terms of an income?

Some freelance travel writers have a sideline; e.g. as a guidebook writer, a tour leader or a freelance sub-editor. Others are so prolific and proficient that they sell several articles from every trip they do. For instance, this year I sent one of my freelances, Jasper Winn, to do a story in Malawi. To date he has sold five different pieces from that trip to different publications and radio stations. Importantly, all were very different from the *Wanderlust* article, so I had no objections there.

What tips would you give to budding travel writers?

a) Know the market: which magazines and newspapers run travel articles, what style of article they go for and who they are aimed at.

b) Think laterally: about where to send your idea or article, and about the angle.

c) Read. Read travel articles of all types. Understand what makes a good piece.

d) Does your idea pass the 'so what?' test? You say you could write an article on Thailand. So what? So could thousands of other people. Why should we go for you?

e) What are editors going to be looking for? What's in the news? What is going to be a hot destination and why?

f) Don't claim to be 'funnier than Bill Bryson'. People who claim that invariably aren't.

Are there any courses or any training that you'd recommend a budding travel writer to undertake?

The courses run by Travellers' Tales (www.travellerstales.org) are excellent. Like any craft, travel writing needs a lot of practice to develop and improve.

What are the most common mistakes that travel writers make in their copy?

Diary-style articles rarely work, so don't even consider those unless agreed by an editor. Avoid tired clichés – snow-capped mountains, sun-kissed beaches, cacophony of sound, the heat hit me like a sauna. Avoid exclamation marks!!! And make sure you've got an eye-grabbing intro and an interesting last paragraph, too – your article is a story, not a school essay.

What are the most common mistakes that travel writers make when pitching to you?

Not understanding who our readers are. Or saying something along the lines of 'I'm off to Peru – would you like an article?' If it's Peru that you're going to, think of two or three different angles or ways to treat a story that would suit my publication. Tell me why they would be of interest to my readers. And why should I use you and not the dozen other people who have just written in with ideas on Peru?

What are the main differences between travel writing for a magazine as opposed to a newspaper?

Magazines have much longer lead times than newspapers and tend to plan much more in advance. Therefore, it is no use pitching an idea on Christmas breaks in November – you should have been suggesting it the previous February or March.

Likewise, rather than responding to topical items [that are currently] in the news, think ahead to what the trends and newsworthy topics will be in six to 12 months' time. Magazines like to think of themselves as setting the trends and influencing their readers. It is absolutely key that you understand who those readers are and what makes them tick.

Photographs are much more important to a magazine – they use more of them and usually in colour. So, even if you can't supply the photos, they are more likely to go for a story if it's going to be visually interesting.

What, in your opinion, constitutes 'good' travel writing?

Good travel writing should transport the reader to the destination or situation that you're describing. They should be able to hear the sounds, smell the smells, and feel the atmosphere.

What constitutes 'bad' travel writing?

I can't stand 'ego' pieces which are about the author, rather than about the place or the experience. The author is there to guide, inform and entertain the reader, not to be the equivalent of the pub bore.

At the other end of the pendulum, very dry articles that are crammed with facts and figures are equally indigestible.

What are the rewards of travel writing as a career?

You get to see places, have experiences and meet people that you may not have under your own steam. Having a notebook gives you the perfect excuse to nose around and ask questions in a situation where you may have felt too shy or overawed.

What is the downside?

If you want to make travel writing pay, you have to very much treat it as a job, cramming extraordinary trips into just a few days. Your idea of a dream trip might not involve inspecting every hotel in town or having a very boring dinner with the local head of tourism.

And once you're a travel writer, you might find it impossible to ever take a proper holiday again – the temptation to just knock up a piece in your notebook or on your laptop will be too much.

INTERVIEW WITH
LIZZY KREMER

Based in the UK, Lizzy Kremer is an agent at David Higham Associates Ltd in London.

What is the best way of getting an agent? How do you know that they are right for you and vice versa?

Although agencies often indicate that they don't pay any attention to the manuscripts that are sent to them on an unsolicited basis, my experience is that good writing stands out a mile and will be read. If an agent is not interested in representing travel writing, they might not read past the letter. However, you might have to make some of those submissions in order to find the right agent for you. You can call before sending your work but you probably won't gain anything by it. Make sure your submissions are well presented, professional (no long chatty letters) and always enclose a two- to three-page book outline, the first few chapters and a self-addressed envelope. Work hard at getting yourself published in other ways. If you have had articles printed in papers, magazines or websites, enclose those with your manuscript. When choosing your representation, trust your instincts. Go with the agent who seems passionate about your writing. Make sure the agency has a good reputation within the industry by reading up on them in the various writers' handbooks available. You should take as much care as possible when choosing an agent. If you have written something wonderful, the power is in your hands. I take on new clients when two things fall into place – when I love their writing and when I think I can sell the ideas they have. Apart from that I just have to get a sense we would work well together.

What does an agent exactly do?

A good agent will work with you on your book proposal or manuscript prior to making submissions if she feels it could benefit from some editorial attention. Then she will draw up a list of editors she believes will enjoy your work and will want to publish you. Hopefully she will communicate with you effectively – letting you know who she is sending your work to, why she has chosen those people and what you can expect to happen next. She will encourage swift responses from the publishers and perhaps arrange for you to meet them, so that you have an opportunity to sell yourself in person and in order for you to gain a better understanding of the publishing team you might be working with. She will then negotiate the best possible deal for you. That deal might be the result of an auction between editors competing to become your publisher. Or it might simply be a nice deal with the one editor or publishing house who you and your agent believe will do the best possible job of editing and promoting your work. The agent will then negotiate your contract, using all the precedents available to her from the other contracts she has negotiated with your publisher in the past. An agent might retain certain rights, such as translation rights or newspaper serialisation rights, in order to make those further deals herself. Once your contract has been signed, the agent will continue to act as a middle person on certain aspects of your relationship with your publishers, from encouraging their publicity or marketing efforts to chasing moneys due. Publishers usually prefer to commission agented authors because they realise that agents can provide invaluable advice and support to writers. Publishers only prefer unagented authors if they are trying to save money.

What tips would you give to budding travel literature writers?
Work hard at getting yourself published in other ways – in newspapers, magazines and online. Enter writing competitions. Don't limit your writing experience to travel writing – the more you write, the more you will develop your own style.

What are the most common mistakes that travel writers make in their first manuscripts?
They probably aren't any different from the mistakes that writers of all genres make. Don't lose sight of the story and what your book is really about. Don't try too hard. Write from the heart. Don't list everything you did and saw. Remember the book has to have a dramatic arc just as a novel does. Once you think you have finished the book, go back to the start and review the first few chapters again. Inexperienced writers often 'write their way in' to a book, using the first few chapters to find their feet.

What, in your opinion, constitutes 'good' travel writing?

Books which offer a personal or emotional journey as well as a physical one have great appeal. When I pick up a book I want to be moved by it, I want it to change my life. I don't see why I should lower these expectations, even if sometimes it is enough to be entertained. I want to find out about a place but also something about life at the same time.

What constitutes 'bad' travel writing?
Many, many things. Mostly writing which is more about the writing than the travelling, or more about the writer than their journey. It is easier to talk about what is good. Find your own voice, have confidence in your unique perspective and go with your passions and you give your writing the chance to shine.

INTERVIEW WITH

JONATHAN LORIE

Based in the UK, Jonathan Lorie is Contributing Editor at *Traveller* magazine and Director of Travellers' Tales media training.

How did you start off in your career as a travel editor?
I trained and worked as a professional journalist and then acquired some serious travel experience, especially in unusual places: 41 countries so far! You need both halves of the equation – professional skills and travel experience.

What is the best way of establishing yourself if you're just starting out in your career as a freelance travel journalist?

A good route is to develop a specialism in something – get yourself known to editors for whatever it is, whether it's extreme-sports travel or humorous writing or Spanish resorts, or whatever. That way they will come back to you, which is a nice position to be in.

How do freelance travel writers get the numbers to add up in terms of an income?
The smart operators sell three or four stories from each trip, rewritten for different outlets. And of

course they get the trips for free by getting themselves known to the PR people who run the press trips.

What tips would you give to budding travel writers?

Come up with the goods and keep your nose clean. Deliver what you promise or what you're asked for, to length and on time. Don't tell people you've got a commission when you haven't, don't leave facts unchecked, don't let editors down. Reliability is as important as talent.

Are there any courses or any training that you'd recommend a budding travel writer to undertake?

Absolutely. I run the leading training agency in this field, Travellers Tales. We offer two- to seven-day courses with top experts in London and around the world, and the difference in people's ability and knowledge and confidence after a little training is amazing. There are also courses in features writing and photojournalism at some universities, which are good general training opportunities.

What are the most common mistakes that travel writers make in their copy?

Simple things like length and style, and unchecked facts. All these are easy to get right, with a little care and attention.

What are the most common mistakes that travel writers make when pitching to you?

They haven't read our magazine and pitch things that we don't want.

What are the main differences between travel writing for a newspaper as opposed to a magazine?

Increasingly, newspaper articles on travel are consumer guides – how to visit this or that place – whereas some magazines still allow a more personal impression of what a place or journey is like.

What, in your opinion, constitutes 'good' travel writing?

Something that takes you there, leads you through those streets, makes you feel the reality of the journey. I don't think good travel writing has to be complimentary about a place – bad trips often make the best articles.

What constitutes 'bad' travel writing?

Formula writing, where the author either hasn't really been there or else hasn't felt anything about the place. This always shows.

What are the rewards of travel writing as a career?

You'll have some great trips and meet some fascinating people. If you're lucky, you'll also be allowed to write articles that you really like writing.

What is the downside?

You won't earn a fortune and you'll spend a lot of time pitching stories that don't work out. But if you're prepared to persist, you'll make it.

INTERVIEW WITH

SARAH MILLER

Based in the UK, Sarah Miller is the Editor of *Condé Nast Traveller* magazine.

How did you start off in your career as a travel editor?

I started off in features, working on monthly magazines and then 12 years on two British national newspapers – the *Sunday Times* followed by the *Daily Telegraph*. I edited features sections on the weekly paper and was also Assistant Editor of the *Sunday Times Magazine*, followed by working in features across the board for the *Daily Telegraph*, where I was also Arts Editor and Features Editor of the *Saturday Telegraph*. I was approached to launch the UK edition of *Condé Nast Traveller* precisely because I'm an editor and a journalist rather than a 'travel' journalist. Condé Nast wanted someone who understood that travel, rather than being a separate compartment, a section of a newspaper, is part of the mainstream, integral to everyone's lives, from the food we eat to the clothes we pack.

What is the best way of establishing yourself if you're just starting out in your career as a freelance travel journalist?

Starting off your career by being a travel writer is extremely difficult – too many people think that just because they can get about the world, they can write. If you can try getting some work experience, you'll be a remembered name (if you leave your CV and have been willing and enthusiastic) when you make a pitch to an editor you know. Pitching correctly is everything. Editors want good, original journalistic ideas which are timely and relevant to a publication and its production schedules. Also, don't muddy the pitch by also claiming to be a good photographer. Get your words accepted first.

How can freelance travel journalists get the numbers to add up in terms of an income?

Be flexible but understand that supplying work that appears everywhere may not be as rewarding a financial option as you think. It's better to build relationships with editors of complementary publications – a monthly travel magazine, a newspaper section, foreign publications – so that each editor doesn't feel you're writing for their direct competitors. Tailor-make your ideas to each. Don't send the same list of ideas to everyone but make each editor feel you are right for their brand. No editor wants to come second or feel that they're being offered second-hand goods. This way you can establish a regular income baseline and build from there. As a general rule, editors prefer working directly with writers rather than through agents, though they are helpful, once you are more established, for expanding your list of outlets. Try to write in areas other than travel – main features, columns, books, scripts. And maximise your earning potential from the four or five 'complementary' publications through syndication round the world. I prefer to work with writers who will sign rights agreements.

And, from a writer's point of view, letting the organisations deal with selling frees up time for pitching and writing.

What tips would you give to budding travel writers?

Ideas are stories, they're not countries. Most people try to cover too much. An entire gap year is a guide book, not an article. The best pieces are relevant, timely and finely focused. And whether you're writing for a newspaper or magazine, think about what would sell it, what is going to make the public buy it. Understanding lead times is essential. It's no good pitching a good idea if by the time it comes out, the peg has gone. It's tough being a freelance writer, particularly in travel. I always say don't specialise only in travel writing unless you're being published really regularly.

Are there any courses or any training that you'd recommend a budding travel writer to undertake?

Good writing is good writing and is usually born from experience. This notion that there are 'travel' writers is something I sometimes think was dreamt up by retailers who like to pigeonhole what they display. There are good journalism courses out there – Cardiff School of Journalism or London College of Printing – but I would always see these as an extra to a good degree and interesting life. On the other hand, I don't know a single writer who hasn't benefited from a subbing course. Accurate, clear expression as much as evocation is the essence of being a good writer.

What are the most common mistakes that travel writers make in their copy?

They talk too much about themselves, getting to a place, and imagine a linear narrative of 'and then, and next'. Plus, while I don't recommend selling yourself as a photographer at the same time, not enough writers have a sense of what a piece could look like visually – both photographically or how it could be 'packaged' on the page.

What are the most common mistakes that travel writers make when pitching to you?

Spelling mistakes which make you doubt their ability to be accurate. Ideas which are encyclopedic and undiscriminating. And it's all too obvious when someone hasn't actually read the publication they're pitching to. Travel writers too often rattle off a list of every destination they've ever visited from A to Z and say they could write a piece on any of them. Also, they tend to forget that there are only so many pieces per publication per year. For instance, a monthly magazine only has 12 issues a year, and it's unlikely a writer would appear more than once in an issue, or even in every issue. Good travel writers are also acutely aware of timing and the seasons. It's no good pitching a skiing idea halfway through the season to a monthly because they are already onto their spring/summer issues.

What are the main differences between travel writing for a newspaper as opposed to a magazine?

Newspapers offer more scope to writers in some ways because there are 52 editions a year – so they need more copy. Also, they don't rely on display photography in the same way so a person with three good ideas would stand a better chance of seeing all three get published in the course of a year. But travel magazines can usually run longer pieces.

What, in your opinion, constitutes 'good' travel writing?

Good travel writing shouldn't read like a dissertation. A good destination piece should make you feel you're there. I stop and listen to how a piece 'sounds', 'smells', 'looks' or whether it makes me laugh. I also look for people – too many writers deliver pieces that feel like the Mary Celeste. News reports should open my eyes to something I didn't know before. And the very best writing always makes me feel I want to read it again, like a good novel.

What constitutes 'bad' travel writing?

Reliance on where the next free trip is coming from and travel clichés – if I read 'As we banked over Rio...', then the piece goes straight in the bin. Also, pieces that leave you thinking you could be anywhere in the world. And finally, writing that is trying too hard to be clever.

What are the rewards of travel writing as a career?

Not losing a sense of wonder.

What are the downsides?

It's very hard to succeed and can get quite lonely out there.

INTERVIEW WITH

AMY RENNERT

Based in the US, Amy Rennert is the former Editor-in-Chief of *San Francisco* magazine and the founder and president of the Amy Rennert Agency, Inc.

What is the best way of getting an agent? How do you know that they are right for you and vice versa?

The best way to get an agent is to do your research first. Publishers Marketplace (www.publishers marketplace.com) is a great resource, as is *Jeff Herman's Guide to Book Publishers, Editors and Literary Agents*. It's also a good idea to check the acknowledgements pages in appropriate books. It's important to take the time and care to follow specific submission guidelines. Some agents want a query first, others will accept sample pages; some will accept email submissions, others won't. It shows that you've done your research and respect the agent's practices if you follow their guidelines.

What does an agent exactly do?

An agent has many roles, but the most accurate definition of a literary agent is the person who guides you and acts as your advocate – from start to finish –

through the publishing process. I'm a former national magazine editor and I consider myself an author's first editor before we sell the book. Agents send proposals and manuscripts to appropriate publishers and then make deals on the authors' behalf. They also provide critical feedback during the editorial process and then help promote, market and advertise your work after publication. Many agents, myself included, have a wide range of media contacts, so we often help sell subrights, including first serial and film.

As an agent I don't just represent the book. I represent authors and I'm very involved in career management as well.

What tips would you give to budding travel literature writers?
Travel! And write while you travel, so you don't forget about specific thoughts and experiences once you return home. Also, it is always smart to try to establish a name for yourself – try to get articles or essays published in smaller, regional magazines, and gradually you'll make a name for yourself.

And read! Read other pieces of travel writing to see what works and what doesn't work. Know the marketplace so that you aren't trying to sell something that's been done numerous times. Also,

it is important to determine what kind of travel writing you want to do.

What, do you find, are the most common mistakes that travel writers make in their first manuscripts?
They give too many details about the trip, the preparation for it, getting visas, packing their bags, telling people about the upcoming trip, why they are taking it, getting to the airport – rather than concentrating on the real heart of the story. Often these are facts and incidents that happen to pretty much everyone who travels – they don't have a unique perspective or point of view. I think new writers feel they need to give all of the background up front. That may be a good and useful writing exercise for the writer but it's not appreciated by the reader. They should go back and cut judiciously – start where the story really starts.

What, in your opinion, constitutes 'good' travel writing?
A strong voice – Pico Iyer, Simon Winchester and Jan Morris are some of my personal favourites. We see a lot of travel writing that doesn't have any real voice. I look for compelling narrative nonfiction that reads like great fiction.

INTERVIEW WITH

ROBERT UPE

Robert Upe is former Travel Editor of the *Age* in Melbourne, Australia.

How did you start off in your career as a travel editor?

Twenty-five years as a journalist at metropolitan newspapers in various roles, from reporter to sub-editor to chief sub-editor of sport and features, production editor, magazines editor and, perhaps most importantly, ski writer, which put me on the edge of travel. Wrote weekly winter ski column for almost two decades, then a couple of ski guidebooks, which helped me into mainstream travel.

What is the best way of establishing yourself if you're just starting out in your career as a freelance travel journalist?

Networking. Join a travel writers' association and mix with fellow freelancers and public relations people. Know the industry and the people in it. The contacts will ultimately pay off. Submit articles far and wide and persist despite knockbacks.

How do you think freelance travel writers get the numbers to add up in terms of an income?

Most don't get the numbers to add up. But the most successful freelancers network continuously and are well known with fellow freelancers, PR people and newspaper travel editors. They sell their stories overseas as well as their home country. They will produce several stories from one trip. They will offer photos or photo sources to go with their stories, thus maximising chances of being accepted.

What tips would you give to budding travel writers?

Instead of pitching destination pieces like everyone else, offer a completed consumer article such as 'how to get the best seat on the plane'. Few freelancers offer these, so your chances of getting published will increase. Once you have a few consumer articles published, the travel editor will be more inclined to consider a destination piece. Try to write a guidebook for a publisher such as Lonely Planet. Guidebook writing is a good discipline and helps establish credentials.

Are there any courses or any training that you'd recommend a budding travel writer to undertake?
No particular courses, but read the good travel writers (in books, newspapers and magazines) and take note of their techniques and story structures.

What are the most common mistakes that travel writers make in their copy?
They don't get into the skin of a destination and they are too general and try to cover too much ground. The reader needs to 'feel' the destination. Copy littered with superlatives is a turn-off and so are intros with statistics. Make sure it's a 'travel' story. That sounds silly, but so many writers stray from the main premise and end up offering social commentary or history pieces.

What are the most common mistakes that travel writers make when pitching to you?
They pitch vague ideas or too many ideas in one go. Complex pitches that are going to take a long time to deal with are usually spiked. I prefer completed stories

to ideas, because almost every idea sounds good.

What, in your opinion, constitutes 'good' travel writing?
Be original.
First-person narrative allows the writer to get into the skin of a destination (but need to be careful not to overdo).
Extra research helps. You may be salmon fishing in Canada and it may make for an atmospheric piece, but what type of salmon are they, are they good fighters, good to eat, prized by the locals etc. You may be writing about Sun Valley and that Ernest Hemmingway shot himself there, but where, what time, how. Extra detail provides extra dimension to the story.

What constitutes 'bad' travel writing?
Copy that is too general and gushing and clichéd and lazy.

What is the downside of travel writing as a career?
Difficult to make a reasonable income and need to be away a lot.

What's the role of the internet in the landscape of contemporary travel writing?
Research.

How do you think would-be travel writers can best utilise the web

for their own professional development?

Discerning research for background information, but NEVER as the main source of a destination article. To be relevant you need to be on the road a lot.

Where do you see travel publishing going in the next five years?

More integration between printed articles and online, with increased and better use of photo galleries and video clips by the author.

~ *Part 3* ~

RESOURCES

HERE'S A HANDY GUIDE TO GET YOU STARTED AND
HELP YOU ALONG THE WAY: A COMPENDIUM OF
VALUABLE RESOURCES IN THE UK, US AND AUSTRALIA,
SUCH AS PUBLICATIONS, ORGANISATIONS, WEBSITES,
REFERENCE BOOKS AND MUCH MORE.

UK RESOURCES

GENERAL GUIDES TO PUBLISHERS, EDITORS & LITERARY AGENTS

The Directory of UK & Irish Book Publishers

by the Booksellers Association
www.ukpublishers.net

The Directory of UK & Irish Publishers is an annually updated guide to publishers in the UK and Ireland, containing details of over 3000 publishers in an A-Z listing. The Online Directory (accessible for subcription period of one year to purchasers of the printed guide) includes an additional 6000 or so entries. Details include named contacts, business type and email and web addresses. You can order through the Booksellers Association (www.booksellers.org.uk or email mail@booksellers.org.uk).

Writers' & Artists' Yearbook

by A&C Black
www.writersandartists.co.uk

Revised and updated annually, the *Writers' & Artists' Yearbook* is the bestselling reference guide that all UK writers and artists have on their bookshelves – whether you are looking at writing a book or a magazine or newspaper article. The *Writers' & Artists' Yearbook* gives comprehensive listings of magazines, newspapers, book publishers, literary and artists' agents, and theatre, television and radio producers. Not to mention its listings of picture agencies, societies, prizes, creative writing courses, festivals and much, much more.

MAJOR TRAVEL PUBLISHERS

TRAVEL GUIDEBOOKS

Berlitz

58 Borough High St, London SE1 1XF
☎ 020-7403 0284, Fax 020-7403 0290
insight@apaguide.co.uk
www.berlitzpublishing.com

Over 130 pocket guidebooks to the world put together by the team that also produces the Insight Guides.

Bradt Travel Guides

23 High St, Chalfont St Peter, Buckinghamshire SL9 9QE
☎ 01753-893444, Fax 01753-892333
info@bradtguides.com
www.bradt-travelguides.com

Bradt Travel Guides focuses on emerging travel destinations. The company has over 70 titles in print.

Cadogan Guides

New Holland Publishers, Garfield House, 86-88 Egdware Rd, London W2 2EA
☎ 020-7724 7773, Fax 020-7258 1293
info@cadoganguides.co.uk
www.newhollandpublishers.com/cadogan-guides.asp

Around 100 titles covering the following series: country & regional guides, city guides, Buying Property Abroad guides, Working & Living Abroad, Take the Kids and a travel literature series.

Crimson Publishing

Westminster House, Kew Rd, Richmond, Surrey TW9 2ND
☎ 020-8334 1600, Fax 020-8334 1601
info@crimsonpublishing.co.uk

www.crimsonpublishing.co.uk

Series include: country guides, Living & Working Abroad, Jobs Abroad, and guides to buying a house overseas.

Dorling Kindersley

Penguin Group (UK), 80 Strand, London WC2R 0RL

☎ 020-7010 3000, Fax 020-7010 6060

travelguides@uk.dk.com

www.dk.com

Highly visual Eyewitness country, city and regional guidebooks and a Top Ten series for world cities.

Footprint Handbooks

6 Riverside Ct, Lower Bristol Rd, Bath BA2 3DZ

☎ 01225-469141, Fax 01225-469461

discover@footprintbooks.com

www.footprintbooks.com

Travel guides for independent and adventurous travellers with over 90 titles.

Insight Guides

58 Borough High St, London SE1 1XF

☎ 020-7403 0284, Fax 020-7403 0290

insight@apaguide.co.uk

www.insightguides.com

Over 200 pictorial guides to the world plus pocket guides and compact guides. Also publishes a range of thematic guides.

Itchy Media

Unit 2, Whitehorse Yard, 78 Liverpool Rd, London N1 0QD

☎ 020-7288 4300, Fax 020-7359 9611

all@itchymedia.co.uk

www.itchymedia.co.uk

Pocket-sized UK city guides for those aged between 18 and 35.

Lonely Planet Publications

2nd fl, 186 City Rd, London EC1V 2NT

☎ 020-7106 2100, Fax 020-7106 2101

go@lonelyplanet.co.uk

www.lonelyplanet.com

One of the world's leading travel media companies, publishing over 600 titles across 17 different languages.

Rough Guides

Penguin Group (UK), 80 Strand, London WC2R 0RL

☎ 020-7010 3000

write@roughguides.com

www.roughguides.com

More than 200 travel guidebooks, plus music and other reference guides. Go online to find details on how to write for them.

Thomas Cook Publishing

PO Box 227, Units 15/16 The Thomas Cook Business Park, Peterborough PE3 8SB

☎ 01733-416477, Fax 01733-416688

books@thomascook.com

www.thomascookpublishing.com

More than 160 titles to cities, countries and regions aimed at a variety of travellers from soft backpackers to more mainstream holiday-makers.

Time Out Guides

Universal House, 251 Tottenham Court Rd, London W1T 7AB

☎ 020-7813 3000

guides@timeout.com

www.timeout.com

More than 100 overseas city guides, separate guides to London shopping, eating, children, sport, pubs and bars, plus national eating and drinking guides and a biannual guide to Europe by air.

Trailblazer Publications

The Old Manse, Power Rd, Hindhead, Surrey GU26 6SU

Enquiries by fax or email only

Fax 01428-607571

info@trailblazer-guides.com

www.trailblazer-guides.com

A range of route guides for the adventurous traveller including walking guides and rail guides.

TRAVEL LITERATURE

Bloomsbury Publishing

36 Soho Sq, London W1D 3QY
☎ 020-7494 2111, Fax 020-7434 0151
aspectguides@bloomsbury.com for the travel guidebooks
www.bloomsbury.com

Bloomsbury does not have a large travel literature list but is always interested in manuscripts with 'legs'. The company also publishes a small range of guides to hotels and restaurants in France.

Eye Books

8 Peacock Yard, Iliffe St, London SE17 3LH
☎ 0845-450 8870, Fax 01746-766665
info@eye-books.com
www.eye-books.com

Small publishing house specialising in travel books about personal journeys and growth – ordinary people doing extraordinary things.

Faber and Faber

3 Queen Sq, London WC1N 3AU
☎ 020-7465 0189, Fax 020-7465 0034
editorial@faber.co.uk
www.faber.co.uk

Publisher of Jan Morris, Tobias Jones and Benedict Allen. Travel literature appears within its nonfiction list.

HarperCollins Publishers

77–85 Fulham Palace Rd, Hammersmith, London W6 8JB
☎ 020-8741 7070
webcontact@harpercollins.co.uk
www.harpercollins.co.uk

Most travel literature is published under the Flamingo imprint.

Hodder & Stoughton

338 Euston Rd, London NW1 3BH
☎ 020-7873 6000, Fax 020-7873 6024
www.hachettelivre.co.uk

Recent travel-related titles include David Moore's *Accidental Pilgrim: Travels with a Celtic Saint* and *Stealing Water: A Secret Life in an African City*, by Tim Ecott.

John Murray (Publishers)

338 Euston Rd, London NW1 3BH
☎ 020-7873 6000, Fax 020-7873 6442
www.hachettelivre.co.uk/publishers/johnmurray

Publishers of distinguished travel literature authors like Dervla Murphy and Patrick Leigh Fermor. The list continues to be built with new travel literature authors.

Little, Brown Book Group

100 Victoria Embankment, London EC4Y 0DY
☎ 020-7911 8000, Fax 020-7911 8100
info@littlebrown.co.uk
www.littlebrown.co.uk

'While we strongly prefer submissions to be sent via an agent, we do occasionally accept unsolicited material.'

Lonely Planet Publications

2nd fl, 186 City Rd, London EC1V 2NT
☎ 020-7106 2100, Fax 020-7106 2101
go@lonelyplanet.co.uk
www.lonelyplanet.com

Lonely Planet's travel literature series was launched in 1996, and features a mix of single-author narratives and anthologies. Proposals for travel literature titles should be sent to the Australia office (see p316).

The Orion Publishing Group

Orion House, 5 Upper St Martin's Lane, London WC2H 9EA
☎ 020-7240 3444, Fax 020-7379 6158
info@orionbooks.co.uk
www.orionbooks.co.uk

Weidenfeld & Nicolson is the imprint where travel literature is published.

Pan Macmillan

20 New Wharf Rd, London N1 9RR
☎ 020-7014 6000, Fax 020-7014 6001
www.panmacmillan.co.uk

Travel Literature is published in all imprints. Only manuscripts submitted by an agent are considered.

Penguin
80 Strand, London WC2R 0RL
☎ 020-7010 3000, Fax 020-7010 6060
customer.service@penguin.co.uk
www.penguin.co.uk
Publishers of Paul Theroux and Redmond O'Hanlon, Penguin does not accept any unsolicited manuscripts.

Random House Group
20 Vauxhall Bridge Rd, London SW1V 2SA
☎ 020-7840 8400, Fax 020-7233 8791
www.randomhouse.co.uk
Publishes travel literature in a range of imprints including Jonathan Cape, Chatto & Windus, Vintage, Ebury and Arrow. All need to be contacted separately – ring the main telephone number for details.

Transworld
61–63 Uxbridge Rd, London W5 5SA
☎ 020-8579 2652, Fax 020-8579 5479
info@transworld-publishers.co.uk
www.booksattransworld.co.uk
Publishers of Bill Bryson; most travel literature comes out in the Black Swan, Bantam and Doubleday imprints.

TRAVEL MAGAZINES

ABTA Magazine
2nd Floor, 197–199 City Rd, London EC1V 1JN
☎ 020-7253 9906, Fax 020-7250 0955
editorial@absolutepublishing.com
www.absolutepublishing.com
Monthly travel trade publication containing in-depth analysis of issues affecting the travel trade from an industry perspective.

Adventure Travel
5 Alscot Workshop, Alscot Park, Atherstone on Stour, Stratford Upon Avon, Warwicks CV37 8BL
☎ 01789-450000, Fax 01789-459046
lara@atmagazine.co.uk
www.adventuretravelmagazine.co.uk
Bimonthly travel magazine aimed at the 25–45 age group, particularly to trekkers and aspiring mountaineers.

Business Traveller
2nd Floor Cardinal House, 39–40 Albemarle St, London W1S 4TE
☎ 020-7647 6330, Fax 020-7647 6331
editorial@businesstraveller.com
www.businesstraveller.com
Monthly consumer magazine with destination features which are business or lifestyle related.

Condé Nast Traveller
Vogue House, Hanover Sq, London W1S 1JU
☎ 020-7499 9080
No enquiries by fax
cntraveller@condenast.co.uk
www.cntraveller.co.uk
Glossy, monthly travel/lifestyle magazine aimed at the high end of the market.

Food & Travel
Suite 51, The Business Centre, Ingate Place, London SW8 3NS
☎ 020-7501 0511, Fax 020-7501 0510
info@foodandtravel.com
www.foodandtravel.com
The best in food and travel from around the world; comes out monthly.

France Magazine
Archant Life Ltd, Cumberland House, Oriel Rd, Cheltenham, Glos GL50 1BB
☎ 01242 216050, Fax 01242 216074
editorial@francemag.com
www.completefrance.com/magazines/france-magazine
Monthly magazine about France. No unsolicited copy; ideas by email.

Geographical (magazine of the Royal Geographical Society)

Circle Publishing, 2nd Floor, 83–84 George St, Richmond upon Thames, Surrey TW9 1HE
☎ 020-8332 2713, Fax 020-8332 9307
magazine@geographical.co.uk
www.geographical.co.uk
Monthly magazine for RGS members and the wider public. Postal submissions.

Globe

Globetrotters Club, BCM/Roving, London WC1N 3XX
☎ 020-8674 6229 (information line only)
danjames@ntlworld.com
www.globetrotters.co.uk
This is the bimonthly magazine of the Globetrotters Club (see General Travel Information & Advice, p295 for details). Articles can be posted or emailed; there's no financial remuneration.

High Life & Business Life

Cedar Communications, 85 Strand, London WC2R 0DW
☎ 020-7550 8000
high.life@cedarcom.co.uk
www.bahighlife.com
High Life is the monthly in-flight magazine for British Airways passengers. Business Life is carried only on short-haul British Airways flights and carries lifestyle stories with a business twist.

Holiday Which?

Consumers' Association, 2 Marylebone Rd, London NW1 4DF
☎ 020-7770 7548, Fax 020-7770 7663
holiday@which.co.uk
www.which.net
Published four times a year (January, March, May and September); provides independent travel features, investigative articles and hard news on all aspects of holidaying in the UK and abroad. Most articles are written by *Holiday Which?* staff; occasionally freelancers are employed. Unsolicited manuscripts not accepted.

Living France

Archant Life Ltd, Archant House, Oriel Rd, Cheltenham, Glocs GL50 1BB
☎ 01242-216092, Fax 01242-216094
editorial@livingfrance.com
www.livingfrance.com
Monthly magazine on France and French property. Submissions by email.

Lonely Planet Traveller

BBC Worldwide, Media Centre, 201 Wood Lane, London W12 7QT
☎ 020-8433 1702
lpmagazine@bbc.com
www.lonelyplanet.com/magazine
Monthly travel magazine providing independent travel advice and information.

Merricks Media

Units 3 & 4, Riverside Court, Lower Bristol Rd, Bath, Somerset BA2 3DZ
☎ 01225 786846, Fax 01225 786861
info@merricksmedia.co.uk
www.merricksmedia.co.uk
Magazines include *French, Greece, Australia and New Zealand, Portugal, Spanish Homes* and *Italian*; monthly or bimonthly, these magazines all have culture, lifestyle, and buying a property features in them.

The Sunday Times Travel Magazine

Level 4, 1 Pennington St, London E98 1ST
☎ 020-7782 7405, Fax 020-7867 0410
travelmag@sunday-times.co.uk
www.sundaytimestravel.co.uk
Monthly glossy newsstand magazine covering all things holiday. Email submissions.

TNT Magazine

TNT Group, 14–15 Childs Place, Earls Court, London SW5 9RX
☎ 020-7373 3377, Fax 020-7341 6600
tnteditor@tntmag.co.uk
www.tntmagazine.com/uk
A weekly free magazine for UK-based travellers, *TNT Magazine* is distributed in

London and Edinburgh. Email submissions. Also interested in photographs.

Travel Trade Gazette
First Floor, Ludgate House, 245 Blackfriars Rd, London SE1 9UY
☎ 020-7921 8005, Fax 020-7921 8032
www.ttglive.com
A weekly newspaper for the travel trade.

Travel Weekly
Quadrant House, The Quadrant, Sutton, Surrey SM2 5AS
☎ 020-8652 3500, Fax 020-8652 3956
travel.weekly@rbi.co.uk
www.travelweekly.co.uk
Weekly travel industry newspaper. Email submissions.

Traveller
Wexas Ltd, 45–49 Brompton Rd, London SW3 1DE
☎ 020-7589 0500, Fax 020-7581 8476
traveller@wexas.com
www.wexas.com/traveller-magazine/
Guidelines: www.wexas.com/publications/traveller_magazine/contributors_guidelines.aspx
Quarterly travel magazine for the Wexas travellers' club aimed at a 35+ age group.

Wanderlust Magazine
1 Leworth Place, Mellor Walk, Windsor, Berks SL4 1EB
☎ 01753-620426, Fax 01753-620474
info@wanderlust.co.uk
www.wanderlust.co.uk
Guidelines: www.wanderlust.co.uk/article.php?page_id=2035
Leading magazine for independent-minded travellers, published eight times a year.

NEWSPAPERS

The Daily Mail
Travel Desk, Associated Newspapers, Northcliffe House, 2 Derry St, London W8 5TT
☎ 020-7938 7153
No enquiries by fax
travel@dailymail.co.uk
www.travelmail.co.uk

Main travel section of between eight and 12 pages is published on Saturday. Also a small travel section on Wednesday.

The Daily Telegraph
Travel Desk, 111 Buckingham Palace Rd, London SW1W 0DT
☎ 020-7931 2391
traveldesk@telegraph.co.uk
www.telegraph.co.uk/travel
The Saturday travel section ranges from between 12 and 42 pages but usually comes out at 18. Also do *Ultratravel.*

The Guardian
Travel Desk, 119 Farringdon Rd, London EC1R 3ER
☎ 020-7239 9591, Fax 020-7239 9935
travel@guardian.co.uk
www.guardian.co.uk/theguardian/travel
Eighteen- to 20-page travel supplement on a Saturday.

The Independent
Travel Desk, Independent House, 191 Marsh Wall, London E14 9RS
☎ 020-7005 2834, Fax 020-7005 2999
travel@independent.co.uk
www.independent.co.uk/travel
Twenty-four-page travel tabloid – *Independent Traveller* – on a Saturday.

Independent on Sunday
Travel Desk, Independent House, 191 Marsh Wall, London E14 9RS
☎ 020-7005 2000, Fax 020-7005 2999
sundaytravel@independent.co.uk
www.independent.co.uk/travel
Ten- to 12-page travel section pubon a Sunday.

Mail on Sunday
Travel Desk, Associated Newspapers, Northcliffe House, 2 Derry St, London W8 5TS
☎ 020-7938 6000, Fax 020-7937 3829
www.travelmail.co.uk
About 12 to 18 pages of travel published on Sunday. Please mail any article proposals.

The Observer

Travel Desk, 119 Farringdon Rd, London EC1R 3ER
☎ 020-7713 4181, Fax 020-7239 9508
escape@observer.co.uk
www.guardian.co.uk/theobserver/escape

From 14 to 30 pages of travel on a Sunday. Occasionally, the paper produces an *Observer Travel Magazine*. Please fax all travel story proposals, rather than ring.

The Sunday Telegraph

Travel Desk, 111 Buckingham Palace Rd, London SW1W 0DT
☎ 020-7931 2000
traveldesk@telegraph.co.uk
www.telegraph.co.uk/travel

Sunday travel section of up to 15 pages.

The Sunday Times

Travel Desk, News International, 1 Pennington St, London E98 1ST
☎ 020-7782 5819, Fax 020-7782 5540
travel@sunday-times.co.uk
www.timesonline.co.uk/tol/travel

Sunday travel section of up to 30 pages.

The Times

Travel Desk, News International, 1 Pennington St, London E98 1TT
☎ 020-7782 5173, Fax 020-7782 5927
travel@thetimes.co.uk
www.timesonline.co.uk/tol/travel

Saturday travel section of up to 26 pages.

ONLINE

Please bear in mind that some of these publications pay for stories and some do not.

Globetrotters e-newsletter

http://globetrotters.co.uk/newsletter

If you enjoy writing, the Globetrotters' e-newsletter would love to hear from you: your travel stories, anecdotes, jokes, questions, hints and tips up to 750 words, together with a couple of sentences about yourself and a contact email address. Over 8,000 people currently subscribe to the Globetrotter e-news.

Highbury Columbus Travel Publishing

www.travel-guide.com
☎ 01322-660070 (ask for Head of Editorial)

Comprehensive online information on every country, 101 major cities and 200 airports worldwide. An in-house editorial team and a network of freelance travel writers update this on a daily basis.

Teletext Holidays

traveldesk@teletext.co.uk
www.teletextholidays.co.uk

Extensive bank of travel guides and information – mostly uses in-house staff to update travel information but occasionally uses freelance travel writers.

TravelMag

ed@travelmag.co.uk
www.travelmag.co.uk

An online travel magazine supported by Wexas, the travel club. Interested in both articles and pictures. Contributor guidelines are found online. There's no payment but it's a good way of getting your name in print.

TravelMole

editor@travelmole.com
www.travelmole.com

Online network of over 90,000 members of the travel and tourism industry. There's a lot on this site including daily trade news reports, chat forums and reference directories. The site uses travel trade writers from time to time.

TravelNotes

www.travelnotes.org

A US online guide to travel. The site needs Roving Reporters, Country Correspondents, Credible City Guides and

Cyberspace Travellers. Contributor guidelines and contact details are online and you can gain exposure for your work (and maybe earn a little extra money) by being published by them.

ViaMichelin UK

www.viamichelin.com

This website mostly offers travel assistance but freelance travel writers are used to update and compile the monthly online magazine section.

World Rover

editor@worldrover.net

www.worldrover.net

A US site which takes contributions from UK writers, although unpaid.

WRITERS' GROUPS & ASSOCIATIONS

Arts Council England (National Office)

14 Great Peter St, London SW1P 3NQ

☎ 0845-300 6200, Fax 020-7973 6590

enquiries@artscouncil.org.uk

www.artscouncil.org.uk

The Arts Council England is the national development agency for the arts, investing public funds in both individuals and organisations. The Arts Council supports writers through Grants for the Arts, through the annual Arts Council England Writers' Awards scheme, through International Fellowships and a whole range of literary prizes.

British Guild of Travel Writers

BGTW Secretariat, 5 Berwick Courtyard, Berwick St Leonard, Salisbury, Wiltshire SP3 5UA

☎ 01747-820455, Fax 020-8975 2801

info@bgtw.org

www.bgtw.org

Over 200 members of journalists, authors, editors, photographers and broadcasters involved in the world of travel. Strict membership criteria are detailed on the guild's website.

Directory of Writers' Circles, Courses and Workshops

Diana Hayden, 39 Lincoln Way, Harlington, Bedfordshire LU5 6NG

☎ 01525-873197, No Fax

diana@writers-circles.com

www.writers-circles.com

There are over 1000 writing circles in the UK and Ireland. You can contact Diana Hayden by email or phone and she will tell you of the writing circle nearest to you. She also publishes a printed directory of writing circles which you can buy.

The English Centre of International PEN

6–8 Armwell St, London EC1R 1UQ

☎ 020-7713 0023, Fax 020-7837 7838

enquiries@englishpen.org

www.englishpen.org

A membership organisation for writers and literary professionals founded in 1921, providing an active and supportive focus in the home community for writers and other professionals working in the literary sector.

Llenyddiaeth Cymru (Literature Wales)

4th fl, Cambrian Buildings, Mount Stuart Sq, Cardiff CF10 5FL

☎ 029-2047 2266, Fax 029-2049 2930

post@literaturewales.org

www.literaturewales.org

Represents the interests of Welsh writers and Welsh writing both inside Wales and beyond. It works in partnership with Ty Newydd, the Cricieth-based residential writers' centre. It runs events, courses, competitions, tours by authors, lectures, international exchanges, readings, literary performances and festivals. It offers bursaries and administers the annual Book of the Year award.

National Association of Writers' Groups

Mike and Diane Wilson, 40 Burstall Hill, Bridlington, East Yorkshire YO16 7GA

☎ 01262-609228, Fax 01262-609228

nawg@tesco.net

www.nawg.co.uk

Launched in 1995, there are over 150 affiliated groups and over 100 associate (individual) members spread across the UK. The Association aims to bring cohesion and fellowship to isolated writers' groups and individuals, promoting the study and art of writing in all its aspects. On its site there's a list of writers' groups, details of the competitions, festival of writing and bimonthly magazine.

National Union of Journalists

Headland House, 308–312 Gray's Inn Rd, London WC1X 8DP

☎ 020-7278 7916, Fax 020-7837 8143

info@nuj.org.uk

www.nuj.org.uk

The National Union of Journalists is the biggest journalists' union in the world, with 34,000 members. There are offices in Dublin, Glasgow and Manchester. You can find help with training, legal services, advice on what freelance writers should be paid, and much more. Ten times a year the union publishes a magazine called the *Journalist*.

Outdoor Writers' Guild

PO Box 520, Bamber Bridge, Preston, Lancashire PR5 8LF

☎ 01772-321243, Fax 0870-137 8888

secretary@owg.org.uk

www.owg.org.uk

Membership is open to writers, journalists, photographers, illustrators, broad-

casters, filmmakers, artists, publishers and editors, actively and professionally involved in sustainable activities in any outdoor setting.

Public Lending Right

Richard House, Sorbonne Close, Stockton-on-Tees TS17 6DA

☎ 01642-604699, Fax 01642-615641

authorservices@plr.uk.com

www.plr.uk.com

Under the UK's PLR Scheme authors receive payments from government funds for the free borrowing of their books from public libraries in the UK. To qualify for payment, you must apply to register your books with them.

Society of Authors

84 Drayton Gardens, London SW10 9SB

☎ 020-7373 6642, Fax 020-7373 5768

info@societyofauthors.org

www.societyofauthors.org

You have to be a published author/writer to join. Benefits include: clause-by-clause contract vetting; advice on professional issues or problems; opportunities to meet other authors, publishers and agents; invitations to talks and seminars; plus you get the quarterly journal called the *Author*.

Travelwriters UK

www.travelwriters.co.uk

A site where travel writers, broadcasters and photographers can advertise (for a fee) their experience and expertise. It might be worth a go but don't hold your breath.

Writers and Photographers Unlimited

PO Box 520, Bamber Bridge, Preston, Lancashire PR5 8LF

☎ 01772-321243, Fax 0870-137 8888

mail@wpu.org.uk

www.wpu.org.uk

WPu is an electronic membership service to English-language professional writers and photographers specialising in all aspects of travel, tourism, the outdoors, adventure sports, food and drink. Membership is by invitation only but you can apply online to be considered. There is an annual fee.

Writers' Guild of Great Britain

15 Britannia St, London WC1X 9JN
☎ 020-7833 0777, Fax 020-7833 4777
eric@writersguild.org.uk
www.writersguild.org.uk

This is a trade union for writers working in television, radio, film, theatre, books and multimedia. They've got Minimum Terms Agreements and advice services plus professional, cultural and social activities.

WRITERS' WEBSITES & TOOLS

ABCtales.com

www.abctales.com

Set up by the guy behind the *Big Issue*, and Gordon Roddick (of Body Shop fame), this is a site where you can post your writings for free.

Askaboutwriting

www.askaboutwriting.net

Useful site aimed at British and Irish writers.

Association of Authors' Agents

www.agentsassoc.co.uk

There's an online directory of members.

Author Network

www.author-network.com

Provides an extensive range of resources for writers.

Bartleby.com

www.bartleby.com

Loads of reference books online, like *Roget's Thesaurus*, the *World Factbook* and *Brewer's Dictionary of Phrase & Fable*.

The Booksellers Association

www.booksellers.org.uk

Contains info on events and online directories of publishers and members.

Booktrust

www.booktrust.org.uk

A site devoted to books, publishing and the book trade, with listings of events, publishers, prizes, writers, finance and factsheets.

The Independent Publishers' Guild

www.ipg.uk.com

The membership organisation for independent publishers with an online directory.

The Literary Consultancy

The Crypt Centre, Munster Sq, London NW1 3PL
☎ 020-7813 4330
info@literaryconsultancy.co.uk
www.literaryconsultancy.co.uk

Independent assessment of your manuscript for a charge.

The Publishers Association

www.publishers.org.uk

There's a useful 'Getting Published' section here.

WriteLink

www.writelink.co.uk

Writers' website with an outstanding list of possible markets, a chat room, opportunities to write for them (in return for small gratuity) and a great deal more.

Writers' and Artists' Yearbook

www.writersandartists.co.uk

Site includes a guide for unpublished writers, a research centre for writers, a web directory, a writers' noticeboard and a calendar of literary events.

WritersServices
www.writersservices.com
A site for writers with information on a wide range of resources, from agents to websites.

CLIMATE & THE ENVIRONMENT

Climate Care
www.climatecare.org
A site which calculates the amount of carbon dioxide you generate by travelling, then offsets it by funding projects that reduce this major greenhouse gas. Besides allowing you to compensate for your own emissions as a travel writer, it's also a useful resource for writing about ethical travel.

The Met Office
www.metoffice.com
UK and world weather forecasts.

ECOTOURISM & RESPONSIBLE TRAVEL

responsibletravel.com
www.responsibletravel.com
'Holidays that give the world a break' is the catch-cry of this website, backed by Gordon Roddick.

Tourism Concern
www.tourismconcern.org.uk
Campaigning for ethical and fairly traded tourism.

EMBASSIES, CONSULATES & PASSPORTS

Thames Consular Services
www.thamesconsular.com

A leading independent passport and visa agency.

UK Foreign & Commonwealth Office
www.fco.gov.uk
Provides details of all embassies and consulates in the UK.

UK Passport Agency, The Home Office
www.ukpa.gov.uk
Online passport applications and advice.

FACTS, FIGURES & STATISTICS

The Audit Bureau of Circulations
www.abc.org.uk
Among other things, the ABC publishes the circulations figures of magazines and newspapers.

The British Library
www.bl.uk
The national library of the UK and one of the world's greatest libraries.

CIA World Factbook
www.cia.gov/cia/publications/factbook
Everything you ever wanted to know about countries but never dared to ask. It's obviously a US site but every travel writer has this site marked down as a Favourite.

Country Calling Codes
www.countrycallingcodes.com
International telephoning made easy.

Encyclopaedia Britannica
www.britannica.com
You can search through the 32-volumed Encyclopaedia Britannica online for practically any topic imaginable.

European Travel Commission
www.etc-corporate.org
A wealth of country information.

IATA
www.iata.org
The International Air Transport Association site features useful reports, facts and figures.

National Statistics Online
www.statistics.gov.uk
Some of these reports have to be bought.

VisitBritain
www.visitbritain.com
Click on to the UK Tourism Industry section of this site for all manner of facts and figures.

The World Heritage List
http://whc.unesco.org/pg.cfm?cid=31
The 878 properties which the World Heritage Committee has inscribed on the World Heritage List.

World Information
http://world-information.org/
Business, economic and political information on every country in the world.

World Tourism Organisation
www.unwto.org
There's a wealth of statistics available on this site, some are for free and others will cost you.

GENERAL TRAVEL INFORMATION & ADVICE

ABTA
www.abta.com
The Association of British Travel Agents.

AITO
www.aito.co.uk
The Association of Independent Tour Operators.

ANTOR
www.antor.com
Association of National Tourist Offices in the UK.

ATTA
www.atta.co.uk
African Travel & Tourism Association.

British Tourist Authority
www.visitbritain.com
VisitBritain is the site of the British Tourist Authority.

Cybercafes
www.cybercafes.com
Contains a database of more than 4200 internet cafés in 141 countries.

Globetrotters Club
BCM/Roving, London WC1N 3XX
☎ 020-8674 6229 (information line only)
http://globetrotters.co.uk
Globetrotters is an international travel club founded in 1945. It meets on the first Saturday of every month in London where guest travellers speak about their adventures. There's a bimonthly printed magazine called *Globe* and a monthly e-newsletter.

National Rail Enquiries
www.nationalrail.co.uk
Information about Britain's appalling train services.

RAC
www.rac.co.uk/route-planner/
Use this site to plan routes for the UK and Europe by car.

Steve Kropla
www.kropla.com
One of the web's most comprehensive listings of worldwide electrical and telephone information.

Thorn Tree Travel Forum
www.lonelyplanet.com/thorntree

The Thorn Tree Travel Forum section of Lonely Planet's website is a bulletin board used by travellers from all over the world to exchange information about a wide variety of travel topics and destinations. You'll also find cultural, literature, food, and political discussions.

Tourist Office Worldwide Directory
www.towd.com

The directory provides links to official US and international tourist information sources: government tourism offices, convention and visitors bureaus, chambers of commerce, and similar organisations that provide free, accurate and unbiased travel information to the public.

Travel Lists
www.travel-lists.co.uk

Independent travel directories for British travellers.

TravelMole
www.travelmole.com

Online network of 90,000 members of the travel and tourism industry. There's a lot here including daily trade news reports, chat forums and reference directories.

travel-quest
www.travel-quest.co.uk

Travel directory – adventure holidays and activity holidays worldwide.

time and date.com
www.timeanddate.com

World time zones, and also the times of sunrise, sunset, international country codes and city coordinates.

UK Foreign & Commonwealth Office
www.fco.gov.uk/travel

Country by country travel advice.

Universal Currency Converter
www.xe.com

Calculate your dwindling finances online in any number of different currencies.

HEALTH

Department of Health
www.nhs.uk/Healthcareabroad/Pages/Healthcareabroad.aspx

Health advice for travellers.

Foreign and Commonwealth Office
www.gov.uk/government/organisations/foreign-common-wealth-office/series/foreign-travel-guidance-documents

Health advice and advisories.

London Hospital for Tropical Diseases
www.thehtd.org

Houses the National Travel Health Network and Centre (www.NaTHNaC.org), which offers travel health advice for each country in the world.

MASTA Travel Health
www.masta.org

For the latest health news, plus travel clinics, chat room and advice.

World Health Organization
www.who.int

The website provides information on health risks around the world as well as recommended precautions, immunisations and vaccines when travelling.

WORLD EVENTS

Artrepublic
www.artrepublic.com/exhibitions.html

Search over 1250 museum listings to find out what exhibitions are on now.

Blogger
www.blogger.com
Have your own online travel diary to
share with your friends.

My Trip Journal
www.mytripjournal.com
Build an online journal of your trip with
maps, photos and email notification of
updates for your friends.

WRITING COURSES

The Arvon Foundation (National Administration Office)
2nd fl, 42a Buckingham Palace Rd, London SW1W 0RE
☎ 020-7931 7611, Fax 020-7963 0961
london@arvonfoundation.org
www.arvonfoundation.org
This registered charity has some of the
best writing courses in the country,
including ones specifically on travel
writing. Courses usually run for
four-and-a-half days between April
and December.

Cardiff School of Journalism, Media and Cultural Studies
Bute Bldg, Cardiff University, King Edward VII Ave, Cardiff CF10 3NB
☎ 029-2023 8832 Fax 029-2087 4000
www.cf.ac.uk
Runs courses in journalism and other contemporary media including international
media, media technologies, media development, film, radio, television, magazine
journalism, and public and media relations.

London College of Printing
Elephant & Castle, London SE1 6SB
☎ 020-7514 6569, Fax 020-7514 6535
info@lcc.arts.ac.uk
www.lcc.arts.ac.uk

Over 240 courses on design, media,
printing, publishing, travel and tourism. Long, short or summer courses are
available.

Mary Ward Centre
42 Queen Sq, London WC1N 3AQ
☎ 020-7269 6000, Fax 020-7269 6001
mwenquiries@marywardcentre.ac.uk
www.marywardcentre.ac.uk
One of the writing courses run by this
college is called Travel Journalism Intro
and lasts for 11 weeks.

National Council for the Training of Journalists (NCTJ)
The New Granary, Station Rd, Newport, Saffron Walden Essex CB11 3PL
☎ 01799-544014, Fax 01799-544015
info@nctj.com
www.nctj.com
One- to four-day courses on aspects of
journalism from Sharpening Your English
to Successful Freelancing. Also full-time
or weekend courses lasting from 40 weeks
to three years.

The Open University
PO Box 197, Milton Keynes MK7 6BJ
☎ 0845-300 6090
enquiries@open.ac.uk
www.open.ac.uk
With a network of centres throughout
the UK, the Open University runs several
writing courses a year.

Skyros
9 Eastcliff Rd, Shanklin, Isle of Wight PO37 6AA
☎ 01983-865566, Fax 01983-865537
office@skyros.com
www.skyros.com
Skyros is a specialist holistic holiday
company offering courses that engage
the mind, body and spirit. A variety of
writing courses run all year round on the
island of Skyros, Greece, and in Cuba,
Thailand and Cambodia.

Travellers' Tales

92 Hillfield Rd, London NW6 1QA

info@travellerstales.org

www.travellerstales.org

Founded and directed by Jonathan Lorie. Faculty has included authors William Dalrymple, Colin Thubron and Chris Stewart, and travel editors from *Wanderlust*, *Traveller*, the *Independent*, the *Guardian*, *Outdoor Photography* and *BBC Wildlife*.

Travel Writing Workshops

PO Box 20479, London SE17 3WF

getintouch@travelworkshops.co.uk

www.travelworkshops.co.uk

Faculty has included Dea Birkett, Rory MacLean, Ed Grenby and Dan Linstead.

University of East Anglia

Norwich, Norfolk NR4 7TJ

☎ 01603-592283, Fax 01603-593799

lit.admiss@uea.ac.uk

www.uea.ac.uk

Many universities offer writing courses (see www.ucas.ac.uk or www.postgrad .hobsons.com) but UEA's MA in Creative Writing is famous, set up by Angus Wilson and Malcolm Bradbury.

Ways with Words

Droridge Farm, Dartington, Totnes, Devon TQ9 6JQ

☎ 01803-867373, Fax 01803-863688

admin@wayswithwords.co.uk

www.wayswithwords.co.uk

A family business running a number of writing courses as well as organising three large literature festivals a year. One- and two-week creative writing courses are run in France and Italy.

REFERENCE PURCHASES

An Author's Guide to Publishing by Michael Legat

Brewer's Dictionary of Modern Phrase & Fable revised by John Ayto and Ian Crofton

Brewer's Dictionary of Phrase & Fable revised by John Ayto

The Cassell Dictionary of Slang edited by Jonathan Green

The Concise Oxford Dictionary of Quotations edited by Susan Ratcliffe

A Dictionary of World History by Edmund Wright and Jonathan Law

The Freelance Writer's Handbook – How to Make Money and Enjoy Life by Andrew Crofts

The Internet: A Writer's Guide by Jane Dorner

Mind the Gaffe by R. L. Trask

Fowler's Modern English Usage revised by R. W. Burchfield

The Modern Law of Copyright & Design by Hugh Laddie, Peter Prescott, and Mary Vitoria

From Pitch to Publication by Carole Blake

Quick Guides by the Society of Authors – see the website (www.societyofauthors .org/publications/index.html) for details

Roget's Thesaurus edited by Peter Roget and George W. Davidson

Starting in Business (IR28) from the Inland Revenue (download from www .inlandrevenue.gov.uk).

The Teleworking Handbook by Alan Denbigh

The Times Comprehensive Atlas of the World, 11th edition – rather expensive at £150 but well worth it

The Times Concise Atlas of the World, 8th edition – slightly cheaper at £75

Understanding Publishers' Contracts by Michael Legat

User's Guide to Copyright by M. F. Flint, Nicholas Fitzpatrick, and Clive Thorne

LIBRARY REFERENCES

The Bookseller Magazine (weekly magazine for the bookselling and publishing world – twice a year there's a special travel issue)

The Directory of Writers' Circles by Diana Hayden; annual

Encyclopaedia Britannica by Encyclopaedia (UK) Ltd

Publishing News (weekly newspaper for the bookselling and publishing world – twice a year there's a special travel issue)

Whitaker's Almanack by A&C Black; annual

Who's Who by A&C Black; annual

TRAVEL LITERATURE CLASSICS

Following is a list of 20 travel literature classics by UK authors compiled with help from Lonely Planet co-founder Tony Wheeler and the staff members of Stanford Bookshop, London:

Arabia Through the Looking Glass by Jonathan Raban

Arabian Sands by Wilfred Thesiger

Frontiers of Heaven by Stanley Stewart

Full Tilt by Dervla Murphy

Holy Mountain by William Dalrymple

I Came, I Saw by Norman Lewis

In Patagonia by Bruce Chatwin

Into the Heart of Borneo by Redmond O'Hanlon

Journey Into Cyprus by Colin Thubron

A Pattern of Islands by Arthur Grimble

The Road to Oxiana by Robert Byron

A Season in Heaven by David Tomory

A Short Walk in the Hindu Kush by Eric Newby

South From Granada by Gerald Brenan

Southern Gates of Arabia by Freya Stark

Terra Incognito by Sara Wheeler

A Time of Gifts by Patrick Leigh-Fermor

An Unexpected Light: Travels in Afghanistan by Jason Elliot

Venice by Jan Morris

The Worst Journey in the World by Apsley Cherry-Garrard

US RESOURCES

GENERAL GUIDES TO PUBLISHERS, EDITORS & LITERARY AGENTS

Bacon's Newspaper/Magazine Directory (2 volumes)

http://us.cision.com/products_services/bacons_media_directories_2009.asp

Lists editors and contact information for nearly 22,000 magazines and newsletters and all US, Canadian, Mexican and Caribbean daily newspapers. Published annually. Includes travel editor pitching profiles for most papers. This directory costs $595; it is available at many public libraries.

BookWire

www.bookwire.com

This website provides a list of and links to various travel publishers.

Editor & Publisher International Year Book, Parts 1 and 2

www.editorandpublisher.com/eandp/resources/yearbook.jsp

The encyclopedia of the newspaper industry. Published annually. Part 1 includes lists for all dailies worldwide. Part 2 covers all community and special interest US and Canadian weeklies. Part 1 costs $150; Part 2 costs $135. These are also available at many public libraries.

ehotelier.com

www.ehotelier.com/browse/magazines.php

This website offers a variety of resources for people in the hospitality industry and provides an extensive list of travel trade publications, linked to their websites.

Jeff Herman's Guide to Book Publishers, Editors, and Literary Agents

by Jeff Herman (Writer, Inc)

A who's who for the publishing industry. Provides contact information for hundreds of top editors and agents. Published annually.

LMP: The Directory of the American Book Publishing Industry (Literary Market Place)

compiled by Information Today Inc staff
(Information Today)
www.literarymarketplace.com

Over 2000 pages of book publisher listings. Published annually. An international directory is also available.

Online Newspapers

www.onlinenewspapers.com

This free site has links to the websites of thousands of US and international newspapers.

Publishers Marketplace

www.publishersmarketplace.com

This resource is especially helpful for writers looking for an agent. Users pay $20/month to access the online databases.

Travel Publications Update

Marco Polo Publications, 1299 Bayshore Blvd, Suite B, Dunedin, FL 34698
☎ 800-523 7274, 727-735 9455, Fax 727-735 9534
http://main.travelwriters.com/tpu/about/index.asp

The *Travel Publications Update* offers concise information about more than 500 travel magazines and 200 newspaper travel sections. Each listing includes editorial contact information, a description of the publication, article and photography guidelines, pay rates and other essential data. Listings are updated continuously (but you need to buy a new copy to get updated information). Cost

is $39. Even if you don't buy a copy it's worth browsing this site for market news and press releases.

Travel Publishers Association

www.travelpubs.com

This website provides links to various independent travel publishers who are members of the Travel Publishers Association. Many of these publishers specialise in books targeted to niche markets (e.g. RV travellers, gay/lesbian market).

Travelwriter Marketletter

43301 Ardmore St, Ashburn, VA 20147
☎ 571-214 9086, Fax 208-988 7672

A monthly newsletter of current market information, news and tips for travel writers and photographers. A sample issue is available online. A one-year online subscription costs $65.

World Hum

www.worldhum.com

This site features links to many of the major travel magazine websites, newspaper travel section websites (in the US and abroad) and a host of other great travel links.

Writer's Market

edited by Kathryn S. Brogan (Writer's Digest Books)
www.writersmarket.com/index_ns.asp

Annual guide to literary agents, book publishers, consumer magazines, contests and awards, and more, from the publishers of *Writer's Digest* magazine. The subscription-based website ($29.99 annual fee) also offers information regarding travel publishers and links to their websites.

Yahoo! Directory

http://dir.yahoo.com

Search for 'Travel Publishers' to access links to the websites of over 75 travel guidebook and travel literature publishers; a 'Travel Magazines' search provides links to over 100 major print and online travel magazine websites, including major travel magazines, as well as in-flight magazines, regional publications and publications targeted to specific travel niches.

MAJOR TRAVEL PUBLISHERS

TRAVEL GUIDEBOOKS

As the aforementioned reference books illustrate, there are dozens of guidebook publishers. Following are eight of the most prominent:

Avalon Travel Publishing
1400 65th St, Suite 250, Emeryville, CA 94608
☎ 510-595 3664
info@travelmatters.com
www.travelmatters.com
Publishers of the Moon Handbook series and of Rick Steves' guidebooks.

Fodor's Travel Publications
Researcher Writer Positions, 1745 Broadway, 15th Floor, New York, NY 10019
☎ 212-782 9000
www.fodors.com
Publishers of the Fodor's guidebook series. Proposals should be mailed to their New York office at the address listed above.

The Globe Pequot Press
246 Goose Lane, PO Box 480, Guilford, CT 06437
☎ 203-458 4500
info@globepequot.com
www.globepequot.com
Publishers of a variety of theme and destination guides.

Let's Go Publications
67 Mt Auburn St, Cambridge, MA 02138
☎ 617-495 9659, Fax 617-496 7070
www.letsgo.com

As a wholly-owned subsidiary of Harvard Student Agencies, employs only Harvard students.

Lonely Planet Publications
150 Linden St, Oakland CA 94607
☎ 510-893 8555, Fax 510-893 8563
info@lonelyplanet.com
www.lonelyplanet.com
One of the world's leading travel media companies, publishing over 600 titles across 17 different languages.

Rough Guides
345 Hudson St, New York, NY 10014
☎ 212-414 3635
write@roughguides.com
www.roughguides.com
The company has an office in New York, but mailed proposals and inquiries should be directed to the UK office (see p285).

Sasquatch Books
119 S Main, Suite 400, Seattle, WA 98104
☎ 206-467 4300, 800-775 0817, Fax 206-467 4301
www.sasquatchbooks.com
Publishers of guides to the Pacific Northwest, Alaska, California and the Southwest.

Wilderness Press
1345 8th St, Berkeley, CA 94710
☎ 510-558 1666, 800-443 7227
mail@wildernesspress.com
www.wildernesspress.com
Publishers of outdoor activity–oriented guides to California, Alaska, Hawaii, the US Southwest and Pacific Northwest, New England, Canada and Baja.

TRAVEL LITERATURE

Numerous publishing companies produce travel literature. Here are 11 of the most prominent:

US RESOURCES

Broadway Books

1745 Broadway, New York, NY 10019
☎ 212-782 9000
bwaypub@randomhouse.com
www.randomhouse.com/broadway

Broadway's Broadway Abroad division specialises in a particular area of narrative travel books: travelogues and memoirs of authors' experiences living in (as opposed to visiting or journeying through) the world's most seductive and unusual places. Authors include Frances Mayes, Bill Bryson and Tony Cohan.

Crown Journeys

1745 Broadway, New York, NY 10019
☎ 212-782 9000
crownbiz@randomhouse.com
www.randomhouse.com/crown

Crown publishes a selection of popular fiction and nonfiction by both established and rising authors. Travel titles are part of the Crown Journeys series.

Harcourt Trade Publishers

15 East 26th St, 15th fl, New York, NY 10010
☎ 212-592 1000
www.harcourtbooks.com

Under the Harcourt name, Harcourt Trade Publishers publishes hardcover editions of fine fiction and literature, nonfiction, poetry, and belles-lettres from authors worldwide.

HarperCollins

10 East 53rd St, New York, NY 10022
☎ 212-207 7000
www.harpercollins.com

HarperCollins has published over 150 travel-related titles, including literary nonfiction and the Access guidebook series. Manuscripts must be submitted through an agent.

Houghton Mifflin Company

222 Berkeley St, Boston, MA 02116
☎ 617-351 5000
www.houghtonmifflinbooks.com

Publishes Paul Theroux and Jeffrey Tayler. Manuscripts must be submitted through an agent.

Lonely Planet Publications

150 Linden St, Oakland CA 94607
☎ 510-893 8555, Fax 510-893 8563
info@lonelyplanet.com
www.lonelyplanet.com

Lonely Planet publishes literary travel anthologies, single-author narratives and pictorial books, in addition to its guidebooks. Proposals for travel literature titles should be sent to the Australia office (see p317).

Penguin Group

375 Hudson St, New York, NY 10014
☎ 212-366 2000
www.us.penguingroup.com

Penguin Group publishes an extensive list of travel literature titles, as well as the Rough Guide and Time Out guidebook series.

Random House Group

1745 Broadway, New York, NY 10019
☎ 212-782 9000
editor@randomhouse.com
www.randomhouse.com

Several imprints that publish travel narratives.

Seal Press

1700 4th St, Berkeley, CA 94710
☎ 510-595 3664
www.sealpress.com

Seal Press, an imprint of the Perseus Books Group, publishes fiction and nonfiction books by women across the globe.

Travelers' Tales

853 Alma St, Palo Alto, CA 94301
☎ 650-462 2110, Fax 650-462 2114
ttales@travelerstales.com
www.travelerstales.com

Travelers' Tales publishes a variety of anthologies and travel advice books. The company currently has more than 100 titles in print; annual publications include an anthology of best travel writing, for which submissions are welcome. Travelers' Tales also publishes stories on its website.

Vintage
1745 Broadway, New York, NY 10019
☎ 212-782 9000
www.randomhouse.com/vintage
This imprint of Random House has published the works of some of the most popular American travel writers, including Tim Cahill, Pico Iyer and Bill Bryson. A list of travel writing titles can be found at www.randomhouse.ca/vintage/travel writing.htm. Manuscripts must be submitted through an agent.

TRAVEL MAGAZINES

Hundreds of magazines publish travel writing. Following are six of the most prominent that specialise in publishing articles on travel. If publications welcome email queries, we include the appropriate email address.

Afar
394 Pacific Avenue, San Francisco, CA 941111
☎ 415-814 1401
www.afar.com
Afar is a high-quality glossy magazine that focuses on experiential, immersive travel and publishes a wide range of service pieces and narrative articles.

Condé Nast Traveler
The Condé Nast Publications, 4 Times Sq, New York, NY 10036
☎ 212-286 2101
www.concierge.com/cntraveler
Condé Nast Traveler is a monthly magazine seeking stories that appeal to upscale, sophisticated travellers.

Islands
460 North Orlando Ave, Suite 200, Winter Park, FL 32789
☎ 407-628 4802
Islands.editorial@bonniercorp.com
www.islands.com
'*Islands* is interested in your ideas, culled from your travel experiences and your knowledge of the world. Our features are primarily assigned to writers with whom we have a relationship. However, there are plenty of opportunities to contribute to *Islands* and to build a relationship with us. We are actively looking for current ideas for our front-of-the-book Discover [section].' Published eight times a year.

National Geographic Traveler
Query Editor, 1145 17th St NW, Washington, DC 20036-4688
☎ 202-857 7000 (ask for the magazine's editorial office)
www.traveler.nationalgeographic.com
Guidelines: www.traveler.nationalgeographic.com/about-us/writers-guidelines-text
Traveler's publishing goals are to find the new and authentic, to showcase fresh travel opportunities, and to be an advocate for travellers and for sustainable tourism.

Outside
Editorial Department, 400 Market St, Santa Fe, NM 87501
☎ 505-989 7100
http://outside.away.com
Guidelines: http://outside.away.com/system/guidelines.html
Outside is a monthly national magazine dedicated to covering the people, sports and activities, politics, art, literature and hardware of the outdoors.

Travel + Leisure
1120 Ave of the Americas, 10th fl, New York, NY 10036
☎ 212-382 5600
www.travelandleisure.com
Guidelines: www.travelandleisure.com/contact
Monthly publication targeting sophisticated, active travellers who plan both pleasure and business trips. About 95 per cent of the magazine is written by

freelance writers on assignment. Online query form available on guidelines site.

NEWSPAPERS

Atlanta Journal-Constitution
72 Marietta St, Atlanta, GA 30303-2804
☎ 404-526 5479
travel@ajc.com
www.ajc.com
Sunday section publishes articles on regional, national and international destinations.

The Baltimore Sun
501 N Calvert St, Baltimore, MD 21278
☎ 410-332 6199
travel@baltsun.com
www.baltimoresun.com
Sunday section of six to 12 pages. The best way to break in is by pitching regional articles.

The Boston Globe
Travel Editor, PO Box 55819, Boston, MA, 02205-5819
☎ 617-929 2079
travel@globe.com
www.boston.com
Sunday section of 16 to 20 pages. Prefers email submissions.

The Chicago Tribune
Travel Editor, 435 North Michigan Ave, Chicago, IL 60611
☎ 312-222 3999
rwerland@tribune.com
www.chicagotribune.com
Only deals with completed manuscripts; does not accept queries by phone. Sunday section of 10 to 22 pages. Interested in the Midwest and shorter stories.

The Christian Science Monitor
210 Massachusetts Ave, Boston, MA 02115
☎ 617-450 7929
www.csmonitor.com

Guidelines: www.csmonitor.com/aboutus/guidelines.html
This national newspaper publishes a variety of travel articles and essays.

The Dallas Morning News
Travel Editor, 508 Young St, Dallas, TX 75202
☎ 214-977 8191
mebotter@dallasnews.com
www.dallasnews.com
Sunday section of six to 10 pages. Requests that stories be submitted via regular mail and that stories have a tight angle or focus. Maximum length for main: 800 words.

The Denver Post
101 W Colfax Ave, Suite 600, Denver, CO 80202
☎ 303-954 1599
travel@denverpost.com
www.denverpost.com
Sunday section of eight to 12 pages. Submissions that are timely, newsy and compelling will have a better chance of making it.

The Los Angeles Times
202 W First St, Los Angeles, CA 90012
☎ 213-237 5000
travel@latimes.com
www.latimes.com
National paper with a Sunday travel section of 10 to 16 pages; publishes articles on a wide variety of international and domestic destinations, with special emphasis on California. 'Our stories are first-person experiential – travel stories as opposed to travel features. As we used to say in Missouri, "Show me, don't tell me."'

The Miami Herald
One Herald Plaza, Miami, FL 33132
☎ 305-376 3629
travel@miamiherald.com
www.miamiherald.com
Sunday section of eight to 10 pages.

The New York Times

229 West 43rd St, New York, NY 10036

☎ 212-556 4692

travel@nytimes.com

www.nytimes.com

This national newspaper has one of the largest travel sections in the US. The *New York Times* publishes articles on a variety of international and domestic destinations.

The Philadelphia Inquirer

400 N Broad St, Philadelphia, PA 19101

☎ 215-854 5727

inquirer.travel@phillynews.com

www.philly.com/inquirer

Sunday section publishes articles on regional, national and international destinations.

The San Francisco Chronicle

901 Mission St, San Francisco, CA 94103

☎ 415-777 7932

travel@sfchronicle.com

www.sfchron.com

Sunday section of six to eight pages. The best way for freelancers to break in is to send California stories.

The Seattle Times

Travel Dept, PO Box 70, Seattle, WA 98111

☎ 206-464 2111

travel@seattletimes.com

www.seattletimes.com

Sunday paper publishes articles on regional, national and international destinations.

The Washington Post

Travel Section, 1150 15th St NW, Washington, DC 20071

☎ 202-334 7750

travel@washpost.com

www.washingtonpost.com

National paper with a Sunday travel section of six to 10 pages; publishes articles on a wide variety of international and domestic destinations.

ONLINE

The following websites have comprehensive links to other online travel sites:

BootsnAll

www.bootsnall.com

Billed as the 'ultimate resource for the independent traveller', this site offers travel booking information, discussion groups, travel guides and traveller's resources. The site also accepts story submissions and publishes travel articles.

Joe Sent Me

www.joesentme.com

A website for business travellers that contains a wealth of information useful to travel writers. Look for the link to Travel Newsstand (www.travelnewsstand.com), where you'll find links to newspaper travel sections and travel magazines worldwide. Also click on Fellow Travelers (www.fellowtravelers.com), another Joe Sent Me site that provides links to all the travel commentators currently published on the web.

Transitions Abroad

www.transitionsabroad.com/index.shtml

This website is designed for people who are interested in studying or working – or simply living – abroad. It includes links to numerous travel writing sites and blogs.

Travelers' Tales

www.travelerstales.com

The Travelers' Tales website features weekly stories from freelance writers, along with information about Travelers' Tales anthologies, upcoming titles and submission guidelines.

World Hum

www.worldhum.com

This website publishes articles, essays and first-person stories that 'reveal the heart

US RESOURCES

of a beating travel experience'. It also provides links to dozens of travel-related journals, magazines, communities, blogs, newspaper sections, book publishers, bookstores, TV and radio stations, and other helpful sites.

Written Road

www.writtenroad.com

This website offers 'the inside scoop to the travel publishing world', with advice for writers, information on writing opportunities, and an extensive list of resources and events.

WRITERS' GROUPS & ASSOCIATIONS

In your local area, you may find travel writing or general writing groups and organisations that are open to writers of all levels. If writing becomes your career, the following national organisations may add clout to your resume, and provide various benefits such as networking opportunities, insider market information and discounted health insurance.

American Society of Journalists and Authors

1501 Broadway, Suite 302, New York, NY 10036
☎ 212-997 0947
www.asja.org

Founded in 1948, this is the US' leading organisation of independent nonfiction writers. Their monthly member newsletter provides valuable information on writing markets. To become a member of ASJA, you must have published a minimum of six bylined articles written on a freelance basis in major magazines. Nonmembers can still receive the Contracts Watch newsletter, a free source of information about the latest terms and

negotiations in the world of periodicals, print and electronic publishing.

International Food, Wine and Travel Writers Association

1142 South Diamond Bar Blvd. #177, Diamond Bar, CA 91765-22030 Box 8249, Calabasas, CA 91372
☎ 877-439 8929; 909-860 6914 (international); Fax 909-396 0014
admin@ifwtwa.org
www.ifwtwa.org

This association has more than 300 members, including travel and food journalists and broadcasters, representatives of tourism boards and convention and visitor bureaus, and other public relations professionals. Their membership standards include a minimum of 10 published travel articles per year.

National Writers Association

10940 S Parker Rd, #508, Parker, CO 80134
☎ 303-841 0246, Fax 303-841 2607
natlwritersassn@hotmail.com
www.nationalwriters.com

Members of the National Writers Association receive discounts on health and dental insurance, car rentals, office supplies, and other products and services. NWA also provides services such as contract reading, editing, and manuscript criticism from other members. Email or call for information on how to join.

National Writers Union

113 University Pl, 6th fl, New York, NY 10003
☎ 212-254 0279, Fax 212-254 0673
nwu@nwu.org
www.nwu.org

The National Writers Union (NWU) is a trade union for freelance writers of all genres who work for American publishers or employers. You are eligible for membership if you have published a book, a play, three articles, five poems, a short story, or an equal amount of newsletter, publicity, technical, commercial, government or institutional copy. You are also eligible for membership if you have written an equal amount of unpublished material and are actively writing and attempting to publish your work.

North American Travel Journalists Association

3579 Foothill Blvd, Box 744, Pasadena, CA 91107
☎ 626-376 9754, Fax 626-628 1854
info@natja.org
www.natja.org

A professional organisation of writers, photographers and editors dedicated to the travel and hospitality industries. You must submit 10 clips of your writing published in the last year to join. Member dues are $150 per year.

Society of American Travel Writers

7044 South 13 St, Oak Creek, WI 53154
☎ 414-908 4949, Fax 414-768 8001
satw@satw.org
www.satw.org

The leading organisation for travel writers and other travel professionals, SATW works to raise the standards of the profession, guard the right of freedom to travel, and encourage conservation and preservation of historic sites and natural wonders. You must fulfil membership publishing requirements and be sponsored by two SATW members to join.

Travel Journalists Guild

PO Box 10643, Chicago, IL 60610
☎ 312-664 9279, Fax 312-664 9701
www.tjgonline.com

Guild members include freelance writers, photographers, artists and filmmakers who focus on travel. To become a member, you must be a self-employed freelance travel journalist in the field of writing, photography, lecturing, art, radio or television who has worked in the field

for at least three years in the past five. You must also be sponsored by two current members and provide at least 12 clips of articles published (or broadcast, distributed etc.) for each of the past three years.

Information on additional writers' associations and groups can be found at:

The Writer Gazette

www.writergazette.com/linksclubs.shtml

This website also provides links to writer-related articles, paying calls for submission and freelance job postings, contests, tips and other resources to help inspire, improve and promote your writing career.

WRITERS' WEBSITES & TOOLS

The following websites contain extensive lists of links to resources for writers:

The 101 Best Websites for Writers by WritersDigest.com

www.writersdigest.com/101bestsites

This is a selective list of helpful websites for writers.

Internet-Resources.com

www.internet-resources.com/writers

A huge collection of links to resources for writers.

Writers Write Links and Resources for Writers

www.writerswrite.com/writinglinks

Assorted links for writers organised by genre and type.

Writing-World.com

www.writing-world.com/links

Provides well-organised lists of hundreds of links for writers.

US RESOURCES

Here are a few specific sites for writers:

Absolute Write
www.absolutewrite.com
Absolute Write is a place for professional writers to meet. The website offers market listings, a newsletter, discussion forums, editorial services, articles and classes, plus a handy warnings page to keep you from making bad decisions.

Alibris
www.alibris.com
This website connects people to thousands of independent book, music and movie sellers around the world. It offers over 35 million used, new and hard-to-find titles to consumers, libraries and retailers.

Bartleby.com
www.bartleby.com
Bartleby.com publishes classics of literature, nonfiction and reference free of charge for visitors to its site.

Bibliofind
www.bibliofind.com
Bibliofind, through a partnership with Amazon.com (www.amazon.com), provides millions of rare, used, and out-of-print books through their community of booksellers.

Carnegie Library of Pittsburgh
www.clpgh.org/research/travel
This website provides information and links to numerous print and online travel-guide publishers as well as booking agents. Links to specialty guides covering subjects from dining out to cruises are included along with general travel guides.

Common Errors in English
www.wsu.edu/~brians/errors/index.html
This site provides information to help avoid common word usage errors.

Creativity for Life
www.creativityforlife.com
This site offers hints, tips and tricks to keep your creativity alive.

Freelance Writers
www.freelancewrite.about.com
Part of the about.com network, this site includes articles, relevant links, how-to information, forums, and answers to questions.

OneLook Dictionary Search
www.onelook.com
OneLook easily helps define, translate or determine the accurate spelling for over 5 million words by linking visitors to more than 900 online dictionaries.

Writers Weekly
www.writersweekly.com
Writers Weekly is an e-zine dedicated to freelance writers. The site features articles, a forum, and sections on markets and writers' 'warnings'. There is also a section dedicated to new writer resources and one dedicated to self-publishing.

CLIMATE & THE ENVIRONMENT

Intellicast.com
www.intellicast.com
Intellicast.com provides extensive specialised weather information to help plan outdoor and weather-sensitive activities, such as golfing, sailing, hiking, skiing or relaxing at the beach. The site offers free, accurate and up-to-date weather information and forecasts for most US and featured international destinations.

The Weather Channel
www.weather.com

The Weather Channel's website features current conditions and forecasts for over 77,000 locations worldwide, along with local and regional radars. The site also offers a variety of maps, along with weather-related news, educational material, a weather glossary, a storm encyclopedia, seasonal features, and other resources for travel planning.

ECOTOURISM & RESPONSIBLE TRAVEL

Ethical Traveler
www.ethicaltraveler.org
Ethical Traveler is a grassroots alliance whose goal is to unite the travel community in the fight to strengthen human rights and to protect the environment. Offers links to other organisations and companies concerned with the same issues.

The International Ecotourism Society
www.ecotourism.org
The largest and oldest ecotourism organisation in the world, TIES is dedicated to generating and disseminating information about ecotourism. The website has links to other ecotourism organisations around the world, as well as information about how you can travel responsibly to natural areas while conserving the environment and sustaining the well-being of the local people.

EMBASSIES, CONSULATES & PASSPORTS

Embassy World
www.embassyworld.com
Embassy World is a website designed to provide a comprehensive directory of

and search engine for contact resources for all of the world's embassies and consulates.

US Department of State
www.travel.state.gov
The US Department of State website provides information to US citizens about passports and visas required to visit other countries.

FACTS, FIGURES & STATISTICS

The Audit Bureau of Circulations
www.accessabc.com
Among other things, provides magazine and newspaper circulation figures.

Country Calling Codes
www.countrycallingcodes.com
International telephoning made easy.

Encyclopaedia Britannica
www.britannica.com
You can search through the 32-volume Encyclopaedia Britannica online.

European Travel Commission
www.etc-corporate.org
Extensive country information for Europe.

Firstgov.gov: Reference Shelf
www.firstgov.gov/Topics/Reference_Shelf.shtml#statistics
Links to data and statistics from the US government's official web portal.

IATA
www.iata.org
The International Air Transport Association site features interesting reports, facts and figures.

Nation Master
www.nationmaster.com/index.php
This website contains information from

US RESOURCES

the CIA Factbook as well as other sources and allows users to generate graphs based on numerical data that compare countries across various statistics. Information can be analysed based on health, politics and ecology.

Office of Travel and Tourism Industries

tinet.ita.doc.gov/research

This office functions as the US federal tourism office. A core responsibility is to collect, analyse and disseminate international travel and tourism statistics for the US Travel and Tourism Statistical System.

time and date.com

www.timeanddate.com

Includes the times of sunrise, sunset, international country codes, and city coordinates.

Universal Currency Converter

www.xe.com

Converts the values of nearly every currency using current market rates.

US Travel Association

www.ustravel.org

Provides an authoritative and recognised source of research, analysis and forecasting for the entire industry. Information on statistics and trends is offered, with enhanced services for members.

The World Heritage List

http://whc.unesco.org/pg.cfm?cid=31

The 878 properties which the World Heritage Committee has inscribed on the World Heritage List.

World Information

www.worldinformation.com

Business, economic and political information on every country in the world.

World Tourism Organization

www.world-tourism.org

There's a wealth of statistics on tourism available on this site; some are for free and others will cost you.

GENERAL TRAVEL INFORMATION & ADVICE

Cybercafes

www.cybercafes.com

Contains a database of more than 4200 internet cafés in 141 countries.

ehotelier.com

www.ehotelier.com/browse/conventions.php#visitor bureaus

This website, which offers a variety of resources for people in the hospitality industry, provides an extensive list of convention and visitors bureaus in the US and abroad.

Joe Sent Me

www.joesentme.com

Joe Brancatelli's site targets business travellers with free access/links to everything from pharmacy and cybercafé locations to travel warnings and airport/flight information. Two levels of annual membership, $49 and $89, are available.

OAG Travel News

www.oag.com

OAG Travel News offers the latest business travel news, with special emphasis on airline-related news and information.

The Practical Nomad

www.hasbrouck.org

Edward Hasbrouck, author of *The Practical Nomad: How to Travel Around the World* and *The Practical Nomad Guide to the Online Travel Marketplace*, runs this website, with links to travel planning and research, logistics and practicalities, tickets and reservations, and tips and resources for using the internet on the road.

Thorn Tree Travel Forum

www.lonelyplanet.com/thorntree

The Thorn Tree Travel Forum section of Lonely Planet's website is a bulletin board used by travellers from all over the world to exchange information about a wide variety of travel topics and destinations. You'll also find cultural, literature, food, and political discussions.

Tourism Offices Worldwide

www.towd.com

The Tourism Offices Worldwide Directory provides links to official US and international tourist information sources: government tourism offices, convention and visitors bureaus, chambers of commerce, and similar organisations that provide free, accurate and unbiased travel information to the public.

Travel Weekly

www.twcrossroads.com

Billing itself as the 'National Newspaper of the Travel Industry', Travel Weekly's website offers travel industry news features, as well as a forum and stories on destinations.

US Department of Homeland Security: Transportation Security Administration

www.tsa.gov

The mission of the Transportation Security Administration is to protect the nation's transportation systems to ensure freedom of movement for people and commerce. The 'Travelers & Consumers' section of its website offers information, links, tips and requirements for air, rail, passenger vessel, highway and mass transit travel. Consumers can sign up to receive Homeland Security Alerts which notify travellers of changes in the Homeland Security Alert status, TSA Policy updates and other critical information to assist with travel plans.

US Department of State

www.state.gov

US Department of State travel warnings provide updates about risks abroad such as civil unrest, natural disasters or outbreaks of serious diseases. The site also provides information about visa requirements and consular details for visiting other countries.

World Travel Guide

www.worldtravelguide.net

Provides histories and travel information on virtually every country in the world.

World Travel Watch

www.worldtravelwatch.com

Larry Habegger and James O'Reilly have been reporting on issues that affect travellers for major newspapers since 1985. Their World Travel Watch site reports on developments around the globe, from crime waves, disease outbreaks and transit strikes to political upheavals and cultural quirks. It also provides links to major news resources.

HEALTH

Travel Health Online

www.tripprep.com

A resource of travel medicine and practitioners around the globe.

US Centers for Disease Control

www.cdc.gov/travel

CDC is the federal agency for developing and applying disease prevention and control, environmental health, and health education activities designed to improve the health of the people of the US. The website provides health information on specific destinations as well as on outbreaks that may affect international travellers.

US RESOURCES

World Health Organization

www.who.int

The website provides information on health risks around the world as well as recommended precautions, immunisations and vaccines when travelling.

MAPS

Atlapedia

www.atlapedia.com

This site provides facts, figures and statistical data on geography, climate, people, religion, language, history, economy and also full-colour physical maps and political maps for regions of the world.

MapQuest

www.mapquest.com

MapQuest provides basic maps of US and select international cities. Visitors can also utilise this site to get directions between two points in the US or Europe.

Mapsonus.com

www.mapsonus.com

This site provides advanced mapping and driving directions throughout the US.

WORLD EVENTS

Artrepublic

www.artrepublic.com/exhibitions.html

Search over 1250 museum listings to find out what exhibitions are on now.

City Search

www.citysearch.com

This local search service allows users to find up-to-date information on businesses, from restaurants and retail to travel and professional services, for major US cities and some international locations.

Whatsonwhen

www.whatsonwhen.com

A world-wide directory of upcoming events.

YOU ON THE WEB

Backflip.com

www.backflip.com

'My Daily Routine' organises all the websites you regularly visit and speeds up the process of browsing through them.

Blogger

www.blogger.com

Allows you to build and maintain your own online diary.

Buildfree.org

www.buildfree.org

Build your own website for free.

My Trip Journal

www.mytripjournal.com

Build an online journal of your trip with maps, photos and email notification of updates for your friends.

WRITING COURSES

The Association of Writers & Writing Programs

www.awpwriter.org

The association is dedicated to the promotion of writers and creative writing programs at universities in the US and Canada. Its website features information on writing programs, conferences and contests. Membership benefits include a subscription to the association's *Writer's Chronicle* magazine, job lists and discounted registration fees for contests and conferences.

Media Bistro

www.mediabistro.com

Media Bistro is dedicated to anyone who creates or works with content, including editors, writers, television producers, graphic designers, book publishers and people in production and circulation departments in industries including magazines, television, radio, newspapers, book publishing, online media, advertising, PR and graphic design. It provides opportunities (both online and offline) to network, share resources, become informed of job opportunities and interesting projects, improve career skills and showcase work, and also runs a variety of writing and related courses in major US cities.

Poets & Writers

www.pw.org

The mission of Poets & Writers is to support and promote the literary community in the US, and to foster communication among and professional development for poets and writers of fiction and nonfiction. The organisation publishes *Poets & Writers* magazine and its website offers links to writer's resources, including national and regional organisations, writing programs and conferences.

ShawGuides' Guide to Writers Conferences and Workshops

www.writing.shawguides.com

This website lists almost 1500 writers' conferences and workshops and is searchable by country, state, date and genre.

The Writer

www.writermag.com

The venerable magazine's website offers information about writers' groups and conferences.

Writer's Digest

www.writersdigest.com

This 'online guide to the writer's life' publishes the monthly *Writer's Digest* magazine and offers a 24-month Writer's Digest school and various online workshops.

Writing-World.com: Writing Classes, Conferences and Colonies

www.writing-world.com/links/classes.shtml

This website provides links to websites, schools, colleges and universities that offer writing classes.

REFERENCE PURCHASES

Every writer must have a good dictionary such as *Merriam-Webster's Collegiate Dictionary* or *The American Heritage Dictionary of the English Language*. A thesaurus such as *Roget's Thesaurus* is also essential. In addition, consider purchasing the following books:

The American Directory of Writer's Guidelines, 3rd Edition: A Compilation of Information for Freelancers from More than 1,400 Magazine Editors and Book Publishers by Brigitte M. Philips, Sussan D. Klassen and Dorris Hall

AP Stylebook and Briefing on Media Law (Associated Press)

The ASJA Guide to Freelance Writing: A Professional Guide to the Business, for Nonfiction Writers of All Experience Levels edited by Timothy Harper

Bartlett's Familiar Quotations by John Bartlett

Bird by Bird: Some Instructions on Writing and Life by Anne Lamott

The Chicago Manual of Style, 15th Edition (University of Chicago Press)

The Elements of Style by William Strunk Jr and E. B. White
Literary Law Guide for Authors by Tonya Marie Evans, Susan Borden Evans and Dan Poynter
On Writing Well by William Zinsser
Rand McNally Goode's World Atlas by J. Paul Goode et al
The World Almanac and Book of Facts (World Almanac; annual)
The Writer's Legal Guide: An Author's Guild Desk Reference by Tad Crawford and Kay Murray

LIBRARY REFERENCES

These useful references are available in many libraries:
Bacon's Newspaper/Magazine Directory (2 volumes) by Bacon's Media Directories; annual
Editor & Publisher International Year Book by Editor & Publisher; annual
Encyclopaedia Britannica by Encyclopaedia Britannica Inc
LMP: The Directory of the American Book Publishing Industry (Literary Market Place) by Inc Staff Information Today; annual
Poets & Writers magazine
The Writer magazine
Writer's Digest magazine

TRAVEL LITERATURE CLASSICS

Don George's list of top 20 works of travel literature by US authors:
Arctic Dreams by Barry Lopez
Blue Highways by William Least-Heat Moon
The Colossus of Maroussi by Henry Miller
Coming Into the Country by John McPhee
Desert Solitare by Edward Abbey
Ghost Train to the Eastern Star by Paul Theroux
The Inland Sea by Donald Richie
Innocents Abroad by Mark Twain
Jaguars Ripped My Flesh by Tim Cahill
Notes from a Small Island by Bill Bryson
On the Road by Jack Kerouac
Pilgrim at Tinker Creek by Annie Dillard
The Snow Leopard by Peter Matthiessen
The Solace of Open Spaces by Gretel Ehrlich
Travels with Charley by John Steinbeck
Two Towns in Provence by M. F. K. Fisher
Video Night in Kathmandu by Pico Iyer
Walden by Henry David Thoreau
Westward Ha! by S. J. Perelman
Zen and the Art of Motorcycle Maintenance by Robert M. Pirsig

AUSTRALIAN RESOURCES

GENERAL GUIDES TO PUBLISHERS, EDITORS & LITERARY AGENTS

The Australian Writer

PO Box 973, Eltham Vic 3095
austwriter@writers.asn.au
www.writers.asn.au

Bimonthly interviews, articles and resources for writers, published by the Victorian branch of the Fellowship of Australian Writers (FAW).

The Australian Writer's Marketplace

www.awmonline.com.au

The prime resource for Australian writers, this annually updated guide to markets and resources includes advice from leading authors and separate indexes to publishers, literary agents, awards and courses.

Australian Books in Print

www.thorpe.com.au

This hefty two-volume reference guide published by Thorpe-Bowker provides contact details and summaries of all Australian publishers and distributors, local distributors of overseas publishers and information on literary associations.

Margaret Gee's Australian Media Guide

Crown Content, Ground Floor, 9 Queen St, Melbourne Vic 3000
☎ 03-8627 5800, Fax 03-8627 5899
www.mediaguide.com.au

Available in both print and online formats, the guide includes listings and details of Australia's newspapers and magazines.

Vicnet Literature

www.vicnet.net.au/culture/literature

Vicnet's Literature website includes a database of books and writers, and links to literary agents, prizes, publishers, references, magazines and organisations.

MAJOR TRAVEL PUBLISHERS

Many publishers' websites provide detailed information and advice on topics such as writing tips, unsolicited manuscripts, style and presentation, agents, contracts and manuscript services.

TRAVEL GUIDEBOOKS

Explore Australia Publishing

Private Bag 1600 South Yarra, Victoria 3141
(85 High St, Prahran, Victoria 3181)
☎ 03-8520 6444, Fax 03-8520 6422
explore@hardiegrant.com.au
www.hardiegrant.com.au

This publisher of road maps, activity guides and the state-based 'Explore' guides has been in business for 25 years.

Little Hills Press

12/103 Kurrajong Ave, Mount Druitt NSW 2770
☎ 02-9677 9658, Fax 02-9677 9152
lhills@bigpond.net.au
www.littlehills.com

This small, locally owned publisher produces regional and activity-based travel guides. A publisher of travel guides since 1987, Little Hills also produces general trade titles in fields such as languages, cooking and gardening.

Lonely Planet Publications

Locked Bag 1, Footscray Vic 3011
☎ 03-8379 8000, Fax 03-8379 8111
www.lonelyplanet.com/contact
www.lonelyplanet.com

Head office of the global travel media company, covering every country in the world in over 600 titles across 17 different languages.

New Holland Publishers (Australia)

Unit 1, 66 Gibbes St, Chatswood, NSW 2067
☎ 02-8986 4700, Fax 02-8986 4799
www.newholland.com.au

This branch of the international New Holland company focuses on nonfiction Australiana including pictorials, natural history and regional travel destinations. Also publishes reference, cookery, gardening, health, lifestyle and current affairs titles.

Universal Publishers

1 Waterloo Rd, PO Box 1530, Macquarie Centre, NSW 2113
☎ 02-9857 3700, Fax 02-9888 9074
www.universalpublishers.com.au

Australia's largest publisher of local mapping and travel-related products, Universal's titles include the Gregory's leisure guides and UBD maps and references.

TRAVEL LITERATURE

Allen & Unwin

PO Box 8500, St Leonards NSW 1590
☎ 02-8425 0100, Fax 02-9906 2218
submissions@allenandunwin.com
www.allenandunwin.com

Distributed worldwide by its UK parent company, Allen & Unwin publishes a wide-ranging list of nonfiction Australian titles including memoir and travel writing.

Five Mile Press

1 Centre Rd, Scoresby, Vic 3179
☎ 03-8756 5500, Fax 03-8756 5588
publishing@fivemile.com.au
www.fivemile.com.au

Small, independent publisher of nonfiction Australiana such as literary anthologies.

Hardie Grant Books

Private Bag 1600 South Yarra, Victoria 3141
(or 85 High St, Prahran, Victoria 3181)
☎ 03-8520 6444, Fax 03-8520 6422
info@hardiegrant.com.au
www.hardiegrant.com.au

Publisher of the best-selling guide to fictional *Molvania*, Hardie Grant also publishes books on contemporary issues and popular culture.

HarperCollins Publishers

PO Box 321, Pymble NSW 2073
☎ 02-9952 5000, Fax 02-9952 5555
www.harpercollins.com.au

HarperCollins Australia's list of contemporary nonfiction titles includes travel and memoir, lifestyle and Australian issues.

Hachette Livre Australia

Level 17, 207 Kent St, Sydney NSW 2000
☎ 02-8248 0800, Fax 02-8248 0810

auspub@hachette.com.au
www.hachette.com.au

Hachette Livre Australia publishes travel nonfiction by Australian authors.

Lonely Planet Publications

Locked Bag 1, Footscray Vic 3011
☎ 03-8379 8000, Fax 03-8379 8111
www.lonelyplanet.com/contact
www.lonelyplanet.com

All travel literature and travel pictorials are commissioned out of Lonely Planet's Australia office.

Pan Macmillan Australia

Level 25, 1 Market St, Sydney NSW 2000
☎ 02-9285 9100, Fax 02-9285 9190
panpublishing@macmillan.com.au
www.panmacmillan.com.au
Guidelines: www.panmacmillan.com.au/submission_guidelines.asp

Pan Macmillan publishes and distributes a range of imprints, including Australian adventure travel and travel literature titles.

Penguin Australia

PO Box 701, Hawthorn Vic 3122
(250 Camberwell Rd, Camberwell, Vic 3124)
☎ 03-9811 2400, Fax 03-9811 2620
www.penguin.com.au

Penguin Australia's Books for Adults list includes travel and memoir, short stories and fiction. Check the website to see if they are currently accepting unsolicited manuscripts.

Random House Australia

Level 3, 100 Pacific Hwy, North Sydney NSW 2060
☎ 02-9954 9966, Fax 02-9954 4562
random@randomhouse.com.au
www.randomhouse.com.au

Australian travel titles published by Random House Australia and its many imprints include Sarah Turnbull's *Al-*

most French and Sarah MacDonald's *Holy Cow.*

Text Publishing Company

Swann House, 22 William St, Melbourne Vic 3000
☎ 03-8610 4500, Fax 03-9629 8621
www.textpublishing.com.au
Guidelines: www.textpublishing.com.au/contact-us/
manuscript-submissions

The publisher of prestigious Australian authors such as Murray Bail, Tim Flannery and Anna Funder.

Wakefield Press

1 The Parade West, Kent Town SA 5067
submissions@wakefieldpress.com.au
www.wakefieldpress.com.au
Guidelines: www.wakefieldpress.com.au/forauthors/
unsolmanuscripts.html

This small, independently owned publishing company from South Australia produces travel anthologies, Australian travel stories, autobiographies and books on food, history, culture and art.

TRAVEL MAGAZINES

AFTA Traveller Magazine

Level 3, 309 Pitt St, Sydney NSW 2000
☎ 02-9264 3299, Fax 02-9264 1085
afta@afta.com.au
www.afta.com.au

The Australian Federation of Travel Agents' free quarterly trade magazine highlights destinations and has updates on campaigns and programs conducted by tourist offices, airlines and hotels.

Arena Magazine

PO Box 18, North Carlton Vic 3054
☎ 03-9416 5166, Fax 03-9416 0684
magazine@arena.org.au
www.arena.org.au

An independent leftist bimonthly forum for the discussion of political, cultural and social issues.

Art Almanac

PO Box 915, Glebe NSW 2037
☎ 02-9660 6755, Fax 02-9660 6799
info@art-almanac.com.au
www.art-almanac.com.au

Monthly reviews of current local exhibitions and news from the international art world.

Aussie Backpacker Magazine

PO Box 1264, Townsville Qld 4810
☎ 07-4772 3244, Fax 07-4772 3250
info@aussiebackpacker.com.au
www.aussiebackpacker.com.au

Monthly collection of information, articles and stories aimed towards budget travellers. Also publishes the *Aussie Backpacker Attractions and Accommodation Guide.*

Australian 4WD Action

Locked Bag 111, Silverwater NSW 1811
☎ 02-9741 3800, Fax 02-9748 3596
www.4wdaction.com.au/

Monthly articles and reviews for outback travellers.

Australian Coast & Country

☎ 1300 667 580
editor@coastandcountry.com.au
www.coastandcountry.com.au

Quarterly magazine focusing on country living.

Australian Geographic

54 Park St, Sydney NSW 2000
☎ 02-9263 9813, Fax 02-9263 9810
editorial@ausgeo.com.au
www.australiangeographic.com.au

Quarterly articles for lovers of adventure and discovery.

Australian Gourmet Traveller

PO Box 4088, Sydney NSW 2001
☎ 02-9282 8758, Fax 02-9264 3621
gourmet@acpmagazines.com.au
www.gourmettraveller.com.au

Monthly magazine devoted to wine, food and travel.

Australian House & Garden
c/o ACP Magazines, 54–58 Park St, Sydney NSW 2000
☎ 02-9282 8000, Fax 02-9267 4361
www.houseandgarden.com.au
Lifestyle and travel magazine.

Australian Table
c/o ACP Magazines, 54–58 Park St, Sydney NSW 2000
☎ 02-9282 8000, Fax 02-9267 4361
www.acp.com.au/MagazineTitles.aspx
Monthly magazine focusing on food, lifestyle and travel.

Australian Traveller
Australian Traveller Media Pty Ltd, PO Box 159, Broadway NSW 2007
☎ 02-9281 6080
info@australiantraveller.com
gbarton@australiantraveller.com
www.australiantraveller.com
Bimonthly, focused on Australian domestic travel.

Backpacker Essentials
GPO Box 5276, Sydney NSW 2001
☎ 02-9261 1111, Fax 02-9261 1969
backpacker.essentials@yhansw.org.au
www.backpackeressentials.com.au
A YHA-focused print and online magazine for Australia's budget and independent travellers. Topics include destination guides, transport and book reviews.

Cuisine
PO Box 6341, Auckland 1036, New Zealand
☎ 64-9-909 6831, Fax 64-9-909 6839
tam@cuisine.co.nz
www.cuisine.co.nz
Trans-Tasman food and lifestyle quarterly from New Zealand; also available in Australia.

Get Lost!
justin@getlostmag.com
www.getlostmag.com

A quarterly, focusing on travel lifestyles and culture, targeting the backpacker and youth markets.

Inside Out
Level 5, 2 Holt St, Surry Hills NSW 2010
☎ 02-9288 3272, Fax 02-9288 2788
insideout@newsltd.com.au
www.insideout.com.au
Bimonthly home and lifestyle magazine.

KiaOra (Air New Zealand)
c/o ACP Media, Private Bag 92512, Auckland 1141, New Zealand
☎ 64-9-308 2700, Fax 64-9-308 2878
www.acpmedia.co.nz
Air New Zealand's monthly in-flight magazine covers regional destinations serviced by the airline.

Luxury Travel
1st fl, 645 Harris St, Ultimo NSW 2007
☎ 02-9281 7523, Fax 02-9281 7529
mkirkwood@luxurytravelmag.com.au
www.luxurytravelmag.com.au
Quarterly magazine focusing on four- and five-star travel.

On the Road
PO Box 310, Williamstown Vic 3016
☎ 03-9397 2611, Fax 03-9397 2711
patrick@ontheroad.com.au
www.ontheroad.com.au
Monthly magazine for camping, 4WD and ecotourism enthusiasts.

Outdoor Australia
c/o ACP Magazines, 54–58 Park St, Sydney NSW 2000
☎ 02-9282 8000, Fax 02-9267 4361
www.outdooraustralia.com
Bimonthly magazine for lovers of bushwalking, camping and other outdoor pursuits.

Overland
PO Box 14428, Melbourne Vic 8001
☎ 03-9688 4163, Fax 03-9687 7614

overland@vu.edu.au

http:\\overland.org.au

Overland is a leftist literary and political quarterly focusing on culture, current affairs, history, reviews and new writing.

Qantas: The Australian Way

c/o QMedia, ACP Magazines, Level 13, 66–68 Goulburn St, Sydney NSW 2000

☎ 02-9282 8856, Fax 02-9261 4791

qantas@acpmagazines.com.au

www.qantas.com.au/info/flying/inTheAir/australianWay

Qantas Airline's in-flight magazine is published monthly.

Quarterly Essay

Level 5, 289 Flinders Lane, Melbourne Vic 3000

☎ 03-9654 2000, Fax 03-9654 2290

quarterlyessay@blackincbooks.com

www.quarterlyessay.com

Award-winning current affairs quarterly providing serious and significant reflections on contemporary issues.

TNT Magazine Australia

Level 4, 46–48 York St, Sydney NSW 2000

☎ 02-9299 4811, Fax 02-9299 4861

editor@tntdownunder.com

www.tntdownunder.com

A free weekly publication for independent travellers and backpackers.

Tracks

Wolseley Media, Level 5, 55 Chandos St, St Leonards NSW 2065

☎ 02-9901 6100, Fax 02-9901 6116

tracksmag@tracksmag.com.au

www.tracksmag.com

This monthly surfing magazine includes travel tips and travel stories.

Travel + Leisure Australia

1 Darling Island Rd, Pyrmont NSW 2009

☎ 02-9282 2602

tleditor@fairfax.com.au

www.travelandleisure.com.au

Published 10 times a year, this glossy covers the globe.

Travel Weekly

Locked Bag 2999, Chatswood NSW 2067

☎ 02-9422 2004, Fax 02-9422 2863

www.travelweekly.com.au

Travel Weekly is a weekly wrap-up of industry news and stories.

Vacations & Travel

Suite 16/1–15 Barr St, Balmain NSW 2041

☎ 02-9555 8100, Fax 02-9818 5625

editor@globalpublishing.com.au

www.vacationsandtravelmag.com

Quarterly publication targeting adventurous travellers.

Vogue Australia

180 Bourke Rd, Alexandria NSW 2015

☎ 02-9353 6666

editor@vogue.com.au

www.vogue.com.au

Monthly fashion and beauty magazine; includes travel articles.

Vogue Entertaining + Travel

170–180 Bourke Rd, Alexandria NSW 2015

☎ 02-8062 2615, Fax 02-8062 2166

www.vogue.com.au/in_vogue/vogue_entertaining_travel

Lifestyle, food and travel magazine published bimonthly.

NEWSPAPERS

The Advertiser

GPO Box 339, Adelaide SA 5001

☎ 1300 130 370, Fax 08-8206 3669

mailedit@adv.newsltd.com.au

www.news.com.au/adelaidenow

This South Australian newspaper has a colour travel section on Saturdays.

The Age

PO Box 257C, Melbourne Vic 3001

☎ 03-9601 2250, Fax 03-9601 2332

newsdesk@theage.com.au

www.theage.com.au

Victoria's major newspaper includes an eight-page travel section on Saturday. Topics include feature stories, specialist city guides, travel tips and advice.

The Australian

GPO Box 4245, Sydney NSW 2001
☎ 02-9288 3000, Fax 02-9288 2250
travel@theaustralian.com.au
www.theaustralian.news.com.au
Saturday's *Weekend Australian* includes a travel and indulgence lift-out, edited by Susan Kurosawa.

The Canberra Times

PO Box 7155, Canberra MC ACT 2610
☎ 02-6280 2122
www.canberratimes.com.au
The capital's newspaper includes a Sunday travel section.

The Courier Mail

PO Box 130, Brisbane Qld 4001
☎ 1300 30 40 20, Fax 07-3666 6696
www.news.com.au/couriermail/contactus
www.news.com.au/couriermail
Tabloid features special interest sections on travel and a regular section on Saturday. The *Sunday Mail* features the Escape 24-page full-colour travel lift-out.

The Daily Telegraph

GPO Box 4245, Surry Hills NSW 2001
☎ 02-9288 3000, Fax 02-9288 2300
news@dailytelegraph.com.au
www.news.com.au/dailytelegraph
This Sydney newspaper includes a travel section every Tuesday.

Herald Sun

PO Box 14999, Melbourne Vic 3001
☎ 03-9292 1226, Fax 03-9292 2112
news@heraldsun.com.au
www.news.com.au/heraldsun
Melbourne's tabloid includes a travel feature section on Friday.

The Sun-Herald

201 Sussex St, Sydney NSW 2000
☎ 02-9282 1679, Fax 02-9282 2151
shnews@mail.fairfax.com.au
www.sunherald.com.au
The Sunday tabloid includes a 20-page full-colour travel magazine.

Sunday Herald Sun

PO Box 14634, Melbourne City Vic 3001
☎ 03-9292 2963, Fax 03-9292 2080
sundayhs@hwt.newsltd.com.au
www.news.com.au/heraldsun/sundayheraldsun
Includes the full-colour, 24-page Escape travel lift-out.

The Sunday Mail

GPO Box 339, Adelaide SA 5001
☎ 1300 130 370, Fax 08-8206 3646
mailedit@adv.newsltd.com.au
www.news.com.au/adelaidenow
South Australia's Sunday paper features the expanded Escape full-colour travel section.

The Sunday Telegraph

GPO Box 4245, Surry Hills NSW 2001
☎ 02-9288 3000, Fax 02-9288 2300
news@sundaytelegraph.com.au
www.sundaytelegraph.com.au
Includes the full-colour Escape and Body & Soul lift-outs.

The Sydney Morning Herald

GPO Box 506, Sydney NSW 2001
☎ 02-9282 2833, Fax 02-9282 3253
travel@smh.com.au
www.smh.com.au
Sydney's major newspaper contains similar travel coverage to the *Age*. Both papers welcome freelance submissions about unsubsidised travel.

The West Australian

GPO Box D162, Perth WA 6001
☎ 08-9482 3111, Fax 08-9482 9070
travel@wanews.com.au
www.thewest.com.au

The *West Australian* was first published in 1833, and features travel in Saturday's weekend edition.

ONLINE

Crikey

www.crikey.com.au

Australia's leading independent online news service promises to 'fill the gaps the Australian media seem unable or unwilling to fulfil' and accepts contributions from journalists who might 'think the Australian media is too cautious, under-resourced, unadventurous and too concentrated'.

National Library of Australia

www.nla.gov.au/npapers

The NLA's huge resources include links to Australia's newspaper media, searchable by state, town and title.

News Medianet

www.newsspace.com.au

Provides an online guide to News Corporation's titles, including circulation figures and market research.

Online Newspapers

www.onlinenewspapers.com/australi.htm

This international guide to online newspapers includes a comprehensive listing of Australia's urban and regional newspaper websites.

Reportage

www.reportage.uts.edu.au

The Australian Centre for Independent Journalism's web magazine focuses on national and international issues, including travel.

Travel News

www.news.com.au/travel/travelnews

News Limited's online travel magazine includes features culled from its national newspapers and some news agency content.

Tourism Victoria

www.tourismvictoria.com.au

Tourism Victoria publishes *Pieces of Victoria*, a monthly electronic news bulletin for travel writers highlighting special events, tours, accommodation and other travel products.

WRITERS' GROUPS & ASSOCIATIONS

Asia & Pacific Writers Network

sydney@pen.org.au

www.pen.org.au

Members are given access to a database and online forums to develop a more comprehensive understanding of the writing, cultures and issues of the Asia-Pacific region.

Australian Society of Authors (ASA)

PO Box 1566, Strawberry Hills NSW 2012

☎ 02-9318 0877, Fax 02-9318 0530

asa@asauthors.org

www.asauthors.org

Promotes and protects the professional interests of Australian writers. Members receive the association's journal, *Australian Author*, and regular newsletters.

Australian Society of Travel Writers

www.astw.org.au

This website is largely for members only, and is dedicated to reporting news for the travel industry and serving the interests of the travelling public. The website includes useful hints for becoming a travel writer, accessible by nonmembers.

Australian Writers' Guild

www.awg.com.au

National Office

8/50 Reservoir St, Surry Hills NSW 2010

☎ 02-9281 1554, Fax 02-9281 4321

admin@awg.com.au

South Australia

The Writers' Centre, 187 Rundle St, Adelaide SA 5000

☎ 08-8232 6852

sa@awg.com.au

Western Australia

PO Box 492, Leederville WA 6903

☎ 08-9201 1172, Fax 08-9201 1173

wa@awg.com.au

The professional association for performance writers provides access to industry information and a wide range of services.

Copyright Agency

Level 15, 233 Castlereagh St, Sydney NSW 2000

☎ 02-9394 7600, Fax 02-9394 7601

enquiry@copyright.com.au

www.copyright.com.au

This not-for-profit copyright-collecting society seeks to secure fair payment for authors and publishers; membership is free.

Fellowship of Australian Writers (FAW)

PO Box 973, Eltham Vic 3095

austwriter@writers.asn.au

www.writers.asn.au

A nonprofit membership-based group dedicated to supporting, promoting and advocating the needs and interests of Australian writers. Current contact information for regional groups given on website.

Sydney PEN

14a Lonsdale Close, Lake Haven NSW 2263

☎ 1300 364 997, 02-4394 0397, Fax 02-4392 9410

sydney@pen.org.au

www.pen.org.au

A member of the international association of writers, founded in 1921 to promote friendship and intellectual cooperation among writers worldwide.

Varuna – The Writers' House

141 Cascade St, Katoomba NSW 2780

☎ 02-4782 5674, Fax 02-4782 6220

varuna@varuna.com.au

www.varuna.com.au

Fellowships are offered annually to writers in all genres and of all levels of experience.

Writers Centres

Australian Capital Territory

Gorman House, Ainslie Ave, Braddon ACT 2612

☎ 02-6262 9191, Fax 02-6262 9191

admin@actwriters.org.au

www.actwriters.org.au

New South Wales

PO Box 1056, Rozelle NSW 2039

☎ 02-9555 9757, Fax 02-9818 1327

info@nswwriterscentre.org.au

www.nswwriterscentre.org.au

Northern Territory

Froghollow Centre for the Arts, 55 McMinn St, Darwin NT 0810

☎ 08-8941 2651, Fax 08-8941 2115

Email through form on website

www.ntwriters.com.au

Queensland

Level 2, 109 Edward St, Brisbane Qld 4000

☎ 07-3839 1243, Fax 07-3839 1245

qldwriters@qwc.asn.au

www.qwc.asn.au

South Australia

PO Box 43, Rundle Mall PO, Adelaide SA 5000

☎ 08-8223 7662, Fax 08-8232 3994

sawriters@sawriters.on.net

www.sawriters.on.net

Tasmania

77 Salamanca Pl, Hobart Tas 7000

☎ 03-6224 0029, Fax 03-6224 0029

admin@tasmanianwriters.org

www.tasmanianwriters.org

Victoria
1st fl, Nicholas Bldg, 37 Swanston St,
Melbourne Vic 3000
☎ 03-9654 9068, Fax 03-9654 4751
Email through form on website
www.vwc.org.au
Western Australia
Alexander Library Building, Perth Cultural Centre WA 6000
☎ 08-9228 9908, Fax 08-9228 9907
www.writingwa.org
The various writers centres provide support for Australian writers, including local advice and the use of resource libraries and facilities.

WRITERS' WEBSITES & TOOLS

Aboriginal Languages of Australia
www.dnathan.com/VL/austLang.htm
A guide to online language resources for Aboriginal and Torres Strait Islander languages.

Aboriginal Studies Virtual Library
www.ciolek.com/WWWVL-Aboriginal.html
An online guide to Aboriginal studies, including history, native title, art and culture.

Allen & Unwin Writing Centre
www.allenandunwin.com/default.aspx?page=20
Allen & Unwin's 'Being a Writer' online compendium of inspirational tips and practical advice for writers includes author interviews, useful links and competition news.

Australian Copyright Council
www.copyright.org.au
All the information you'll ever need to know about copyright, plus a guide to the organisation's training programs, publications and information sheets.

Australian Law Online
www.australianlawonline.gov.au/accesspoint
This government-run site provides Australians with access to information about the Australian legal system.

Australian Publishers Association
www.publishers.asn.au
Includes useful information for getting published and general trade information.

Australian Writers Online
www.groups.yahoo.com/group/Australian_Writers_Online
Includes useful links and a chat room for Australian writers.

Australia's Copyright Act 1968
www.austlii.edu.au/au/legis/cth/consol_act/ca1968133
View the Act on line.

Department of Communications, Information Technology & the Arts
www.arts.gov.au
The Australian government's guide to arts and culture.

Go Australia
www.goaustralia.about.com
An online guide to travel in Australia; includes Aussie colloquialisms and slang.

Macquarie.Net
www.macquariedictionary.com.au
Provides access to a range of information and images on history, science, geography, literature and the arts, with a strong Australian emphasis. You can also subscribe to the online Macquarie Dictionary.

National Library of Australia
www.nla.gov.au/oz/litsites.html
A guide to Australian literature on the internet.

AUSTRALIAN RESOURCES

Ozguide
www.journoz.com
A comprehensive list of internet information sources for Australian journalists.

PATA Award for Travel Writing
www.pata.org
The Pacific Asia Travel Association sponsors annual awards in the fields of journalism, photography, guidebook writing, websites and electronic newsletters.

Writers on the Web
www.toadshow.com.au/rob/default.asp
Articles, advice and links on writing for the web, plus an extremely useful cliché-thesaurus.

CLIMATE & THE ENVIRONMENT

Bureau of Meteorology
www.bom.gov.au
Weather forecasts, warnings and observations nationwide.

Caring for Our Country
www.nrm.gov.au
The government's initiative to restore and conserve Australia's environment and natural resources.

CSIRO
www.dar.csiro.au
The atmospheric research division of the Commonwealth Scientific & Industrial Research Organisation studies Australia's weather, climate and atmospheric pollution.

ECOTOURISM & RESPONSIBLE TRAVEL

Big Volcano Ecotourism Resource Centre
www.bigvolcano.com.au/ercentre/eaacode.htm

Includes guidelines for operators, the *Code of Practice for Ecotourism Operators* and tips for how to choose an ecotourism holiday or program.

Ecotourism Australia
www.ecotourism.org.au
Heaps of information on Australia's ecotourism industry.

Wilderness Society
www.wilderness.org.au
Community-based environmental advocacy organisation committed to defending and protecting Australia's wild country.

EMBASSIES, CONSULATES & PASSPORTS

Department of Foreign Affairs & Trade
www.dfat.gov.au
Includes details of overseas high commissions, embassies and consulates, as well as information on visa regulations, passport advice and the government's travel advisory service (www.smartraveller.gov.au).

FACTS, FIGURES & STATISTICS

Australian Automobile Association
www.aaa.asn.au/index.php
Includes a statistics database of motoring-related topics.

Australian Bureau of Statistics
www.abs.gov.au
Australia's official statistical organisation publishes a range of information including national economic and social indica-

tors, the consumer price index and papers from the 2006 census.

Australian Heritage Council
www.environment.gov.au/heritage/ahc/index.html
Up-to-date news on heritage issues in Australia.

Australian Honours List
www.itsanhonour.gov.au/index.cfm
The List provides a who's who of esteemed Australians.

Australian National Museum
www.austmus.gov.au
Includes an online guide to the museum's research and collections.

Commonwealth Parliamentary Library
www.aph.gov.au/library
Publishes monthly economic and social indicator reports.

Country Calling Codes
www.countrycallingcodes.com
International telephoning made easy.

Geoscience Australia
www.ga.gov.au/education
All kinds of fabulous facts about Australia.

National Heritage List
www.environment.gov.au/heritage/places/national/index.html
The Australian Heritage Council's listing of places of natural, historic and indigenous significance.

National Library of Australia
www.nla.gov.au/oz/stats.html
Links to all kinds of Australian statistical information on the web.

National Trust of Australia
www.nationaltrust.org.au
Website includes links to state branches

and information on properties and collections.

Tourism Australia
www.tourism.australia.com
The Tourism Research section includes a breakdown of visitor arrivals data and other market intelligence.

Universal Currency Converter
www.xe.com
Calculate your dwindling finances online in any number of different currencies.

GENERAL TRAVEL INFORMATION & ADVICE

Atlas Travel Club
www.atlascluboz.com
A nonprofit travel and leisure club.

Australian Automobile Association
www.aaa.asn.au
Includes links to state-based organisations.

Australian Federation of Travel Agents
www.afta.com.au
The representative body of Australia's travel agents, highlighting industry events and hot deals.

Australian Internet Cafes
www.gnomon.com.au/publications/netaccess/index.shtml
Where to go online across Australia.

Australian Regional Tourist Associations
http://members.ozemail.com.au/~fnq/rta
Tourist information websites and organisations across the land.

Australian Wireless Hotspots
www.wi-fihotspotlist.com/browse/au

AUSTRALIAN RESOURCES

State-by-state listings of cafés, restaurants and businesses with Wi-Fi access.

Civil Aviation Safety Authority

www.casa.gov.au

Includes aviation industry information and air travel safety tips.

Cybercafes

www.cybercafes.com

Contains a database of more than 4200 internet cafés in 141 countries.

PATA (Pacific Asia Travel Association)

www.travelwithpata.com

A travel guide to the Asia-Pacific region, with destination features, travel deals and advice.

Thorn Tree Travel Forum

www.lonelyplanet.com/thorntree

The Thorn Tree Travel Forum section of Lonely Planet's website is a bulletin board used by travellers from all over the world to exchange information about a wide variety of travel topics and destinations. You'll also find cultural, literature, food, and political discussions.

Tourism Offices Worldwide

www.towd.com

The Tourism Offices Worldwide Directory provides links to official international tourist information sources: government tourism offices, convention and visitors bureaus, chambers of commerce, and similar organisations that provide free, accurate and unbiased travel information to the public.

Travel Weekly

www.travelweekly.com.au

Highlights breaking news in Australia's travel industry, with links to airlines, travel agents and hotels.

HEALTH

My Doctor

www.mydr.com.au

A comprehensive health information resource provided by the MIMS Consumer Health Group.

Smart Traveller

www.smarttraveller.gov.au/tips/travelwell.html

Health tips and recommendations from the Department of Foreign Affairs & Trade.

Travel Doctor

www.tmvc.com.au

The Traveller's Medical & Vaccination Centre site features health advice, clinic details and current health alerts for overseas travel.

World Health Organization

www.who.int

The WHO website provides information on health risks around the world as well as recommended precautions, immunisations and vaccines when travelling.

MAPS

Australian Place Name Search

Geoscience Australia

http://www.ga.gov.au/products-services/maps.html

Free downloadable topographic and geophysical maps of Australia.

Street Directory.com

www.street-directory.com.au

A virtual street directory.

Whereis

www.whereis.com.au

A virtual street directory.

City Search
www.citysearch.com.au
A guide to what's on where and when throughout Australia.

Culture and Recreation
www.acn.net.au/events
Reviews, previews and listings of Australian events.

My Trip Journal
www.mytripjournal.com
Build an online journal of your trip with maps, photos and email notification of updates for your friends.

WRITING COURSES
Good Guides (www.thegoodguides.com.au) publishes a print and online guide to every university and college course available in Australia.

Cengage Education
Level 7, 80 Dorcas St, South Melbourne Vic 3205
☎ 03-9685 4111, Fax 03-9685 4199
www.cengage.edu.au/journalism-writing-courses/professional-freelance-journalism
The Professional Freelance Journalism course includes travel writing.

Centre for Adult Education
21 Degraves St, Melbourne Vic 3000
☎ 03-9652 0611, Fax 03-9652 0748
writing@cae.edu.au
www.cae.edu.au
Offers short entry-level courses and professional-development courses in travel writing and professional writing and editing.

Macleay College
PO Box 433, Paddington NSW 2021
☎ 02-9360 2033, Fax 02-9331 7368
www.macleay.edu.au
Macleay College provides full- or part-time courses in journalism and editing at diploma level.

Massey University
School of English and Media Studies, PN 241, Massey University, Private Bag 11 222, Palmerston North, New Zealand
☎ 64-6-356 9099 ext 7311, Fax 64-6-350 5672
www.massey.ac.nz
Offers courses in travel writing; its interactive website is open to all writers.

Offbeatrips Travel & Tourism Journalism
9 Compass Close, Edge Hill, Cairns Qld 4870
☎ 07-4032 1708
info@offbeatrips.com
www.offbeatrips.com
Online, part-time distance education course specialising in freelance travel journalism.

Open Learning Institute of TAFE
Adult Community Education, GPO Box 1326, South Brisbane Qld 4101
☎ 07-3259 4111, Fax 07-3259 4377
enquiries.tol@deta.qld.gov.au
www.oli.tafe.net
The short, vocationally oriented correspondence courses include freelance journalism levels I and II.

OTEN Distance Education
51 Wentworth Rd, Strathfield NSW 2135
☎ 02-9715 8333, Fax 02-9715 8111
oten.courseinfo@tafensw.edu.au
www.tafensw.edu.au/oten
Correspondence courses include a one-year Writing for Publication commercial certificate and Writing in Plain English communications course.

Open Universities Australia

GPO Box 5387 Melbourne, Vic 3001
☎ 03-8628 2500, Fax 03-8628 2900
www.open.edu.au

Australia's distance learning university offers a Bachelor of Communications with media studies components including journalism and new media.

Southern Cross University

School of Arts, PO Box 157, Lismore NSW 2480
☎ 02-6620 3000, Fax 02-6622 3700
www.scu.edu.au

The School of Arts offers distance, full- or part-time training in journalism as part of a BA or associate degree via its Lismore, Coffs Harbour and Tweed Heads campuses.

University of Newcastle

School of Design, Communication and Information Technology, University Dr, Callaghan NSW 2308
☎ 02-4921 5000, Fax 02-4921 4200
EnquiryCentre@newcastle.edu.au
www.newcastle.edu.au

A journalism major is included in the university's communications program.

University of Sydney

Centre for Continuing Education, Locked Bag 2020, Glebe NSW 2037
☎ 02-9036 4789, Fax 02-9036 4799
cceinfo@usyd.edu.au
www.cce.usyd.edu.au

The centre's short courses for adults include How to Get Published and Writing for Cash. It also operates a writing retreat in Italy.

University of Technology, Sydney

PO Box 123, Broadway NSW 2007
☎ 02-9514 1222
www.uts.edu.au

One of Australia's leading undergraduate and postgraduate schools of journalism, UTS hosts the Australian Centre for Independent Journalism.

Writers Centres

The various writers centres listed earlier also offer short courses and workshops in all aspects of writing and publishing. See p323 for contact details.

REFERENCE PURCHASES

Aboriginal Words edited by Nick Thieberger & William McGregor

Aussie Slang by Sarah Dawson

Australian Book Contracts by Barbara Jefferis

The Australian Oxford Dictionary edited by Bruce Moore

The Australian People: An Encyclopedia of the Nation, Its People and Their Origins by James Jupp

A Dictionary of Australian Colloquialisms by G. A. Wilkes

The Dictionary of Australian Quotations edited by Stephen Murray-Smith

A Guide to Australian Law for Journalists, Authors, Printers and Publishers by Geoffrey Sawyer

The Little Aussie Fact Book by Margaret Nicholson

Macquarie Dictionary, 4th edition, edited by A. Delbridge, J.N.L. Bernard, D. Blair, S. Butler, P. Peters & C. Vallop

Macquarie Australian Slang Dictionary edited by James Lambert

Macquarie Thesaurus edited by J.N.L. Bernard

Macquarie Writer's Friend: A Guide to Grammar and Usage

Modern Australian Usage by Nicholas Hudson

The Oxford Companion to Australian History, edited by Graeme Davison, John Hirst & Stuart Macintyre

The Penguin Working Words: An Australian Guide to Modern English Usage edited by Barrie Hughes
The SBS World Guide, 11th edition
Style Manual: For Authors, Editors and Printers, 6th edition, Department of Finance and Administration, revised by Snooks & Co.
Writing as a Business by Ken Methold
Writing Feature Stories by Matthew Ricketson

LIBRARY REFERENCES

Australian Books in Print (DW Thorpe)
Australian Bookseller & Publisher (DW Thorpe)
Australian Dictionary of Biography (Melbourne University Press)
Australian Literary Awards & Fellowships (DW Thorpe)
Directory of Australian Booksellers (DW Thorpe)
Guide to New Australian Books (DW Thorpe)

Weekly Book Newsletter (DW Thorpe)
Who's Who in Australia (Information Australia)
International Literary Market Place (Information Today)

TRAVEL LITERATURE CLASSICS

The following 10 travel literature titles reveal quite different responses to Australia and its culture, penned by both locals and visitors:
Down Under by Bill Bryson
In the Land of Oz by Howard Jacobson
One for the Road by Tony Horowitz
Sean & David's Long Drive by Sean Condon
A Secret Country by John Pilger
The Songlines by Bruce Chatwin
Thirty Days in Sydney by Peter Carey
Tracks by Robyn Davidson
Sydney by Jan Morris
The Winners' Enclosure by Annie Caulfield

AUSTRALIAN RESOURCES

SAMPLE PAPERWORK

In this section we have gathered contributor guidelines from four eminent publications representing newspaper, magazine and digital outlets. Our goal is to give you a good sense of the kinds of information such guidelines provide, while also spotlighting the specific kinds of articles these particular publications want to receive. In addition to these guidelines, we also reproduce sample model and property release forms for photographers. Get those journals, laptops and cameras ready – and good luck!

LOS ANGELES TIMES TRAVEL SECTION
(http://www.latimes.com/la-trw-guidelines-story,0,2454724.story)

Guidelines for Freelance Writers

Dear Travel Writer:

Welcome to the cornerstone of what we do.

What follows is the most important information contained in these several pages. The Los Angeles Times values honesty, fairness and truth. We understand the difficulties of the profession, but we also know that our reputation--and yours--rests on ensuring that our readers receive the best information possible.

These guidelines are from our own code of ethics, constructed over many months and with much care.

The Los Angeles Times Ethics Guidelines for Freelance Writers

The work of freelance journalists appears in our paper and on our website alongside staff-produced photos, articles and graphics. Freelancers must therefore approach their work without conflicts and must adhere to the same standards of professionalism that The Times requires of its own staff. It is the responsibility of assigning editors to inquire about a freelancer's potential conflicts of interest before making an assignment.

Conflict-of-interest provisions may apply differently to contributors to the Op-Ed pages. They are expected to bring institutional and personal perspectives to their work. They are not expected to avoid conflicts, but they are expected to disclose them.

More information about our expectations follows. If you have any questions, please call me or e-mail me.

Thank you again for your interest in and articles submitted to the *Los Angeles Times*.

Sincerely,
Catharine M. Hamm
Travel editor

Guidelines for Submitting Manuscripts to the LA Times Travel Section

With the increasing power of the Internet, it *is* a small world after all. We are awash in information: guidebooks, blogs, chat rooms, travel websites, maps etc.

The Travel section is looking for bold, original travel features that tell a great story and are strong character-driven or first-person narratives – the more experiential the better. Stories should be sophisticated, compelling, complete and written with flair. They should evoke a strong sense of place (sounds, colors, smells, tastes), time (when did you go?), expertise and personal perspective, and they should be written with a very precise story angle in mind. We are not looking for everything you need to know about Shanghai; we are looking for the city from the vantage of its architecture or its fine arts. Find a salient angle in your story, be selective with your descriptions and historical facts and spin a tale that tells of a unique experience that can be replicated. We want stories that will make readers get out of their chairs and go – or at least enjoy the ride from their armchairs. We want stories that will make readers get out of their chairs and go – or at least enjoy the ride from their armchairs. We also want destination stories that reflect travel trends, stories that put us out ahead of the curve. Destinations will vary according to our needs, but stories should have a compelling reason to be told, an "of-the-moment" quality that make them relevant rather just an "I went to Italy and did this, then I did this."

In these stories, we require an equal emphasis – in length and in scope – on the Guidebooks sidebar that accompanies each destination feature. This nuts and bolts information is as important to readers as the ride you take them on. Be creative and be detailed about attractions, hotels, restaurants etc.

Above all, be honest. Not every trip goes well. We know that not all hotels are great and that meals are sometimes lousy. We know that tour guides aren't equally well-versed and that weather can be bad. And, more important, our readers know it too because they are travelers. So if something unpleasant happens, that's part of the story, although this isn't supposed to be carpfest either.

Freelancers must approach their work and travel arrangements without conflicts and must adhere to the same standards of professionalism that *The Times* requires of its staff. The Travel section will not consider pieces written about trips that have been subsidized in any way (even if part of a trip was not comped). We may ask for receipts.

Completed stories are considered on speculation only. Stories must be based on trips taken within the previous two years. To be considered, the story may not have run elsewhere or be pending publication elsewhere.

NATIONAL GEOGRAPHIC TRAVELER
(http://travel.nationalgeographic.com/travel/traveler-magazine/about-us/writer-guidelines/)

Writers Guidelines
Thank you for your interest in contributing to *National Geographic Traveler,* which is published eight times a year by the National Geographic Society. *Traveler's* publishing goals are to find the new, to showcase fresh travel opportunities, to be an advocate for travelers. *Traveler's* tag line is "Nobody knows this world better," and accordingly, a *Traveler* story must capture a place's essence in a way that inspires readers to follow in the writer's footsteps – and equip them to do so with useful destination information.

What types of stories does Traveler publish?
Each issue of the magazine contains five or more features, roughly balanced between U.S. and foreign subjects. Generally, we are interested in places accessible to most travelers, not just the intrepid or wealthy. The types of destinations we cover vary widely, from mainstream to adventure travel.

Traveler features are usually narrow in scope; we do not cover whole states or countries. Subjects of particular interest to us are national and state parks, historic places, cities, little-known or undiscovered places, train trips, cruises, and driving trips. Service information is generally given separately at the end of each feature in a section that includes how to get to the destination, things to see and do there, and where to obtain more information. The writer is expected to send along as much service information as possible with the manuscript to help us prepare this section.

We also publish several regular service-oriented departments, with the emphasis on meaty, practical information. Subjects include photography, food, lodgings, ecotourism, adventurous learning experiences, and short getaways. Essays offering reflections on the travel experience round out the department mix.

What kinds of proposals is Traveler looking for?

We accept freelance queries for most of our departments. Ideas for features are generated both by the Traveler staff and by freelance contributors. We do assign features to writers we have not used but only to those whose published clips demonstrate the highest level of writing skill. We do not accept phone queries from writers, and we discourage the submission of unsolicited manuscripts for feature articles. We do not accept proposals about trips that are subsidized in any way.

How should an idea be proposed?

If we have to sell readers to consume our magazine, then writers must sell us with more than just notions and place-names, so please do not send us any unfocused wish lists of multiple queries. Restrict each submission to one or two well-developed proposals that have been crafted especially for us. A carefully considered proposal combines support for doing a particular destination with some premise or hook. A good query has a headline that suggests what the story is, a deck that amplifies on that, a strong lead, and not much more than a page that clearly sets out the premise and approach of the piece. The query should represent the writer's style and should answer these questions about the story: Why now, and why in *Traveler*?

Check the *Traveler* index to make sure we have not recently run a piece on the topic you are proposing. **Please include your credentials, relevant published clippings and a SASE to ensure that the requested materials are returned. Mail your proposal to Query Editor, National Geographic Traveler, 1145 17th St NW, Washington DC 20036.** Prospective contributors doing preliminary research for a story must avoid giving the impression that they are representing the National Geographic Society or *Traveler*. They may use the name of the magazine only if they have a definite assignment. When *Traveler* gives an assignment, the terms are clearly stated in a written contract.

How long are Traveler feature stories and departments?

Most *Traveler* features range from 1,500 to 2,500 words, depending on the subject. *Traveler* departments generally run from 750 to 1,500 words. Compensation varies depending on the type of feature or department but is competitive with other national magazines. Payment is made upon acceptance. We buy all rights to manuscripts, although copyright is returned to the author 90 days after publication.

What does Traveler look for in writing style?

There are no limitations on style, as long as the writing is lively and interesting, although a sense of discovery should be at the heart of every *Traveler* story. We want our writers to project a curious and knowing voice that captures the experience of travel – the places and personalities, the insights and idiosyncrasies. Writers who work for us must see destinations with fresh eyes and real insight. We place a premium on surprise and good storytelling – the compelling anecdote, the colorful character, the lively quote, the telling detail. And we prefer that our readers be allowed to experience a destination directly through the words and actions of people the writer encounters, not just through the writer's narrative.

Beyond being strongly evocative of place, our articles attempt to speak to the soul of traveling. Every traveler, no matter how seasoned, wonders what awaits at a new destination. This goes beyond weather and accommodations and language and scenics and museums. There's a certain frisson of expectation: How foreign is this destination? What new experience will I have? This is travel as texture—the feel of a place, its essential differentness, its look, its flavor. We seek that texture in every story we publish.

WRITER'S QUERIES
Mail to:
National Geographic Traveler
Attn: Query Editor
1145 17th Street N.W.
Washington, D.C. 20036-4688

WANDERLUST
(http://www.wanderlust.co.uk/aboutus/writers)

Writer Guidelines
Want to write for *Wanderlust*? Read these guidelines first.

With only 10 issues a year, the opportunities for getting work published in *Wanderlust* are very limited. The vast majority of our articles are commissioned specifically for the magazine, and written by experienced journalists, guidebook authors or travel experts. Please read our guidelines carefully and note that we do not accept enquiries or proposals by telephone. Here are answers to some of the commonest queries we receive:

Should I send a manuscript or a proposal?
Please do **not** send us manuscripts – we simply do not have the time to read them.

If you have already completed the trip(s) you wish to write about, please email submissions@wanderlust.co.uk, or write to us with:

- A one-paragraph proposal outlining the story
- The proposed first paragraph of your story
- Brief details of how you undertook your journey, including any tour operators used
- If you have pictures, please include up to five low-resolution images to give a flavour of your trip (if emailing, your whole message should not be larger than 2MB)
- Any relevant experience you have, with links to / cuttings from previously published stories if possible
- Note: please make sure your email subject line sums up the them and destination of your proposal, eg trekking in Nepal; Siena short break guide

If you have not yet undertaken the trip you wish to write about – or your proposal is for a different kind of feature, please email submissions@ wanderlust.co.uk, or write to us with:

- A one-paragraph proposal outlining the story
- Your proposed dates of travel
- Brief details of how you will be undertaking your journey, including any proposed tour operators
- Any relevant experience you have, with links to previously published stories if possible
- Note: please make sure your email subject line sums up the them and destination of your proposal, eg trekking in Nepal; Siena short break guide

Please note we cannot respond to postal contributions unless a self-addressed envelope (SAE) is enclosed, which must be stamped or accompanied by sufficient International Reply Coupons (IRCs).

I've submitted a proposal – what do I do next?

Although we endeavour to reply to proposals, at busy times this is not always possible. If we are interested, we'll respond by email, asking you for further details or a draft article for consideration. But please bear in mind that this may take several weeks.

If you have not heard back from us within a month, feel free to email or write again. If you need an answer by a specific date, let us know – and if the date passes, please assume we are not interested.

Please do not telephone the office to follow up submissions – if you do not hear back from us, you should assume we are unable to use your proposal.

I'm a first-timer writer – will my proposal be considered?

Yes, but you need to demonstrate writing flair and professionalism. You should also target one of our shorter regular slots, for example a news story, pocket guide, or a consumer feature.

How do I know if you've already covered somewhere?

Most of our articles from the past five years are now archived on this website, and can be searched by destination. Study a copy of the magazine before considering a submission.

It is no coincidence that the majority of our contributors are regular readers! Ensure you are familiar with the magazine. Copies can be bought from our shop or the Apple App Store.

Do you accept articles without accompanying photographs?

Yes. The photographs in the magazine come from a variety of sources – writers, professional photographers, stock libraries – and we can normally find or commission images to accompany a good article. However, if you have print-quality, professional standard images, please let us know when submitting a proposal.

Do you accept articles without accompanying photographs?

Yes. The photographs in the magazine come from a variety of sources – writers, professional photographers, stock libraries – and we can normally find or commission images to accompany a good article. However, if you have print-quality, professional standard images, please let us know when submitting a proposal.

What do you look for in an article?

Our mission is simple – we want to provide our readers with the best writing, the best photographs and the most authoritative facts.

Wanderlust aims to cover all aspects of independent, semi-independent and special-interest travel. We do cover 'soft' adventure but leave the crampons and adrenalin stuff to other magazines. Off-the-beaten-track destinations, secret corners of the world and unusual angles on well-known places are always of particular interest.

We are particularly interested in local culture and try to provide more of an insight than travel articles in other publications – hence, we prefer pieces to be written by someone with an in-depth knowledge of a topic or destination.

You should make yourself familiar with the style, tone and content of Wanderlust, and be aware of recent articles to ensure your chosen subject has not be covered in the past year or so. Many of our articles from the past five years are now archived on this website, and can be searched by destination.

If tackling a topical subject then do bear in mind that we plan the contents of each issue up to a year ahead.

Always ask yourself what makes your article different from all the others that may have been sent to us on the same topic, and why you are qualified to advise others.

What kinds of feature / regular formats do you publish?

Wanderlust includes various features open to submissions:

1. DESTINATION FEATURES

Covering a specific destination – a country or a region – or an activity, eg, horseriding in Chile, walking in Morocco. Should be both anecdotal and informative, written in the first person and in the past tense, and between 1,800–2,200 words.

2. DISPATCHES

Shorter, topical pieces (700–1200 words) describing a recent development in a destination of interest to our readers. Examples include an eyewitness account of a royal wedding in Uganda, a new walking trail in the Middle East, and slum tourism in Mumbai.

3. SPECIAL INTEREST FEATURES

Do you have specialist knowledge on a travel-relevant subject? Topics covered to date include safaris, cycling holidays, New Zealand walks, family adventure trips. Must be authoritative – authors should have in-depth and regional or global knowledge.

7. CONSUMER ARTICLES

A practical guide of value to travellers. Explain how people can save money, or make their travels better and easier. The style should be direct and instructive, but easy to read and understand. Recent articles have included: finding cheap flights online; road safety abroad; making better travel videos.

What kind of articles DON'T you publish?

If your proposal falls into any of these categories, it's not for us:
- Luxury hotels, resorts or spas
- Activity holidays – golf, skiing, bungee-jumping etc. If an activity provides a unique perspective on a destination or a way of travelling through it (for example, hiking or kayaking) that's fine, but activities are not of interest in themselves.

- 'Big trip' diaries. Round-the-world odysseys, charity challenges, 'wacky races' across continents in unusual vehicles – all make great trips, but long-winded, cumbersome and often superficial articles.
- Family travel. We do not run full-length features.
- One-off expeditions. All featured journeys must be achievable by our readers.
- Trips to FCO-blacklisted destinations, for example war- or disaster-zones. We will not feature destinations the FCO advises against visiting.
- Previously published articles of any kind.

Who reads Wanderlust?

Our readers encompass all ages and budgets, and at least 50% are female. They are well educated and reasonably affluent, and are mostly active travellers, perhaps more experienced than you. Although most are British we have readers in more than 80 countries worldwide.

Some travel independently, others with specialist small-group or tailor-made tour operators. Major interests include wildlife, trekking and photography. A high proportion take 2–3 long haul breaks a year.

Do you commission articles purely for your website?

We don't publish narrative travel features on the site, but we do accept interesting blogs and inspirational round-ups. Please note there are generally no fees available for online content, but we are happy to link back to your or other relevant sites. To suggest an idea, please email us at website@wanderlust.co.uk.

Do you have any general advice for aspiring travel writers?

Here are some general tips:

- Your article should have a beginning, a middle and an end – do not just tail off. Make the opening paragraph one of your strongest, in order to pull the reader in. You do not have to tell a story in chronological order – you can open with a tense situation and then flashback to how it began.
- Ensure that your piece has a strong central theme that moves the reader forward and provides a point to it all.
- Do not try to cover too much in one article – there may be several different articles hiding inside one large piece. You should be able to sum up the contents of your article in a single sentence.
- Show the good and bad side. Disasters and tricky situations often make for a more entertaining read than harmonious, straightforward trips.
- Present an honest account – *Wanderlust* is not a travel brochure. If you hated a place, then say so (and why).
- Feature articles should have personality – though often not yours; dialogue and comment from local people add colour to a story.

- Think about how you can avoid blandness in your descriptions of a destination – recounting a seemingly unimportant incident can bring a place to life more than a detailed adjectival description of its physical appearance. And don't forget smells, sounds, flavours and even temperature or air quality as well as sights and emotions.
- Be aware of the political, environmental and social background to the places you describe – they may not be pertinent to your story, but be sure of this, especially if you are going to allude to them.
- Be aware of the consequences of what you write – for example, ecological issues such as the damaging effect that snorkellers may have on a coral reef. Be wary of endangering the subjects of your article if describing an illegal activity or political views.
- Avoid Americanisms (unless you are recounting speech or quotations from an American!), jargon, foreign terms that are not generally understood, and the numerous travel clichés that many writers fall back on – snow-capped mountains, lands of contrast, kaleidoscopes of colour and seething masses of humanity will all get the chop.
- If we have recently run an article on a particular destination or topic then it will probably be some time (perhaps several years) before we cover that area again.
- Check your facts and be wary of making generalisations that you cannot be sure of.
- It goes without saying that *Wanderlust* will not tolerate any racist, sexist or otherwise discriminatory writing, but be careful too of patronising the peoples you describe and making generalisations about characteristics that could be deemed insulting.
- We have readers in 80+ countries worldwide – try to avoid references that would confuse other nationalities.

What are your rates?
Current rates for most features are £220 per 1,000 published words. Unless otherwise agreed, the fee is based on printed, not submitted, words. Fact pages are paid at £90 per page (approx 750 words) pro-rated. Fees for other sections (including Dispatches and interviews) are set per-article rates, agreed on commissioning.

These rates are based upon copy being available by email, and First British Serial Rights being offered. An invoice request and complimentary copy of the magazine will be sent upon publication. Payment will be made within 30 days.

How do I contact you?
For the print magazine, by email: submissions@wanderlust.co.uk
For the website, by email to: website@wanderlust.co.uk
Editor, Wanderlust: Phoebe Smith; Editor-in-chief: Lyn Hughes

Please do not telephone the office to follow up submissions – if you do not hear back from us, you should assume we are unable to use your proposal.

WILDJUNKET MAGAZINE

Editorial Guidelines (http://www.wildjunket.com/magazine/editorial-guidelines/) WildJunket stories are generally first-person narratives of epic journeys, outdoor adventures and deep cultural experience – written in a lively tone and a strong human touch. We aspire to bring readers on the journey with us and also encourage them to pursue their own adventure. With a focus on independent and sustainable travel, we cover far-flung destinations and experiential journeys instead of family vacations and city breaks. Each section presents a different travel angle, ranging from photo essays to short dispatches and food articles.

Articles should have the audience in mind: Adventurous, independent travelers in the age group of 25-44 seeking deep immersions and unique experiences. All photos must be accompanied by high-resolution images – please include links to low-res photos in your story pitch.

Here are some sections that are open to submissions:

Departments

Destination Features: Inspirational first-person, narrative accounts of your travel experience through a country/region – examples include trekking through the Amazon Jungle and traveling overland in Central Asia. The piece should encompass all-rounded aspects of travel: adventure, culture and history. The anecdote should be entertaining and informative.

- Photos: 10-15
- Writing: 1,800-2,200 words including boxes and sidebar
- Payment: US$150
- Sidebar: Getting There, Getting Around, When to Go, Cost of Travel, Packing and Accommodation

Photo Essay: Using striking, high-quality photos to showcase a destination or culture. Whether they are portrait shots of people in Nigeria, landscapes images of Antarctica or wildlife snapshots from the Galapagos Islands, they should piece together to tell a story.

- Photos: 15-20
- Writing: Introduction (400words) and short captions for each selected photo
- Payment: US$80

Travel Guide: A practical guide on a destination with a general introduction, list of must-see attractions and suggestions of up to 5 itineraries around the country. Itineraries can be themed (wildlife, culture, cities etc.) or based on geographical locations (north, central, south etc.) The style should be lively but informative. Include how long each itinerary takes, and what type of traveler it caters to.

- Photos: 10-15
- Writing: 1,800-2,200 words including boxes, sidebar and list of must-sees
- Payment: US$150
- Sidebar: Getting There, Getting Around, When to Go, Cost of Travel, Packing and Accommodation

Dispatches/Just Back: Short first-person narratives of an unusual experience such as coasteering in Wales or staying in a temple in South Korea (narrower scope than destination feature).

- Photos: 8-10
- Writing: 1,300-1,500 words
- Payment: US$80
- Sidebar: Getting There, When to Go and Accommodation

Under the Radar: A short feature on a country/region that has yet to be discovered by mass tourism and have reasons to be in the tourist limelight. This is a general overview of what to see and most of all, why go now. Style should be factual but lively and includes some narratives.

- Photos: 8-10
- Writing: 1,300-1,500 words
- Payment: US$80
- Sidebar: Getting There, When to Go, Must-See Attractions

Feast: Stories that bring you on a journey through a country's gastronomy. Story scopes range from street food in Seoul to bizarre eats of Marrakech to award-winning tapas joints in Barcelona. It should be narrative and quirky yet informative.

- Photos: 8-10
- Writing: 1,000-1,200 words
- Payment: US$50

Smart Travel: This section discusses travel-related topics: from tipping to couchsurfing. Article should be thought-provoking and evocative.

- No photos needed
- Writing: 700 words
- No payment

Snapshots: On the first few pages of our magazine, we feature contributions from readers who are interested in showcasing their photos. We look for very striking and outstanding images of landscape, people or culture. Photos must be landscape oriented and bigger than 4MB.

- Writing: A 200-word explanation of how, when and where you took the photo
- No payment

General Guidelines

- All articles are written in American English. Prices should also be stated in local currency and USD.
- Please include sub-headings and boxes (at least 1 per feature).
- An author's bio and headshot will be included on the magazine's first page. Please keep your bio short (2-3 sentences).
- Articles should be submitted in a Word document and high-res photos (either in RAW or jpg of at least 4MB) via YouSendIt.com.

Publishing Rights

- Contributors will retain the rights to your articles or photographs.
- Please state if the article or photographs you're pitching are original or have been published previously. While we do not have a first run only policy, please assure that all parties involved are aware of the republication.

Query Process

Once you've read through our past issues to get a good understanding of the style we're looking for, please send us a brief query summarizing the scope of your story with a proper title, subheading and bullet point summary of the content.

Please include links to photos that would accompany your story or send us low-res versions of the photos. It's advisable to include your credentials and samples of your previous writings or blog links to give us an idea of your writing style.

Contact Details

For all magazine pitches, please contact Nellie Huang at editor@wildjunket.com.

SAMPLE RELEASE FORMS

MODEL RELEASE

By signing this document:

I irrevocably consent to the Photographer (and its licensees and assigns) incorporating my image or likeness in photographs or illustrations in any form or media (images) and reproducing, publishing and communicating the Images in any form and media for any purpose, whether commercial or otherwise (including advertising), and to the use of my name and any other text or works in connection with the Images. I waive any right to inspect or approve the Images or any publication incorporating the Images and any right to compensation for the use of the Images by the Photographer, its licensees and assigns. I release the Photographer, its licensees and assigns from any or all claims, actions, proceedings, demands and expenses and other liability that may arise in connection with the use of the Images by any person. I confirm that I am either over 18 years of age or that my parent or guardian has also agreed to these terms by signing in the space provided below.

I understand and agree to the above.

Signed: _____ Signed by parent/guardian: _____

Print name: _____ Print name: _____

Address/email/phone number: _____

Date: _____

Description of image: _____

_____

PROPERTY RELEASE

By signing this document:

I irrevocably consent to the Photographer (and its licensees and assigns) incorporating an image or likeness of the property described below in photographs or illustrations in any form or media (images) and reproducing, publishing and communicating the Images in any form and media for any purpose, whether commercial or otherwise (including advertising). I waive any right to inspect or approve the Images or any publication incorporating the Images and any right to compensation for the use of the Images by the Photographer, its licensees and assigns. I release the Photographer, its licensees and assigns from any or all claims, actions, proceedings, demands and expenses and other liability that may arise in connection with the use of the Images by any person.

I warrant that I am the owner of the property and/or am fully authorised to enter this property release.

Signed: _____ Print name: _____

Address/email/phone number: _____

Date: _____

Property description: _____

Property address: _____

_____

Description of image: _____

_____

GLOSSARY

advance monies paid to an author in advance of actual sales, as part of a royalty-based agreement

back-of-the-book magazine section reserved for promotions, round-up pieces and classified advertisements

brief an assignment given to an author, usually indicating the subject, style and word-count expected by the publication

bright a short, front-of-the-book article

byline a line in a newspaper, etc., naming the writer of the article

clips copies of a writer's previously published articles

commission an assignment given to a writer that is guaranteed to be published by a publication

contributor guidelines rules, principles and advice from a publication as to how to submit material for their consideration or publication

copy-edit to edit text by checking its grammatical and factual consistency and accuracy

embargo a contracted period of time during which the original assigning publication forbids you to reprint the story with another publication

fact box essential information to complement a travel article, such as how to get there, where to stay, where to eat

flat fee method of payment where author receives a set fee for their writing

front-of-the-book magazine section that includes short articles or 'brights'

in medias res without preamble; in the middle of

kill fee compensation given when a publication decides not to publish a commissioned or accepted article

lead introductory segment of a story

lead time amount of advance time a publication needs to plan its content and articles

lede US spelling for *lead*

masthead in a newspaper, etc., the section at the front of the publication or top of the editorial page where the publication's staff is listed

middle-of-the-book section of a magazine where the high-profile, feature articles are published

nut graf a 'nutshell paragraph'; journalism slang for the editorial heart of the story

on spec 'on speculation'; in the hope of success but without formal agreement or instruction from a publication

peg an occasion, theme or pretext, which often forms the basis of or reason for an article

pitch a proposal for an article idea

query see *pitch*

SASE self-addressed, stamped envelope

section break a line break or graphic element (in text) that tells the reader one sequence has ended and another is beginning

sidebar see *fact box*

sub-edit see *copy-edit*

transition connecting word or phrase that acts like a bridge between parts of an article

vox pop popular opinion represented by comments from members of the public

well see *middle-of-the-book*

ABOUT THE AUTHOR

Don George

National Geographic has described Don George as 'a legendary travel writer and editor.' Don has been exploring new frontiers as an author, editor and adventurer for more than 30 years. Currently Editor at Large and Book Columnist for *National Geographic Traveler* magazine, Features Editor and blogger for Gadling.com, Editor of *Recce: Literary Journeys for the Discerning Traveler* (www. geoex.com/blog), and host of the Adventure Collection's blog, The Adventurous Traveler (www.adventurecollection.com), Don has also been Global Travel Editor for Lonely Planet, Travel Editor at the *San Francisco Examiner & Chronicle* and founder and Editor of Salon.com's Wanderlust travel site. Don's stories have been selected to appear in numerous collections, and he has edited nine travel anthologies, including Lonely Planet's acclaimed *Better Than Fiction, The Kindness of Strangers, By the Seat of My Pants,* and *Tales from Nowhere.* Don has won numerous awards for his writing and editing, including the Society of American Travel Writers' Lowell Thomas Award.

Don has lectured on travel writing and travel literature at conferences and workshops around the world. He has been a visiting lecturer in travel writing at the University of California, Berkeley, Graduate School of Journalism, and is the co-founder and chairman of the Book Passage Travel Writers & Photographers Conference, held annually near San Francisco. Complementing his travel writing and editing, Don often appears as a travel expert on TV and radio and in print, and hosts a national series of onstage conversations with prominent travel writers and adventurers. Don has visited more than 75 countries and has worked as a translator in Paris, a teacher in Athens, and a television talk-show host in Tokyo. He lives in the San Francisco area with his wife; their two children are now embarked on their own worldly adventures, but still occasionally make buoyant visits home.

From the Author

This book represents the accumulation of more than five decades of life-experience, and it is impossible to name all the people to whom I am indebted for the inspiration and education embodied herein. But a few deserve special mention. First of all, I want to thank my parents for setting me on the right

About the Author

path with our family adventures when I was still a young and impressionable traveller, and for always encouraging me to follow that path. I want to thank Tony and Maureen Wheeler for making dreams – theirs and mine – come true at Lonely Planet. I'd like to thank the teams that commissioned and edited the first edition of this book (Roz Hopkins, Peter d'Onghia, Janet Austin and Laetitia Clapton) and the second edition (Ben Handicott, Ellie Cobb and Erin Richards) for believing in it from the beginning, and for guiding and supporting its journey. And I want to thank the team that worked on this third edition, Ben Handicott, Will Gourlay, Justin Flynn, Wibowo Rusli and Katherine Marsh for their enthusiastic support and meticulous editing and production efforts.

In updating this edition, I reached out to many Lonely Planet colleagues for their advice and assistance. In particular I want to thank Rana Freedman and Andy Murdock in the U.S. office, Tom Hall in the U.K. office, and Errol Hunt and Will Gourlay in the Australia office for their generous help. I also invited fellow writers, editors and bloggers to send me their ideas and opinions about what to include in this update, and received dozens of thoughtful and valuable suggestions. Thanks to all of you who invested your precious time and energy to respond to my request; your contributions have made this a better book. I especially want to thank travel writers-bloggers Pam Mandel and Candace Rose Rardon, who read the second edition from cover to cover and sent me extensive suggestions to improve and update this edition. I also want to thank all the distinguished travel editors, writers and agents who took the time to contribute their perspectives, experiences and wisdom to these pages, and to update those contributions for this edition.

Thank you to the thousands of students who have endured my classes over the years and whose boundless curiosity and passion have taught and retaught me in ways large and small; to the wonderful writers and editors with whom I have had the privilege of working over the past three decades, who have honed my own appreciation of good writing; and to the innumerable travellers – at home and on the road – I have encountered in my wanderings, who have enriched and enlightened my life beyond measure and instilled in me an abiding, sustaining sense of gratitude and wonder.

Life is a journey. Over the lifetime of this book, my dad has passed away, and my mom has moved away from the beloved house they built when I was born, where I was raised and where she lived for half a century. She thrives now in a new, warm and welcoming home in a neighboring town. The road winds ever on.

Our children have left home, too, for their own explorations. But as I wrote in the author's note to the second edition, some things stay the same. The lessons and love my parents bestowed still interlace my days. And as they have since before this book was born, my own intimate circle of fellow travellers – Kuniko, Jenny and Jeremy – continue to grace my journey with the grandest magic, and meaning, and love.